1965

Also by Andrew Grant Jackson

Still the Greatest:
The Essential Songs of the Beatles' Solo Careers

Where's Ringo?

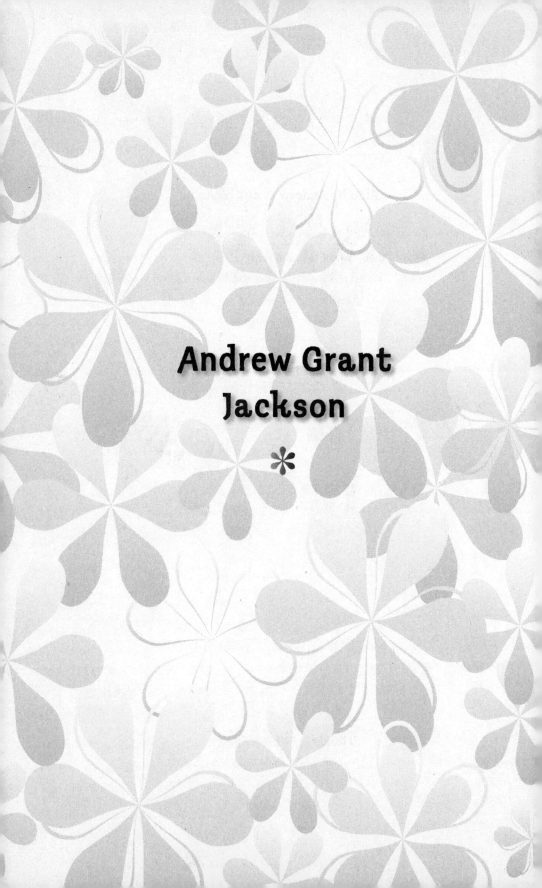

Andrew Grant Jackson

*

1965

*

The Most Revolutionary Year in Music

THOMAS DUNNE BOOKS
St. Martin's Press
New York

THOMAS DUNNE BOOKS.
An imprint of St. Martin's Press.

1965. Copyright © 2015 by Andrew Grant Jackson. All rights reserved. Printed in the United States of America. For information, address St. Martin's Press, 175 Fifth Avenue, New York, N.Y. 10010.

www.thomasdunnebooks.com
www.stmartins.com

Designed by Kathryn Parise

The Library of Congress Cataloging-in-Publication Data is available upon request.

ISBN 978-1-250-05962-8 (hardcover)
ISBN 978-1-4668-6497-9 (e-book)

St. Martin's Press books may be purchased for educational, business, or promotional use. For information on bulk purchases, please contact the Macmillan Corporate Premium Sales Department at 1-800-221-7945, extension 5442, or write to specialmarkets@macmillan.com.

First Edition: February 2015

10 9 8 7 6 5 4 3 2 1

To Dad, for getting *Big Hits (High Tide and Green Grass)*

at the used-record store, and to Keira, for singing

"Stop! In the Name of Love"

Contents

Acknowledgments

I am deeply grateful to my editor Rob Kirkpatrick for taking on the project, sharing his insights born of experience, helping to shape the narrative, and keeping it focused and moving forward.

Infinite thanks to editorial assistant Jennifer Letwack for pulling all the pieces together. The efforts of copy editor Jenna Dolan were crucial in strengthening the piece. Thanks to jacket designer Rob Grom for capturing the spirit of *Rubber Soul* and the early Acid Test posters, to production editor David Lott, publicist Joe Rinaldi, and marketing manager Karlyn Hixson.

It was a pleasure to work with freelance copy editor Laura Adiletta, who was vital in helping me see the forest for the trees. Many thanks to writers Morgan Hobbs, David Jenison, and Erick Trickey for their feedback, and to Jeff McCarty and Jay Burnley for going above and beyond the call of duty.

My agent, Charlie Viney, encouraged the project from the very beginning and has always provided inestimable guidance. Thanks also to Sally Fricker of the Viney Agency.

If I couldn't live through 1965, at least I'm lucky enough to have YouTube to research the more obscure fringes of its music, along with the dusty bins of record conventions. Thanks to the night I heard "A Hard Rain's A-Gonna Fall" on the porch for the first time just before dawn, while the rain hissed on trees silhouetted by lightning and the great breeze of the summer thunderstorm blew through the screen. Thanks to my parents for passing on a sense of the '60s' epic romanticism, to Barb for being such a great mother to Keira, and to Keira for sharing her toys with me (sometimes).

1965 Selected Time Line

Unless otherwise noted, all chart positions reflect the Billboard *U.S. pop chart.*

January

1 The Beatles' "I Feel Fine" holds the top spot for the second of three weeks with the first intentional use of feedback on a record.

4 President Lyndon Johnson announces plans for Great Society government programs such as Medicare to create "abundance and liberty for all."

11–12 The Rolling Stones record their version of the Staple Singers' gospel ("The Last Time") and baroque chamber pop ("Play with Fire").

13–15 Dylan records *Bringing It All Back Home*, fusing psychedelic folk lyrics with rock and roll.

16 Connie Smith's "Once a Day" ends its eight-week run at the top of the country chart, the record for a female artist until 2012.

20 Lyndon Johnson's inauguration draws the largest crowd until Barack Obama's in 2009.

20 The Byrds record "Mr. Tambourine Man," matching the Beatles' jangling guitar and beat with Dylan's surreal lyrics and an intro inspired by Bach.

February

1 John Coltrane releases his magnum opus, *A Love Supreme*, in February (exact date unknown).

1 James Brown records "Papa's Got a Brand New Bag" in one hour, inventing the funk genre.

6 "You Lost That Lovin' Feelin'" becomes the longest No. 1 record to date, at 3:45.

10 Martha and the Vandellas release "Nowhere to Run," a future anthem to soldiers and rioters, and inspiration for the riff of "Satisfaction."

18 While demonstrating for the right to vote, a black man, Jimmie Lee Jackson, is fatally shot in the stomach by a state trooper in Selma, Alabama.

20 Buck Owens's "I've Got a Tiger by the Tail" tops the country chart, epitomizing the Bakersfield sound.

21 Malcolm X is assassinated.

March

2 President Johnson orders the Operation Rolling Thunder bombing campaign against North Vietnam.

6 The Temptations' "My Girl" (co-written/co-produced by Smokey Robinson) tops the charts.

6 Sam Cooke's civil rights anthem "A Change Is Gonna Come" peaks at No. 31.

7 ABC interrupts the Sunday Night Movie (*Judgment at Nuremberg*) to broadcast images of civil rights demonstrators being beaten by Alabama state troopers, an incident that will be dubbed "Bloody Sunday."

8 The Deacons for Defense and Justice, an armed civil rights organization, incorporates in Louisiana.

8 The first combat troops arrive in Vietnam. Thirty-five hundred marines land at China Beach, joining twenty-three thousand American military advisers training the South Vietnamese.

8 Brian Wilson's precursor to *Pet Sounds*, *The Beach Boys Today!*, is released, boasting a stunning array of instrumentation.

15 President Johnson vows "We Shall Overcome" in a televised speech supporting protestors in Selma.

16 Eighty-two-year-old activist Alice Herz sets herself on fire in Detroit to protest U.S. involvement in Vietnam.

24–25 Thirty-five hundred people attend a teach-in about Vietnam held at the University of Michigan and organized by Students for a Democratic Society (SDS).

25 The March from Selma to Montgomery concludes with twenty-five thousand gathered at the Alabama State Capitol. Martin Luther King Jr. gives his "How Long? Not Long!" speech.

27 Curtis Mayfield and the Impressions' civil rights anthem "People Get Ready" peaks at No. 14. Bob Marley and the Wailers rework it into "One Love" in Jamaica later in the year.

27 Dylan's *Bringing It All Back Home* is released.

27 John Lennon and George Harrison are dosed with LSD without their consent for the first time by Harrison's dentist.

April

3 Solomon Burke's "Got to Get You Off My Mind," inspired by the death of his friend Sam Cooke, tops the R&B charts.

4 The Staple Singers record "Freedom Highway," about the Selma-to-Montgomery March, at Chicago's New Nazareth Church (on an undetermined Sunday during April).

13 Guitarist Eric Clapton leaves the Yardbirds because he considers the harpsichord-laden "For Your Love" too pop. The band tries to recruit Jimmy Page, who declines and suggests Jeff Beck.

20 *The Pawnbroker* is released in American movie theaters, featuring the first bare breasts approved by the U.S. Production Code.

May

1 The civil rights anthem "We're Gonna Make It," by Little Milton, tops the R&B charts.

5 The Grateful Dead (under the name the Warlocks) debut at Magoo's Pizza, in the San Francisco Bay Area.

6 James Brown recuts "I Got You (I Feel Good)" in Miami, Florida, in his new funk style.

6 The Rolling Stones write "Satisfaction" at a hotel pool in Clearwater, Florida, as a Dylanesque folk song.

8 The British Invasion of the United States peaks as eight of the U.S. Top 10 singles are English (and one Australian).

.12 The Rolling Stones rework "Satisfaction" with the beat of the Four Tops' "I Can't Help Myself (Sugar Pie, Honey Bunch)."

21–23 Between ten thousand and thirty thousand people attend an anti-war teach-in in Berkeley, California.

21 The Who release "Anyway, Anyhow, Anywhere," with an avant-garde feedback instrumental.

22 Marvin Gaye's "I'll Be Doggone" (produced/co-written by Smokey Robinson) tops the R&B charts with a riff influenced by the Searchers' proto-folk-rock "Needles and Pins."

22 The Beatles top the charts with the jangle pop of "Ticket to Ride."

22 Van Morrison and Them's garage rock anthem "Gloria" peaks in the United States at No. 93.

June

1 Bob Marley and the Wailers release the ska anthem "Rude Boy" (approximate date).

2 James Brown's "Papa's Got a Brand New Bag" is released; starting on August 14, it will top the R&B charts for eight weeks.

5 Sam the Sham and the Pharaohs' "Wooly Bully" reaches No. 2. *Billboard* later determines it the best-selling song of the year.

6 "(I Can't Get No) Satisfaction" is released. Starting July 10, it will top the pop charts for four weeks.

7 The U.S. Supreme Court decides in *Griswold v. Connecticut* that states cannot outlaw the birth control pill (a.k.a. the Pill) because the Constitution guarantees "marital privacy."

12 The Supremes and production team Holland-Dozier-Holland score their fifth consecutive No. 1 with "Back in My Arms Again."

19 Phil Ochs performs "I Ain't Marching Anymore" at the New York Folk Festival.

20 Three members of the Rat Pack (Frank Sinatra, Dean Martin, and Sammy Davis Jr.) give their last performance for twenty-three years.

21 The Byrds release their *Mr. Tambourine Man* album with a psychedelic cover shot taken using a fish-eye camera lens.

23 Smokey Robinson and the Miracles release "The Tracks of My Tears."

26 The Byrds' "Mr. Tambourine Man" single hits No. 1.

28 The Red Dog Saloon opens in Virginia City, Nevada, with a performance by the Charlatans and LSD provided by Owsley Stanley, kick-starting the San Francisco psychedelic scene.

July

 4 The East Coast Homophile Organizations (ECHO) protests at Philadelphia's Independence Hall. It becomes a yearly event for the rest of the decade as the "Annual Reminder" for gay rights.

 8 Nina Simone's "I Put a Spell on You" peaks in the United Kingdom at No. 49. Later in the year, the Beatles adapt the song's "I love you" bridge for "Michelle."

15 Barry McGuire records "Eve of Destruction" in one take.

17 Curtis Mayfield and the Impressions' civil rights anthem "Meeting Over Yonder" peaks at No. 48.

19 The Beatles release John Lennon's confessional single "Help!" Their film of the same name premieres ten days later.

20 Dylan releases "Like a Rolling Stone," which reaches No. 2 in September. At 6:13, it's by far the longest single to hit the pop charts, with the most expressionistic and jaded lyrics heard on AM radio to date.

20 The Lovin' Spoonful debuts with their folk-rock anthem "Do You Believe in Magic."

23 Paul Simon performs "I Am a Rock" solo on the British television program *Ready Steady Go!* in London.

24 Jackie DeShannon hits No. 7 with Burt Bacharach and Hal David's idealistic anthem "What the World Needs Now Is Love."

25 Bob Dylan is booed at the Newport Folk Festival for playing an electrified "Maggie's Farm."

26 John Coltrane performs *A Love Supreme* live for the only time, at Festival Mondial du Jazz Antibes, in France.

26 The *New York Times* proclaims model Edie Sedgwick Andy Warhol's latest star.

28 President Johnson doubles the number of men per month to be drafted to Vietnam, boosting the figure from seventeen thousand to thirty-five thousand.

30 As part of the Great Society and the War on Poverty, Johnson signs into law Medicare and Medicaid.

30 The Kinks release "See My Friends," imitating the music and vocals they heard while in India.

August

5 The *CBS Evening News with Walter Cronkite* airs footage of American soldiers burning the huts of Vietnamese villagers. An outraged Johnson complains to the network's president.

6 President Johnson signs the Voting Rights Act into law in the Capitol Rotunda with Martin Luther King Jr. in attendance.

7 Herman's Hermits top the charts with "I'm Henry VIII, I Am," a cover of a 1910 music hall song. Soon other British bands will rediscover the genre, akin to American vaudeville.

7 Hunter S. Thompson, the Hells Angels, Allen Ginsberg, and Neal Cassady attend an LSD-fueled party at Ken Kesey's.

7 Wilson Pickett's "In the Midnight Hour" hits No. 1 on the R&B chart with the delayed drumbeat that will become a Stax Records staple.

9 Massachusetts Institute of Technology implements the Compatible Time-Sharing System (CTSS) with the earliest-known form of e-mail, MAIL.

11–15 Riots erupt in the Watts neighborhood of Los Angeles.

13 The Jefferson Airplane debuts at the San Francisco club Matrix.

14 Cher defends Sonny's long hair in "I Got You Babe," which tops the chart for three weeks.

15 Donovan releases his cover of Buffy St. Marie's antiwar anthem "Universal Soldier," which goes head to head with Glen Campbell's version. In October, Campbell will say draft card burners should be hanged.

15 Otis Redding releases his composition "Respect."

15 The Beatles play the first concert in a sports arena, Shea Stadium, with an attendance record (55,600) that will stand until 1973.

21 Waylon Jennings releases his first Nashville single, "That's the Chance I'll Have to Take."

24 The Beatles trip with the Byrds and Peter Fonda in Los Angeles, and then visit Elvis Presley three days later.

25 Three members of the Sexual Freedom League are sentenced to three months (suspended) for staging a "Nude Wade-in" in San Francisco.

28 The Beach Boys reach No. 3 with "California Girls," featuring Brian Wilson's Bach-inspired intro.

30 Bob Dylan releases his visionary masterpiece *Highway 61 Revisited*.

31 President Johnson decrees the burning of draft cards a crime punishable by a five-year prison sentence and a thousand-dollar fine.

September

1 Mary Quant's eight-city "Youthquake" tour of U.S. department stores climaxes in New York, featuring models in miniskirts dancing to the band the Skunks.

6 Bakersfield's Merle Haggard releases his first album *Strangers*.

13 Simon and Garfunkel's "The Sound of Silence" is rereleased after being electrified by Dylan's producer, Tom Wilson, in the style of the Byrds.

15 Bill Cosby becomes the first black actor to star in a TV drama with his role in *I Spy*. Four southern stations decline to air the show.

25 Barry McGuire's "Eve of Destruction" becomes the most topical song to hit No. 1. Along with attacking southern racism, it spotlights the injustice of being too young to vote but old enough to be drafted.

25 The Yardbirds reach No. 9 with "Heart Full of Soul," in which Jeff Beck imitates the Indian sitar on his guitar with a fuzz box.

25 The Animals' "We Gotta Get out of This Place," by Brill Building songwriters Mann and Weil, peaks at No. 13.

25 The Barbarians make it to No. 83 with their long-hair anthem "Are You a Boy or Are You a Girl?"

October

1 The Yardbirds emulate Gregorian chants in the U.K. B side "Still I'm Sad."

9 The Beatles' "Yesterday," with baroque string quartet, tops the pop chart for four weeks and becomes the most covered song of the decade.

15–16 The Vietnam Day Committee helps coordinate the International Days of Protest against American Military Intervention, with antiwar groups in more than forty cities in the United States and Europe.

15 Country Joe (McDonald) and the Fish perform the "I-Feel-Like-I'm-Fixin'-to-Die Rag" at a Berkeley teach-in.

15 The Great Society, with Grace Slick, debuts at the Coffee Gallery in San Francisco's North Beach.

16 Despite Allen Ginsberg chanting "Hare Krishna," members of the Hells Angels attack antiwar protestors in Oakland.

16 Scenesters from the psychedelic Red Dog Saloon, named the Family Dog, organize the dance party "A Tribute to Dr. Strange" at the International Longshore and Warehouse Union (ILWU) hall, in San Francisco, with Jefferson Airplane, the Charlatans, and the Great Society.

23 The pro-war "Hello Vietnam," recorded by Johnnie Wright, tops the country charts for three weeks.

24 The Family Dog holds "A Tribute to Sparkle Plenty" at the ILWU hall in San Francisco, with the Lovin' Spoonful and the Charlatans.

26 Queen Elizabeth II declares the Beatles "Members of the Order of the British Empire" at Buckingham Palace.

26 The Rolling Stones record "As Tears Go By" with strings, in imitation of "Yesterday."

30 Otis Redding tops the R&B album charts with *Otis Blue*, which includes his cover of the Rolling Stones' "Satisfaction."

30 Supermodel Jean Shrimpton is criticized for wearing a minidress to the Victoria Derby in Australia.

30 Fontella Bass tops the R&B charts for four weeks with "Rescue Me."

November

1 Smokey Robinson and the Miracles release their *Going to a Go-Go* album.

6 Bob Dylan's attack on his former folk community, "Positively 4th Street," peaks at No. 7.

6 The Rolling Stones' "Get off My Cloud" b/w "I'm Free" hits No. 1 for two weeks.

13 The Lovin' Spoonful releases "You Didn't Have to Be So Nice," inspiring the melody of Brian Wilson's "God Only Knows."

19 Nancy Sinatra records future women's liberation anthem "These Boots Are Made for Walkin'."

19 The *Berkeley Barb* publishes Allen Ginsberg's essay "Demonstration or Spectacle as Example, as Communication, or How to Make a March/Spectacle," which extols the use of flowers in protest marches, the concept later dubbed "flower power."

19 The Leaves release the garage rock anthem "Hey Joe."

22 Bob Dylan secretly marries Sara Lownds; their first son, Jesse Byron, is born January 6.

22 Stevie Wonder releases "Uptight," with a beat inspired by "Satisfaction."

27 Ken Kesey holds the first public Acid Test, in Santa Cruz, with punch bowls spiked with LSD.

27 The Turtles' anti-conformity anthem, "Let Me Be," peaks at No. 29.

29 Johnny Cash records his folk spoof "The One on the Right Is on the Left."

30 Ralph Nader publishes his exposé of the automobile industry, *Unsafe at Any Speed*.

December

3 On their *Rubber Soul* album, the Beatles use the sitar for the first time in a pop song to make "Norwegian Wood" seem less Dylanesque, with lyrics depicting the burgeoning sexual revolution.

3 The Beatles try to match "Satisfaction" with their own soul-inflected dance hit, "Day Tripper," and try to out-jangle the Byrds with "Nowhere Man."

3 The Rolling Stones begin recording *Aftermath*, featuring Brian Jones on a variety of exotic instruments.

3 *The Who Sings My Generation* album explodes with some of the most aggressive guitar, drum, and bass work yet committed to vinyl.

4 James Brown's second funk single, "I Got You (I Feel Good)," tops the R&B chart for six weeks with the most prominent bass on the airwaves, courtesy of band member Bernard Odum.

4 The Byrds own the No. 1 spot through Christmas Eve via their cover of Pete Seeger's "Turn! Turn! Turn! (To Everything There Is a Season)," with lyrics from the Bible.

4 The Grateful Dead play the second Acid Test, in San Jose, becoming Ken Kesey's house band.

7 The Massachusetts Supreme Court upholds high school officials' right to suspend students with long hair.

8 With the help of their friend Barry McGuire, the Mamas and the Papas release the folk-rock "California Dreamin'," with baroque flute accompaniment.

9 *A Charlie Brown Christmas* debuts on CBS.

11 The Velvet Underground opens for the Myddle Class at New Jersey's Summit High School.

16 Mary Beth Tinker and Christopher Eckhardt are sent home for wearing black armbands to their Iowa high school to protest the war. The students will take their case to trial, and in 1968 the U.S. Supreme Court will rule in favor of their right to self-expression.

18 The Animals' anthem of independence, "It's My Life," reaches No. 24.

20 The Student Nonviolent Coordinating Committee newsletter announces the formation of the Lowndes County Freedom Organization. Its symbol is the black panther.

31 With the help of their new manager, Andy Warhol, the Velvet Underground appears in a segment of the *CBS Evening News with Walter Cronkite.*

31 U.S. troops in Vietnam number 184,000 at year's end.

1965

INTRODUCTION

A Change Is Gonna Come

"I guess the Fifties would have ended in about '65."
—BOB DYLAN

Nineteen sixty-five is the moment in rock history when the Technicolor butterfly burst out of its black-and-white cocoon. The combined forces of TV, the civil rights movement, the antiwar movement, the Pill, psychedelics, and long hair gave people a heightened awareness of the ways they were being repressed and led to a demand for freedom in all spheres of life, from the political to the sexual to the spiritual. Musicians gave voice to these passions with an immediacy unmatched by other artistic forms. Unlike artists in film, TV, and print, musicians were largely uncensored and could get their new singles out in a matter of days. The epic cultural changes ignited an unprecedented explosion in creativity, and the performers' rivalries resulted in the most groundbreaking twelve months in music history. It was the year rock and roll evolved into the premier art form of its time and accelerated the drive for personal liberty throughout the Western world, as artists such as the Beatles, Bob Dylan, James Brown, the Rolling Stones, John Coltrane, Johnny Cash, Bob Marley, the Byrds, the Supremes, the Beach Boys, the Who, Buck Owens, the Kinks, Otis Redding, the Lovin' Spoonful, Smokey Robinson, the Yardbirds, Frank Sinatra, Waylon Jennings, the Grateful Dead, the Mamas and the Papas, the Four Tops, Simon and Garfunkel, and Marvin Gaye raced to outdo one another with each successive release.

New sounds were explored, such as the jangle, the sitar, and feedback. Baroque pop blended rock with elements of classical music, using harpsichords, flutes, string quartets, Bach-inspired melodies, and Gregorian chants. Ken Kesey's Acid Tests with the Grateful Dead—with their liquid light shows, strobes, multimedia projections, and extended instrumental jams (not to mention spiked Kool-Aid)—established the model for rock concerts and raves to follow.

While the musicians birthed psychedelia, Dylan brought surrealism to lyrics. When he and the Byrds defied acoustic purists and matched the visionary depth of folk music with the raw power of electric rock, they proved it was possible to have both artistic freedom and a hit. Dylan's tracks on *Bringing It All Back Home* and *Highway 61 Revisited* liberated his peers to write about anything they wanted and, along with the Beatles' *Rubber Soul*, ushered in the era of the rock album as a cohesive work of art, as opposed to a random collection of hits and filler songs.

As the civil rights movement reached its crescendo, the golden age of soul fused the transcendence of gospel with the catharsis of rhythm and blues. Motown broke pop's glass ceiling, fueled by competition both inside the company and with other soul labels such as Stax Records. Meanwhile, James Brown invented funk by stripping everything out except the rhythm, and thus built the foundation for all dance music to follow.

In country, Johnny Cash, Waylon Jennings, Buck Owens, and Merle Haggard rebelled against the Nashville sound.

Even Frank Sinatra managed one of his most remarkable comebacks in a career full of them, with the Grammy Award–winning albums *September of My Years* and *A Man and His Music*.

You couldn't turn on the radio without hearing a new classic: "Like a Rolling Stone," "(I Can't Get No) Satisfaction," "Papa's Got a Brand New Bag," "My Generation," "People Get Ready," "Nowhere Man," "Mr. Tambourine Man," "The Sound of Silence," "Eve of Destruction," "Freedom Highway," "It's My Life," "Respect," "I Fought the Law," "My Girl," "Go Where You Wanna Go," "One Love," "A Change Is Gonna Come," "Do You Believe In Magic," "We're Gonna Make It," "You've Lost That Lovin' Feelin'," "In the Midnight Hour," "California Dreamin'," "Heart Full of Soul," "I Can't Help Myself," "California Girls," "Stop! In the Name of Love," "Norwegian Wood," "I'll Be Doggone,"

"I Got You Babe," "Nowhere to Run," "Let Me Be," "I'll Feel a Whole Lot Better," "I Ain't Marching Anymore," "Till the End of the Day," "Get Off of My Cloud," "Turn! Turn! Turn!"

The Beatles loomed over their era like possibly no other artist has since. From January 1965 through January 1966 they enjoyed six No. 1 U.S. singles in a row, a feat unbroken until the Bee Gees tied it in 1979 and Whitney Houston topped it with seven singles in 1988. The emotional arc of those six singles reflects the shifting mood of that extraordinary year. The sunny "I Feel Fine" and "Eight Days a Week" matched the optimism both of America rebounding from President Kennedy's assassination and Britain proud to be the swinging capital of pop culture. The hopefulness continued through the first half of the year, as blacks secured the right to vote in the South and President Johnson vowed to end poverty with such Great Society programs as Medicare and Medicaid.

But the Beatles turned melancholy in "Ticket to Ride," and desperate with "Help!," just as President Johnson began drafting thirty-five thousand men a month to Vietnam and Watts exploded in the worst case of urban unrest since the Detroit race riot of 1943.

The desolate "Yesterday" resonated with millions who felt a stable past was crumbling in the face of social upheaval. Parents began to see rockers as Pied Pipers leading their children to long hair and drug-soaked promiscuity. Rioters, black militants, antiwar radicals, and Acid Test partiers would soon scare enough voters to sweep Ronald Reagan into the governorship of California, an election that prophesized a nationwide shift away from liberalism. The pensive "We Can Work It Out" bemoaned the fussing and fighting that dominated the rest of the decade.

Dylan's albums followed a similar emotional arc. The ebullience of his first rock album, *Bringing It All Back Home*, was in marked contrast to the darkness of *Highway 61 Revisited*, recorded just days after he was vilified at the Newport Folk Festival for going commercial. Buck Owens also weathered the outrage of puritans, for daring to mix country with rockabilly.

In fact, the argument over authenticity was a major theme of the year: the Beatles versus the Stones; the polished sounds of Motown's session musicians the Funk Brothers and the Detroit Symphony Orchestra versus Stax's Booker T. and the M.G.s and the Memphis Horns. Nashville's slick A-Team versus Bakersfield's steel guitars and Fender Telecasters. Ironically, many folk-rockers were backed by the LA studio pros dubbed the Wrecking Crew.

The biggest battle of all was America's fight to reclaim its title as the center of pop music from the British Invasion. There were twenty-seven U.S. No. 1 hits that year; thirteen were British and fourteen American. On the British side, five were from the Beatles, two from the Rolling Stones, two from Herman's Hermits, and four from other British artists. The American effort comprised six Motown hits (four by the Supremes), four folk-rock hits (two by the Byrds), three from the Brill Building hit factory, and one from the Beach Boys.

Probably the musicians' most recurring struggle that year was the inner battle not to self-destruct. As they raced neck and neck to be the biggest acts on earth, artists such as the Beach Boys, the Byrds, the Supremes, the Who, the Kinks, Marvin Gaye, and Johnny Cash threatened to implode, either from outside pressure or from personal demons.

At the dawn of 1965, thanks to the postwar baby boom, half the U.S. population was younger than twenty-five, and 41 percent were younger than twenty.[1] (By contrast, in 2012 only 23.5 percent of Americans were below the age of eighteen.) It was the most educated generation in history, buoyed by unprecedented prosperity. But the "generation gap" had not yet kicked in; teens mainly followed in the footsteps of their parents as they grew up. The Beatles were shaggy, but Paul McCartney soothed adults by singing show tunes. High school principals ensured that boys' hair was kept short and that girls' skirt hems reached below the knee.

If you needed to unwind, you drank alcohol or took pills. Amphetamine and barbiturate use was so widespread that Congress would pass the Drug Abuse Control Amendments on July 15, to rein in the consumption of stimulants and depressants. Eastern traditions such as yoga and meditation were mostly unknown, particularly as Asian immigration was heavily restricted. Many Americans considered psychologists and counselors "funny doctors," and would not have considered seeing one themselves, as that might have implied there was something wrong with them.

In 1964 only 3.1 percent of American TV owners had a color set, though NBC started broadcasting almost all its shows in color in the fall of 1965, for those who did. Eighty percent of the country was white (11 percent black),[2] and many whites were still rural residents, as demonstrated by the shows that were popular then: *Bonanza, The Andy Griffith Show, Petticoat Junc-*

tion, The Beverly Hillbillies, Gomer Pyle, Lassie, The Big Valley, The Virginian, Daniel Boone, The Wild Wild West, and *Gunsmoke.* Other highly rated programs included *The Lucy Show, The Red Skelton Hour, Walt Disney's Wonderful World of Color, The Lawrence Welk Show, The Donna Reed Show,* and *Gidget.* The Cold War was reflected in spy shows such as *The Man from U.N.C.L.E.* and *Get Smart.* The wife had magic powers in *Bewitched,* but her husband tried to squelch her using them.

On the big screen, the top-grossing films were *The Sound of Music, Doctor Zhivago,* and the James Bond feature *Thunderball.* Movies almost always had happy endings, unless they were foreign. The Motion Picture Production Code prohibited nudity and scenes that were "unacceptably sex suggestive and lustful."[3] Comedian Lenny Bruce had been convicted for obscenity in April 1964 for, among other outrages, observing that Eleanor Roosevelt had the nicest breasts of all the First Ladies.[4]

The American economy was booming, and if you wanted a job, you could move to a factory town such as Flint, Michigan, and get one. "Oh God, I'm telling you, you could quit a job one day and get a job across town in another GM plant. They needed workers," recalled former General Motors employee Don Spillman.[5] The company was forced to send officials into the streets to find locals who could staff the assembly lines.

But down south, if you were black, the situation was different. The voting registrar administered literacy tests to dissuade you from voting. If you passed and still tried to vote, there would be reprisals from the Ku Klux Klan. Interracial marriage was still banned in twelve states. Many concert venues had only just stopped roping off the black section from the white section, per the 1964 Civil Rights Act's ban on segregation. The Beatles had to put riders in their contracts stipulating they would not play segregated venues.

If you were gay or had bisexual tendencies, your parents might take you to a psychiatrist who would give you shock therapy, as happened to future Velvet Underground member Lou Reed. If you had socialist beliefs, you kept quiet, because the Communist Control Act of 1954 made it illegal to be a member of the Communist Party, and the House Un-American Activities Committee was still investigating citizens with Communist ties.

Yet, recent technological and pharmaceutical innovations had begun to affect the collective unconscious. In 1965 their influence exploded in an unprecedented chain reaction.

Citizens in the North had been able to disregard the horrors of Jim Crow in the southern states, but now television beamed out images of southern police officers siccing their German shepherds on black teenagers and blasting them across the street with fire hoses, which ripped hair off their heads. After ABC interrupted *Judgment at Nuremberg* to broadcast footage from the "Bloody Sunday" march in Selma, Alabama, public outcry pushed the Voting Rights Act through Congress, and federal monitors were sent to protect blacks as they voted in the South.

When Johnson started the ground war in Vietnam, TV broadcast images of soldiers burning huts while peasant families sobbed, causing many people back home to question the conflict. And televised antiwar demonstrations revealed that there was not complete consensus among the American public with regard to the war, causing many viewers to think harder about their own stance.

Up until now, women mostly had to choose between family and career, and few chose career. If you were an unmarried female, you were either a good girl or "fast." Officially doctors prescribed the Pill only to married women, lest they be seen as contributing to wanton promiscuity, but more unmarried women were beginning to gain access to it. As pregnancy ceased being a concern, at a time when sexually transmitted diseases had been largely eradicated, many people began to rethink the "Madonna/whore" paradigm they'd been brought up with. In June, when the Supreme Court struck down state laws prohibiting the sale of contraceptives, it became possible to dispense the Pill to low-income married women on a mass scale as part of the War on Poverty, paving the way for the sexual revolution and unlocking passions pent up for eons.

LSD use was still largely under the radar, but many of its proselytizers, such as Timothy Leary and Allen Ginsberg, found that the drug's offer of a momentary glimpse of cosmic enlightenment jibed with the philosophies espoused by Asian religions. The two promoted ancient holy Tibetan texts and meditations and mantras. In the spring, both the Beatles and the Beach Boys would be dosed with acid for the first time; in autumn, Ken Kesey started holding his Acid Tests in public. Psychedelics offered a whole new way of perceiving reality, and their arrival created a hunger for a drug-free, permanent version of the same state of mind, which laid the groundwork for the spiritual revival and the human potential and consciousness movements.

At the time, only novels and foreign films could rival music in its ability to discuss civil rights, politics, sex, and drugs. But those other forms took a long time to produce. Dylan recorded whole albums in one to three days in which he advised against following leaders and warned that society would try to exploit you. And when he moved out of the (smaller) folk market and into the mainstream pop charts, he took the message from the already converted to mainstream teenagers—just as they began to receive their draft notices.

Singer-songwriter Arlo Guthrie said:

> The corporations, the businessmen and women who were controlling the entertainment business, did not understand the lyrics of the songs that they were selling. The guys on the radio didn't get it. The guys that owned the radio had no connection with the music, in terms of understanding it. For the first time, there was an explosion of all different kinds of music being played. And the lyrics were unintelligible. Not just the lyrics—the philosophy, the heart of it, was unreadable, unknowable, to the people who controlled the industry. So all of a sudden, all around the world, for a very short time . . . imagine a world where everybody's got a radio, and all of a sudden everybody's saying what they really think, in words you could understand, but your parents couldn't . . . A floodgate had opened, because we were using a language that couldn't be understood over whose system we were using to communicate it. And it was so wonderful. People were walking down the street plain laughing, just having a great time, because all of a sudden, it was free.[6]

These heavy ramifications were still being conveyed, for the most part, by musicians using an upbeat pop structure that, to our ears today, carries a sense of innocence and, sometimes, naïveté. In a 2012 paper entitled "Emotional Cues in American Popular Music: Five Decades of the Top 40," researchers at the University of Toronto and Freie Universität of Berlin studied the tempo and key of more than a thousand hits from 1965 to 2009 and determined that music today is statistically slower and sadder.[7] Our culture interprets songs in major keys with fast tempos as happy and uplifting, whereas slow, minor-key songs are interpreted as sad, serious, complex, and sophisticated. In the 1960s, 85 percent of Top 40 songs were in a major key, whereas in the first decade of the 2000s, only 42.5 percent were. In the 1960s, songs averaged 116 beats per minute, with the average song length being just under three minutes, while today, 100 beats per minute is the norm, with an average song length of just under four minutes. Contemporary songs often combine a minor key with a fast beat, fostering a more ambiguous, mixed mood than the "feel-good" oldies.[8]

The music itself is vastly different in other respects. In 1965, much of it was still recorded live. Stax Records had just a one-track mono recorder for artists such as Otis Redding. Other facilities, such as Abbey Road, where the Beatles recorded, had four-track recorders. The bands would record the rhythm track live, and then overdub their vocals and perhaps additional instruments. A large portion of bands in 1965 excelled at harmonies, from the Beatles, the Byrds, and the Beach Boys to Motown groups—an art much less prevalent today. Nineteen sixty-five was a year with one foot in the world of doo-wop, still embraced by the Four Seasons and Smokey Robinson, and the other in the future as British art school rockers transmogrified the blues with fuzz boxes and distortion. It is that tension of awakening awareness and experimentation inside the old-school framework that makes 1965 unique, the ground zero moment when the monochrome door opened onto a kaleidoscopic Oz waiting on the other side.

PROLOGUE

I Shall Be Free

The Beatles and the Animals lure Bob Dylan toward rock; while Dylan, the Who, and the Kinks influence the Beatles' first No. 1 single of the year.

*

At the end of 1963, after President Kennedy was assassinated, the Beatles, the Rolling Stones, and the Beatles' manager, Brian Epstein, were hanging out at The Ad Lib, a nightclub in London. Two *New York Post* writers, Al Aronowitz and Pete Hamill, joined them.

Aronowitz, who in 1959 had done a twelve-article series on the Beat Generation for the *Post*, was trying to convince the Beatles to listen to the folk singer Bob Dylan, whose third album, *The Times They Are A-Changin'*, was about to be released. John Lennon, a notoriously bad drunk, scoffed, "To hell with Dylan, we play rock and roll."[1]

The funny thing was Lennon had started out playing a British combination of folk music, blues, and ragtime called skiffle. And when Dylan was in high school, he was quoted in the yearbook as saying that his ambition was to "join Little Richard." At the high school talent show, he and his band blasted a cover of Danny and the Juniors' "Rock and Roll Is Here to Stay"—until the principal cut the mike.

Dylan's producer, Tom Wilson, actually wanted Dylan to play with a band, and the singer-songwriter had recorded a rock-and-roll single, "Mixed Up Confusion," a year earlier. But his manager, Albert Grossman, who wanted to market Dylan as a folk singer, had the single retracted almost as soon as it was released. At the time, the intellectual folkies looked down on rock and roll as commercial kid stuff.

Still, that evening at The Ad Lib, Lennon, who didn't know about Dylan's rock past, sneered, "Dylan, Dylan. Give me Chuck Berry, give me Little Richard. Don't give me fancy crap. Crap, American folky intellectual crap. It's crap."[2]

"Ach, come off it, John," Paul McCartney said.[3]

Soon McCartney and George Harrison had *The Freewheelin' Bob Dylan* on heavy rotation in the Beatles' hotel rooms.

The following February, the week the Beatles made their first appearance on *The Ed Sullivan Show*, Dylan was on a road trip with some friends when he heard "I Want to Hold Your Hand" on the radio. He "nearly jumped out of the car," his tour manager later recalled.[4]

"Did you hear that?" Dylan cried. "That was fuckin' great! Oh man."[5]

Dylan later said, "They were doing things nobody was doing. Their chords were outrageous, just outrageous, and their harmonies made it all valid . . . But I kept it to myself that I really dug them. Everybody else thought they were for the teenyboppers, that they were gonna pass right away. But it was obvious to me that they had staying power. I knew they were pointing the direction where music had to go."[6]

Dylan also felt a kinship with the band because he believed that they were singing "I get high" in the bridge of "I Want to Hold Your Hand." Dylan smoked marijuana regularly and had a bag of it perched on the station wagon's dashboard for the length of the trip.

When he returned to New York, he got an electric guitar.

On March 23, 1964, Lennon appeared on the BBC TV show *Tonight* to promote the release of his first book, *In His Own Write*, a collection of cartoony sketches and short satirical pieces. His shtick in both *Write* and its sequel, *A Spaniard in the Works*, was to spell words as they sounded and then twist them into absurd puns ("Last Will and Testicle"), partially masking gleefully mean tales of death, violence, deformity, and marital ambivalence. There were vignettes about pubic crabs, putting dogs to sleep, men marrying horses, and beating your friends to death on Christmas. They would have shocked read-ers' parents had they bothered to decipher them.

Backstage, host Kenneth Allsop challenged Lennon to write more per-sonal songs like the bits in his book, rather than the generic love songs the group had been releasing.[7] The encouragement to dig deeper coincided with Lennon's gradual conversion to Dylan. When the group recorded "I'm a Loser" on August 14, Lennon included a lyric inspired by the clown who cried in the alley in Dylan's "A Hard Rain's A-Gonna Fall." "I objected to the word 'clown,' because that was always artsy-fartsy, but Dylan had used it so I thought it was all right, and it rhymed with whatever I was doing."[8]

Aside from the apocalyptic visions of "A Hard Rain's A-Gonna Fall" and some absurd comedy tracks, the bulk of Dylan's early songs were grounded in reality. That was beginning to shift, though. In his autobiography, *Chron-icles*, Dylan writes that when his girlfriend Suze Rotolo introduced him to the French Symbolist poet Arthur Rimbaud, "That was a big deal." In 1871, the sixteen-year-old Rimbaud had written, "I say that one must be a seer, make oneself a seer. The poet makes himself a seer by a long, prodigious, and ratio-nal disordering of all the senses. Every form of love, of suffering, of madness; he searches himself, he consumes all the poisons in him, and keeps only their quintessences . . . He reaches [for] the unknown and even if, crazed, he ends up losing the understanding of his visions, at least he has seen them."

Dylan's senses started getting disordered in "Chimes of Freedom." Caught in a thunderstorm, he and his friends hear the lightning and see the thun-der. Synesthesia, in which a sensation is perceived by a sense other than the one being stimulated (for instance, seeing sounds or hearing images), was an effect sometimes attributed to the hallucinogen LSD. According to music producer Paul Rothchild, he and Dylan's road manager Victor Maymudes in-troduced Dylan to the drug at the end of April 1964, following the wrap of his spring tour. Some accounts say Dylan wrote "Mr. Tambourine Man" after staying up all night listening to music while on acid.[9]

The tambourine man himself was Bruce Langhorne, Dylan's session gui-tarist for numerous albums. "On one session, Tom Wilson had asked [Bruce] to play tambourine," Dylan remembered. "[The tambourine] was as big as a wagon wheel. He was playing, and this vision of him playing this tambourine just stuck in my mind."[10] Called a Turkish frame drum, the instrument had small bells attached inside that gave it the "jingle jangle" sound referenced in the lyrics. The song's "magic swirlin' ship" was a giant float Dylan and his friends saw in a Mardi Gras parade on that February road trip, after being awake for three days on speed, weed, and booze.

But regardless of whether drugs were an influence, "Mr. Tambourine Man" captures Dylan's joy of writing until dawn, when the weariness turned to trance and his mind opened into a dreamlike space between waking and sleep, freeing him to wander beyond time, drunk on alliteration and the pure sounds of words.

In June 1964 he recorded *Another Side of Bob Dylan* in one day, and taped a version of "Mr. Tambourine Man" accompanied by Ramblin' Jack Elliott. But he decided he could do the song better, at a later date, and kept it off the album, though he played it live at London's Royal Festival Hall and the Newport Folk Festival.

"It Ain't Me Babe" was another new song he performed at the Royal Festival Hall. Both a London *Times* critic and Dylan fan Johnny Cash thought its "no, no, no" chorus was a spoof of the "yeah yeah yeah" chorus of the Beatles' "She Loves You." By then, Dylan had cooled on the Beatles, in the face of their continued deluge of the media, and told his journalist friend Aronowitz that he thought they were bubble gum.

Still, ten days after Dylan recorded *Another Side*, his fourth acoustic album, a band from Manchester released a rock version of a song from his self-titled debut album, called "House of the Rising Sun." The Animals' organist, Alan Price, was a huge Dylan fan, and the group had been covering the song on tour with Chuck Berry. It had been going over so well that their producer, Mickie Most, had decided to make it their next single, even though the subject matter was about gambling in whorehouses. The band captured the tune in one take, and it hit No. 1 on both sides of the Atlantic, one of the darkest songs ever to top AM radio. Rock critic Dave Marsh called it the first folk-rock song.

Price laughed in an interview, "I got told this story by Joan Baez. She said when Bob Dylan heard it they were driving up the coast, past Monterey, California, and he stopped the car and got out and beat the bumpers. He was miffed because he wanted to play electric folk music and when he heard that we'd got there first he was really annoyed."[11]

The Beatles also became harder for Dylan to write off when their first feature film, *A Hard Day's Night*, was released in August of that year. United Artists had originally undertaken the film merely for the soundtrack money, but the team assembled to produce it was exemplary. Cinematographer Gilbert Taylor's previous film was Stanley Kubrick's *Dr. Strangelove*; Liverpudlian Alun Owen's screenplay would be nominated for an Oscar; director Richard Lester's quick edits and hand-held moving camera would set the template for all rock videos to follow; and the witty exuberance of the Fab Four garnered comparisons to the Marx Brothers, much like Dylan's first album's liner notes compared his stage mannerisms to those of Charlie Chaplin.

So on August 28, 1964, Aronowitz took Dylan to meet the group at New York's Delmonico hotel. When Dylan arrived, the Beatles offered him amphetamine pills. While Dylan was certainly no stranger to speed, he said that he'd prefer "cheap wine" instead.[12] "I've got some really good grass," he offered.

When the group admitted that they didn't smoke pot, Dylan was nonplussed. But what about their song about getting high?

The band explained the lyric in "I Want to Hold Your Hand" was not "I get high" but "I can't hide," as in the singer couldn't hide his love for his woman.

At that point, the Beatles had smoked marijuana only a few times, and none of these had been transcendent experiences. One evening they learned the Twist. Another time Lennon and his wife, Cynthia, smoked a joint with some other couples, but the already trashed Lennon threw up in the bathroom and staggered home.[13]

Still, the Beatles were tentatively game. The road managers stuffed towels in the door cracks and drew the shades so none of the fans singing Beatles songs outside could see. Dylan rolled some joints and offered one to Lennon. Perhaps flashing back to his earlier bad night, Lennon passed it on to Ringo Starr—"My royal taster."

There were cops guarding the hallways from fans, so Starr and Dylan went into the back room. Starr didn't know he was supposed to share the joint with Dylan and smoked the whole thing. When he returned, the others asked how it was.

"The ceiling's coming down on me," he replied.

The others leaped up and went into the back with Dylan to try it.

McCartney said, "For about five minutes we went, 'This isn't doing anything,' so we kept having more. 'Sssshhh! This isn't doing anything. Are you feeling . . . gggggzzzz!' and we started giggling uncontrollably."[14]

Soon everyone was in hysterics. Dylan answered the constantly ringing phone with "This is Beatlemania here."[15] McCartney became convinced he had discovered the meaning of life and, after spending an eternity trying to find a pencil, had road manager Mal Evans write down his words of wisdom.

The next morning the group looked at the paper, which read, "There are Seven Levels!" "And we pissed ourselves laughing," McCartney said. "I mean, 'What the fuck's that? What the fuck are the seven levels?'"[16] Soon the band was smoking marijuana for breakfast.

The group finished their American tour in late September and flew back to England. On October 8, on the way to Abbey Road Studios, McCartney came up with the Little Richard/Ray Charles–inspired "She's a Woman," and they recorded it for the B side of their next single. They stuck in a message for their new friend Dylan, a line about how McCartney's woman turned him on when he got lonely. "Turn on" was slang for getting high, and Lennon recalled, "We were so excited to say 'turn me on,' you know, about marijuana and all that, using it as an expression."[17]

The record's A side, "I Feel Fine," was another of Lennon's ebullient thank-yous to the fans, with a euphoric riff borrowed from Bobby Parker's "Watch Your Step." Between the band's resplendent harmonies and Starr's drumming in the style of Ray Charles's "What'd I Say," the song was a guaranteed hit.

But for an extra twist, Lennon added a yowl of feedback to the intro, generating it by leaning his guitar against the amp. Critical consensus says that it was the first use of intentional feedback on a record. Maybe it was the marijuana that made him appreciate the beauty in sonic distortion, though he'd heard two other London bands use feedback before he started smoking pot.

Back on August 2, the Kinks had opened for the Beatles in Bournemouth, England. Kinks leader Ray Davies later recalled, "John Lennon made a remark that we were only there to warm up for them, but we got a great reaction to 'You Really Got Me.'" The London band tore the house down with the song, which featured the most distorted guitar sound to date, thanks to guitarist Dave Davies's slashed speaker cone. "It was an early validation that we had something that stood up for us, like being bullied in school and having something that was bigger than the bully, it was that sort of feeling."[18]

Two weeks later, on August 16, the Who, going by the name the High Numbers, joined the Beatles and the Kinks on the bill in Blackpool. Onstage, Pete Townshend shook his guitar in front of the amps to conjure a feedback maelstrom. But the High Numbers' first single had flopped, and Townshend didn't feel he had enough clout to ask the band's producer to put anything avant-garde on their records. The Beatles' producer George Martin, however, would prove extremely receptive to his group's increasingly unusual ideas.

"I Feel Fine" shot to No. 1 on December 26, and stayed there for three weeks. Its brief five seconds of feedback reverberated like the jarring Emergency Broadcast System signal—then in use in the United States to verify that the airwaves were working properly—thus announcing that a new era of experimentation was about to begin.

Dylan was writing his next album in his studio apartment above Café Espresso in Woodstock, New York. Usually he'd smoke marijuana while drinking red wine or coffee at the typewriter. Café owner Bernard Paturel, who later worked as Dylan's chauffeur, saw that Dylan would tear pictures out of magazines and newspapers, spread dozens of them on the floor, and sit in the middle of them with his guitar. As David Hadju writes in his biography of Dylan, *Positively 4th Street*, "Bob would start with a simple musical framework, a blues pattern he could repeat indefinitely, and he would close his eyes—he would not draw from the pictures literally but would use the impression the faces left as a visual model for kaleidoscopic language. He appeared to sing whatever came to him: disconnected phrases with a poetic feeling. When something came out that he liked, he scrawled it down hurriedly so as to stay in the moment, and he would do this until there were enough words written for a song."

Dylan's producer Wilson, an African American, had been saying for years that if they matched Dylan with a band, they "might have a white Ray Charles with a message."[19] Now, after the success of the Animals, Wilson had his regular session musicians overdub Fats Domino–style rock and roll onto some old acoustic Dylan tracks, including "House of the Risin' Sun," to demonstrate what the combination could sound like.[20] Also, Dylan had recently jammed with a group of folkies in Los Angeles called the Byrds, who were working up an electric version of "Mr. Tambourine Man" that you could dance to. He decided it was finally time to pull the trigger.

I.

WINTER

I Got a Head Full of Ideas

The Rolling Stones record their version of gospel and chamber pop on January 11–12. Dylan records *Bringing It All Back Home* on January 13–15, fusing psychedelic folk lyrics with rock and roll and turning the album into high art. The Byrds record "Mr. Tambourine Man" on January 20.

The Rolling Stones' twenty-one-year-old manager, Andrew Loog Old-ham, saw how much money Lennon-McCartney were making through their songwriting royalties and pushed Mick Jagger and Keith Richards to develop their own partnership. The two Stones had written pop songs for other artists, but for their own band's records they stuck mostly to Chess blues classics. With a handful of atmospheric exceptions such as "Tell Me" and "Good Times, Bad Times," their originals were dominated by puppy love clichés that made them unsuitable for the Stones' tough image. Richards said that gooey love ballads were much easier to write than good rock-and-roll songs.[1] Even the best of the originals, "So Much in Love," covered by the Mighty Avengers, sounded only slightly more bitter than the Brit pop of Herman's Hermits.

Their breakthrough came when Jagger gave up the phony role of good guy and took for himself the persona of the rake, in "Heart of Stone." Set to country blues à la Otis Redding's "Pain in My Heart," the song warns little girls to stay away because the singer enjoys making them sad. The eerie backing vocals mirror the group's sullen album covers.

The song made it to No. 19, so the Stones went back into the studio on January 11 with two more Jagger/Richards compositions. At the suggestion of Phil Spector's arranger and conductor, Jack Nitzsche, whom they had met at the *Teen Awards Music International (T.A.M.I.) Show* the previous October, they recorded at RCA Studios in Hollywood.

In light of the Stones' nefarious image, it's ironic that their first quasi-self-penned U.K. No. 1 was derived from a gospel song. During one of the band's U.S. tours, Richards had picked up a Staple Singers album, and when he was home in the United Kingdom, he played along with the record to learn the chords. One of the tracks was the traditional spiritual "This May Be the Last Time," recorded in 1955 and distinguished by the spectral blues guitar of Pops Staples. (Though they performed under the name the Staple Singers, their surname was Staples.) James Brown had adapted the song for his B side to "Out of Sight" the previous July. Though bloggers have grumbled that Jagger/Richards should have credited Pops Staples for their version, Brown did not credit him, either. With traditional (that is, pre-copyright) songs, you didn't need to share the cash as you did with covers. Jagger/Richards sped up the song and changed the lyrics to make it a love song—or, rather, a "threat song": if his woman didn't shape up and try to please him, he was going to take off.

Their earlier A side "It's All Over Now" has a massive, echoing intro thanks to Chess Studio's engineer Ron Malo, but after nine seconds the lead guitar recedes to let Jagger sing. In "The Last Time," however, guitarist Brian Jones's riff keeps droning throughout the entire tune, a move unusual in pop at the time. Soon after the song's release on February 26, hypnotic riff-based hooks came to predominate in British rock, from the Beatles' "Ticket to Ride" to the Yardbirds' "Heart Full of Soul."

Richards played acoustic and then performed the solo. On many tunes, he'd play rhythm and sing harmony until the instrumental, at which point he would switch to the lead.

Perhaps the highlight of the song is the climax in which Jagger screams into the sonic vortex like a wild primate while the backing vocals and beat endlessly repeat—the epitome of Oldham's "wall of noise," his attempt to emulate his hero Phil Spector's Wall of Sound production technique. Spector himself was on hand to give the song a listen, and predicted it would reach No. 10. It went to No. 9 in the United States.

Jagger later commented, "I suppose we'd been writing for almost nine months to a year by then, just learning how to put songs together. And with 'The Last Time,' it became fun. After that, we were confident that we were on our way, that we'd just got started."[2]

For the B side, "Play with Fire," Jagger returned to the "Heart of Stone" theme, warning a girl not to get involved with him. But he fleshed in her character by making her a socialite with diamonds and a chauffeur, and added a decadent storyline.

Like the Beatles, the Stones had become sought-after party guests of the aristocracy. At a dance hosted by the British ambassador to the United States, Sir David Ormsby-Gore, Jagger even befriended Princess Margaret. (It was said Queen Elizabeth disapproved of their decades-long friendship, which is why she avoided the 2003 ceremony in which Jagger was knighted wearing Adidas sneakers.)[3]

Naturally there was some ambivalence toward social climbing in a group formed to emulate working-class black bluesmen. Jagger has it both ways. In "Play with Fire," the contempt in his voice says he doesn't need the socialite, but he's also bragging to us about the rarified circles that want him.

Jagger's warning to the young lady becomes gradually more unsettling because of the amount of personal information he knows about her mother, an heiress who owns a block in one of London's richest neighborhoods. Jagger knows that the father was never home so the mother went out for "kicks" in the exclusive London district of Knightsbridge—presumably with Jagger. In retaliation, the father took the mother's jewelry away and gave it to the daughter, and now the mother has to party on the poorer side of town, Stepney. Jagger warns the daughter that she had better not fool around with him if she wants to keep her jewelry, or the father will cut her off, too, and she'll have to go live with her mother.

It's a (more cynical) precursor to the mother-daughter rivalry in the Mike Nichols film *The Graduate*. In an interview decades later, *Rolling Stone*'s editor Jann Wenner said, "At the time to write about stuff like that must have been somewhat daring."

Jagger replied, "I don't know if it was daring. It just hadn't been done. Obviously there had been lyric writers that had written stuff much more interesting and sophisticated—say, Noel Coward, who I didn't really know about. He was someone that your parents knew."[4]

Even if it wasn't daring, it was innovative considering that while the Stones were recording the song, the Beatles' lyrically basic "I Feel Fine" was on top of the charts. A few months after "Play with Fire" was released, in February 1965, Dylan would write his own epic about a rich girl's descent to the streets, "Like a Rolling Stone."

In painting a detailed story and naming specific parts of town, Jagger/ Richards brought a lyrical specificity to rock that, to date, only Chuck Berry and his disciples the Beach Boys had explored, with the latter band's milieu confined to the innocent world of drive-ins and malt shops.

Initially the Stones attempted an up-tempo version called "Mess with Fire," which fizzled.[5] But, as Nitzsche recalled, the band was flexible; when something didn't work, they didn't hesitate to try it in a different style. Still, by 7:00 a.m., drummer Charlie Watts, bassist Bill Wyman, and Brian Jones had fallen asleep on the studio couches while a janitor swept up. Jagger and Richards left them there as they went into the echo chamber. Phil Spector took over bass on a tuned-down electric guitar while Richards played what he called "Elizabethan blues" on his acoustic. In his playing, Richards had been influenced by Big Bill Broonzy, a guitarist who toured the college circuit in the 1950s, playing music from the era of Queen Elizabeth I (1558–1603) alongside folk and blues songs.[6] Nitzsche played harpsichord, creating an atmosphere almost akin to that of a horror film. Jagger's muted performance increased the menace by underselling it. His tambourine and Nitzsche's tam-tams rounded out the sound.

Half a mile away, at the Gold Star and Western Studios, Brian Wilson was simultaneously adding a cornucopia of instruments to *The Beach Boys Today!*. Spector had already been melding pop and classical, as had Burt Bacharach, but the era of baroque pop, a.k.a. chamber pop, in which bands fused elements of classical with rock, had now officially begun.

The next day, January 13, in the Columbia recording studio in New York City, Dylan played solo on acoustic guitar or piano for the first day of sessions. On the 14th, however, producer Tom Wilson brought in a whole platoon of musicians: three guitarists (blues guitarist Bruce Langhorne, pop guitarist Kenny Rankin, and general session guitarist Al Gorgoni), two bassists (William E. Lee, father of filmmaker Spike Lee; and Joseph Macho Jr.), a pianist (Paul Griffin), and a drummer (Bobby Gregg).

In three hours, from 2:30 to 5:30 p.m., the eight of them recorded almost all of *Bringing It All Back Home*'s first side: "Love Minus Zero/No Limit," "Subterranean Homesick Blues" (captured in one take), "Outlaw Blues," "She Belongs to Me," and "Bob Dylan's 115th Dream." They didn't rehearse; Langhorne later described their chemistry as telepathic. That evening, Dylan did another session with future Lovin' Spoonful John Sebastian on bass and John Hammond Jr. on guitar, but no cuts from that session made the album.

The following day the original musicians returned for another 2:30–5:30 p.m. session, except pianist Paul Griffin, who couldn't make it. (Frank Owens covered for him.) The day went as smoothly as the one before. Dylan would demonstrate a track on piano, and then the ensemble would try it at a couple of different speeds. "Maggie's Farm" was captured in one take, and they also got the electric rocker "On the Road Again" in the can.

Dylan recorded the entire second side that same day. Langhorne played electric guitar for "Mr. Tambourine Man," and Lee joined Dylan on bass for "It's All Over Now, Baby Blue." Dylan recorded "It's Alright, Ma (I'm Only Bleeding)" and "Gates of Eden" by himself on guitar. (Electric versions of the songs of side two were recorded but never released.)

The album's single "Subterranean Homesick Blues" synthesizes the Beat Generation, Chuck Berry, and Woody Guthrie. The title is a reference to Jack Kerouac's *The Subterraneans*. The rhythm comes from Berry's "Too Much Monkey Business." The opening lines come from "Taking It Easy," written by Guthrie and recorded by Pete Seeger's Weavers. The latter song features a father in the basement mixing up the hops while the brother watches out for the cops. In "Subterranean Homesick Blues," Dylan's associate mixes up a different sort of (unnamed) medicine, but the cops are shaking them down nonetheless, and planting bugs in preparation for a bust. The protagonist realizes it's time to go straight: get sick (street slang for giving up heroin), get clean, join society, and try to be a success. Soon, however, he's homesick for the underground lifestyle and jumps back down the manhole. But even there, he's screwed—there's no water because vandals have stolen the pump handles. The song prophesizes the journey of the hippies, who would soon begin to drop out of mainstream society and into the drug culture, only to find that lifestyle to be equally stressful. Some credit the song with being one of the first proto-hip-hop tracks, more than twenty years ahead of white rappers such as the Beastie Boys, Beck, and Anthony Kiedis (whose group, the Red Hot Chili Peppers, would cover the tune).

Dylan was regarded as the king of the topical song but had become disinterested in writing solemn political tracts. "Maggie's Farm" was a new kind of protest song, one he could write without being bored. He sings the darkly hilarious portrait of a plantation with such hipper-than-thou confidence that it's amazing to think the band had been working together for only a few hours. As the song's sharecropper refuses to go along with the program anymore, Bill Lee booms wryly along on bass; twenty-five years later, his son, Spike Lee, would grow up to embody black dissent.

Dylan's euphoria at finally living his rock-and-roll dream infuses side one, epitomized by the spontaneous laughter opening "Bob Dylan's 115th Dream." The song itself is a near remake of his aborted rock single "Mixed Up Confusion," almost as if he were resuming where he left off two years before. Set to a piano that evokes Chaplin's silent comedies, the song is an endless cartoon about pirates let loose in an anarchic New York where bowling balls come rolling down the road to knock you off your feet and where feet pop out of telephones to kick you in the head. It's the moment when rock lyrics go psychedelic.

Most of the songs of side one are variations on the same basic blues-rock groove, but two are mellow tributes to Dylan's muses, Joan Baez and Sara Lownds. (Like the heroine of "She Belongs to Me," Baez wore an Egyptian ring.) Baez visited the studio during the sessions.[7] She had been the much bigger star when she and Dylan first met, almost two years before, and took Dylan on tour with her, giving him a solo spot during her shows. They were now perceived by many to be the "first couple" of folk.

But within the last few months, Dylan had secretly begun seeing Sara Lownds, a former model and bunny from the New York Playboy Club who was friends with his manager's wife (Sally Grossman, the woman on the cover of *Bringing It All Back Home*).[8] Lownds lived in an apartment at New York's Chelsea Hotel with her young daughter, whom she'd had with a fashion photographer, and Dylan rented a room there to be near her. She was the more likely inspiration for "Love Minus Zero/No Limit," as the song concerns a woman who has no ideals and speaks like silence—the opposite of Baez, who'd founded the Institute for the Study of Nonviolence and constantly pushed Dylan to use his fame for political good. In a year and a half, Dylan would retreat into silence with Lownds as his wife.

The remaining two tracks on the side ("Outlaw Blues" and "On the Road Again") are comparatively weak retreads of the other rock numbers. Their inclusion is baffling, considering the band had captured "If You Gotta Go, Go Now," a far superior song and already a regular part of Dylan's act; but perhaps he was sick of it or felt it was too straightforward. He set it aside, allowing Manfred Mann to take it all the way to No. 2 in the United Kingdom. He also demo'd "I'll Keep It with Mine" and "Farewell, Angelina," but they were ballads in the vein of his previous album, and Dylan was eager to show off his own blues band (which the Rolling Stones' Bill Wyman noted in his memoir sounded much like theirs).⁹ After all, the title of the album, *Bringing It All Back Home*, essentially proclaims that Dylan is taking the rock-and-roll crown back from the Brits.

After six tries, Dylan and Langhorne finally got the perfect take of "Mr. Tambourine Man." It opens the acoustic side two, which completes Dylan's transformation from protest singer to full-time surrealist. For the transition, he had found another role model along with Rimbaud, and this one was alive.

Beat Generation poet Allen Ginsberg lived on the fault line between social hero and exhibitionist loony, as might be expected from his upbringing. His father was a poet–high school teacher, and his mother was a schizophrenic nudist Communist; Ginsberg authorized her lobotomy in 1947. He was expelled from Columbia University for writing dirty words on his window, and in his poems he boasted that he was everything that repressed postwar America hated: gay, druggie, a Communist when he was a kid. But he maintained that he wasn't a bad person: he deserved love as everyone deserved love. When Ginsberg went to trial for obscenity in 1957 but was not convicted, it gave courage to outsiders and helped loosen things up, paving the way for the counterculture to follow.

Dylan absorbed the stream-of-consciousness style that Ginsberg and his fellow Beat Jack Kerouac developed together, a musical hipster patois that transformed gritty reality into incandescent wordplay. They found beauty in the modern urban landscape and expressed it in a cadence influenced by their beloved bebop, informed by their quest for spiritual transcendence. Ginsberg cried the first time he heard Dylan's "A Hard Rain's A-Gonna Fall" because he felt the torch had been passed to a new generation.[10] The two artists quickly struck up a friendship.

Ginsberg saw himself in the prophetic tradition, confronting America with its soul-sucking dark side in order to heal it. In "Gates of Eden" on *Bringing It All Back Home*, Dylan chants stridently as if he were a biblical prophet. What exactly he is prophesizing is unclear, though, as he deliberately replaces the easy interpretation of his earlier morality tracts with Zen koan-like images that veer into the bizarre. Perhaps Eden was the state of enlightenment, the only thing real in a hopelessly twisted world, or perhaps the song was designed to be impenetrable.

The main message of "It's Alright, Ma (I'm Only Bleeding)" seems to be that society will exploit you if you don't get hip (a theme that especially resonated as the Vietnam draft kicked in that spring). But what blew people's minds more than any individual aphorism or cinematic image was Dylan's ability to endlessly play folk-blues riffs while reeling off stanza after spellbinding stanza in enigmatic emotionless delivery, leaving his live audiences stunned and unsure if he was a mystic oracle channeling divinations, a genius, a charlatan, or all the above.

The album's final track, "It's All Over Now, Baby Blue"—with the sky folding under you and orphans crying like a fire in the sun—showed that he had surpassed Rimbaud, just one of many spirits in his magpie synthesis of ancient folk bards, Ginsberg, Guthrie, Berry, Johnny Cash, and the Stones. With *Bringing It All Back Home*, he had created the first rock album that sucked the art of poetry into its bloodstream, the moment in which LPs became not just collections of pop songs but works to stand alongside masterpieces in any form, from Picasso's *Guernica* to James Joyce's *Ulysses*. But unlike those pièces de résistance, Dylan's would soon be heard by youth across the planet, listening, as Ginsberg put it, "to the crack of doom on the hydrogen jukebox."

The Byrds' first single had failed to chart after its release the October before, and their manager, Jim Dickson, knew they needed something special to break through. He'd heard Dylan sing "Mr. Tambourine Man" live, but the song hadn't been released yet, so Dickson got a copy of the acetate and pushed the Byrds to record it. None of them really liked it at first. Vocalist

Gene Clark gave it a shot, but rhythm guitarist–vocalist David Crosby convinced him it wasn't worth pursuing.[11]

Lead guitarist Jim McGuinn resisted initially as well. Back when he was a folk singer in Greenwich Village, he knew Dylan, "but he was my enemy . . . I felt competitive. He had like twenty little girl fans and I didn't so I was mad at him. I didn't particularly dig his imitation of Ramblin' Jack Elliot or Woody Guthrie. I thought, okay, anybody could get up there and do that. But he was sincere about it so he carried it. That's why he made it, because he was sincere about everything he tried. And he used to play these trust games with all his friends back then. Like he'd tell me confidentially that he was really down and out and hooked on heroin—you know, a complete lie—just to see if it would get back to him. He was pretty weird."[12]

But McGuinn gave "Mr. Tambourine Man" a shot. He cut down the lyrics, focusing on the line about boot heels wandering because it made him think of the Beatles' Cuban-heeled boots and Jack Kerouac wandering across America.[13] They set it to the beat of Beatles and Phil Spector songs. The track needed some kind of intro, so McGuinn took eight notes from Bach's "Jesu, Joy of Man's Desiring."

On January 20, five days after Dylan recorded his official version, the Byrds went into Columbia Records' Los Angeles studio to record "Mr. Tambourine Man." Their producer was Terry Melcher, the son of Doris Day. Melcher decided that no one in the band except McGuinn was technically good enough to play their instruments on record yet, so he hired LA's top session musicians to accompany McGuinn on guitar and lead vocals: Hal Blaine on drums, Leon Russell on electric piano, and Larry Knechtel on bass. (Along with other musicians such as guitarist Glen Campbell and bassist Carol Kaye, these three formed the core of a loose-knit band of session musicians called the Wrecking Crew, which played on countless hits, including those by the Beach Boys and Phil Spector.) Clark and Crosby added their harmonies. Melcher tweaked the beat to imitate "Don't Worry Baby," the Beach Boys' take on the Spector drums.[14]

They wanted the guitar sound the Beatles had gotten on the *Beatles for Sale* cuts "What You're Doing" and "Words of Love." But Columbia's engineers had not worked with rock musicians before and were afraid McGuinn's twelve-string Rickenbacker guitar would blow out their expensive equipment. So engineer Ray Gerhardt ran the guitar through a compressor, a mixing tool that lowered the loud audio signals but left the quieter ones untouched. Then to be safe, he double-compressed it—which ended up making the guitar sound especially trebly and bright, and allowed each note to sustain a few extra seconds. At the mixing board, they tweaked McGuinn's vocals to sound like a cross between Lennon and Dylan.[15]

Now it was just a matter of waiting for these three records' release dates: February 26 for the Stones, March 27 for Dylan, April 12 for the Byrds.

Hitsville USA and the Sovereigns of Soul

The Supremes enjoy their first No. 1 of the year with "Come See about Me" on January 16, while Smokey Robinson's songs help the Temptations and Marvin Gaye unlock their potential. Also in January, the Impressions release one of the greatest civil rights anthems, "People Get Ready," while Solomon Burke records his ode to the slain Sam Cooke. Martin Luther King Jr. turns to gospel greats the Staple Singers and Mahalia Jackson when he needs solace.

*

Detroit, Michigan, was the nation's fourth-biggest city, an integrated promised land for countless workers bustling round the clock at General Motors, Chrysler, and Ford. Department stores and nightclubs teemed in the evenings. Women of either color could walk by themselves most hours through the metropolis of marble, sandstone, and granite.

Berry Gordy named his record label after the nickname for the Motor City, a combination of the words *motor* and *town*. Headquarters was a two-story house at 2648 West Grand Boulevard, with a sign reading "Hitsville, USA" above the front window. The ground floor housed the office, tape library, and Studio A, a.k.a. "the Snake Pit," where the session men known as the Funk Brothers recorded the backing tracks. After sessions, musicians such as bassist James Jamerson and drummer Benny Benjamin played jazz all night at the 20 Grand club or the Chit Chat Lounge, coming up with ideas for tomorrow's cuts, then hung out on the corner of John R. and E. Canfield Streets, where a guy sold sausages and tamales, telling dirty jokes till dawn.[1]

Gordy's production method was inspired by his time served on the Ford Motors assembly line. He wrote in his memoir, "At the plant, cars started out as just a frame, pulled along on conveyor belts until they emerged at the end of the line—brand spanking new cars rolling off the line. I wanted the same concept for my company, only with artists and songs and records."[2] The songwriters wrote the track, the Funk Brothers laid down the music, and then the singers overdubbed their vocals.

Gordy instituted his own form of quality control in production evaluation meetings. Every Friday morning, Motown staffers would gather in his office to listen to twenty new recordings and decide which should be released, rating each cut on a scale of one to ten. The big question was: if you had only a buck and you were hungry, would you buy the record or a hot dog? Staffers would usually pick the hot dog, but the time they took to decide indicated how good the record was. Sometimes records got shot down only to be reworked and brought back. Gordy promised the staff that they would never be punished for being honest; in turn, he was ruthless in his own dissections. The end result was that 75 percent of the 537 singles Motown released during the decade made the charts, and 79 were Top 10 *Billboard* pop hits.[3]

The key was a relentless, pounding beat. A songwriter-pianist from the rival label Stax named Isaac Hayes said, "Now it was a standard joke with blacks, that whites could *not*, cannot clap on a backbeat. What Motown did was very smart. They beat kids over the head with it. That wasn't soulful to us down at Stax, but baby it sold."[4]

In February's "Nowhere to Run" by Martha and the Vandellas, the Funk Brothers accentuated the drums and tambourine by hitting snow chains. Written and produced by the team of Holland-Dozier-Holland, the song is a variation on the storyline that ran through many of the producers' hits: the singer knows she's in a bad relationship but is unable to forget her lover and move on. But its foreboding groove turned it into a theme song for both Vietnam soldiers and inner-city rioters in the second half of the year.

Lamont Dozier and Brian Holland wrote the music and produced the sessions, while Brian's brother Eddie wrote the lyrics and arranged the vocals. Dozier recalled, "We would listen to John (Lennon) and Paul (McCartney) and Brian Wilson and see what everybody was doing. They probably inspired us to be better than we even felt we could be. When they got hot, we tried to get hotter. When they did something spectacular, we tried to be even more spectacular. In that regard I think we were doing the same thing for them. When I talked with John Lennon, he said, 'You guys inspired us to do things.' I said, 'That's funny, you guys did the same thing for us.'"[5]

Except for the Beatles, no one sold more records through the decade than Holland-Dozier-Holland, or HDH, and the Supremes: Diana Ross, Mary Wilson, and Florence Ballard. They had scored three No. 1's in 1964, and would score three more this year. "Come See about Me" was No. 1 in December, and then interrupted by the Beatles' "I Feel Fine," but it returned to the top spot on January 16. Ross's sexy come-hither groove was so catchy in "Come See about Me" that even garage rockers Mitch Ryder and the Detroit Wheels covered the song.

In March, Gordy shepherded a number of his biggest acts across the Atlantic for a European tour. On March 18, Britain's blue-eyed soul diva Dusty Springfield taped *The Sounds of Motown* TV special, hosting the Supremes, the Miracles, the Temptations, Martha and the Vandellas, Marvin Gaye, Little Stevie Wonder, and the Earl Van Dyke Sextet. (Van Dyke was the bandleader of the Funk Brothers.) The Supremes didn't have any choreography for their new single "Stop! In the Name of Love," so Melvin Franklin and Paul Williams of the Temptations led them into the men's room and brainstormed the famous traffic officer hand signal move. The song hit No. 1 that month.

In the track, Ross begs her man not to have an affair with another woman. But in real life, Ross became the "other woman," to the married Gordy. During the British tour, Ballard and Wilson believed Gordy was imposing a curfew on the Supremes because he was obsessed with Ross. Gordy later recalled that it was in Paris that he realized he loved her, the night they fought over Dean Martin's "You're Nobody Till Somebody Loves You."[6]

Martin's song was currently No. 1 on the easy listening chart, and that was the audience Gordy wanted the Supremes to cross over to. The big money was in the supper clubs, nightclubs where dinner was served while people watched performers, places such as New York's Copacabana and Howard Hughes's Sands nightclub in Vegas, where Frank Sinatra's Rat Pack held its summits. Nat King Cole had integrated the Sands just a decade earlier. Gordy wanted

Motown to become the soundtrack not only to blacks but also to whites, and not just white kids but also white adults. It was about the numbers—the black population made up about 11 percent of the United States; the white population, about 80 percent.

So Gordy wanted Ross to do Martin's hit, but Ross felt she couldn't sing it properly. A bad argument erupted, and he stormed out, assuming she was going to defy him. But when he returned to watch the Supremes' performance later that evening, he was surprised to hear Ross sing Martin's song onstage. In her dressing room, he asked her why, and she said she'd done it for him.

They spent the night together for the first time in Paris—or rather, tried to. To his chagrin, Gordy was impotent. "I was so engrossed in her. It was something I'd wanted, and I was in love with her long before she was in love with me, so when she fell in love with me in Paris, I couldn't believe it. Of course, nothing happened on my part, and it was so embarrassing. I wanted to smother myself. Then Diana said, 'It's not that bad. Look at it this way, at least you have power over everything else.'"[7]

The problem was rectified soon enough; they had a love child at the end of the decade. But he never told her he loved her. Gordy said later that they both vowed not to let their personal life interfere with her quest for stardom.

There was a lot of passion flowing backstage at Motown. Before Gordy, Ross had gone out with Smokey Robinson, and then Eddie Kendricks of the Temptations;[8] then she began a flirtation with Brian Holland—until his wife stormed over to Detroit's 20 Grand club and had to be restrained from attacking Ross.[9] Mary Wilson also reportedly dated Eddie Kendricks, and later Abdul "Duke" Fakir of the Four Tops. Meanwhile, Florence Ballard saw the Temps' Otis Williams.

In terms of writing and producing hits, HDH's greatest rival inside Motown was Smokey Robinson. Robinson, Warren "Pete" Moore, and Ronald White had sung doo-wop together since they were eleven, and eventually coalesced into the Miracles. Both Moore and White cowrote many of the hits with Robinson. Moore, the bass vocalist, also arranged the background harmonies, drawing on his gospel influence. Robinson's wife, Claudette, was in the group as well. Guitarist Marv Tarplin was the Miracles' "secret weapon," writing the riffs to many of their greatest hits.

Robinson was Gordy's first breakout artist in his effort to have his sing-ers cross over beyond R&B and become the "Sound of Young (read: White) America." Robinson was a suave front man à la Sam Cooke, but his beauti-ful falsetto made him particularly nonthreatening to white audiences; it led rock journalist Nik Cohn to call him "pop's first female impersonator."[10] Rob-inson's great-grandmother was Caucasian, and when he was born, the seg-regated hospital put him in the whites-only section of the nursery. It was because he was light-skinned that his uncle gave him the nickname Smokey, as a joke.

As a songwriter, Robinson was one of Lennon's biggest influences, and for years just about every piece written on Robinson mentioned that Dylan had dubbed him the "greatest living poet." (Though Motown's head of PR, Al Abrams, admitted in his memoir that journalist Al Aronowitz had advised him to make that up, since Dylan would never remember whether he'd said it.[11] In fact, Dylan had included Robinson when a reporter asked him on December 3 in San Francisco, "What poets do you dig?") Robinson was a Don Juan who wrote candidly about it. "I felt that because of my love and respect for women, I could maintain relationships with more than one," he says in his memoir.[12] (In the Miracles' March release "Ooo Baby Baby," he tearfully begs his woman to forgive him for cheating and reminds her that she's made mistakes, too.) No doubt the fact that he was married to some-one in his band while dealing with the temptations of being a heartthrob exacerbated these tensions. Claudette looked the other way, but she warned him not to have a child with another woman (and when he did, she divorced him, in 1986).

Gordy had taught Robinson about writing and producing, and Robinson now handled the duties not only for his own band but also for many other Motown acts. With the Temptations, he initially wrote many of the hits for their singer Eddie Kendricks, whose falsetto made it sound almost as if Rob-inson were singing. But Robinson sensed that background vocalist David Ruffin was "this sleeping giant in this group because he had this—it's sort of like a mellow gruff-sounding voice. And all I needed was the right song for his voice and I felt like I would have a smash hit record. So I sat down at the piano to write a song for David Ruffin's voice. So I wanted to make it something that he could belt out, but yet make it melodic and sweet."[13] Rob-inson hit the jackpot when he flipped the gender of his previous No. 1 hit, Mary Wells's "My Guy," with the help of Miracle Ronald White.

The pumping bass, finger snaps, and halcyon guitar perfectly evoke the lyrics "sunshine on a cloudy day." On TV appearances, the Temps twirled their arms, lunged, and spun while the strings of the Detroit Symphony Orchestra swelled in the song's bridge. Ruffin, tall and lanky enough to make thick black-framed glasses cutting-edge cool, raised his open hand to testify that all he needed was his woman's love. Gordy gave Robinson a thousand-dollar bonus because he knew "My Girl" was going straight to No. 1—which it did on March 6.

Like Ruffin, Marvin Gaye was a moody prima donna, but he had the artistic genius and productivity to back it up. He also had understandable cause for his bad behavior, in the person of father Marvin Sr., a Hebrew Pentecostal minister who regularly beat Gaye in his youth, became jealous of his son's phenomenal success, and eventually shot him to death—the Oedipus tragedy in reverse.

Originally, Gaye was the Miracles' session drummer, and co-songwriter on his own early singles and on Martha and the Vandellas' "Dancing in the Streets." He wanted to be a crooner like Sinatra and Nat King Cole and not have to "shake my ass."[14] He was married to Gordy's sister Anna, so that gave him some leverage as he struggled to find his voice. But his albums of show tunes and standards didn't sell, so, reluctantly, Gaye would bang out the next R&B single. He recalled that in the mid-sixties, "When I wouldn't want to record—just flat out refuse—Berry would get mad, his voice would get real high, he'd lose his cool. I'd feel bad and finally get my ass back in the studio."[15] Gordy had given Anna and Gaye his old house to live in, and producer Clarence Paul would pick up Gaye there and give him some coke in the car on the way to the studio[16]—and somehow Gaye amassed a string of classics despite the fact that he'd rather have been singing Cole Porter.

The rugged vocals of David Ruffin and the Four Tops' Levi Stubbs compelled Gaye to make his own sound grittier. "I heard in their voices a strength my own voice lacked. Listening to these singers every day inspired me to work even harder on my natural midrange—my tough-man voice. I developed a growl. The Temps and Tops made me remember that when a lot of women listen to music, they want to feel the power of a real man."[17] The edge was there in January's "I'll Be Doggone," Gaye's first million-selling single, cowritten by Robinson, Pete Moore, and guitarist Marv Tarplin. The song was the closest Motown came in the mid-sixties to the riff rock of white bands. Tarplin was influenced by the proto-folk-rock of "Needles and Pins"; the Byrds pinched the same riff for "I'll Feel a Whole Lot Better."

Robinson took a page from Gaye's life for the lyrics for "I'll Be Doggone." Gaye insists that a woman should try to be whatever her man wants her to be, especially when all he wants is for her to be true. "You see, Anna and I had a strange sense of when we were being untrue to each other. We always knew," Gaye recalled. "One night, for example, I found myself getting in the car and driving to a motel, walking up to a certain room and knocking on the door. All by instinct. How could I be so sure that Anna was in there with another man? I had no way of knowing the motel and the room number. Some force led me on. I think that's the same force that transforms my happiness to misery." When he confronted his wife and her lover, Gaye said, "I think I laughed. I might have cried. But certainly there was some enjoyment in finding them. It was definitely an adventure."[18]

The entire soul music community, Motown and beyond, was haunted by the killing of founding father Sam Cooke on December 11. It was Cooke and Ray Charles who had created the genre a decade earlier, when they combined gospel and rhythm and blues, a controversial move that enraged many churchgoers, just as Dylan's going electric would soon enrage folk idealists. Following Cooke's death, his label released "A Change Is Gonna Come" as a single, and it made it to No. 9 on the R&B chart and No. 31 on the pop charts in February.

The song was inspired by Dylan's "Blowin' in the Wind" and by civil rights organizers Cooke had met who were trying to integrate restaurants such as Howard Johnson's in Durham, North Carolina. The lyrics about life being too hard but death being too frightening echo those in Jerome Kern and Oscar Hammerstein's "Ol' Man River," from *Show Boat*, most famously sung by African American actor and activist Paul Robeson. But the month after Cooke wrote his first draft of the song, the lyrics took on a devastating second meaning when his eighteen-month-old son, Vincent, drowned in the family swimming pool. A few months later, Cooke and his touring party were arrested when they tried to check into a whites-only motel in Louisiana. A French horn echoes Cooke's weary desolation as he sings line after line describing adversity, including even being backstabbed by his own brother. But by the time he makes it to the song's close, he thinks that he can carry on, and he knows a change is coming.

Soul singer Solomon Burke went to dinner with Cooke on December 11, but said good night before Cooke took off with a young lady to a motel for a tryst. When the woman disappeared with Cooke's clothes and money, an enraged Cooke thought the female motel manager was hiding her and attacked her. The manager shot Cooke in self-defense.

Back at his own hotel that night, Burke found a special-delivery letter waiting for him from his wife, saying she wanted a divorce. Then a friend called him to tell him that Cooke had been shot. "I thought he was joking. 'Sam wasn't shot, man. I just left him.' It was no joke. Sam's death was devastating. He meant so much to me. He meant a lot to all of us. He represented the next level for us. He opened doors that haven't been stepped through since. He was gonna be the next Nat Cole. He was a dear friend, and now he was gone. I had to get on the train to get on a plane to get back to Sam's funeral in Chicago. I had no sleep, and I couldn't get Sam off my mind. There's the song. I wrote 'Got to Get You Off My Mind' to get Sam Cooke off my mind."[19] Recorded in January with the help of Atlantic Records producer Jerry Wexler, the song's lyrics are about Burke's wife's leaving him, but Burke sings it in Cooke's style.

Another of the civil rights movement's most enduring anthems entered the pop Top 20 in February, making it to No. 14. Curtis Mayfield and the Impressions' "People Get Ready" was inspired by Martin Luther King Jr.'s "I Have a Dream" speech and by the traditional gospel song "This Train's Bound for Glory." Like Dylan's "The Times They Are A-Changin'," "People Get Ready" states that integration is inevitable. But in place of Dylan's strident voice of conquest, the Impressions sing in a healing way that makes the song a timeless resource for anyone who needs to make it through hard times. A few months after its release, Bob Marley rewrote the song for his band the Wailers' original version of "One Love."

The Staple Singers frequently opened rallies for Dr. King. Roebuck "Pops" Staples was born in 1915 and grew up on the same Mississippi plantation as Delta blues guitarist Charley Patton. Pops got a guitar at age twelve and developed his own sound, what guitarist-musicologist Ry Cooder called "those spooky chords."[20] But blues was the music of house parties and roadhouses, and Pops was a religious family man, so he turned to, as Duke Ellington called it, "gospel in a blues key."[21] He formed the Staple Singers with his children, with lead vocals often taken over by daughter Mavis. Though she was the youngest (born 1939), she possessed a voice that Dylan said made his hair stand on end when he first heard it over the radio as a kid in Minnesota.[22] Mavis was Aretha Franklin's greatest rival on the gospel circuit, though the two were friends, having grown up together along with Sam Cooke.

Dylan met the Staples during the taping of a Westinghouse TV special in 1963. While the performers waited in line at the cafeteria, Dylan called out, "Pops, I want to marry Mavis."

Everyone laughed, and Pops called back, "Don't tell me, tell Mavis."[23]

Dylan and Mavis's first kiss was at the 1963 Newport Folk Festival, and they saw each other intermittently through the rest of the decade, even after marrying other people. "Oh yeah, Dylan was a player," Mavis said, laughing.[24] "It got serious. It was boyfriend-girlfriend stuff. We loved each other, and still do."[25] (Her name was scrawled on Dylan's 1965 handwritten lyric sheet for "Like a Rolling Stone," which sold at auction for two million dollars in 2014.)

It was Mavis who put the brakes on, as she feared that Dr. King would not like her marrying a white man. (Dylan was of Ukrainian and Lithuanian-Jewish descent, with a Turkish great-grandmother.) Pops later called Mavis's reluctance foolish, pointing out all the white people who had been marching with them. Later she rued her decision: "I could kick myself, because we were really in love. It was my first love, and it was the one I lost."[26] (Dylan married his black backup singer Carolyn Dennis in 1986.)

It was the "Queen of Gospel," Mahalia Jackson, whom Dr. King called when he was depressed. She'd sing for him over the phone, and sometimes he'd cry listening to her. During the March on Washington for Jobs and Freedom in 1963, King's speech wasn't truly catching fire until Jackson suddenly called out, "Tell them about the dream, Martin!" She was referring to a speech he'd given a few months earlier in Detroit, where he imagined a day when black children could go to school and play together with white children. So King pushed his notes aside and started improvising "I Have a Dream" in front of nearly three hundred thousand people, Baptist preacher style. Jackson's 1965 album *Mahalia* features "Like the Breeze Blows," which tied Dylan's "Blowin' in the Wind" with King's manifesto—you couldn't "stop the breeze from blowing" or "stop a dream in the hearts of men from growing," she sang in her indomitable contralto. Events in Selma, Alabama, would soon prove her song (as well as Cooke's and Mayfield's) to be correct.

The Brill and the
Beach Boys Fight Back

Phil Spector's "You've Lost That Lovin' Feelin'" tops the charts on February 6, followed immediately by a second hit from the Brill Building songwriting factory, "This Diamond Ring." Meanwhile, Brian Wilson begins his evolution from poet laureate of high school to baroque visionary on *The Beach Boys Today!*, released on March 8, featuring the chart topper "Help Me, Rhonda."

Thanks to the Beatles-led British Invasion, Americans had succumbed to a ravenous thirst for all things English—a culture simultaneously exotic yet similar enough to relate to. Of the twenty-seven records that hit the U.S. No. 1 spot throughout the year, thirteen were from the United Kingdom. Motown was the biggest bulwark against the onslaught, with six chart toppers. New York's Brill Building would fight back with three.

Before the Beatles, the songwriters and producers associated with the Brill Building, at 1619 Broadway, had been pop's most prolific source of hits. (Technically, a number of the artists moved out of the actual building and up the street to 1650 Broadway, but the term "Brill Building sound" stuck.) Aldon Music's publisher, Don Kirshner, would find out which recording artists needed a new song, and then goad his songwriting teams to compete to write the best one. Three of Aldon's teams were married couples: Barry Mann and Cynthia Weil, Carole King and Gerry Goffin, and Ellie Greenwich and Jeff Barry. They were all young and Jewish, working in small cubbyholes with a piano, a bench, and a chair, hearing the other teams composing right next to them. King bounced her baby on her lap at the piano or kept her in a play-pen. The writers were one another's greatest competitors but also best friends. On holiday road trips, they'd make bets to see whose songs would be played most on the radio.[1] They wrote for the Drifters and girl groups such as the Ronettes, the Shirelles, the Chiffons, the Crystals, and the Dixie Cups. Gerry Goffin even had a child with the Cookies' lead singer, though he stayed married to Carole King.[2]

Phil Spector produced epics for the Crystals and the Ronettes. A tiny man with a Napoleon complex, he compensated by making the biggest-sounding records possible with his Wall of Sound, often with LA session musicians the Wrecking Crew. He would have several guitarists, bassists, pianists, drummers, and percussionists play simultaneously, and then bury instruments in the mix, so they could be felt but not heard, and swathe the cacophony in echo.

But now Motown had taken over the girl group genre with the Supremes, the Vandellas, and the Marvellettes. The Beatles made it seem effortless to write, sing, and play your own material, inspiring bands to try it themselves and rely less on outside sources. Suddenly the Brill seemed out of date. The Ronettes' "Walking in the Rain," Spector's cowrite with Mann and Weil, couldn't crack the Top 20 after its release in December.

To shake things up, Spector decided to work with men, the blue-eyed soul singers the Righteous Brothers. Spector lived in Los Angeles, so he flew Mann and Weil out to stay at the Chateau Marmont and rented them a piano. Inspired by the Four Tops' "Baby I Need Your Loving," they came up with "You've Lost That Lovin' Feelin'."[3] When they played it for Spector, he got choked up at the lines about something beautiful dying. He would turn it into his most desolate blockbuster yet, its adult sophistication in stark contrast to the juvenilia that made up much of the current hit parade. But at three minutes and forty-five seconds, it was longer than most radio stations would play. Spector remedied that by printing labels that said the song was only three minutes, five seconds. In 1999 the performing rights organization BMI declared that the song had been played on radio and television more than any other song of the century.[4]

"Feelin'" held the top spot for two weeks before being supplanted by Gary Lewis and the Playboy's "This Diamond Ring," by Brill songwriting team Brass-Kooper-Levine. Later in the year, Al Kooper would play the organ in Dylan's "Like a Rolling Stone."

Around the time "Feelin'" peaked on the charts, Mann and Weil were sleeping when their phone started ringing in the middle of the night. It was Brian Wilson, the leader of the Beach Boys. "Your song is the greatest record ever. I was ready to quit the music business, but this has inspired me to write again. I want to write with you guys."[5]

"Now?" a groggy Weil managed to reply.

Originally, Wilson saw his band as a combination of the Four Freshmen's vocal harmonies and Chuck Berry's rock and roll. He wasn't a surfer. It was his younger brother Dennis who surfed, originally to get out of the house to avoid fighting with their overbearing father, Murry. But Brian picked up the lingo from Dennis and used it in their songs, with Brian on bass, Dennis on drums, little brother Carl on guitar, cousin Mike Love on lead vocals, and a folk musician from Brian's football team named Al Jardine on rhythm guitar. The rest of the country, stuck back in the snow, daydreamed about catching waves in an endless summer with the girls on the beach and sent the boys ever higher up the charts. Hot rods, drag racing, and high school were the other big themes. The Beach Boys felt like the kings of rock. Then the Beatles pulled into town.

Eleven days after the Beatles' first appearance on *The Ed Sullivan Show*, Wilson went into the studio to record "Don't Worry Baby," which tells the story of a guy who was bragging about his car but now doubts whether he can win the upcoming race. His woman looks him in his eyes, makes love to him, and tells him not to worry. "I knew we were good," Wilson said, "but it wasn't until the Beatles arrived that I knew we had to get going . . . So we stepped on the gas a little bit."[6] "Don't Worry Baby's" A side, "I Get Around," became their first No. 1.

But the day before Christmas Eve, the pressure caught up to Wilson. His good friend Loren Schwartz, an assistant at the William Morris talent agency, had recently introduced him to marijuana.[7] Brian had been married to his sixteen-year-old wife, Marilyn Rovell, for only two weeks, and now he had to go back on tour to Texas. Not only was Brian singing and playing bass, but he was also writing, producing, arranging, and managing the group.

On the airplane, he started crying into his pillow. As soon as the plane took off, he shrieked and fell to the floor, sobbing. Carl Wilson and Al Jardine tried to help him, as did the flight attendant, but Brian told her to get away from him. He did the Houston show that night, but it was his last live performance for twelve years.[8] The morning after, he woke up sick to his stomach and cried in his hotel room all day, even turning Carl away. He flew back to LA, where his mother picked him up and comforted him as he cried some more.

Wilson told the rest of the band he wasn't going to tour with them anymore. Love and Jardine cried; Dennis freaked out and threatened to strike the road manager with an ashtray, but Carl calmed him down.[9] Brian told the group not to worry, that it would all be worth it because he would write them some good songs. Wrecking Crew member Glen Campbell had cut many of the Beach Boys' tracks in the studio, so he stepped in to play bass and sing falsetto onstage through early March. (The rest of the band performed live, just not on record anymore, though they had for their first six albums.) Campbell didn't know the lyrics, but the girls were screaming so much that it didn't matter.

Thus, in January, Brian Wilson could focus on his passion, the Beach Boys' next album *Today!*, reinvigorated by marijuana. "It opened some doors for me, and I got a little more committed to music than I had done before, more committed to the making of music for people on a spiritual level," he said.[10]

The Beach Boys couldn't necessarily top the Beatles as writers or singers, but Wilson knew he could create the most luxuriant soundscapes captured on vinyl. While the Beatles were a tight combo who played everything themselves in the studio (frequently accompanied by producer George Martin on piano), the Beach Boys now laid their gorgeous vocal harmonies over the Wrecking Crew performing on everything from mandolins, English and French horns, saxophones, and harmonicas; to organs, harpsichords, and accordions; to timbales, congas, vibraphones, xylophones, and sleigh bells.

Today!'s first side has the hits: "Dance, Dance, Dance" (No. 8), "When I Grow Up (to Be a Man)" (No. 9), and a cover of Bobby Freeman's "Do You Wanna Dance?" (No. 12). Dennis sang lead on the last, and the track holds its own against the original 1950s classic by turning into a hard-pounding rocker with the Wall of Sound kicking in at the chorus, fitting for Dennis's wild-man personality. He was the kind of guy who kicked in dressing room doors to make an entrance when introducing himself to other bands on the bill. Once, when the Beach Boys were cornered in a stairwell by a gang of jealous local boys, Dennis kicked one in the nuts and split his scrotum.[11] While the rest of the band still looked like the Four Freshmen, in sweaters and with neatly parted hair, Dennis's bleached mane got shaggier, and he was the most popular with the female fans.

The second side of *Today!* was a dry run for the Beach Boys' landmark album *Pet Sounds*, with its opulent orchestration, multilayered vocals, and lyrical concerns moving away from teenage Americana. Though the band was not usually renowned as wordsmiths, the songs on *Today!* grew surprisingly mature. In "She Knows Me Too Well," the singer admits he treats his woman bad and then expects to be forgiven by making her laugh. "In the Back of My Mind" sees the singer striving to rationalize the fears that haunt him.

Brian originally didn't think much of "Help Me, Rhonda," perhaps because he had borrowed the melody from Buster Brown's "Fannie Mae." Love wrote the lines about a man who, after being dumped by his fiancée, asks Ronda—as her name was originally spelled in the lyrics—to help him forget her. Before his current marriage, Brian had once proposed to another woman and was rejected, so perhaps that was the inspiration, though Brian told Jardine that Ronda was a made-up character.[12] Jardine sang lead, only his second time as lead vocalist on a Beach Boys track; Love or Brian usually handled that duty.

It was just an album cut until Terry Melcher, the Byrds' producer, wanted to cover it for his own group the Rip Chords. Melcher's interest made Brian realize that "Help Me, Rhonda" was something special, so on February 24, the Boys and the Wrecking Crew went back into the studio to cut a new version for a single. Brian shaved twenty seconds off, Campbell added guitar to the instrumental, and an *h* was added to Ronda's name.

The group was laying down new vocals when Murry Wilson arrived, drunk, and started trying to direct the proceedings as he had done in the early days as their manager, before they fired him. The father had terrorized the boys when they were young. Brian said in 1999 that "[Murry] hit me with a two by four, right to the side of my head. He totally put my right ear out.

He made me so deaf."[13] Murry would also take his glass eye out and make his kids look in the socket.

But Brian wasn't intimidated anymore, as revealed in the session tape that, years later, was circulated as a bootleg.

"Brian, you're coming in shrill," Murry told him. "Al, loosen up a little more, say sexy 'Rhonda' more . . . Dennis, don't flat anymore . . . you're so tight fella, I can't believe it . . . loosen up, sweetie."

"Oh shit! You're driving me nuts, shut up!" Brian finally screamed. "That's it; I've got one ear left, and your big loud voice is killing it."

"You're an ingrate when you do this . . . When you guys get so big that you can't sing from your hearts, you're going downhill."

"We would like to record under an atmosphere of calmness, and you're not . . . presenting that."

"The kid got a big success and he thinks he owns the business . . . Brian, I'm a genius, too."[14]

The contretemps would inspire the next album's "I'm Bugged at My Ol' Man," in which Brian bemoans how his dad has sold his surfboard, cut off his hair in his sleep, locked him in his room, boarded up his windows, taken his phone, and given him breadcrumbs to eat. Still, despite Murry's interruption of the recording session, the revamped "Help Me, Rhonda" hit No. 1 after its release on April 5.

Resolution: *A Love Supreme,* Malcolm X, and the March from Selma to Montgomery

John Coltrane releases his magnum opus in February. Malcolm X plants the seeds of Black Power before his murder on February 21. Martin Luther King Jr. leads protestors on the Voting Rights Trail, March 21–25.

When saxophonist John Coltrane became strung out on heroin again in 1957, Miles Davis fired him from the first Great Quintet, the American jazz band Davis had formed two years earlier. Coltrane played with pianist Thelonious Monk for a year, and then had a spiritual epiphany and got clean. He did not want to go down in flames like bebop sax pioneer Charlie Parker, dead at thirty-four in 1955 from advanced cirrhosis of the liver and a heart attack. It was with Monk that Coltrane invented his "sheets of sound" playing style (so named by *Down Beat* critic Ira Gitler in 1958). Coltrane would play arpeggios and patterns running from the lowest note to the highest ultrafast, play several chords at the same time, and then play each note in each chord. The style was so new that even the French booed Coltrane when he rejoined Davis on tour there in 1959.

Coltrane practiced all day, playing scales endlessly in his room, and then played live for hours, attaining a state of ecstasy. With his own quartet he played up to forty-five weeks a year, six nights a week, three to four sets a night, crossing the country in a Chrysler station wagon.[1] He began studying diverse forms of music from across the globe—classical composers such as Stravinsky and Debussy, Indian ragas, African rhythms—and'elements from these found their way into his own compositions.

After the birth of his son, Trane, as he was known, took a break from touring and meditated in his room for five days. There he wrote *A Love Supreme*, a suite broken into four movements that symbolized the path of achieving spiritual clarity: "Acknowledgement" (acknowledging the desire for enlightenment), "Resolution" (resolving to attain it), "Pursuance" (striving for it), and "Psalm" (attaining it).

On December 9, with his band (McCoy Tyner on piano, Jimmy Garrison on double bass, and Elvin Jones on drums), he recorded the album in one session, from 8:00 p.m. till midnight, in engineer Rudy Van Gelder's New Jersey studio.[2] The studio looked a bit like a church, with its thirty-nine-foot ceiling comprised of two huge wooden arches and exposed brick walls. The album's majesty owes much to Van Gelder's spatial balance of sound: the musicians played close to one another, the drummer not separated by a baffle, the lights set low for mood.

The band didn't know what Coltrane planned for them to do, but they all had near-telepathic communication after years of playing together live. When the rare mistake was made, Coltrane would gently say, "Excuse me," and they'd start again.[3]

"Acknowledgement" opens with the benevolent crash of a gong and the gentle tap of cymbals, and then the bass kicks in with a four-note motif echoing the words "a love supreme." Five minutes into the track, Coltrane picks up the motif and plays it thirty-seven times with his sax in all twelve keys, and then chants it vocally like a mantra, the first time his voice is heard on record.

For the final piece, "Psalm," Jones's tympani and cymbals evoke the grandeur of ocean waves crashing against mountains as Trane's sax blows out across the cosmos. Coltrane "plays" the words of a sixty-nine-line poem he wrote (and includes in the liner notes), an exhortation to seek God every day and ask God to help "resolve our fears and weaknesses."[4] (Fan-made videos on YouTube play the music while highlighting the lines of the poem; Coltrane follows the words almost exactly.) He gives thanks and praises the wonders of the universe. "One thought can produce millions of vibrations," he writes/sings. "Thought waves, heat waves . . . and they all go back to God . . . and He cleanses all." The movement climaxes with "Elation. Elegance. Exaltation. All from God. Thank you God. Amen."

As to what sort of God Coltrane believed in, on his liner notes for his album *Meditations*, he writes, "I believe in all religions." Both his grandfathers were African Methodist Episcopal Zion ministers, and he studied the Bible. His first wife, Juanita, converted to Islam, and he studied the Koran. He also studied the Hindu Bhagavad Gita, the Buddhist Tibetan Book of the Dead, Zen, the Kabbalah, Greek philosophy, and astrology.

Impulse! Records released the thirty-three-minute album in February and it became Coltrane's most popular work. Usually his albums sold around thirty thousand copies, but this one would go on to sell half a million. Phil Lesh of the Grateful Dead remembered that he would hear the album wafting out of windows constantly as he walked around Haight-Ashbury.[5] Coltrane played *A Love Supreme* live only once, however, at the Festival Mondial du Jazz Antibes in France on July 26. His usual venue was nightclubs, where the audience was drunk and distracted—not the proper atmosphere for his hymn of devotion.[6]

Malcolm Little (born 1925) was the son of Earl Little, a leader in the Universal Negro Improvement Association. Whites killed three of Earl's brothers, and then an offshoot of the Klan called the Black Legion burned down the Littles' house. Finally, Earl was killed in a streetcar accident when Malcolm was six; his mother believed the Black Legion was responsible. She had a nervous breakdown six years later and was institutionalized, and Malcolm's siblings were split up and sent to different foster homes.

Malcolm became a pimp, drug dealer, gambler, thief, and sometimes a male hustler. It was his incarnation as a criminal that later gave him the street cred Martin Luther King Jr. lacked, as many blacks couldn't relate to MLK's upbringing as the college-educated son of a Baptist pastor. In 1946, Little was sentenced to ten years for burglary and joined the Nation of Islam in prison. Founded in 1930, the Nation forbade drugs and alcohol, rehabilitated convicts and addicts, and strove to achieve economic independence by supporting its own businesses and creating its own schools.

In 1950, Malcolm Little took the name Malcolm X and, after his parole in

1952, became the Nation of Islam's most powerful speaker. At six foot three, he had physical and intellectual swagger and captivated crowds with his fiery rhetoric. He pushed for the words *black* or *African* to replace *Negro*, denouncing *Negro* as a label from slave owners. He encouraged blacks to throw off the feelings of inferiority internalized since slavery and be proud of their African heritage.

Yet, over time, tensions began to rise between the Nation's star and its leader Elijah Muhammad. Some speculate that Muhammad was envious that Malcolm received the bulk of the media attention. Malcolm was disillusioned that Muhammad had impregnated many of his teenage secretaries. After the FBI's covert COINTELPRO program was revealed in the 1970s, many came to believe that the Nation's national secretary, John Ali, was an undercover agent who had deliberately stoked discord between Elijah Muhammad and Malcolm X.

On March 8, 1964, Malcolm announced that he was leaving the Nation of Islam to start his own organization. His successor as Nation of Islam spokesman, Louis X (today Louis Farrakhan), branded Malcolm a traitor and said he was worthy of death.

The Nation of Islam discouraged black people from voting and getting involved with the white world's politics. But Malcolm now wanted to work together with civil rights organizations such as Dr. King's Southern Christian Leadership Conference (SCLC) to mobilize the black vote. A month after he left the Nation, he delivered his famous "The Ballot or the Bullet" speech in which he defined Black Nationalism as the black man controlling the politicians of his community. To do so, he advised putting one's religion "in the closet," because whether a black person was Christian, Muslim, or atheist, he had the same problem. The white man owned the stores in the neighborhood but took the money out of town at the end of the day. Malcolm insisted that the key to liberation was blacks owning and operating the businesses in their own neighborhoods, generating employment, and keeping the money in the community.

Malcolm and King met only once, briefly, eighteen days after Malcolm left the Nation of Islam, when both traveled to Washington, DC, for the debate over the congressional Civil Rights Act. Outside the Senate Caucus Room, they smiled and shook hands.

"Well, Malcolm, good to see you."

"Good to see you."

President Johnson passed the Civil Rights Act of 1964 in July, but southern blacks were still subject to red tape designed to dissuade them from casting ballots, such as poll taxes and "literacy tests," not to mention questions such as "How many bubbles are in a bar of soap?" Beyond the harassment at the registrar, blacks could also lose their jobs or bank credit for daring to vote. And the looming threat of the Klan was ever present. The Student Nonviolent Coordinating Committee (SNCC) had been working to register voters in Selma, Alabama, for two years, but by the beginning of 1965 it had managed to register only three hundred out of fifteen thousand local blacks. So other Selma residents reached out to King's SCLC for help.

Many different cities were competing for the SCLC's attention, but Selma had a loose-cannon sheriff named Jim Clark, who the SCLC knew would generate outrageous press. Clark was the archetypal redneck cop with no anger management skills. He would stand in front of the courthouse to block blacks from registering, wearing a lapel pin that read "Never" (in reference to integration). Armed with pistol, club, and cattle prod, he menaced black student protestors, using the electric prod on them when marching them to holding areas. Author James Baldwin stated that Clark even put the prod against a woman's breast.

Clark formed an anti–civil rights force comprised of highway patrolmen and the KKK to drive the activists out of his jurisdiction, and was present for the momentous protest march of February 18 that set in motion the forces that would finally overcome voter repression. When state troopers started to club the mother and grandfather of Jimmie Lee Jackson, a twenty-six-year-old church deacon, Jackson rose to their defense and was shot in the stomach by state trooper Corporal James Bonard Fowler.

Malcolm had long spoken out in favor of self-defense, a stance that seemed incendiary to a large majority of whites at the time (though most whites believed in self-defense for *themselves*). "We are nonviolent with people who are nonviolent with us, but we are not nonviolent with anyone who is violent with us . . . Any time you live in a society supposedly based upon law and it doesn't enforce its own law because the color of a man's skin happens to be wrong, then I say those people are justified to resort to any means necessary to bring about justice where the government can't give them justice."[7]

Malcolm saw himself as the essential bad cop to King's good cop, and warned, "I think that the people in this part of the world would do well to listen to Dr. Martin Luther King and give him what he's asking for, and give it to him fast, before some other factions come along and try to do it another way. What he's asking for is rights and that's the ballot. And if he can't get it the way [King's] trying to get it, then it's going to be gotten one way or the other."[8]

The Nation of Islam maintained it owned Malcolm's house in Queens and sued him for it. It lost the case, but it went back to trial. On February 14, the night before the next scheduled court date, the house burned down. Malcolm's wife and kids got out safely, but the event deeply shook him.

On February 21, four hundred people gathered at Manhattan's Audubon Ballroom to hear Malcolm speak. Suddenly, men in the crowd shouted, threw a smoke bomb, and shot Malcolm twenty-one times with a shotgun and two handguns.

The killers ran, though the crowd caught one, Nation of Islam's Talmadge Hayer, and beat him until the police showed up. He said that four others were involved, but he wouldn't name them; two other men were jailed.

Elijah Muhammad said, "Malcolm X got just what he preached."[9]

King sent a condolence telegram to Malcolm's wife, Betty, and told the press, "While we did not always see eye to eye on methods to solve the race problem, I always had a deep affection for Malcolm and felt that he had a great ability to put his finger on the existence and root of the problem. He was an eloquent spokesman for his point of view, and no one can honestly doubt that Malcolm had a great concern for the problems that we face as a race."

Crowds of up to thirty thousand attended the public viewing in Harlem on February 23–26. Actor Ossie Davis, known to later generations by his many appearances in Spike Lee films, delivered the eulogy. Davis' wife Ruby Dee (who would also later be a Lee alum) and Sidney Poitier's wife Juanita raised money for Malcolm's family. He had died at age thirty-nine with no savings for his survivors; he hadn't wanted to profit from his organization.

The *New York Times* obituary on February 22 labeled him "an extraordinary and twisted man, turning many true gifts to evil purpose." On March 5, *Time* wrote that Malcolm was "an unashamed demagogue. His gospel was hatred . . ." But theirs would hardly be the last word. Malcolm had been in the process of authoring his *Autobiography* with Alex Haley, who would later write *Roots*. Published in November, it went on to sell millions of copies over the ensuing decades.

In Alabama, on February 26, Jimmie Lee Jackson died in the hospital from his gunshot wounds. King railed at Jackson's funeral on March 3, "He was murdered by the timidity of a federal government that can spend millions of dollars a day to keep troops in South Vietnam and cannot protect the rights of its own citizens seeking the right to vote."

In response to Jackson's shooting, the SCLC planned a fifty-four-mile march from Selma to the state capital, Montgomery. It was to be in the style of Gandhi's marches, which lasted for days and provided lots of time for media coverage. Governor George Wallace quickly forbade the march, but 525 protestors embarked on March 7 anyway.

Sheriff Clark ordered all white males over twenty-one in his county to report to the courthouse for deputation. Then Clark's men watched as Governor Wallace ordered the state troopers to stop the march. When the demonstrators proceeded to cross the Edmund Pettus Bridge, 200 troopers, many on horseback, attacked them with tear gas, billy clubs, bullwhips, and rubber tubes wrapped in barbed wire. When the marchers fled, the mounted troopers chased them and continued beating them while white crowds on the sidelines cheered.

A local church was turned into a makeshift medical facility to help over fifty marchers suffering serious injuries, and at least sixteen were admitted to Selma's Good Samaritan Hospital. Many enraged blacks wanted to return with guns to exact vengeance and had to be talked down by the nonviolent organizers, who pointed out the troopers had more guns, and more powerful guns at that.[10]

Contrary to Gil Scott-Heron's 1971 rap "The Revolution Will Not Be Televised," with the attack on the marchers, the nonviolent civil rights revolution would begin its televised climax. The ABC Sunday Night Movie that evening was *Judgment at Nuremberg*, in which Americans put white supremacist Nazis on trial in the weeks after World War II. ABC News interrupted the movie to show forty-eight million viewers footage of women, children, and clergy being assaulted in what was quickly named "Bloody Sunday."

The nationwide revulsion was immediate. King arrived in Selma and put out a call for all religious leaders and sympathetic citizens to come to Alabama for a new march, to take place on March 9. Hundreds came by bus, car, and plane.

The SCLC requested a court order to prevent the police from obstructing the new demonstration. Instead, Federal District Court judge Frank Minis Johnson, though one of the only southern judges not hostile to the movement, issued a restraining order to delay the March 9 march until he could hold a hearing on the issue in a few days. Nevertheless, twenty-five hundred marchers set out again for the state capital. State troopers ordered them, again at the bridge, to turn back. King, at the front of the marchers, requested that they be allowed to pray, and he knelt in the street.

Having not yet crossed the bridge, the marchers had not yet violated the restraining order. The SCLC believed that the sympathetic Judge Johnson would eventually lift the restraining order. So they decided to turn around and head back to Selma, avoiding bloodshed—though frustrating many of the marchers.

That day, President Johnson called King. He asked him to wait until the court lifted the restraining order and vowed to get a Voting Rights Bill before Congress in a few days. As the marchers returned to Selma, King asked all the supporters who had come in from other states to stay a little longer.

That night, three out-of-state idealists, white Unitarian ministers, after leaving a local restaurant made a wrong turn and got lost. Suddenly they heard white men calling after them, "Hey, you n——s."[11] They were attacked with clubs, and thirty-eight-year-old Reverend James Reeb from Massachusetts died from head injuries two days later.

President Johnson called Reeb's wife, now a widow with four children, to offer his condolences. Protests increased across the country, though some blacks were upset that a white death generated bigger demonstrations and media coverage than Jackson's death the previous month. On March 13, Governor Wallace arrived at the White House. LBJ put his arm around him, asking the governor how he wanted to be remembered by history. Wallace still wouldn't agree to protect the marchers.

On March 15, LBJ went on TV to address the nation from Capitol Hill, in a joint session of Congress. Outside, civil rights protestors sang "We Shall Overcome." "I speak tonight for the dignity of man and the destiny of democracy. I urge every member of both parties, Americans of all religions and of all colors, from every section of this country, to join me in that cause. At times, history and fate meet at a single time in a single place to shape a turning point in man's unending search for freedom. So it was at Lexington and Concord. So it was a century ago at Appomattox. So it was last week in Selma, Alabama."

Johnson announced that he was sending forth a bill to remove all restrictions used to prevent blacks from voting. "Their cause must be our cause, too. Because it is not just Negroes, but really it's all of us who must overcome the crippling legacy of bigotry and injustice. And we shall overcome."

SCLC activist C. T. Vivian recalled, "I looked over . . . and Martin was very quietly sitting in the chair, and a tear ran down his cheek. It was a victory like none other. It was an affirmation of the movement."[12]

The restraining order on the march was removed the next day. Johnson sent three thousand National Guardsmen to protect the thirty-two hundred activists walking out of Selma and toward Montgomery on March 21. Threats against King prompted many marchers who shared King's build to wear similar blue suits to confuse potential assassins. When the roads narrowed to two lanes, only three hundred people were allowed to march for the next four days, because that was the maximum number of people the Guardsmen felt they could reliably protect.

The marchers covered between seven and seventeen miles a day, singing and clapping to spirituals such as "Ain't Gonna Let Nobody Turn Me 'Round," sometimes in the rain. People waved and brought them food and drink; the marchers slept in black farmers' fields. When they arrived in Montgomery four days and fifty-four miles later, on March 25, more than twenty-five thousand people had joined them for the final leg of the journey.

King gave a speech on the steps of the State Capitol Building, a few hundred feet from the Dexter Avenue Baptist Church where he had begun his ministry in 1954. The church was where the 1956 Montgomery Bus Boycott had been headquartered, after Rosa Parks set off a chain reaction by refusing to give up her seat and move to the back of the bus.

SCLC cofounder Rev. Joseph Lowry would later say diplomatically of King's singing ability, "His gift was speaking more than singing,"[13] but the musicality of King's cadence, in the black southern preacher tradition, made him the most memorable orator of his century. He would regularly incorporate the lyrics of hymns into his sermons, and the ancient call-and-response tradition was alive in him and in men such as Rev. Ralph Abernathy, who stood beside King at the Capitol that day, echoing his lines with "Yes, sir," and "Speak, sir." King's deep vibrato and sustain on key words—"letting the worrrrrrllldddd know"—and his repetition of key phrases turned his speeches into a cappella blues spirituals.

King exhorted the crowd to remain committed to nonviolence in order to win the friendship and understanding of the white man, and not to seek his defeat or humiliation. Looking forward to a society at peace beyond color, he soared into one of his greatest speeches, "How long? Not long!" He quoted William Cullen Bryant's poem "The Battlefield" ("Truth, crushed to earth, shall rise again") and paraphrased the Bible's Galatians, about reaping what one sows, as well as mentioning abolitionist Theodore Parker's aphorism that the arc of the moral universe was long but "bends towards justice." His speech climaxed as he shouted the lyrics of "The Battle Hymn of the Republic" into the roar of the crowd. Julia Ward Howe had written the song in 1861 by refashioning the melody of "John Brown's Body," a song in honor of the white abolitionist, into a marching song for the soldiers of the Civil War. In alluding to it, King was implying that the March from Selma to Montgomery had finally achieved what Brown started 106 years before.

King later remarked in his Annual Report at the SCLC's Ninth Annual National Convention on August 11, "Montgomery led to the Civil Rights Acts of 1957 and 1960; Birmingham inspired the Civil Rights Act of 1964 and Selma produced the voting rights legislation of 1965."[14]

Despite the victory in Montgomery, the KKK wasn't about to fade away. The night of King's speech on the steps of the State Capitol, members of the Klan murdered white female activist Viola Liuzzo, a housewife who had come down from Michigan to help with the march. When the Klansmen saw her driving black marchers back to Selma, they chased her down and shot her in the car. One of the Klansmen was revealed to be an FBI informant who did nothing to stop the murder, so Hoover and COINTELPRO spread the rumor that Liuzzo was a Communist who had left her kids to have sex with black men.[15] The FBI's role in the smear campaign was revealed in documents obtained in 1978 through the Freedom of Information Act. The killers were given a standing ovation at a Klan parade on May 3, 1965, but were sentenced to ten years seven months later. That same month, the three white men who beat James Reeb were acquitted of murder.

In April, the Staple Singers picked up on the theme of "Ain't Gonna Let Nobody Turn Me 'Round" with "Freedom Highway." They recorded the song, and the rest of the album of the same name, backed by a full gospel choir, in Chicago's New Nazareth Church, with the congregation clapping along.[16] In the title track, an exasperated Mavis Staples boomed that the whole world was wondering what was wrong with the United States, but gave props to LBJ for saying, "We shall overcome."

Pops's "Why (Am I Treated So Bad)" was inspired by the time the National Guard stopped Little Rock black students from entering a white school despite the Supreme Court decision that segregation was unconstitutional. The song became one of King's favorites. Thereafter, whenever the Staple Singers opened for King, the civil rights leader would ask, "Stape, you gonna play my song tonight?"[17]

II * SPRING

Nashville versus Bakersfield

Nashville's Roger Miller and Bakersfield's Buck Owens fight for the country No. 1 spot in March, while the Outlaws take on Music City and Johnny Cash self-destructs.

Like Motown writ large, Nashville (or Music City, as it was nicknamed) was a well-oiled assembly line. Producers got their songs from the publishing houses on Music Row and then brought them to life with a group of session musicians called the A-Team, renowned for their ability to cut three songs in three hours. The artists would perform at the Grand Ole Opry and then regroup at bars such as Tootsies or Linebaugh's. After the bars closed, they could go to the home of Sue Brewer, dubbed the Boar's Nest, where singer-songwriters such as George Jones, Faron Young, Waylon Jennings, and Kris Kristofferson picked guitars all night long.[1]

The year's quintessential country anthem came from Faron Young. "Walk Tall" tells the story of a convict looking back on how he ignored the wisdom of his mama and fell in with the wrong crowd. He vows he'll make her proud once he gets out. Porter Wagoner's "Green, Green Grass of Home" was another archetypal country ode, in which a man revisits his beloved hometown, and then wakes up and realizes he's in prison, about to be executed in the morning.

The biggest country hit of the year was Roger Miller's ode to hobos, "King of the Road." (Hobos loomed large in country music, as did truck drivers. They were both descendants of the drifting cowboy.) After its release in January, the song spent five weeks on top of the country chart, and it made it to No. 4 on the U.S. pop charts—and No. 1 in the United Kingdom. As a thank-you to the Brits, Miller penned "England Swings" in the same gently rollicking manner.

Alternately dubbed the "hillbilly intellectual," "cracker-barrel philosopher" (*Life*), and the "unhokey Okie" (*Time*), Miller cleaned up with six Grammys for "King of the Road," including Song of the Year, Record of the Year, Best Country Song, Best Country and Western Male Vocal, Best Country and Western Single, Best Country and Western Album (for *The Return of Roger Miller*)—and even Best Rock and Roll Male Vocal and Best Rock and Roll Single, which betrays the age of the Grammys voters. But though Miller was a favorite on the talk show circuit, he had peaked. Like innumerable contemporaries of his in country and rock, he was undone by pills.

To a large extent country artists were in their own self-contained universe, though Nashville executives such as Chet Atkins and Owen Bradley strove to cross over with the "Nashville Sound." They stripped out the banjo and replaced the fiddle with violins, as in the urban pop of New York. They moved away from cowboys singing in the nasal "high lonesome" style and concentrated on polished crooners, backing them with vocal groups such as the Anita Kerr Quartet. Eddie Arnold was the most successful with this formula, making it to No. 6 on the pop charts with "Make the World Go Away."

The Nashville Sound did to country what Motown did to R&B: made it slick. Also, just as that slickness created a space for Stax Records as the gritty alternative to Motown, so Bakersfield, California, rose as the earthier rival to Music City.

In the Great Depression, Oklahoma was hit by drought, and many farmers left the Dust Bowl to become farmworkers in Bakersfield, 110 miles northwest of Los Angeles. Bakersfield was just north of Weedpatch Camp, the labor camp built by the federal Farm Security Administration immortalized in John Steinbeck's epic novel *The Grapes of Wrath*. Bakersfield was close enough to Hollywood for session work but far enough away that the residents could develop their own unique form of entertainment. They embraced the steel guitars and fiddles Nashville had left behind and added the loud twang of electric Fender Telecasters. The music was designed for dancing in the clubs and fused Western swing and honky-tonk with rockabilly's backbeat.

The king of Bakersfield, Buck Owens (born 1929), was originally a Capitol Records session man for rockabilly artists Gene Vincent and Wanda Jackson. In the mid-1960s he enjoyed a streak of fifteen No. 1 singles on the country chart and was the James Brown ("hardest working man") of country, playing hundreds of shows a year. He had his own publishing company and booking agency, and started buying radio stations.

Owens kept the music flowing with sparkling singles such as "Buckaroo" and his March album *I've Got a Tiger by the Tail*. Its title song is a typically wry vignette about a guy struggling to keep up with his club-hopping woman. The album also includes "Crying Time," which Ray Charles covered at the end of the year. A decade earlier, Charles had outraged purists by combining gospel with R&B into soul, but when that was no longer controversial, he turned his attention to an even more radical experiment: fusing soul with country. Charles took "Crying Time" to No. 6 on the pop charts, No. 5 R&B, and No. 1 easy listening. "I'm crazy about Buck," said Charles, who won two Grammys for the song.[2]

Owens and the Beatles were label mates at Capitol Records, and Owens added the Beatles' version of "Twist and Shout" to his set. He and guitarist-fiddler Don Rich would imitate Liverpool accents for between-song banter, and wore Beatle wigs when their band, the Buckaroos, played Carnegie Hall.[3] The Beatles in turn picked up all Owens's albums when they came to Los Angeles, and started writing their own country-rock songs, such as "I'll Cry Instead," "I Don't Want to Spoil the Party," and "I'm a Loser." The pinnacle of the Beatles' country exploration would be Ringo Starr's cover of Owens's "Act Naturally." The song's theme of movie stardom fit for the Beatles' second soundtrack album, *Help!*, released in August.

When Owens acknowledged publicly that he liked the Beatles, he later recalled, "People would say, 'You shouldn't be sayin' that. You should be talkin' about country music.' And I said, 'Why not? It's the truth! Why can't I say I'm a Beatles fan?' I used to get criticized for that."[4]

When Owens covered Chuck Berry's "Memphis, Tennessee" on *I've Got a Tiger by the Tail*, country doctrinaires began questioning his authenticity, again, in an echo of the attacks Dylan would soon endure for playing rock. But Owens took the opposite tack of the defiant Dylan. In March he bought an ad in the Nashville paper *Music City News* that read, "I shall sing no song that is not a country song. I shall make no record that is not a country record. I refuse to be known as anything but a country singer. I am proud to be associated with country music. Country music and country music fans made me what I am today. And I shall not forget it."[5]

But like a skilled lawyer, he later clarified, "I see [the song] 'Memphis' as bein' rockabilly. I didn't say I wasn't gonna do rockabilly. I just said I ain't gonna sing no song that ain't a country song. I won't be known as anything but a country singer. I meant that, I still mean that. Listen to the lyrics. If they're not country lyrics . . . the melody . . . if that ain't a country melody. The only thing was, a black man was singin' it, a black man who I was a big fan of. So, my famous saying for my little pledge—I didn't date it. I really meant it at the time. I don't mean for it to be taken lightly."[6]

Merle Haggard was Bakersfield's brooding flip side to Buck Owens's crowd-pleaser. Haggard's youth had been filled with the kind of tangles with the law that gangsta rappers would later try to make press releases out of. He was repeatedly sent to detention centers for truancy, petty larceny, writing bad checks, and burglary. He would often escape and live out his future hit "I Am a Lonesome Fugitive," fleeing by train or hitchhiking to a new locale, where he would work odd jobs. After trying to rob a Bakersfield roadhouse, he ended up in San Quentin Prison. He was tempted to make one final escape—he'd heard his wife was pregnant by another man—but finally decided to stay put. The fellow convict he was going to escape with got out, shot a cop, and was executed. Haggard was further inspired to get his life together when Johnny Cash played the prison.

When Haggard got out, he started writing his own tunes, and briefly served as Buck Owens's bassist, giving Owens's band the moniker the Buckaroos. Haggard recorded the duet "Just Between the Two of Us" with Owens's ex-wife Bonnie—she and Owens had split back in 1951—a songwriter and country singer in her own right. The two won the Academy of Country Music Award for Best Vocal Group of 1965 and were married on June 28. Haggard also won Most Promising Male Vocalist and formed his own group, the Strangers, named for his Top 10 country hit of the previous year, "(All My Friends Are Gonna Be) Strangers." Bonnie served as the group's backing vocalist. The band's self-titled debut album was released in September.

The most surprising country debut of the year was Charley Pride, a Mississippi-born black man whose sharecropper father thought the blues were immoral and turned his son on to the Grand Ole Opry and Hank Williams instead. Pride was a pitcher in the Negro League and other minor leagues when country artists Red Sovine and Red Foley heard him singing and hooked him up with producer Chet Atkins, who got Pride signed before telling the label that he was black. Pride's manager, Jack D. Johnson, suppressed all pictures of the artist for two full years.

Pride's first RCA session in August yielded "The Snakes Crawl at Night," backed with "Atlantic Coastal Line." The A side title sounded like it might be a polemic against the Klan, but it was actually in the country tradition of a man murdering his cheating wife. The B side was a beautifully detailed hobo song sung in Pride's warm baritone.

When Pride walked out onstage in the redneck clubs, you could cut the tension with a knife. But the unflappable Pride would say, "Howdy, folks, I know I've got a mighty dark suntan, I got it picking cotton down in Sledge, Mississippi. I hope you don't mind if I sing a few country songs for you."[7] And after launching into Hank Williams's "Lovesick Blues," he'd have the audience in the palm of his hand.

Pride's big break would come the following year, when singer-songwriter Willie Nelson brought him on a package tour. Some club owners in Klan-heavy counties received death threats, and had to hire police officers to guard the stage. Nelson said that while facing down one rowdy crowd as he introduced Pride, "I knew something special was called for at that moment, so I grabbed Charlie and laid a big kiss on his lips, and once the crowd recovered they listened to Charlie and went crazy over him."[8]

Nelson had written a number of classic country hits, including Patsy Cline's "Crazy" and Faron Young's "Hello Walls," but his own singles couldn't get higher than country No. 43. At the time, he still acted the hillbilly, but his music reflected a jazzy influence as he mostly talked the lyrics of moody pieces such as "Night Life."

Nelson had cut his first record nine years earlier. One of the Nashville artists with whom he would later form the Outlaw country movement, Waylon Jennings, had been kicking around almost as long, but Jennings was lucky just to be alive. In 1958, fellow Texan Buddy Holly had produced Jennings's "Jole Blon" and "When Sin Stops (Love Begins)" and then picked him to play bass for his Winter Dance Party Tour. Holly arranged for a tour plane, but Jennings gave away his seat the night the plane went down and claimed the lives of Holly, the Big Bopper, and Richie Valens. "The day the music died," Don McLean called it in his elegy "American Pie."

Jennings moved to Arizona and formed the rockabilly Waylors. He got signed by Herb Alpert's A&M Records but was ignored because he wasn't folk, the hot trend of the moment. Things started rolling once Chet Atkins signed him to RCA and he moved to Nashville; his first recording session in Music City was on March 16.

June Carter had brought Johnny Cash to see Jennings play in Arizona. Both men had worked in the cotton fields, and knew all the same obscure music by country guys from the 1920s. Cash wanted a place to crash when he was in Nashville, so he and Jennings got a one-bedroom with two king-size beds. They'd always forget their keys, lock themselves out, and have to kick the door in. Jennings hid his pills behind the air conditioner; Cash hid his behind the TV.[9]

In his autobiography, Jennings wrote of Cash,

We were so much alike in many ways, it was scary. We both dressed in black . . . It's a worn-out word, but we were soul mates . . . We flipped over each other from the moment we met, though at first we stood back. It was so sudden we were kind of afraid of each other. John and I were both manly men, and we liked to walk macho and talk macho; but after a while we learned we could be ourselves . . . We'd just get giddy and silly around each other, and laugh a lot. That would be when I'd be calling him John. Or Maynard. He had a lot of names. "Johnny Cash" was formal, as in "Mr. Cash." There was Johnny when he was just lounging around. And then there was Cash. Sometimes you couldn't tease John or he would become Cash. He was very seldom Cash with me. Cash was usually when he was mean, or when he was on drugs.[10]

Jennings's first country hit, "That's the Chance I'll Have to Take" opens with a lonesome harmonica that echoes like the wide-open spaces of Arizona and Texas. A little folk seems to have rubbed off on it. In fact, his first Nashville album was called *Folk-Country*, recorded from March to July. Like Cash, Jennings dug Dylan and had covered "Don't Think Twice, It's Alright" live; later he'd tackle Dylan's "I Don't Believe You" and the Beatles' "Norwegian Wood." Another of his singles, "Anita, You're Dreaming," was based on the same traditional Mexican folk melody Dylan had used for "To Ramona."

After Jennings's rocking "Stop the World (and Let Me Off)" made it to

No. 16 (country), a film tailored around Jennings, called *Nashville Rebel*, went into production and was released the following year.

Johnny Cash had started the year on a positive note by performing the Impressions' "Amen" on the American musical variety show *Shindig!*, on January 13, and then covering three of his friend Bob Dylan's songs on his album *Orange Blossom Special* the following month. He then proceeded to go off the rails. In a fit of amphetamine-stoked rage, he smashed the floor lights of the Grand Ole Opry with his mike stand and was blackballed for years. Unable to sleep, he'd break furniture in hotel rooms long before the Who and Led Zeppelin would make it part of their PR. At home in Casitas Springs, California, he'd drink beer, pop pills, and pace around his room listening to music and feeling alienated from his wife, Vivian, while yearning for June Carter, member of the storied Carter Family folk/country group and often his backup singer on tour. Cash and Vivian would argue, and he'd squeal off into the desert and get into a car wreck.[11] He flipped a camper after falling asleep at the wheel and crashed a car after thinking someone was tailing him with a gun. He'd disappear for days, not eating until his pastor came to find him. (It was ironic that his bass-baritone drawl was as slow as it was, considering he was so addicted to speed.) On May 11 he got arrested for picking flowers while intoxicated and wrote "Starkville City Jail" about spending the night in a cell. (In 2007 the town held a Johnny Cash Flower Pickin' Festival.)

The next month, while fishing in the California backcountry, his camper truck's muffler split from the exhaust pipe. When he tried to start the auto, the heat set the grass on fire. Wasted, he staggered around trying to put it out with his leather jacket, but the blaze quickly spread into a five-hundred-acre forest fire that burned the foliage off three mountains and drove away forty-four endangered condors.[12] "I didn't do it, my truck did, and it's dead, so you can't question it," he told the judge, later adding, "I don't care about your damn yellow buzzards." Cash paid a penalty of $82,001.

He got himself in the hottest water yet just a few months later. On October 4, while crossing the Mexican border from Juarez into El Paso, he was arrested by federal narcotics agents with no fewer than 688 Dexedrine speed capsules and 475 Equanil downers hidden in his guitar case. Out on bail, he spent the rest of the year recording comedy songs for his next album, *Everybody Loves a Nut*, trying to put a funny spin on a year of drug busts, fires, and Ole Opry freak-outs.

6

West Coast Nights

The Byrds ignite the Sunset Strip with their residency at Ciro's in March and April, while Brian Wilson's April LSD trip inspires the Beach Boys' most archetypal single but haunts him with auditory hallucinations.

Before the Byrds, Jim McGuinn was a young guitar and banjo player who accompanied folk acts such as the Limeliters, the Chad Mitchell Trio, and Judy Collins. When Bobby Darin wanted to go folk, he brought McGuinn into his band. Darin also gave McGuinn a job as a songwriter at his company, T.M. Music, in the Brill Building. One of McGuinn's ditties, "Beach Ball," cashed in on the surf music craze and was a hit in Australia; the Bee Gees sang backing vocals on it.

By day, McGuinn worked in the pop world; by night, he played the Greenwich Village folk clubs and then had jam sessions back at the Earl Hotel, where both he and John Phillips (later of the Mamas and the Papas) lived. Then the Beatles gave him an epiphany that he believed could bridge the two camps in which he existed.

McGuinn started adding what he called the Beatles beat to folk songs, speeding up classics such as "The Water Is Wide" to four/four double time.[1] It was a discovery not unlike the one made ten years earlier by Elvis Presley and his bassist Bill Black, when they sped up the country song "Blue Moon of Kentucky" and the blues song "That's All Right Mama." "Fine, man. Hell, that's different," Presley and Black's producer, Sam Phillips, exclaimed. "That's a pop song now, nearly 'bout."[2] When different genres cross-pollinated, the hybrid vigor often inaugurated new golden eras, be it rock and roll (R&B plus country), soul (R&B plus gospel), grunge (metal plus punk), or folk-rock.

But the Greenwich Village purists didn't like what McGuinn was doing, so the musician thought he'd give Los Angeles a try. The Troubadour club hosted regular hootenannies, and there McGuinn met a young folkie named Gene Clark, who'd been playing with the New Christy Minstrels. Clark suggested they form a twosome like the British pop duo Peter and Gordon. They were practicing in the stairwell of the Troubadour when suddenly another folkie named David Crosby started harmonizing with them unbidden. His tenor took their vocals to an entirely new level; without him, McGuinn and Clark's voices were so close they blended into unison.

McGuinn had been trying to figure out how the Beatles got their sound. Then, when the trio went to a screening of *A Hard Day's Night*, he spotted George Harrison's brand-new twelve-string Rickenbacker. "That's it!" he exclaimed.[3] Crosby recalled, "We knew exactly what we wanted to do. It probably blew my mind more than [the Beatles' appearance on] *Ed Sullivan*. The whole movie was magic. I'm told that I came out of the theater, grabbed a stop sign and swung around it like I was pole dancing. I was just so happy. It was like, 'Oh, man . . . I know how to do that! We can do that!'"[4] Folk singers were supposed to use only acoustic twelve-strings, but McGuinn went out and bought his own electric Rickenbacker.

Crosby had been working with a manager-producer named Jim Dickson, who now took on the whole group and brought in a Southern California bluegrass musician named Chris Hillman to play bass. The final piece of the puzzle was Michael Clarke (no relation to Gene). Hillman had chops, but Michael Clarke had a blond Beatle cut like those of Brian Jones and Yardbirds singer Keith Relf. At seventeen, he'd hitched from Washington State to San Francisco and played bongos in North Beach with the post-beatniks. Crosby had met him in Big Sur, playing the conga drums. So when the new group saw Clarke one day walking down Santa Monica Boulevard toward the Troubadour, Crosby said, "Hey, man, you wanna be a drummer?" and Clarke said, "Sure," even though he'd never played a full drum set before.[5] They called themselves the Jet Set, then briefly the Beefeaters, to fool people into thinking they were British. Luckily they settled on the Byrds (misspelled, in Beatle fashion).

After their version of "Mr. Tambourine Man" was released on April 12, it went on to become the second-biggest worldwide hit of the year after "Satisfaction." "Never had lyrics of such literary quality and ambiguous meaning been used on a rock record," wrote critic Richie Unterberger.[6] With its lines about taking a trip on a magic swirlin' ship and fading into one's own parade, it was the weirdest No. 1 yet. By year's end, though, the Beatles and Stones would have their own "tripping" singles.

The song also inaugurated "jangle pop," the subgenre that has intermittently resurged throughout rock's history, both with the sound of the guitar and the "jingle jangle morning" lyric. In the mid-1960s the jangle was embraced by everyone from the Beach Boys, the Hollies, Paul Revere and the Raiders, to even (occasionally) the Stones.

Though the Wrecking Crew played on "Mr. Tambourine Man," the Byrds took over playing their own instruments for their two albums of the year, which included six Dylan covers between them. Gene Clark wrote many superb originals, while McGuinn found classics to cover such as "He Was a Friend of Mine," molded into a eulogy to JFK. Chris Hillman covered Porter Wagoner's country hit "Satisfied Mind," hinting at the country-rock direction he'd lead the band in a few years.

Not only did the Byrds discover a new sound, but also their scene gave birth to the West Coast hippie dance style, kicking off the golden years of the Sunset Strip.

The band rehearsed in a room where underground hipster–dance instructor Vito Paulekas held a clay-sculpting class. A marathon dancer in the 1930s, Paulekas spent four years in prison in the 1940s for trying to hold up a movie theater, and then moved to LA and amassed a coterie of proto-hippies. He had a dance troupe and a tree house commune that functioned as a crash pad for runaways. When the Byrds began their residency at the Sunset Strip nightclub Ciro's in March, Paulekas's troupe was almost as much a part of the scene as the Byrds were.

Author Barry Miles (a close friend of the Beatles) called Vito and his wife Zsou's group of approximately thirty-five dancers "the first hippies in Hollywood, perhaps the first hippies anywhere . . . Calling themselves Freaks, they lived a semi-communal life and engaged in sex orgies and free-form dancing whenever they could."[7] Zsou ran a clothing boutique and outfitted the women in see-through velvet and lace (often worn without underwear).

Vito's right-hand man, Carl Franzoni (a.k.a. "Captain Fuck"), said,

The Byrds were, in my estimation, the best dance band that Hollywood ever saw, because they made people dance with that kind of music. Those guys were forever fighting with each other, but when they got up there, they really cooked. [The group] Love weren't the dance band that the Byrds were, and neither was Frank Zappa. The combination of [the band members], the different factions of what kind of music they came from, it just was such a fantastic blend that it was so folk, from all different parts of the United States. I always think of dancing to "The Bells of Rhymney" and like, it's a church, you know? So when they brought that kind of music in to Minnesota, Iowa, places like that, those kids were just: "Wow, where did *you* come from?" They could have started their own church with that kind of music they were playing.[8]

In *Girls Like Us*, author Sheila Weller writes,

Paulekas and Franzoni trained a troupe of young "freakers" in the sensual body movement that soon became synonymous with late-1960s dancing. When you walked into Ciro's in 1965, heard the music, and saw the (stoned) dancing, you were jolted by its radical fluidity, gentleness, and introspection. "You knew a new world had arrived," says one habitué . . . The dancing style . . . was sensual and languorous, a welcome replacement for the corny, thumping Twist-era dances that had prevailed for seven years.[9]

Paul Jay Robbins in the underground *Los Angeles Free Press*, wrote, "Dancing with the Byrds becomes a mystic loss of ego and tangibility; you become pure energy someplace between sound and motion and the involvement is total."[10]

On March 26, Dylan joined the band onstage for Jimmy Reed's "Baby What You Want Me to Do." As teenagers crowded the sidewalks outside, Ciro's quickly became the favored scene of Hollywood's burgeoning acid contingent—Peter Fonda, Jack Nicholson, Bruce Dern, and Dennis Hopper—who in two years would team to write and star in Roger Corman's LSD feature *The Trip*. Also present were musicians such as Jackie DeShannon (whom the Byrds covered on their first album), singer/producer Kim Fowley (later creator of the band the Runaways), and Sonny and Cher (who would scoop one of the Byrds' upcoming Dylan covers, "All I Really Wanna Do").

The Byrds turned their amps, treble boosters, and compressors up to the max to become the loudest band on the scene, and also worked to perfect their image as the new vanguard of hip.[11] Gene Clark rocked the Prince Valiant haircut while banging the tambourine. Crosby mugged in his green suede cape. McGuinn, who'd first seen rectangular specs on John Sebastian in Greenwich Village, got his own set made with cobalt lenses in wire frames. The producer of the TV show *Shindig!* told him that everyone needed a gimmick, and the glasses became McGuinn's.[12]

In April, Brian Wilson's friend from the William Morris Agency, Loren Schwartz, gave him LSD for the first time. In the midst of the trip, Brian suddenly yelled that he was afraid of his parents and fled to his room to hide his head under a pillow. He pulled himself together, though, by riffing off Bach on the piano, an exercise that evolved into the introduction to the Beach Boys' ultimate anthem "California Girls." The next day, he tried to recount his trip to his wife Marilyn. He began crying and hugged her, saying, "I saw God and it just blew my mind."[13] She became deeply upset that he was using drugs and moved out, but when he begged her to come back, she returned.

After the trip, Wilson began experiencing auditory hallucinations. "Oh, I knew right from the start something was wrong. I'd taken some psychedelic drugs, and then about a week after that I started hearing voices . . . All day every day, and I can't get them out. Every few minutes, the voices say something derogatory to me, which discourages me a little bit. But I have to be strong enough to say to them, 'Hey, would you quit stalking me? Fuck off! Don't talk to me—leave me alone!' I have to say these types of things all day long. It's like a fight . . . I believe they started picking on me because they are jealous."[14]

Wilson plowed forward with "California Girls," recorded on April 6. Both it and "Mr. Tambourine Man" had intros inspired by Bach. Though "Mr. Tambourine Man" wasn't officially released until six days later, Wilson had probably already heard it. The Byrds' manager, Terry Melcher, had been in a number of bands with the Beach Boys' newest member, Bruce Johnston. On April 9, Johnston took over from Campbell as Wilson's permanent replacement on the road, and would soon be an integral member. (As a thank-you to Campbell for his help, Wilson gave him "Guess I'm Dumb." Campbell sang over a Wrecking Crew instrumental track that had originally been recorded for the Beach Boys. Campbell's version was released on June 7, and its cinematic orchestration set the blueprint for his future hits.)

The "California Girls" session was Wilson's favorite of his career, and he thought his intro was the finest piece of music he had written. It was recorded on eight-track, the cutting edge in studio technology at the time. Wilson wanted to create an introductory segment that was completely different from the rest of the song. After Wilson's intro, Mike Love took it from there with a celebration of all the different types of women the band had met in their travels across the globe. The track made it to No. 3.

Love was an unusual front man, balding at a young age and compensating by going shirtless on album covers; singing the "Monster Mash" hunched over onstage in the band's candy-striped shirts. But he wrote numerous classics with Wilson, such as "Let Him Run Wild," the B side of "California Girls." His passion for performing kept the band onstage through Wilson's many ups and downs, but tension was growing as Love became wary of Wilson's more avant-garde impulses.

Both Love and Capitol Records thought Wilson's mellow, minor-key music on *Today!* was uncommercial, and they wanted more of the Beach Boys' old, happier style. So their next album, *Summer Days (and Summer Nights!!)*, features tracks such as "Amusement Parks USA" and the ode to "Salt Lake City" (the latter because Mormons were big fans of the group's wholesome image).

Still, Wilson continued to explore more subdued, melancholy moods. He wrote "Girl Don't Tell Me," to be his younger brother Carl's first lead vocal. (Carl looked a bit like a mini-Brian, sometimes leading the casual observer to wonder who was who on album covers.) The song concerns the singer's bitterness that a girl never wrote him after their summer romance, and it is the youthful gawkiness of Carl's voice that makes it especially convincing. The song itself re-appropriates the melody of the Beatles' latest No. 1, "Ticket to Ride," right down to the "i-i-i" vowel elongation. Lennon shared Wilson's introspective side and enjoyed the homage. They were going through the same trip—in more ways than one. Two of the Beatles were given LSD on the other side of the Atlantic within ten days of Wilson's introduction to the drug, but unlike his experience, theirs was not by choice.

England Swings

The Beatles get dosed with LSD on March 27 and release "Ticket to Ride" on April 9. The Brits hold eight spots in the U.S. Top 10 on May 8 as art schools, pirate radio, and Carnaby Street fuel Swinging London. The Who release "Anyway, Anyhow, Anywhere" on May 21. Them, the Animals, and the Yardbirds all score as well, but the Kinks almost implode with their disastrous tour through the un-swinging United States, beginning June 17.

As marijuana drifted out of the folk and soul scenes, it captured the minds of artists such as the Beatles, the Beach Boys, the Byrds, and the Stones. George Harrison said it allowed them to hear sounds they hadn't been able to hear before, though Starr pointed out that they didn't *record* well when they were stoned; it was better to smoke the day before, so they'd have a creative memory to work with.[1]

Lennon took the twelve-string arpeggio Harrison had played at the fade-out of "A Hard Day's Night" and slowed it down for the haunting sparkle of "Ticket to Ride." The drone of the rhythm guitar is the first hint of musical influence from Britain's former colony India. The Beatles also started experimenting with drums. McCartney demonstrated the unusual beat he had in mind, and let Starr take it from there. Starr's off-kilter, rolling drums on

"Ticket to Ride" cap a massive sound that Lennon later proudly deemed "pretty fuckin' heavy for then." For an added twist, they kick the tempo up to double-time just before the fade-out. But perhaps the biggest departure is the downbeat mood. Though the group had released dark album cuts, until then, their *singles*—their main statements to the world—were happy. "Ticket to Ride" was the first time a sad song actually made the A side.

The Beatles' recreation regimen had consisted of amphetamines, whiskey, and Coca-Cola, but after meeting Dylan, they switched to marijuana, which made them feel more relaxed. But marijuana is a hallucinogen, amplifying whatever emotion the smoker is in, and Lennon had been troubled by a difficult childhood. He was abandoned by both parents and given to his aunt; he then suffered the early deaths of his mother, best friend, and favorite uncle. The speed (stimulant), booze (depressant), and thrill of success had blocked all this out, but marijuana brought more complex moods to the fore.

"Ticket to Ride" continues the theme of "I'm a Loser" as Lennon's woman leaves because she can't be free while living with him. The idea in itself was somewhat unusual for the time, as it implies divorce, separation, or "living together," still years away from being accepted. In their early days, the Beatles played the red light district of Hamburg, Germany, where the doctors examined the hookers and issued cards to indicate that they had a clean bill of health. Lennon dubbed these "tickets to ride." McCartney's cousin also had a pub in the town of Ryde, England. Given the Beatles' love of puns, the title probably reflects both meanings.

Just as the Beatles were integrating marijuana into their art, they were hit by a much more potent hallucinogen. After shooting part of their next movie, *Help!*, in the Bahamas and Austria, the group returned to England to shoot from March 22 through April 28. Their first week home, they had March 27 off; it was two nights after King's Montgomery victory speech. Harrison was friends with his dentist, thirty-four-year-old John Riley.[2] So Harrison; his future wife, Pattie Boyd; Lennon and Lennon's wife, Cynthia, went to Riley's flat for dinner. His girlfriend was the twenty-two-year-old "bunny mother" at the London Playboy Club, the person who hired the women who worked there.

Either Riley or his girlfriend had procured LSD from the man who ran the Playboy Club, who had himself gotten it from Timothy Leary. At the time, LSD was still legal, though not many people had heard of it. Riley and his girlfriend hadn't tried acid before and, Harrison later suspected, believed it to be an aphrodisiac. Without asking the Beatles, Pattie, or Cynthia, Riley or his girlfriend slipped acid-dosed sugar cubes into their coffee.[3] Riley himself didn't take any.

After dinner, Lennon and Harrison intended to see a close friend from their Hamburg days, Klaus Voormann, play at the Pickwick Club with his trio Paddy, Klaus and Gibson. But Riley told them, "I advise you not to leave."

When they replied that they had to, Riley explained to Lennon what he'd done. Lennon told Harrison, "We've had LSD."[4]

Riley admitted that he didn't know what it was, just that it was "all the thing" with the London swingers. Harrison had heard about it but wasn't alarmed—this was before the press had demonized the drug. Since LSD took some time to kick in, he wasn't even feeling it yet, and presumed that their host was trying to coerce them into an orgy.

To Cynthia Lennon, on the other hand, "It was as if we suddenly found ourselves in the middle of a horror film. The room seemed to get bigger and bigger. Our host seemed to change into a demon."[5]

Like marijuana, LSD intensifies whatever state of mind the person taking it is already in. It is best to do it in a secure setting, with friends you trust. Fleeing a sex-crazed dentist and his bunny while driving into London evening traffic is not ideal. "It was like having the Devil following us in a taxi," Cynthia said.[6]

When they arrived at the Pickwick and ordered their drinks, Harrison suddenly felt "the most incredible feeling come over me. It was something like a very concentrated version of the best feeling I'd ever had in my whole life. It was fantastic. I felt in love, not with anything or anybody in particular, but with everything. Everything was perfect, in a perfect light, and I had an overwhelming desire to go round the club telling everybody how much I loved them—people I'd never seen before."[7] This from the grumpy Beatle, whose previous compositions included such missives to fans as "Don't Bother Me." Later, he would elaborate that "LSD gave me the experience of: I am not this body. I am pure energy soaring about everywhere that happens to be in a body for a temporary period of time."[8]

Then an explosion jolted Harrison. Actually, it was the waiters throwing chairs onto the tables as the lights came on and the club closed down.

The group had planned to meet Starr at the nearby Ad Lib club, the

ultra-hot spot that played only black music. They walked over, dazzled by
the traffic lights and taxis. Harrison had to talk a hysterically laughing Pattie
Boyd out of smashing a window. In the elevator to the club, the red light
made them feel the elevator was in flames, and they started shrieking. The
door opened, and they screamed to Starr, "The lift's on fire!"

The Ad Lib always had a table reserved for them. As they made their
way to it, the other patrons' thick makeup struck them as masks.[9] When they
sat down at the table, it seemed to stretch out before Lennon. He'd read books
by Romantic writers about their experiences on opium, and as he stared at
the elongating table, amazed, he realized that the same thing was happening to him. A singer came and asked if he could sit next to him; Lennon
agreed, only if the singer didn't talk, because he couldn't think.[10]

The new Mad Hatters sat there till dawn, at which point Harrison drove
them home very slowly, telling Lennon to stop making jokes because if he
laughed, he might crash the car. Boyd wanted to run into the fields and play
football. At Harrison's house, Lennon drew picture after picture and had the
sensation of driving a submarine.

If March 27 is the correct date, as is generally believed, the next day, they
were obliged to perform for the British TV show *Thank Your Lucky Stars*. In
the footage, Lennon smiles as they lip-synch to their latest songs, and they
don't seem hungover or wacked out. But the experience would profoundly
alter the course of the Beatles' lives and art.

Within a year, the controversy over LSD would reach the headlines. While
some psychiatrists proposed that LSD affected the neural mechanism of the
brain in ways similar to mystical experiences, detractors pointed to the de-
formed webs spun by acid-dosed spiders. During interviews for the *Beatles
Anthology* in 1995, Harrison concedes that acid had its dark side, but he said
that the first time he took it, a lightbulb went on in his head that caused him
to ask who he was, where he came from, and where he was going.[11]

A clue arrived a week later, on April 5, as the Beatles shot a scene in the
Rajahama Indian restaurant. Indian musicians played in the background, and
the exotic sound intrigued Harrison. He picked up one of their stringed instruments, called the sitar. "The only way that I can describe it was my intel-
lect didn't know what was going on, and yet this other part of me identified
with it. It just called on me. The pure sound of it and what was playing just
appealed to me so much."[12]

His mother, Louise, said she "always used to fiddle with our wireless to get Indian music. I'd tuned into Indian stuff once by accident, and I thought it was lovely."[13]

Many other musicians were becoming entranced with the instrument. The same month, the Yardbirds tried to use it on "Heart Full of Soul," their follow-up to "For Your Love." The guitar riff on the demo sounded Indian to them, so their manager hired a real Indian sitar player and tabla player to join the band in the studio. But the tabla player couldn't count in four/four time like the English, and he couldn't stop when the band wanted him to stop. They also couldn't get the mix right. So guitarist Jeff Beck imitated the sitar with a Sola Sound Tone Blender fuzz box.[14] The dynamics of shifting from the fuzz guitar in the chorus back to the propulsive acoustic guitar in the verse, along with the echoey backing harmonies, sent "Heart Full of Soul" to No. 2 in the United Kingdom and No. 9 in the United States in June.

The week of May 8, 1965, saw the English holding down eight spots in the U.S. Top 10, the high-water mark for the British Invasion. (And another one of the ten was an Australian folk act, the Seekers.) Gary Lewis and the Playboys were the lone Americans, at No. 2 with "Count Me In."

Herman's Hermits from Manchester held both the top spot, with "Mrs. Brown You've Got a Lovely Daughter," and the No. 7 spot, with their cover of "Silhouettes." They outsold the Fab Four in the States, due to front man Peter Noone's supremacy with the prepubescents. And while the group was considered unhip, "Mrs. Brown" was actually the first contemporary tune to look back to the British music hall tradition, something the Beatles, the Kinks, and the Stones would frequently do in the years ahead.

The Beatles were at No. 3, with "Ticket to Ride." Then another Manchester group, named Wayne Fontana and the Mindbenders, held No. 4 with "Game of Love," which had topped the charts on April 24. At No. 5 was "I'll Never Find Another You," by the Seekers, who enjoyed a number of folk-pop hits throughout the year, including "The Carnival Is Over" and "A World of Our Own."

Petula Clark had scored a No. 1 in January, with "Downtown," and now she was back at No. 6, with her ode to nightclubs, "I Know a Place." The song takes a line from the title of Beatles' manager Brian Epstein's memoir, *A Cellarful of Noise*, about the Cavern Club, where he discovered the group.

(Lennon joked that the title should have been *A Cellarful of Boys*, due to Epstein's penchant for rough trade and rent boys.)

A third Manchester band, Freddie and the Dreamers, were at No. 8 with "I'm Telling You Now," which had held the top spot for two weeks a few weeks earlier. Their bespectacled front man was known for doing "the Freddie," in which he kicked out his arms and legs like a kindergartener—perhaps the whitest dance of all time. In marked contrast, the Stones held No. 9, with "The Last Time." And the Top 10 was rounded out by Sounds Orchestral's "Cast Your Fate to the Wind," written by Vince Guaraldi, who would score *A Charlie Brown Christmas* later in the year.

Beyond the pop charts, England dominated the Academy Awards. Julie Christie won Best Actress for John Schlesinger's *Darling*, and David Lean's *Dr. Zhivago* took home Best Picture. Other Brits nominated in the Best Actor or Actress category included Richard Burton, Laurence Olivier, Julie Andrews, Samantha Eggar, and a raft of Supporting Actors and Actresses. Leading men such as Peter O'Toole, Michael Caine, and Richard Harris were popular on both sides of the Atlantic, and British New Wave directors like Tony Richardson and Richard Lester were years ahead of Hollywood in dealing candidly with sex and class; Hollywood's golden age of realism wouldn't kick in until the end of the decade. *Thunderball*, with Sean Connery, was the biggest box office hit of the James Bond franchise, when adjusted for inflation.

London rose to challenge Paris as the epicenter of the fashion world, led by designers such as Ossie Clark, Bill Gibb, and Mary Quant, the mother of the miniskirt. Carnaby Street kicked into gear, and John Stephen became the rockers' clothier of choice, with his tight suits and fitted shirts. Barbara Hulanicki's store, Biba, popularized her black-and-white Pop Art dresses. The boutique I Was Lord Kitchener's Valet sold military jackets. In December, the boutique Granny Takes a Trip opened, specializing in both vintage clothing and, as the "Trip" implied, the colorful threads the new hippies embraced.

England's blossoming cultural scene benefited from the government-sponsored art colleges, which took in the creatively inclined who did not seem to fit in the more traditional paths of study. Many of the leading British bands were fronted by art school rockers such as John Lennon, Keith Richards, Pete Townshend, Ray Davies, and Eric Clapton (not that they had actually graduated or even paid attention while there). Beatniks, existentialists, activists, and jazz aficionados abounded in the environment. It was the En-glish bohemians' synthesis of hard-core American blues and R&B with the avant-garde sensibility they picked up at art school that resulted in psyche-delia as the groups began mutating the music with distortion, feedback, and foreign instruments.

The palpable sense that Londoners were living through a pop-cultural renaissance was boosted immeasurably by the rise of pirate radio. At the time, the BBC had a monopoly within the United Kingdom and did not broad-cast the Top 40 records that were popular on the street. But starting mid-decade, ships moored just outside England's territorial boundaries be-gan transmitting whatever they wanted. Radio Caroline, Radio London, and Radio Jackie often played unknown and experimental groups, further en-couraging the explosion of bands already under way.

TV's *Ready Steady Go!* did the same. Hosted by mod Cathy McGowan, the program was freewheeling enough to let groups such as the Rolling Stones introduce Brits to their older blues idols such as Howlin' Wolf. Many of the blues greats such as Muddy Waters and Willie Dixon had experienced dif-ficulty supporting themselves because their genre seemed out-of-date to con-temporary black audiences. It reminded many blacks of the American South they had deliberately left behind in their Great Migration north and west. So when bands such as the Stones and the Yardbirds popularized these artists with a new white audience, it helped revive the bluesmen's careers.

But there were only so many American blues songs to cover. The savvier British groups began to realize they had to find original material, though only some would prove up to the challenge of writing their own songs. Of the pop-oriented groups, the Hollies and Moody Blues made the transition. The blues-based groups—the Rolling Stones, the Animals, the Yardbirds, the Who, the Kinks, Manfred Mann, and Ireland's Them with Van Morrison—struggled to walk the line between staying true to their roots and releasing singles commercial enough to allow them to survive. The purist tension was most clearly exemplified when Eric Clapton left the Yardbirds because he felt their February release "For Your Love" was too pop.

Ironically, New York's Brill Building actually ended up providing some of the greatest songs of the British Invasion. The Animals' manager, Mickie Most, would fly from London to New York to visit Don Kirshner, listen to his latest tracks, and buy the best.[15] "We Gotta Get Out of This Place" was an electrifying vow to make it, no matter what the cost, by Mann-Weil. Equally fierce was Roger Atkins–Carl D'Errico's declaration of independence, "It's My Life." The Animals also recorded Goffin-King's "Don't Bring Me Down," but felt they were too cool for Mann-Weil's antidrug anthem, "Kicks," and left that for Paul Revere and the Raiders. The Animals' incendiary triumvirate of Brill-written hits made it briefly irrelevant that lead singer Eric Burdon was not evolving as a songwriter as rivals Jagger/Richards and Van Morrison were.

Though even Morrison benefitted from the Brill, when songwriter/producer Bert Berns gifted Them with the dynamic "Here Comes the Night," released in March. Morrison's raspy lament and Jimmy Page's reverbed guitar were given panoramic punch by Berns's production and underscored with moody organ. (Page was the king of the British session musicians, playing for Donovan, Herman's Hermits, Petula Clark, Tom Jones, Marianne Faithfull, Jackie DeShannon, Nico, and even the early Kinks and the Who, before joining the Yardbirds and later forming Led Zeppelin.)

The other key to sustainability was moderation when it came to partying, but as Swinging London kicked into high gear, this would become a tricky row for many to hoe. Originally cabarets and casinos were the only places open late at night where bands could grab a bite and unwind after a gig or a night in the recording studio (hence the casino sequence in the Beatles' *A Hard Day's Night*). But with the rise of the new class of pop stars, a string of super-"in" night clubs rose to cater to them, such as The Ad Lib and Scotch of St. James, where luminaries as varied as the Stones, the Kinks, Mary Quant, Julie Christie, and even on occasion Princess Margaret held court. Rock critic Nik Cohn wrote that the club scene was so addictive that many rockers never got it together to become world-famous because they enjoyed the high life too much.[16] The Pretty Things admitted as much in "Midnight to Six Man." In the song, they manage to drag themselves out of bed only after dark, in order to hit the club to hear some new sounds and score (in both senses of the word).

Guitarist Pete Townshend went to high school with bassist John Entwistle and vocalist Roger Daltrey, and the trio formed a band, eventually settling on the name the Who. But while Townshend and Entwistle were friends, their relationship with Daltrey was touchier. Daltrey was a hard-ass who didn't let being only five foot seven stop him from settling arguments with his fists. He was ultimately expelled from school for smoking.

Of the London blues bands that went on to fame, the Who was the only one to dare cover James Brown, hence their slogan "Maximum R&B." When drummer Keith Moon asked to sit in with them one night, he blasted them to the next level. A beyond-hyper speed freak, he synthesized the thunderous tom-toms of Gene Krupa with the surf-rock bedlam of the Surfaris' "Wipe Out" into his own iconoclastic style, and was never afraid to deviate from the standard beat to embellish with outlandish drum fills. Sometimes his fills themselves became part of the melody.

The band's first manager, Pete Meaden, decided to make them *the* band of the mod subculture. Mods were usually young people who worked in offices and spent all their money on stylish clothes, obsessed with cutting-edge Italian suits, vests, and shoes. Their ideal weekend was to take amphetamine pills and stay up for days dancing to R&B and soul.

Mods' rumbles with the rockers became legend. Typically, rockers were from the tradesmen class. They were the descendants of the Teddy Boys, the first teenage subculture in post–World War II Britain, and their motorcycles and leather were in sharp contrast to the mods' Vespas and parkas.

In the beginning, the rockers and mods didn't fight—it was actually the mods and the police—but sensationalistic newspapers changed it to "mods versus rockers," and soon, life imitated art.[17] During the spring holiday of 1964, both sides massed to brawl on the beach in resort towns such as Brighton, Margate, Hastings, and Broadstairs, though how different this really was from typical post-football game hooliganism is open to conjecture. Still, it was enough of a newspaper story for a journalist to ask Ringo Starr in *A Hard Day's Night* if he was a mod or a rocker. He'd been a Teddy Boy as a teen, but the Beatles' manager had remolded the band with a proto-mod look. Starr deftly answered that he was a "mocker."

The Who took the mods' style and, equally important, as author Nicholas Schaffner writes in *The British Invasion*, channeled the spirit of the mod-versus-rocker feud into their music.[18] Townshend was the first guy on the circuit to use two amps at the same time, which made his distortion and feedback richer. He rubbed his guitar on his mike stand and shook the guitar in front of the amp to get a throbbing pre-psychedelic cacophony. He created a Morse code effect by flipping the pickup of his guitar off and on, and then hitting another switch to make it sound like he was gunning the audience down, pointing the end of his guitar at them like an Uzi, making his way murderously from one end of the stage to the other.

When Townshend opened for the Stones, he saw Richards warming up by windmilling his arm. When Townshend realized it wasn't part of Richards's act, he took the pose for himself onstage, one of many he would develop to compensate for his nose, which he felt was too big.[19] A few ballet lessons taken as a kid helped his natural grace as he jumped and bent down on his knees, transforming himself into one of the great posers of rock.

One night, while the band played "Smokestack Lightning" at the Railway Hotel in West London, Townshend lifted his twelve-string over his head and it went through the venue's low ceiling. It broke his guitar, but he acted like he'd meant for that to happen, and continued slamming the guitar into the ceiling over and over. The crowd loved it, but next week he didn't have an extra guitar to smash, so he pushed over his amps. Not to be outdone, Moon shoved over his drum kit.[20] (Later, Moon took to stocking his bass drum with explosives to detonate at the climax of their sets.) The press, who had started coming by, told the band that if they did it again, they'd put them on the front page. So Townshend would ram his guitar into the speaker, throw it in the air and catch it, then bring it down over his shoulder and smash it on the ground.

In art school, he had seen the "auto-destructive" work of Gustav Metzger, who would spray hydrochloric acid onto nylon sheets to make the nylon disintegrate, as a symbol of the destructive power of nuclear weapons.[21] Townshend branded his instrument smashing an "auto destruction" happening, which went along with the band's Pop Art clothing, such as Moon's bull's-eye T-shirt and Townshend's coat made out of the Union Jack.

The destruction was also Townshend's catharsis for an abusive childhood. He had been left in the care of his cruel grandmother, who spanked him excessively, possibly as a result of dementia. In Townshend's memoir, he writes of being haunted by a few foggy, horrible incidents with her and her boyfriends, though the experiences were traumatic enough that he still couldn't write about them in therapy in 1982.[22] Then, when he joined the Sea Scouts, scoutmasters sexually abused him in the showers. He and a friend developed a penchant for setting fires.

When the Who recorded their single "I Can't Explain," Townshend didn't feel he could push the producer to let him include the feedback tricks they were exploring onstage. But when the Beatles' scooped them by using feedback at the beginning of "I Feel Fine," Townshend decided to make the effect the centerpiece of the Who's next single, May's "Anyway, Anyhow, Anywhere," perhaps the most avant-garde song to hit the U.K. Top 10 to date.

"I was inspired by listening to Charlie Parker, feeling that this was really a free spirit, and whatever he'd done with drugs and booze and everything else, that his playing released him and freed his spirit, and I wanted us to be like that, and I wanted to write a song about that, a spiritual song."[23]

Townshend came up with the title; macho Daltrey toughened it into a universal ode to self-confidence, asserting that he could go anywhere and live any way he dared; nothing could stop him. Moon's hyperkinetic drums synched with Townshend's guitar as if the band were speeding through hyperspace like the Silver Surfer dodging asteroids. They incorporated all their stage tricks: machine-gunning, surf-rock drum rolls, rim shots, jazz lines, Morse code insanity. Onstage, Daltrey began swinging his microphone above his head like a lasso.

Originally, Townshend had written "I Can't Explain" as an imitation Kinks song. He loved the Kinks' sound so much he wanted their producer, Shel Talmy, to produce the Who as well (which he did). Kinks' guitarist Dave Davies discovered the sound after his girlfriend's parents said he couldn't marry her. He was so angry that he slashed the speaker cone of his crappy amplifier—inflicting damage that resulted in the fiercest, most distorted guitar on record in "You Really Got Me," from whence heavy metal and punk eventually sprang.

It seemed that the Kinks were destined to make it big on American shores. "You Really Got Me" and its follow-up, "All Day and All of the Night," had both made it to No. 7 in the States the previous year. They slowed things down for the jangling "Tired of Waiting for You," which made it to No. 6 (No. 1 in the United Kingdom) in February. Lead singer–rhythm guitarist Ray Davies wrote all but two of March's *Kinda Kinks* tracks, at a time when the Stones were still primarily a cover band. "Everybody's Gonna Be Happy," backed with "Who'll Be the Next in Line," continued the run of strong singles. The band also had the perfect uniform for the U.S. Anglophiles: red riding jackets and frilly shirts.

But they almost blew apart before they even made the trip overseas. On May 19, when an onstage fight escalated in Wales, Kinks drummer Mick Avory knocked Dave out with his hi-hat stand in front of five thousand people.

Avory hid out from the cops while the group auditioned Mitch Mitchell (who later joined Hendrix) to replace him on drums. Eventually, however, the charges were dropped, Avory returned, and the group remade "Tired of Waiting for You" as "Set Me Free" for their trip across the Atlantic. The B side, "I Need You," had more power chords in the "You Really Got Me" vein.

Dave led the single rocker lifestyle, but Ray was a married homebody whose first daughter was born just a few weeks before their first tour. Thus he wasn't in the best frame of mind when they arrived in the States on June 17 and the JFK customs agent asked, "Are you a boy or a girl?"

"That's right, I'm a girl, and so is my brother," Ray replied, a retort that held up the band and delayed their press conference.[24]

On NBC's *Hullabaloo*, Frankie Avalon and Annette Funicello introduced the band, and Ray and Avory danced cheek to cheek, which alarmed various homophobic powers that be. But Ray believed the incident that resulted in their ban from the States occurred during their appearance on Dick Clark's TV show *Where the Action Is*. A man who may have been a union official in the American Federation of Television and Radio Artists (AFTRA) asked Ray if his wife, who was Lithuanian, was a Communist. Ray pushed him, and the man fell over.[25] The band also failed to pay their dues to AFTRA. After that, they were denied permits to reenter the United States for the next four years, the period when English artists made the most money touring overseas.

Still, perhaps they were lucky even to have made it back to Olde England. After playing a concert in Illinois on June 23, the Kinks were invited to the home of a member of the local branch of the Jaycees, a civic organization. He plied them with drinks, but something unnerved the guys about him, so they left abruptly. Later, they discovered that the man was John Wayne Gacy, who was executed in 1994 for killing thirty-three young men and boys.[26]

Back in Britain, they released "Till the End of the Day," an ebullient remake of "All Day and All of the Night" that celebrated their freedom to do whatever they wanted. Along with the Stones' "I'm Free" and the Who's "Anyway, Anyhow, Anywhere," it was the year's happiest statement of youthful empowerment. But the B side, "Where Have All the Good Times Gone," reflected Ray's worries about the group's future in the shadow of the American entry ban. He would go on to write many songs about dead-end streets over the next few years. Yet the ban was what would transform him into the most quintessentially English lyricist, nostalgic for the simpler traditions of old Britannia in the face of social upheaval.

One artist who was barely on the radar was a mod named Davy Jones, who shared the same producer as the Who and the Kinks, Shel Talmy. (Next year, when the Monkees' Davy Jones appeared, the mod Jones would be forced to come up with a new last name, derived from pioneer Jim Bowie's knife.) In his third single, "You've Got a Habit of Leaving" (his first self-penned A side), the young Bowie's voice sounds almost wimpishly juvenile upon first listen. But then his band, the Lower Third, bursts into a Who/Yardbirds-style feedback rave-up for the instrumental. When they swing back to the verse, proto-Ziggy Stardust has hit his groove. The B side is stranger; in "Baby Loves That Way," he lets his girl fool around with other guys. It's the first stirrings of the sexual ambivalence he would ride to the top as glam rock's ultimate androgyne in a later kind of swinging London.

Satisfaction

Jagger and Richards release the anthem of the decade on June 6.

In his flat in St. John's Wood, London, Keith Richards woke up with a
guitar riff in his head and recorded it on his portable tape deck. The hook
recalled two Martha and the Vandellas hits, "Dancing in the Streets" and "Nowhere to Run." Stones manager Andrew Loog Oldham was pushing the group
to move away from 1950s blues and toward contemporary soul.

The half-conscious Richards scrawled the words "I can't get no satisfaction" to go with riff. He was between girlfriends at the time. The line was
similar to one from a Chuck Berry song called "Thirty Days," though Richards later opined, "It could just as well have been 'Auntie Millie's Caught Her
Left Tit in the Mangle.' "[1] Then the tape recorder captured the sound of him
dropping his pick and snoring for the next forty minutes. Richards later rued
not saving the tape.

When he woke up the next day, the riff struck him as unexceptional, just
something for another album track. When the Stones resumed touring, he
played it for Jagger as they relaxed by the hotel pool in Clearwater, Florida,
on May 6. It sounded like a folk song then, perhaps in the vein of the "Walk
Right In," a No. 1 hit by the Rooftop Singers two and a half years before,
complete with lyrics about letting your hair hang down and losing your mind.

Richards had the one line but no melody so Jagger came up with the lyrics. Since it sounded like a folk song, he started griping about advertising, as Dylan had in "It's All Right, Ma (I'm Only Bleeding)." In the United Kingdom the BBC didn't have ads, and Jagger was freaked out by all the commercials bombarding him from American radio and TV.

As Jagger and Richards worked, the rest of the band started congregating by the pool. The night before, Bill Wyman and Brian Jones picked up two models who spent the night with them. Wyman and his model joined the others, and then the model who had been with Jones emerged, battered and bruised. He had beaten her in the night.[2]

Disgusted, the band's assistant, Mike Dorsey, found Jones and confronted him. Wyman wrote, "Blows were exchanged and Brian suffered two cracked ribs, to the satisfaction of everyone." Jones had to wear an elastic belt, which the others dubbed his "corset." The press was told that he had hurt himself practicing karate by the pool.

That night at the Jack Russell Stadium, people in the audience started throwing toilet paper and cups at cops guarding the stage. The confrontation between two hundred fans and the cops got so heated that the concert was stopped after only four songs.

Three days later the band pulled into blues mecca Chicago to record at Chess Records. They had already recorded there twice the previous year because it was the home of their idols: Chuck Berry, Muddy Waters, Bo Diddley, Howlin' Wolf, and many others. As a British teenager, Jagger had written away to Chess to order their albums by mail, since they were hard to find in the U.K., and it was these albums that sparked the formation of the Stones. Jagger and Richards had been childhood schoolmates until Jagger's family moved to a different town. Then, when the two were seventeen, they bumped into each other on a train, and Jagger was carrying Muddy Waters and Chuck Berry albums under his arm. Richards was a fan as well, and surprised, since hardly anybody in England knew who Muddy Waters was. Their friendship was quickly rekindled.

Now, as the Stones covered Don Covay and Otis Redding at Chess on May 10 and 11, it was apparent they'd grown tighter since their last album. They coasted through the grooves with streamlined speed, in the pocket, having locked into an effortless swing to rival Motown's Funk Brothers and Stax's Booker T. and the M.G.s. At the end of the session, they banged out a version of "Satisfaction" with Jones on the harmonica, wrapping at 5:00 a.m.

Deejay Scott Ross, a friend of the band, bet Jones a pair of boots that the tune was going to be a hit.[3] Richards still thought it was suitable only for a B side or an LP track. It was the last time they recorded at Chess. In a nice bit of symmetry, the final track they laid down in Chicago was the song that graduated them from blues students to soul trendsetters.

The group lived out the song's line about riding 'round the world when they flew to Hollywood to take another crack at the song at RCA Studios on May 12–13. Richards decided that a horn section à la "Nowhere to Run" should perform the "Satisfaction" riff. But that wasn't doable on short notice, so Richards decided just to record a "little sketch" with his guitar to show how the horns should play. To make the guitar sound like brass, Richards recalled, "I was screaming for more distortion: *This riff's really gotta hang hard and long*, and we burnt the amps up and turned the shit up, and it still wasn't right."[4]

Someone realized that a fuzz distortion box on the guitar would sustain the notes. George Harrison said, "When Phil Spector was making 'Zip-A-Dee-Doo-Dah' [recorded by Bob B. Soxx and the Blue Jeans], the engineer who'd set up the track overloaded the microphone on the guitar player and it became very distorted. Phil Spector said, 'Leave it like that, it's great.' Some years later everyone started to try to copy that sound and so they invented the fuzz box."[5] Link Wray and the Ventures had used it. Big Jim Sullivan, the session musician Oldham hired for his other clients, used it. In April the Yardbirds used it on "Heart Full of Soul," though that song wouldn't be released till June. So, Richards recalled, roadie–piano player "Ian Stewart went around the corner to Eli Wallach's Music City or something and came around with a [Gibson Maestro] distortion box. *Try this*. It was as off-hand as that. It was just from nowhere."[6]

Richards kicks off with what *Newsweek* would later dub the "five notes that shook the world." Wyman struts in on the third note, his jaunty bass bouncing off Richards like a subliminal second hook. Jones slices away at the acoustic guitar. In the second bar, Watts begins hitting the snare on every beat and does so unchanging for the entire song. His new beat is the key—by adopting the four/four beat of the Four Tops' "I Can't Help Myself," he changes the song from folk to soul. On the third bar, Nitzsche starts banging the tambourine.

Then Jagger saunters in, all nonchalant innocence, merely observing that he can't get any satisfaction, despite the fact that he tries and tries. But his tension rises until, in the reverse of usual rock dynamics, he bursts out of the quieter chorus and into the irate verse, ranting in the humorous style that he would return to in later songs such as "Shattered" but never top, giving lyrics such as "on the radio" his own funky sustain.

You can hear Richards stomp on the fuzzbox pedal to turn it off and on. After opening with the fuzz, he switches to clean electric rhythm guitar. At 35 seconds he clicks the fuzz pedal back on between "get" and "no." At 1:35 he comes back in with the fuzz later than he did the last round—perhaps a mistake. At 2:33 you can hear a burst of fuzz before the chorus—Richards making sure he's got the pedal ready in advance this time.

On the third verse, Jagger leers in and suggestively enunciates "girl reaction," the lusty twist that disturbed the censors the most. He returns to the heavy breathing for the final "no satisfaction"s before giving up in cathartic exasperation.

Oldham, engineer Dave Hassinger, and the entire band except Jagger and Richards were convinced it should be the single. Richards thought it still needed "working up," perhaps overly concerned about its similarity to the Vandellas' "Dancing in the Streets" and "Nowhere to Run." So they put it to a vote: Watts, Wyman, Jones, Oldham, Hassinger, and Ian Stewart voted for it to be a single, while Jagger and Richards voted no.

They knew the lines about trying to "make some girl" could get them banned, so Oldham and Jagger told Hassinger to mix the vocals deeper into the track so they weren't easily understandable. Also mixed practically to inaudibility were Jones's acoustic guitar and Nitzsche's piano, the remnants of the song's folk-rock origins, though alternate mixes released in the 1980s allowed them to be heard.

Five days after Jagger had written the lyrics, the song was in the can. Oldham released it on June 6 in the United States, Richards's misgivings be damned. "I guess he thought, 'They can work it up all they want, but it's about the freshness and the timing.' Which is, after all, everything," [7] Richards conceded. "Andrew spotted the spirit of the track . . . It was still not finished as far as we were concerned, but sometimes an artist's sketches are better than the finished painting, and that's probably one of the perfect examples."[8]

The riff cut like a scythe across the airwaves. The Doors' Ray Manzarek remembered, "The first time I heard 'Satisfaction' on the radio I couldn't believe it. The lyrics were so terrific; they were talking to all young American males. This guy is singing a song to *us*."

When kids weren't yelling along with the "Hey! Hey! Hey!," they tried to decipher the lyrics with the same scrutiny they had given "Louie, Louie" a few years before. Was the bit about how white his shirt could be racial commentary? Was the cigarette he smoked a joint or a Marlboro? Was it a critique of how people let consumer products determine masculinity and self-esteem?

There was no doubt about the sexual dissatisfaction of the third verse, though its finer points were debated. Jagger clarified the next year, " 'Girlie action' was really 'girl reaction.' The dirtiest line in 'Satisfaction' they don't understand, see? It's about 'You better come back next week 'cause you see I'm on a losing streak' "—that is, the woman Jagger is hitting on is having her period. "But (people) don't get that. It's just life. That's really what happens to girls. Why shouldn't people write about it?"[9]

The bottom line of the song was "I Hate Commercials and I Can't Get Laid," and millions across the planet related, just as they had to Eddie Cochran's "Summertime Blues" seven years earlier. The song knocked "I Can't Help Myself" off its No. 1 perch and stayed there for four weeks, till Herman's Hermits "I'm Henry VIII, I Am" pushed it down—as if the sexual aggression of "Satisfaction" had scared teen girls back to their least threatening heartthrob. The Stones and the Hermits were tied for second most popular Brit band in the States, with two chart toppers each.

When various cities banned "Satisfaction," and *Newsweek* blasted the "tasteless themes" by the "leering quintet," it no doubt helped the record become the year's best seller. The ultimate validation came when Otis Redding covered it in July with the horns Richards originally envisioned.

"I never thought that song was commercial anyway," Richards would later muse. "Shows how wrong you can be."[10]

In "Satisfaction," the Stones found their golden formula, mixing the beat of Motown, the lyrics of Dylan and Berry, and the novelty of new technology to synthesize their own style of R&B/pop/rock. The Beatles were the biggest band of the 1960s, and Dylan the most innovative artist, but the Stones released the greatest rock song without even trying, because they were permanently trying.

9

Long Hair and the Pill on Trial

The Massachusetts Supreme Court takes its time to decide the fate of long hair in high school, while the U.S. Supreme Court renders its decision on the Pill on June 7.

In 1845, President Polk had a mullet running down the back of his neck, but during the world wars, hair was kept short to keep lice and fleas at bay, and it stayed short for the next twenty years. Numerous dress code handbooks even expressly stated that boys' hair could not be combed forward.[1] But after the Beatles showed up, newspaper stories of boys being sent home from school until they got their hair cut proliferated.

Massachusetts' Attleboro High School student George Leonard Jr. went to court over the issue. By night he was Georgie Porgie, the front man for a band called the Cry Babies, which played sock hops, churches, and amusement parks. On September 11, 1964, three days into his senior year, the school's principal sent him home and said he couldn't come back till his hair was decent. A hearing before the school committee upheld the principal's ruling three weeks later. Porgie's manager was his father, and in a brilliant PR move, George Leonard Sr. filed a lawsuit saying his son was a professional musician who needed to have long hair for his job. Besides, it was his constitutional right. Leonard Sr. asserted that the school was overstepping the parents' domain and illegally keeping his son from graduating. He asked for a speedy hearing, but the Superior Court did not accommodate him—it would not be until a year later, on October 8, 1965, that "George Leonard, Jr., vs. School Committee of Attleboro" would go before the Massachusetts Supreme Court, with a decision rendered on December 7 (see chapter 25, "Christmas Time Is Here").

Though the waiting was interminable, the front-page news coverage led to Porgie opening for the Stones in Rhode Island and playing with the Barbarians, the garage band that wrote the anthem "Are You a Boy or Are You a Girl?" In real life, the Barbarians had long hair, but in the song, they took on the role of roughnecks taunting a proto-hippie, sneering that his long blond hair and skintight pants meant he had to be either a girl or from Liverpool.

Rolling Stones' memoirs are peppered with anecdotes of brawls with people who insulted their hair. In New York City, people spat at their feet, and Wyman recalled four or five men screaming "faggots" at them. "Brian yelled: 'Let's go get the colonists.' So Mick, Keith and Brian jumped into their convertible and started fighting with them."[2] Wyman didn't say who won that fight. But at the Heathrow Airport restaurant, when an American started taunting them, Mick approached and, per author Philip Norman, "received a punch in the face that knocked him backwards. Keith tried to come to his aid, but was also felled."[3] Another time, when a Frenchman asked Richards if he was a Supreme, Richards slugged him in the face and scared him off.

High school student John Lauber found himself forced to contend with the same sort of animosity in the spring, when the bleach-blond hair draped over his eyes angered fellow student and future presidential candidate Mitt Romney (son of Michigan governor George Romney) and a pack of his conservative buddies.

"He can't look like that. That's wrong. Just look at him!" Romney exclaimed to his friend Matthew Friedemann, as Friedemann recalled years later.[4] Romney and his gang tackled Lauber, pinning down his arms and legs. Lauber cried for help as Romney cut off clumps of his hair. Years later, Romney said he did not remember the incident but admitted, "I participated in a lot of hijinks and pranks in high school. Some may have gone too far, and for that I apologize."[5]

Still, things were nowhere near as draconian as they were in the Soviet Union, where "hairies," as young people with mop tops were called, were hauled into police stations and given haircuts.[6]

One of the first pop songs to reference overtly the flak young men were getting for the new style was by Sonny and Cher, who recorded "I Got You Babe" in late spring backed by the Wrecking Crew. Sonny Bono had cannily fashioned himself into an ersatz Ringo Starr, while Cher's offbeat Armenian beauty made her the ultimate beatnik babe. In the song, she speaks for all the young women who encouraged their boyfriends to grow out their manes despite the cultural blowback, telling Sonny to disregard those who say his hair is too long.

After the song hit No. 1, Bono followed it with his own solo single, "Laugh at Me." "I never thought I'd cut a record by myself, but I got somethin' I wanna say. I want to say it for Cher, and I hope I say it for a lot of people." In the song, he demands to know why people made fun of him and tried to make him run because of the hippie clothes he wore. (Maybe it was because his vest was made of bobcat fur?) He knew that such harassment had to stop someplace, sometime—and meanwhile he accepted their laughter as the price he had to pay for freedom. The song made it to No. 10 in the United States, No. 9 in the United Kingdom, and No. 1 in Canada, despite being sung by a voice that was even less traditionally "pop" than Bob Dylan's.

A subgenre of protest songs rose up, with lyrics directed not at a political problem but rather at oppressive conformity itself. Both the Turtles' "Let Me Be" and the Leaves' "Too Many People" rail against a society trying to "rearrange" them. In "Let Me Be" the Turtles triumphantly declare that they aren't fools and won't be used as pawns for others' selfish ends. The Animals roar that they will think and do what they want in "It's My Life." The Beatles, too, advise listeners to "Think for Yourself." The Stones bellow to "Get Off of My Cloud." Both they and the Kinks had songs named "I'm Free." Even Dean Martin's son released "The Rebel Kind" with his band Dino, Desi and Billy. (Desi was the son of Desi Arnaz Sr. and Lucille Ball.)

Why *were* people so uptight over such a simple thing as hair?

The "Greatest Generation" of World War II had bonded in its monumental fight to overcome the Axis Powers and returned from war to create the most widespread prosperity history had yet seen. It embarrassed jingoistic, homophobic parents to have their boys look effeminate—even if most of the boys adopted the haircut to get girls.

As the months passed, the hair began to represent more than just fashion. Last year the new long-haired British bands sang songs as innocuous as those of the previous generations. But, obliquely at first, musicians were now starting to sing about drugs, premarital sex, and Eastern religion while questioning the Vietnam War and the entire capitalist system.

Ironically, in the artists' subversion of "old-fashioned American values," they had an unlikely ally: businessmen. Plenty of hustlers in the music, TV, and print industries found that the latest form of teenage rebellion meant money, just as it had with the 1950s rock and beatnik crazes. So, despite the growing displeasure of parents, the flood of music, movies, and TV shows with long-haired boys kept coming. Later in the decade, many baby boomers would experiment with dropping out of society, claiming to loathe technology and capitalism. But, ironically, the counterculture owed its existence to both.

Across the heartland, kids suddenly realized there were alternative lifestyles beyond Main Street. Rebellion was a choice they could see others making on TV, whether in the form of wearing Cuban-heeled Beatles boots or protesting the draft. Music had primarily served as entertainment, but now it began influencing life-and-death decisions. Do I help voter registration in the South? Do I go to Vietnam? Do I take a job I don't want for the paycheck so I can keep up with the Joneses?

Soon, to the older generation, long hair symbolized antiwar cowardice; an "in your face" advertisement for the kids' political stance. (Even worse were earrings on young men, and it was not unheard of for fathers to rip them out of their sons' ears.[7]) For the other side, the insistence on long locks asserted a primal American value—"Give me liberty, or give me death!" As one's mane became the battleground of the American culture war, the musicians found themselves increasingly in the crosshairs.

Long hair was changing the identity men had assumed for decades, but the Pill was affecting the identity women had embodied for centuries.

In 1951, Planned Parenthood pioneer Margaret Sanger arranged for a grant for Dr. Gregory "Goody" Pincus to study how to inhibit ovulation via hormones. Nine years later, on June 23, 1960, the FDA approved the oral contraceptive pill Enovid. By 1965, five to six million American women—one out of every four married women under forty-five—were taking it.[8]

Still, a number of states banned the use of contraceptives even for married couples. In 1879, Connecticut legislator P. T. Barnum (of the Barnum and Bailey circus) had sponsored a law that outlawed making or selling birth control. So when the Planned Parenthood League of Connecticut opened in November 1961, it was shut down within two weeks. Its directors, Estelle Griswold and C. Lee Buxton, were arrested and charged with distributing contraception, and each fined a hundred dollars.

Griswold v. Connecticut went all the way to the Supreme Court, where the case was argued on March 29. On June 7 the Court decreed that the Constitution protected the "right to marital privacy." Its decision meant that state laws that banned birth control could be overturned, and the U.S. Department of Health, Education, and Welfare could now begin distributing the Pill and other birth-control services to low-income, married women as part of President Johnson's War on Poverty, not only in the United States but also internationally, through the U.S. Agency for International Development. Nixon continued the approach, and by 1969, 8.5 to 13.0 million women were taking the Pill. By the mid-1980s, that number had grown to 80 million; and in 2000, to 100 million.

The Court also struck down restrictions on the Pill's distribution to unmarried women, but oral contraceptives were still not readily available for them in many states. Whether unmarried women could receive the Pill was left to the prerogative of the doctor writing the prescription, and many people still believed that premarital sex was wrong. College students would sometimes wear fake wedding bands or engagement rings to doctor's appointments. Often, doctors realized the rings were phony but wrote the prescriptions anyway, believing that it might prevent future abortions.[9]

In the fall, a female reporter for the *Pembroke Record*, the newspaper of the women's college at Brown University, asked the university's Dr. Roswell Johnson for a prescription. When he provided one, the reporter wrote about it, and the story unleashed a firestorm of criticism against the doctor. Johnson responded that he denied many requests and had dispensed prescriptions—after "a great deal of soul searching"[10]—only to two students who were each engaged and over twenty-one. He also stressed that they both had parental consent. "I want to feel I'm contributing to a solid relationship and not contributing to unmitigated promiscuity," he said.[11]

The *New York Times*, *Newsweek*, and *Time* reported on the brouhaha. A

Gallup poll found that 77 percent of American women disapproved of the Pill being prescribed to unmarried college students.[12] It wouldn't be until the 1972 Supreme Court case *Eisenstadt v. Baird* that unmarried people's right to possess birth control was formally decided.

But however unmarried women got it, the Pill did indeed lead to a surge in premarital sex, just as moralists had feared. In 1965 approximately 75 percent of female college graduates were virgins. By 1969 that number had decreased to 45 percent.[13] The National Center for Health Statistics reported that "the proportion of women who delayed sexual intercourse until marriage [had] declined from 48 percent among women who married in 1960 to 1964, to 21 percent among women who married in 1975 to 1979."[14]

In the mid-1960s, most colleges and universities did not allow women to stay out past curfew, and being caught having sex could lead to suspension or expulsion. In many schools, when a man visited a woman's dorm room, three out of the couple's four feet had to stay on the floor at all times. But by the start of the next decade, many dorms at schools such as Harvard and Radcliffe had gone coed.[15]

The beginning of the sexual revolution corresponded with the loosening of censorship laws. For the first time, the U.S. Production Code allowed breasts to be shown on screen, in Sidney Lumet's feature film *The Pawnbroker*, which premiered at the Berlin Film Festival in June 1964 but could not secure U.S. distribution until April 1965 due to the controversy. In December, the U.S. Supreme Court argued whether John Cleland's erotic novel *Memoirs of a Woman of Pleasure*, or *Fanny Hill* (1748) was obscene, and decided it was not as long as it was not marketed only for "prurient appeal."

Hugh Hefner's *Playboy* magazine attempted to make sexuality as wholesome as the girl next door and conflate it with upward mobility and intellectualism. He interspersed nude pictorials with reviews of all the consumer products a man of leisure needed in a time of unparalleled prosperity (hi-fi, sports car) and interviews with luminaries of the day such as Martin Luther King Jr., Malcolm X, Marshall McLuhan, Lenny Bruce, Dick Gregory, the Beatles, and Bob Dylan.

But the ultimate symbol of the new era was the miniskirt. In the 1800s, laws required woman to wear long skirts and petticoats and prohibited them from donning pants, boots, or overalls. After women won the right to vote in 1920, liberated flappers raised hemlines to the knee, but they dropped back down during the Depression.

Skirts crept higher throughout the 1950s and had arrived back at the knee by the early 1960s, whereupon King's Road designer Mary Quant raced Paris's André Courrèges and Pierre Cardin to push the boundaries. Courrèges's collection showed some thigh, and the designer maintained that he had invented the new form. Quant said, "It was the girls on the King's Road who invented the mini. I was making easy, youthful, simple clothes in which you could move, in which you could run and jump, and we would make them the length the customer wanted. I wore them very short, and the customers would say, 'Shorter, shorter.'"[16] Quant was the one who named the skirt, though—after her favorite car, the Mini.

In the summer, Quant took her latest collection to the United States and went on a multicity tour of department stores with a fashion show dubbed "Youthquake." Its models wore skirts that showed seven inches of leg above the knee as they danced the Frug and the Twist to rock played by a Milwaukee band called the Skunks (complete with black hair with a white line dyed down the middle, and a song called "Youthquake," composed for the occasion). The tour climaxed in New York on September 1. Soon Boston's (ironically named) Puritan Fashion Group began producing the miniskirt and distributing it through J.C. Penney.[17]

But the world wasn't necessarily ready for it, as Jean "The Shrimp" Shrimpton would soon learn. The world's first internationally known model, Shrimpton flew to Melbourne, Australia, for the Victoria Derby on October 30. According to legend, her dressmaker, Colin Rolfe, ran out of material, and thus her dress ended 3.9 inches above the knee. Shrimpton assured him that no one would notice.

She later recalled, "The day of the races was a hot one, so I didn't bother to wear any stockings. My legs were still brown from the summer, and as the dress was short, it was hardly formal. I had no hat or gloves with me for the very good reason that I owned neither."[18] She also wore a man's watch. Soon the women at the racetrack were yelling derisively at her, while the men wolf-whistled. In the days that followed, the press excoriated her for her scandalous ensemble.

Australia was more conservative than the other former British colonies, but the United States also took some time before accepting the shorter U.K.

fashions. Ultra-trendy scenesters wore miniskirts in New York's private disco Ondine (a favorite Warhol hangout), but most high schools had strict dress codes. Pittsburgh's North Hills High School decreed that skirts could be no shorter than the middle of the knee. Shorts, slacks, and "after five–style dresses" were prohibited, as were blue jeans (for both sexes).[19]

Those who did don minis were aided by the rise of pantyhose. Originally, women's stockings required garters. But during the 1940s, actresses and dancers began wearing stockings sewn to their underwear. In the 1950s, manufacturers began mass-producing similar garments, called "Panti-Legs" or "combination stockings and panty," and in the 1960s, Spandex made these more comfortable.

The first early miniskirt battles became the female version of the boys' haircut wars, though the girls had a little more flexibility. High-schoolers could roll up the waistbands to make skirts shorter, and then pull the hem back down to their knees if administrators came around. School officials would sometimes measure the length from the knee with a yardstick, and send home the most brazen transgressors.

The accessory that went hand in hand with the miniskirt was the knee-high vinyl go-go boot, popularized by Barbra Streisand in the August edition of *Vogue*. Designed by the usual suspects of Courrèges, Saint Laurent, and Quant, in the United Kingdom the go-go boot was called the "kinky boot," since it had originally been worn by dominatrixes in the underground S/M scene.

Dancers on TV music shows such as *Hullaballoo* and *Shindig!* wore go-go boots, as did the singer of the group We Five ("You Were on My Mind"). But they were immortalized by the track Nancy Sinatra recorded on November 19 in collaboration with songwriter-producer Lee Hazlewood. For "These Boots Are Made for Walkin'," Hazlewood encouraged her to sing like a "14-year-old girl who goes with truck drivers,"[20] and the result was one of the greatest anthems of women's liberation.

After vowing to use her boots to walk all over the guy, Sinatra followed it up by redeeming Lennon's "Run for Your Life." In Lennon's version of the song, he warns his "little girl" that she'd better toe the line; Sinatra flips the song so she is bullying her "little boy."

Numerous folk chanteuses repurposed songs by noncommittal men into paeans to their independence. Nico covers Gordon Lightfoot's "I'm Not Sayin'" to inform a guy that she can't guarantee she'll be true. She will try, but he shouldn't be surprised if he sees her around with someone else. She might not even show up when she promises she will.

Cher used Dylan's "All I Really Want to Do" to assure her lover that she didn't want to confine him or meet his kin. Joan Baez covered Dylan's "Daddy You've Been on My Mind" (originally "Mama"), singing that it didn't matter to her whom he was waking up with tomorrow; she wasn't asking him to make commitments. (It is an achingly sad performance, recorded sometime after Baez went to visit Dylan when he was recovering from a stomach illness in an English hospital at the end of May, only to find him accompanied by future wife Sara Lownds.)

Michelle Phillips's penchant for infidelity inspired husband John to write "Go Where You Wanna Go" for the Mamas and the Papas. The group sings that you have to do what you want to do with whomever you want to do it with. Gale Garnett wrote her own hit, "We'll Sing in the Sunshine," which won the Grammy for Best Folk Song. In the track, Garnett sings that she'll stay with the guy for one year—but she'll never love him, and then she'll be on her way. Jackie DeShannon wrote "Come Stay with Me" for Marianne Faithfull, in which she promises that her man can remain free if he stays with her. It was another song hinting at the still-edgy concept of premarital cohabitation.

That the men had their own slew of songs reflecting the New Morality was less surprising. Lennon mourns that his woman wouldn't keep living with him because she had to be free in "Ticket to Ride," and sings of how a woman "had him" in her apartment in "Norwegian Wood," then left him there in the morning when she went to work.

In "She Belongs to Me," Dylan gets on his knees to peek through a keyhole at a woman who's nobody's child, beyond the control of the law. Manfred Mann's cover of Dylan's "If You Gotta Go, Go Now" informs the lady that the singer respects her, but she either has to spend the night with him or take off—and it isn't like he is asking for something she hasn't given before. The Turtles' cover of Dylan's "It Ain't Me Babe" frankly states that the singer isn't the kind to give his woman flowers or base his existence on her. Dylan's original was the song that inspired Gordon Lightfoot's antiromance songs epitomized by "For Lovin' Me." And for many, "Like a Rolling Stone" captures both the terror and exhilaration women felt at the dawn of a new age where all the rules had vanished.

In the Stones' cover of Larry Williams/Sonny Bono's "She Said Yeah," Jagger barely has time to wonder where the girl has come from before she's saying she'll make love to him. Matt McGuinn wrote "The Pill" about a mother who was forced to stay at home having kid after kid while the father went out and had fun, but now, thanks to the Pill, she is wearing miniskirts and hot pants and making up for lost years with a vengeance. The Who issued one of the first divorce songs, "A Legal Matter," inspired by the breakup of Roger Daltrey's marriage. It was a theme that more and more people would be able to relate to.

Free love had existed as concept for centuries, with proponents ranging from thirteenth-century sects such as the Brethren of the Free Spirit, to the eighteenth century's Mary Wollstonecraft (whose daughter ran off with married poet Percy Shelley and wrote *Frankenstein*), to the Greenwich Village bohemians of the early 1900s. In those earlier times the idea was not so much about rampant promiscuity. Rather, it was about being free to be with whomever you wanted without having to be married.

Now, with the advent of the Pill, and with deadly venereal diseases such as syphilis cured, it was perhaps the first time in history when people could have sex without fearing pregnancy or disease. The repression left over from the Victorian age was no longer needed to rein in either problem, and quickly eroded along with the belief that sex was acceptable only inside heterosexual marriage. But if parents were appalled by their sons' long hair and antiwar sentiments, they had nervous breakdowns over their daughters' rejection of the "Madonna/whore" paradigm.

In her book *Girls Like Us*, Sheila Weller writes, "New York's Paraphernalia—and its designers Betsey Johnson and Michael Mott—took the Mary Quant look one novel stop further (paper dresses, neon dresses), but all of which put forth a look of *sexuality-with-innocence*." Models such as Edie Sedgwick and Twiggy were "waifish and full of wonder. In concert with the widened availability of the new, slightly lowered-dose birth control pill, this *winsomeness*—the jaunty miniskirts and boots, the big, wide eyes—repelled adjectives like 'cheap' and 'tramp,' words that seemed relics of a recent but long-ago Dark Age. An act (casual sex among unmarried people) that had always been shameful and tragic now acquired a butterfly-winged lightness."[21]

For women graduating college in the middle of the decade, Weller writes,

Some of your friends were planning post-graduation weddings, while others were secretly rebelling against those first boys they'd had sex with. One day, on a break between classes, a girl of the second sort might pick up a stranger, bring him back to her apartment and crisply sever her long (if indifferently) held belief in love as a prerequisite for sex in one half hour. As she slipped afterward into her lecture hall seat, she would realize, *I can do this*. But *this* wasn't sex, per se. That *would* have been cheap. What she had done was all about sophistication and risk.[22]

In *Do You Believe in Magic?* Anne Gottlieb recounts,

On liberal campuses, 1965 was the year the balance tipped; on conservative and Catholic campuses, 1970–1972. Before that, if a girl slept with guys she was "fast"; after that, if she didn't she was "frigid" (mid-sixties) or "uptight" (late sixties). What was surprising was not the pressure from men (our mamas done told us about that), but the pressure from other women. "I can remember being a sophomore in a dorm with a group of girls that had already slept with boys, and they really wanted everybody else to do that," says New York art historian Carolyn Treat Davidson (born 1946).[23]

Gottlieb goes on to write that the peer pressure to be sexually liberated was not something all young women were ready for. Nor were all of them prepared for the attention they received by wearing miniskirts, which continued to shrink, soon becoming short shorts and then Quant's hot pants. Says Gottlieb, "Anne Strieber (1946) recalls, 'Of course, you had to be fashionable. But it was like walking down the street naked. You had people grabbing at your body all the time, because you were sending out all these signals that you'd never meant to. And we were unprotected.'"

For a majority of men, it was an overwhelmingly positive development that many women felt the desire to have casual sex to prove to themselves they were free from outdated cultural programming. But, Gottlieb reflects, "Looking back, the gap between the 'sexual revolution' and feminism—from about 1965 to 1970—was a bad time for women, despite some good times."[24]

And not just because confusion reigned in the bedroom. Women were discovering that men who fought for peace and racial equality didn't necessarily believe in sexual equality. Student Nonviolent Coordinating Committee leader Stokely Carmichaèl cracked, "What is the position of women in SNCC? The position of women in SNCC is prone." Even though female activists had been inspired by the war for civil rights, they began to realize they needed their own movement.

The U.S. Equal Employment Opportunity Commission (EEOC) was formed on July 2 to carry out the Civil Rights Act of 1964, but in September, the commission decided it was acceptable to segregate job advertisements into "Help Wanted Male" and "Help Wanted Female." The decision raised the ire of Betty Friedan, author of *The Feminine Mystique*. The following year, she would spearhead the formation of the National Organization for Women (NOW), to combat sexual discrimination, serving as president alongside former EEOC commissioner Aileen Hernandez as vice president. It was the first new feminist organization in half a century, but by the end of the decade the women's liberation movement would be in full swing.

III ✳
SUMMER

10

The King of Pop Art and the Girl of the Year

On July 17, Pop artist Andy Warhol's film *Beauty No. 2* premieres and the *New York Times* proclaims its actress Edie Sedgwick a star.

Pop Art was both a cheeky middle finger to pretension and a way to find beauty in the consumer-industrial society we were drowned in, whether we liked it or not. Roy Lichtenstein reproduced the panels of romance comic books with the newsprint dots plainly visible. Thought balloons expressed the soap opera angst of his troubled women. James Rosenquist applied his skill at painting billboards to the massive *F-111* collage of A-bombs, hair dryers, babies, airplanes, and spaghetti. Ed Ruscha depicted a burning Standard Oil gas station from a low cinematic angle and rendered it epic. Wallace Berman made a collage of Muhammad Ali, James Brown, and the Rolling Stones dubbed *Papa's Got a Brand New Bag*.

Andy Warhol surpassed his rivals by turning his own persona into a cartoon. With silver wig, shades, black leather jacket, striped T-shirt, and nail polish, he transformed from a balding mid-thirties nerd into a Pop (art) star who would eventually guest on *The Love Boat*. When he did interviews, he'd come on both fey and moronic. He'd make the questioner squirm with his airy, monosyllabic answers, partly because he really was shy, partly because it was some sort of Zen koan, partly because it was the pre-punk aggression of being deliberately vapid, pretty vacant—the ultimate put-on. "If you want to know all about Andy Warhol," he said, "just look at the surface of my paintings and films and me, and there I am. There's nothing behind it."[1] He sent an impersonator out on the college lecture circuit.

The post-beatniks and folkies and proto-hippies all hewed the party line against mainstream Middle America. Pete Seeger dismissed the "little boxes" of suburbia that all looked just the same. But Warhol rebelled against the rebels by saying he *liked* plastic. Warhol tossed off the aphorism "In the future, everyone will be famous for 15 minutes" for the program of one of his exhibits, yet it prophesized the rise of reality TV and YouTube. He made no bones about wanting money and fame, all the things the Village folkies crucified Dylan for chasing. The 1960s were the peak for strident, self-righteous artists to proclaim art as a tool to stop the war and end racism (and thus save the world). Warhol was the ultimate counterprogramming. He denied that "depth" and "substance" were worth pursuing. With his rejection of hippie idealism, he was the forefather of punk.

Warhol had used assistants when he manufactured ads in the 1950s, and continued to use them as he moved into painting, as indeed many masters had over the centuries. Like Berry Gordy with Motown, he appreciated the efficiency of the assembly line. His assistants would make his silkscreens and lithographs by day in his loft space on Forty-Seventh street while Warhol popped Obetrols (a 1960s version of Adderall) and kept the R&B hit "Sally Goes Round the Roses" on constant repeat, like Tom Sawyer convincing others to whitewash his fences for him. Naming his loft the Factory was another rejection of bohemia orthodoxy, as he embraced capitalism's ability to mass-produce product.

He painted the Factory silver and lined it with aluminum foil to go with his wig. By night, it became a legendary salon to rival that of Gertrude Stein, who in the 1920s opened her Paris apartment to artists such as Picasso and Hemingway. Warhol's place had a much more liberal open-door policy. His guests ranged from the rich and glamorous to skid row outcasts. In the former category were rock stars such as the Stones and models such as Anita Pallenberg; wealthy debutantes and European socialites; free-thinking bohemians, movie stars, and gay icons such as Judy Garland, Montgomery Clift, Rudolf Nureyev, Tennessee Williams, Truman Capote, and Allen Ginsberg.

On the seedy side were the porn stars, drag queens, speed freaks, junkies, gay hustlers, and general weirdos.

In the middle were the Factory regulars, such as Warhol's assistant Gerard Malanga, who helped with the silkscreen and sculpture. Billy Name was the speed freak photographer who "silverized" the Factory and lived in the dark room. Warhol befriended the catty actor Ondine after he had Warhol thrown out of an orgy for not participating. Andy's own mother lived downstairs, cooking roasts covered with radishes and applesauce. And soup, of course. His mother had always fed him the soup, which was why he'd painted Campbell's Soup cans three years before.

It was the combination of the chic and the sordid that informed the milieu of songs by the Factory house band the Velvet Underground, and perhaps some of Dylan's albums *Highway 61 Revisited* and *Blonde on Blonde*. In the decades to follow, the legend of the Factory loomed large in the minds of black-clad art students, as it combined the youthful love of parties and popularity with the adolescent romanticism of decadence, of addictions leading one closer to death. Warhol filmed the drug abuse and S/M orgies and found black humor in them, and his nihilism was another way in which he was punk's forerunner.

His movies started out as a way to top his soup can joke: *Empire* was one shot of the Empire State Building that lasted eight hours. *Couch* displayed different people having sex on said piece of furniture. In 1965 he made approximately twenty-eight films, including versions of *Batman* and *A Clockwork Orange*. Viewed today on the Internet, with their bad acting and long takes, they're on par with video camera sketches made by naughty teenagers. But some were screened in underground theaters such as New York City's Gramercy Arts Theatre, either because of their conceptual humor or their sexual content, alongside other experimental films like Kenneth Anger's homoerotic biker/occult films (*Scorpio Rising* and *Kustom Kar Kommandos*). If someone edited them all down to a thirty-minute compilation, it might make an entertainingly debauched reality show.

But hand in hand with the darkness and inanity came Warhol's bravery in pushing the envelope. It was a decade where books such as William Burroughs's *Naked Lunch* and Henry Miller's *Tropic of Cancer* still went on trial for obscenity.

Warhol lived as an "out" gay man making films that celebrated all forms of LGBT difference in an era of immense legal and cultural oppression. The

U.S. Immigration and Nationality Act of 1952 banned homosexuality, and it was listed in the American Psychiatric Association's *Diagnostic and Statistical Manual of Mental Disorders*. Sodomy was a felony in every U.S. state except Illinois. You could get fifteen years for it in Michigan and a life sentence in Idaho. It was also illegal in Britain.

In 1924 the Society for Human Rights had formed in Chicago to fight for "homosexual emancipation" but disbanded only months later due to the arrest of many of its members. It would be nearly thirty years before another gay rights organization was formed, the Mattachine Society by Harry Hay, followed by the first lesbian organization five years later, the Daughters of Bilitis, and the Janus Society in the early 1960s. Influenced by the civil rights struggle, these organizations teamed up to form ECHO (East Coast Homophile Organizations).

On April 25, approximately 150 demonstrators held a sit-in at Dewey's Restaurant for refusing service to people who the manager believed looked gay.[2] On May 29, seven men and three women picketed the White House to call attention to the fact that gays were being denied civil rights and were blocked from "life, liberty, and the pursuit of happiness." Numerous demonstrations followed throughout the summer, at sites including the Pentagon and the United Nations. ECHO's July 4 protest at Philadelphia's Independence Hall became a yearly event, the Annual Reminder for gay rights, until the Stonewall riots of 1969, at which point it was replaced by the annual Christopher Street Day celebration. But while the battle for gay equality had begun, legal protection was a long way off.

✳

Warhol dubbed the outrageous characters who populated his films "superstars," and one of the earliest prototypes was model and society girl Baby Jane Holzer, the Paris Hilton of her day.[3] She appeared in Warhol's films *Batman Dracula*, *Soap Opera*, and *Couch*. Tom Wolfe dubbed her "The Girl of the Year" in a famous profile for *New York Magazine*, in which Holzer opines, "The Beatles are getting fat. The Beatles—well, John Lennon's still thin, but Paul McCartney is getting a big bottom. That's all right, but I don't particularly care for that. The Stones are thin. I mean, that's why they're beautiful, they're so thin. Mick Jagger—wait'll you see Mick."[4]

But Holzer receded in the spring. "It was getting very scary at the Factory. There were too many crazy people around who were stoned and using too many drugs. They had some laughing gas that everybody was sniffing. The whole thing freaked me out, and I figured it was becoming too faggy and sick and druggy."[5]

At some point between January and March, Warhol met Edie Sedgwick and became entranced by her beauty and vivacious personality. "He was probably in love with Edie," future superstar Viva later theorized. "A sexless kind of love, but he would take up your whole life so you had no time for any other man."[6]

Some Factory denizens pinpoint Tennessee Williams's birthday party as the evening where Warhol befriended Sedgwick. If so, it was a fitting locale, as Sedgwick's tale was as tragic as that of any of Williams's doomed heroines. She was born in 1943 to an heiress mother and a rancher-sculptor father who struck oil. Sedgwick's father had suffered three nervous breakdowns in his youth, and she later maintained that he made advances on her when she was seven. He was a ruthless womanizer, seducing the friends of his wife and children. Once, Sedgwick walked in on him cheating and tried to tell her mother, but he denied it and got a doctor to put Edie on tranquilizers. In boarding school, she developed anorexia and spent time in various psychiatric hospitals. Her beloved brother Francis hanged himself when she was twenty.[7]

In 1964 Sedgwick moved to New York City to pursue modeling, living in her grandmother's fourteen-room Park Avenue apartment until her trust fund kicked in and allowed her to get her own place. She developed a unique waiflike "look": short hair, heavy black eyeliner, large chandelier earrings, long legs in black leotards, mini dresses, striped shirts, and leopard-skin coats.

In December 1964, Bob Dylan's right-hand man, Bobby Neuwirth, heard there was a wild beauty whom he and Dylan had to meet. They called Sedgwick, and she met them at the Kettle of Fish on MacDougal Street, arriving in a limo. They had a great evening, walking together through the snow down Houston Street, laughing and looking at the church displays. Along with the humor, Neuwirth saw that Sedgwick had a "tremendous compassion" for those "who had seen the big sadness."[8] The same month she met Dylan and Neuwirth, another brother, Robert, was carried out of Harvard in a straitjacket and taken to Bellevue. When he got out, he crashed his Harley into a bus on New Year's Eve. He died from the injuries on January 12.

After meeting Warhol sometime in early 1965, Sedgwick started hanging out regularly at the Factory and had nonspeaking roles in his films *Vinyl* and *Bitch*. In April she appeared in *Horse*, which centered on cowboys in jockstraps on poppers (akin to laughing gas) playing strip poker with a horse in the room. A cue card instructed people to "Approach the Horse Sexually Everybody," and the horse kicked one of the actors, Tosh Carillo, in the head.

Warhol decided to make a film built around Sedgwick. In April's *Poor Little Rich Girl*, she puts on makeup, smokes cigarettes, tries on outfits, and talks on the phone about how she blew through her inheritance in six months. The main drawing point of the film was that she was in her underwear, though the first reel was out of focus. *Kitchen* followed in June. Again, half the film is out of focus. She is in her lingerie and talks with other actors until one of them strangles her on the kitchen table.

Critical consensus is that the high point of her oeuvre is *Beauty No. 2*, in which she reclines almost naked in skimpy underwear on a bed with a young man from the Factory named Gino Piserchio. For sixty-five minutes Piserchio gropes her legs and makes out with her, while, off camera, Sedgwick's friend Chuck Wein asks her increasingly hostile and personal questions until she finally throws an ashtray at him. The film premiered at New York's Cinematheque on July 17, and nine days later the *New York Times* ran the article "Edie Pops Up as Newest Star":

> For the restless hedonists who purport to lead the new, fashionable society, novelty is the staff of life. Last fall, they raised up a new goddess after she had been suitably baptized in the pages of *Vogue* and christened her Baby Jane. Before six months were over, they were whispering the obsolescence of Baby Jane. Now on Page 91 of the Aug. 1 issue of *Vogue*, her successor can be found. The magazine . . . has a full-page photograph of Miss Edith Minturn Sedgwick, 22, doing an arabesque in her living room. *Vogue* labels her a Youthquaker.[9]

In November, *Life* ran a fashion spread on her, proclaiming, "The cropped-mop girl with the eloquent legs is doing more for black tights than anybody since Hamlet."

Initially, Sedgwick's folks had disapproved of her modeling. Then, when they got wind that she was being groped in freaky art films in her underwear, they pleaded with her to go back to modeling. But by now, Sedgwick and Warhol were the "it couple" of New York, her hair dyed silver to match his, both wearing boat-necked, striped T-shirts, jetting to his exhibit in Paris.

In October, they appeared on *The Merv Griffin Show* to the strains of "Pop Goes the Weasel." Sedgwick wore her scandalous tights. The gum-chewing Warhol refused to speak, instead whispering to Sedgwick his responses to Merv's questions.

That month they attended an exhibit of his in Philadelphia, and screaming kids mobbed the scene requesting autographs. (Warhol let Sedgwick sign his name.) The paintings had to be taken off the walls to protect them from being damaged. Warhol was delighted—an art opening with no art. The couple took refuge at the top of a stairwell. To make their getaway, they had to cross the roof to the fire escape next door. It was the closest the art world got to Beatlemania.

Warhol announced he had abandoned painting because films were "easier"—which, considering he didn't even focus the camera half the time, was definitely true. His new dream was to go to Hollywood, and he believed Sedgwick could be his ticket. He began to think his film team should start developing coherent narratives for her.

Rumor had it that Sedgwick had also served as the muse for the song Dylan released three days after *Beauty No. 2*'s premiere, a song *Rolling Stone* would later rank as the greatest rock song of all time.

Masterpiece Highs and the Boos of Newport

Dylan shatters the rules of pop music with "Like a Rolling Stone," released July 20; outrages the Newport Folk Festival by going electric on July 25; and records *Highway 61 Revisited* from July 29 to August 4.

Bob Dylan's early singles covered the civil rights movement. Then "Subterranean Homesick Blues" turned darkly comic and grappled with whether to live in the straight world or the counterculture. Then came the cautionary "Like a Rolling Stone," the story of "Miss Lonely" who used to have it made. She used to attend the finest school, wore the finest clothes, casually gave and received gifts. She tossed the bums change and laughed about them. She partied too much, ignoring her friends' warnings that she was heading for trouble.

In Dylan's song, Miss Lonely goes out with a diplomat who takes everything from her that he can steal, like Holly Golightly in *Breakfast at Tiffany's*. In the Hollywood film, a Brazilian diplomat strings Golightly along as his mistress before abandoning her. The struggling writer Paul Varjak (George Peppard) yells at Golightly that she needs to wake up and accept *his* true love. "You call yourself a free spirit, a wild thing, and you're terrified somebody's going to stick you in a cage. Baby, you're already in that cage. You built it yourself."[1] She finally grows up, and they kiss in the rain. At last, she's found a home in Peppard's arms.

But "Like a Rolling Stone" sounds like Dylan made his appeal to Miss Lonely and she still spurned him, so he takes gleeful vengeance in spelling out what awaits her as soon as her looks and money run out. She ends up broke and homeless, pawning her diamond ring and making deals with "mystery tramps" with vacuum eyes and "Napoleon in rags."

The deals could be drug deals—or the kind made by the real-life inspiration for Holly Golightly in Truman Capote's book. Capote said she "was not precisely a call girl. She had no job but accompanied expense-account men to the best restaurants and night clubs with the understanding that her escort was obligated to give her some sort of gift, perhaps jewelry or a check . . . If she felt like it, she might take her escort home for the night."[2] If Dylan's Miss Lonely has any reservations about making such deals, she soon realizes she doesn't even have a reputation to lose anymore, because she's fallen so far she's been forgotten.

Since the song's release, many have speculated that it was inspired by Sedgwick, who shared some of Hepburn/Golightly's poise and slender glamour. Sedgwick had gone to fine boarding schools like the character, she did blow her inheritance (on limos), and she would die from drug addiction. Films such as *Factory Girl* and *I'm Not There* suggest that Dylan had an affair with her. The latter film portrays Sedgwick as a heartbroken mess because Dylan ignores her after hooking up with her. She finds comfort in the arms of his friend-assistant, the Bobby Neuwirth character, a "betrayal" that antagonizes Dylan. Whether that is true, in real life she did become Neuwirth's girlfriend at some point during the year, until her addiction to barbiturates became too much for him to handle and, in 1967, he broke up with her. Dylan scholar Greil Marcus said, "I heard a lecture by Thomas Crow, an art historian, about 'Like a Rolling Stone' being about Edie Sedgwick within Andy Warhol's circle, as something that Dylan saw from the outside, not being personally involved with either of them, but as something he saw and was scared by and saw disaster looming and wrote a song as a warning, and it was compelling."[3]

Others have postulated that Dylan's muse for the song might have been Marianne Faithfull. She was the queen of British folk-pop when Dylan came to England for his May tour. The *Daily Mail* had run a story about her headlined, "Miss Lonely Sobs into the Pops" when she recorded Jagger and

Richards's "As Tears Go By."[4] In her memoir, Faithfull recounts Dylan's attempts to seduce her in his hotel suite between sessions of ignoring her while banging away furiously on his typewriter. "The Out-tuning and Seduction Machine," she called him. She was told he was working on an epic poem about her (the memoir doesn't specify if Dylan or his entourage told her), but when he hit on her, she declined because she was pregnant and engaged to be married the next week. He "turned into Rumpelstiltskin," tore up the papers he was writing, and threw her out.[5] Sadly, Faithfull was also derailed for a number of years due to heroin addiction, homeless before getting her life back together for her late '70s comeback.

Others speculate that Dylan was writing about himself and his alienation from the folk music world. He was bored to death but feared that if he left the safety of his genre for pop and flopped he could end up homeless himself. He told *Playboy*, "Last spring, I guess I was going to quit singing. I was very drained, and the way things were going, it was a very draggy situation . . . It's very tiring having other people tell you how much they dig you if you yourself don't dig you . . . But 'Like a Rolling Stone' changed it all. I mean it was something that I myself could dig."[6]

Regardless of who inspired the song, Dylan wrote "this long piece of vomit, 20 pages long, and out of it I took 'Like a Rolling Stone' and made it as a single. And I'd never written anything like that before, and it suddenly came to me that was what I should do . . . After writing that I wasn't interested in writing a novel or a play."[7]

In 2004 he told music journalist Robert Hilburn, "It's like a ghost is writing a song like that. It gives you the song and it goes away, it goes away. You don't know what it means. Except the ghost picked me to write the song."[8]

The documentary of Dylan's spring tour, *Don't Look Back*, captures Dylan singing "Lost Highway" with Joan Baez in his hotel room. Written by Leon Payne and made famous by country icon Hank Williams in 1949, the song starts with the singer calling himself a lost rolling stone, paying the cost for a life of sin. In 1950, blues master Muddy Waters released "Rollin' Stone," after which the British band named themselves.

When Dylan's song was first announced but before anyone had heard it, many assumed that it was about the band, since to record the album *Bringing It All Back Home* Dylan had formed a group that sounded very much like the Stones.

On June 15, nine days after "Satisfaction" was released, Dylan went into the studio and recorded "Like a Rolling Stone." He brought back the same pianist, bassist, drummer, and Bruce "Mr. Tambourine Man" Langhorne from his previous album, plus blues guitar wunderkind Michael Bloomfield.

A key part of his sound actually found him unexpectedly. Brill Building songwriter–session musician Al Kooper ("This Diamond Ring") was a friend of producer Tom Wilson, so Wilson allowed Kooper to visit Dylan's session to watch. But Kooper sneaked into the empty organ seat.

"Man, what are *you* doin' out there?" Wilson asked. He knew that Kooper didn't even play organ. But then Wilson was distracted, and didn't get around to telling Kooper to move, so Kooper stayed.

Bobby Gregg struck his snare, the band kicked in, and Kooper listened for the other musicians' chords for half a moment before playing them himself.

Afterward, everyone gathered to listen to the playback. When the song entered the second verse, Dylan told Wilson to turn the organ up.

"Hey, man, that cat's not an organ player," Wilson said.

"Hey, now don't tell me who's an organ player and who's not. Just turn the organ up."[9]

Dylan then almost let the song die when he refused to cut the six-minute, thirteen-second track in half for the single. Columbia's sales and marketing department considered it a cancelled release.

But Shaun Considine, Columbia's coordinator of new releases, sneaked out with an acetate of the song and asked the deejay at the über-hip New York nightclub Arthur to play it. The huge crowd response prompted two of New York's top deejays to call the label asking for the new Dylan single.[10] The song was released on July 20 and shot to No. 2—breaking the barrier of how long pop singles could be.

Bruce Springsteen recalled, "The first time that I heard Bob Dylan I was in the car with my mother, and we were listening to, I think, maybe WMCA, and on came that snare shot that sounded like somebody kicked open the door to your mind . . . Dylan was—he was a revolutionary, man; the way that Elvis freed your body, Bob freed your mind."[11]

Not only did the song break the length barrier, but the willful innocence of Top 40 was forever pierced by lyrics stranger and more suggestive than had been heard on pop radio before. But even though the words were dark, there was joy in Dylan's weather-beaten voice, the joy of being all his heroes

at once—Hank Williams, Muddy Waters, the Animals, the Beatles, the Rolling Stones—the joy of smashing out of the industry's little boxes, beyond
folk, beyond rock, beyond country, beyond blues, to a space where you
could be all of them at the same time. The subliminal message was that the
accepted rules weren't necessary; you could have complete artistic control
and a Top 5 hit. You were bound only by the limits of your imagination.
The song's wide-open possibility spoke to everyone from fellow musicians to
young people living on their own for the first time. Others took it as their
theme as they began "dropping out" of society in myriad ways. Some women
heard their own mixed emotions as they considered alternatives to being a
housewife (college, divorce, career), giving up the protection of parents or
husband to stand alone. It was the sound of an old country (traditional, stable, repressive) giving way to something frightening and free.

*

Folk singer emeritus Pete Seeger and Dylan's manager Albert Grossman
were two of the founders of the Newport Folk Festival in 1959, and two of
the men most responsible for the folk revival of the early 1960s. The Kingston Trio's cover of Seeger's antiwar "Where Have All the Flowers Gone"
reached the Top 20 in 1962, the same year the folk group that Grossman
had assembled, Peter, Paul and Mary, got to the Top 10 with "If I Had a Ham-
mer." In 1963, Dylan joined Peter, Paul and Mary and Joan Baez onstage at
Newport to sing his own civil rights anthem "Blowin' in the Wind," and became the darling of the scene.

At Newport '64, Ronnie Gilbert of the Weavers (Seeger's old group) introduced Dylan with "And here he is . . . Take him, you know him, he's yours." In
his memoirs, Dylan wrote that his internal reaction was "What a crazy thing
to say! Screw that. As far as I knew, I didn't belong to anybody then or now."[12]

On the evening of July 25, Peter Yarrow of Peter, Paul and Mary announced, "Ladies and gentlemen, the person that's going to come up now
has a limited amount of time. His name is Bob Dylan."[13]

Dylan took the stage, and his band launched into "Maggie's Farm," his
coded good-bye to writing protest songs. Just like the song's protagonist,
Dylan had a head full of new ideas to try, and he wasn't going to keep singing the way they wanted him to. Ironically, the song was inspired by the old
folk song "Down on Penny's Farm," which Pete Seeger had covered. But as
Dylan played his modernized version with Seeger in the wings, the band

was so loud that Seeger couldn't understand the words. Seeger's father was there, and wore a hearing aid, and the blasting distortion of the speakers upset him. Seeger tried to get the sound mixer to lower the band's volume, but he refused, saying it was how Dylan wanted it.[14] Seeger cursed, "Damn it, if I had an axe, I'd cut the cable right now!"[15]

Mike Bloomfield ripped on the guitar, but in the footage, boos can be heard mingled with the cheers. Dylan said later, "Well, I did this very crazy thing. I didn't know what was going to happen, but they certainly booed, I'll tell you that. You could hear it all over the place."[16]

The extent—and reason—for the booing has long been debated. Probably most were booing because Dylan was no longer writing civil rights anthems but trying to be a pop star. "Like a Rolling Stone" uses the same chords as "La Bamba," "Twist and Shout," and "Louie, Louie," and at New York's Ondine nightclub, go-go girls were frugging to it. Many of the older folk singers, such as Seeger and Burl Ives, erstwhile Communist idealists, had been blacklisted, losing a decade from their careers due to their convictions.

Al Kooper thought the crowd was booing also because the drummer changed the beat mid-song and confused all the musicians.[17] Others say people were booing the poor sound mix, as the festival wasn't set up for rock bands. Kooper also thinks it was because Dylan was the headliner but did only "Maggie's Farm," "Like a Rolling Stone," and "It Takes a Lot to Laugh, It Takes a Train to Cry" before hurrying offstage. At Yarrow's onstage prompting, he did finally return to play acoustic songs, but only two: "Mr. Tambourine Man" and "It's All Over Now, Baby Blue."

Over the course of the next year, Dylan would grow to thrive fiendishly off the audience's boos, tapping into that part of himself back at the high school talent show that howled "Rock and Roll Is Here to Stay"—"African shrieking," a teacher dubbed it—and prompted the principal to turn off the mic's power. Even then, the teenage Dylan kept pounding the piano, breaking the pedal off.[18]

But while Dylan presumably did not care about his principal, he had once turned down an appearance on the popular *Hootenanny* TV show because they wouldn't let blacklisted Pete Seeger play. In an interview with Martin Scorsese decades later, Dylan recalled how hearing that "Someone whose music I cherish, someone who I highly respect is going to cut the cable, was like, oh God, was almost like a dagger." Dylan clutched his heart. "Just the thought of it made me go out and get drunk."[19]

After the adoration he'd received on his spring tour, it was the first time in a long while that he had faced a negative reaction. At the after-party, while the others celebrated, he brooded by himself. When folkie Maria Muldaur asked him to dance, he replied gnomically, "I would dance with you, Maria, but my hands are on fire."[20]

"I was kind of stunned," he later told *Playboy*. "There were a lot of people there who were very pleased that I got booed. I saw them afterward. I do resent somewhat, though, that everybody that booed said they did it because they were old fans."[21]

Four days later, he went into the studio and unleashed an attack on his old folk stomping grounds with "Positively 4th Street," a reference to the street in Greenwich Village that was home to Gerde's Folk City and other clubs Dylan used to play. In it, he sneers that the folkies are envious drags. The song became one of the most specific examples of dirty laundry to make the Top 10. As in the music of Motown, Dylan knew to milk the elements of his previous hit, so the organ is front and center, chortling "ho ho ho" at the smiling faces who think they can backstab him. The beautifully distorted guitar arpeggios give the song a burned-out, mellow groove in sharp contrast to its spiteful words.

For some reason, Dylan stopped working with Tom Wilson, who had done his last three albums and helped guide him toward rock. Years later, Wilson told one interviewer that he had been offered better money to go to a different label, in response to which Dylan shrugged, saying, "Maybe we should try Phil Spector."[22] Instead, the songwriter was paired with producer Bob Johnston, who so far had produced Patti Page and written an underrated Presley classic called "It Hurts Me" with Charlie Daniels. Johnston would also handle Simon and Garfunkel and Johnny Cash.

From July 29 to August 4, Dylan recorded *Highway 61 Revisited*, named for the freeway that ran all the way from his hometown in Minnesota to the southern states where blues, R&B, and rock were born. As Dave Marsh said of his work from this era, "This was rock and roll at the farthest edge imaginable, instrumentalists and singer all peering into a deeper abyss than anyone had previously imagined existed."[23]

The careening comedy of *Bringing It All Back Home*'s "Bob Dylan's 115th Dream" returned in songs such as "Tombstone Blues" and the title track, but the Bloomfield-led band was more ruthless, and the jokes were now jet-black. Dylan synthesized all his previous strands—his humorous songs with his

"Hard Rain" imagery songs with his protest songs—into a phantasmagoria befouled by the stoning he'd received less than a week before at Newport. Now he had his formula down: throw characters from history, literature, movies, and the Bible into a blender with thieves, undertakers, nuns, and jugglers; write off a doomed society in cinematic aphorisms; and then give it an unwieldy title with a modifier that ends in "ly."

"Tombstone Blues" hints at Vietnam, with city fathers trying to drum up fear of imminent invasion and super-macho presidents sending slaves to the jungle to torture and burn out camps with blowtorches. So does "Highway 61 Revisited," in which God warns an irreverent Abraham he'd better kill Him a son.

Nobody could say for certain what the hell "Ballad of a Thin Man" was about. The song is a nightmarish mix of William Burroughs's *Naked Lunch* with the piano of Ray Charles's "I Believe to My Soul." As with "Like a Rolling Stone," there are many candidates for the identity of the song's "Mr. Jones." Journalists often raised Dylan's ire with their inane or repetitive questions, and the documentary *Don't Look Back* shows him savaging one on camera. Journalist Jeffrey Jones later claimed to have been heckled by Dylan in a hotel dining room during the Newport Folk Festival. "Mr. Jones! Gettin' it all down, Mr. Jones?"[24]

Some thought Dylan was continuing his Rolling Stones fixation. He palled around with the drug-addled Brian Jones and was known to greet him with "Hello, Brian, how's your paranoia?" Also, "keeping up with the Joneses" was the great American pastime.

All that can be said for sure is that, to the strains of Al Kooper's creepy organ, a guy enters a room alone, holding his pencil, and has to put his eyes in his pockets as he's besieged by strange men in a whirlpool of phallic imagery. Geeks, sword swallowers, one-eyed midgets, lumberjacks, and kneeling naked men clicking their high heels borrow Mr. Jones's throat, turn him into a cow, and hand him bones. It is as if he's been dosed with LSD and shepherded into a gay orgy at Andy Warhol's Factory (where Dylan made intermittent appearances throughout the year).

New York artist Steve Kaplan (born 1944) remembered the first time he heard the song. "I was living at my mom's house in Queens. And I remember going to bed one night and listening to the AM radio, and I heard this song at about 2 a.m. . . . . It was Bob Dylan, and I was listening to the words. And I remember thinking to myself, *'What the fuck is this? What is this guy talking about?'* It was absolutely hypnotic. It was as if I had just been changed to a different frequency, zapped right into the radio. I was listening with my ears the size of cauliflowers. I could not get enough of that song. But it ended, and I went back to school the next day."[25]

Huey Newton, who would form the Black Panthers the following year, listened to the album ritualistically. He told his comrades that the song was a metaphor for how the white man was screwing over the black man.

The album's eleven-minute final song, "Desolation Row," hints at the reasons Dylan once felt such kinship with the civil rights movement. The opening lines refer to a postcard of a hanging, which Dylan's father actually witnessed. When his father was eight years old, on June 15, 1920, three black men in a traveling circus were accused of raping a white woman and lynched two blocks from his house. Postcards with photos of their corpses were sold. (Dylan's grandparents had fled Ukraine from the pogroms of 1905, where Jews were raped and murdered, so being lynched wasn't such a remote possibility to his father.) A few lines later, Dylan sings of restless riot squads needing somewhere to go; the track was recorded on August 4, a week before the Watts riots.

Al Kooper said the main inspiration for "Desolation Row," however, was Manhattan's Eighth Avenue, "an area infested with whore houses, sleazy bars and porno supermarkets."[26] The song climaxes on the *Titanic*, where people shout, "Which side are you on?," also the title of a folk song about a coal miner strike. Dylan believed that during his performance at Newport, someone had been shouting at him, "Are you with us? Are you with us?"[27] Here he seems to be hinting that the old-fashioned acoustic scene was sinking like the *Titanic*, into irrelevance. ("Positively 4th Street" also has a verse about being on the winning side.)

Ironically, the song was acoustic; Dylan tried an electric version of "Desolation Row" but didn't like it. Luckily, Bob Johnston's Nashville friend Charlie McCoy was in town. McCoy had played for everyone from Presley to Johnny Cash to Quincy Jones and Perry Como. McCoy's fluid guitar work in the style of Grady Martin so captivated Dylan that he recorded in Nashville for the next five years. Producer Johnston spliced together takes six and seven to capture Dylan's stunning harmonica solo at the end. (Dylan's playing was often underrated, but his earliest recorded gig was as session harmonica player for Harry Belafonte on "Midnight Special," four years prior.) Jagger said he heard "Desolation Row" referred to as Dylan's version of "The Waste Land," which is fitting, as T. S. Eliot is one of the song's "all-star cast."[28]

Dylan scholar Mark Polizzotti theorizes that the title came from mixing John Steinbeck's *Cannery Row* with Jack Kerouac's *Desolation Angels*, which was published in June.[29] *Angels* looks back on the glory days of the Beat Generation of a decade earlier. In a *New York Herald Tribune* review of the book, writer Nelson Algren excoriated Kerouac for the same reason the Newport folkies castigated Dylan: for being apolitical. Algren, the author of *Walk on the Wild Side*, was just a little older than the Beats and, like many of the folkies, had been blacklisted by the FBI. Algren charged that although both beatniks and Hugh Hefner–style sexual hedonists proudly considered themselves "nonconformists," they existed only because "a country enjoying such a plenitude of physical luxuries . . . could actually support infantilism as a trade . . . Their nonconformity was of no significance: No Congressional investigator is any more likely to ask anyone whether he knew Allen Ginsberg than he is to ask whether he knew Hugh Hefner."[30]

The negative feedback from the folk community blended with the exhaustion Dylan suffered from his relentless professional schedule—*Revisited* was recorded in just five days—the hurricane of fame, and the drugs he relied on and that kept him up for days at a time. In "Just Like Tom Thumb's Blues," the weariness of Paul Griffin's piano brings the heavy sound of the 1970s five years early. "From a Buick Six" is a psychic flash of the motorcycle accident that will take Dylan off the road a year later. Even in the upbeat "It Takes a Lot to Laugh, It Takes a Train to Cry," he muses that he might die on top of the hill. The bleak nihilism of *Highway 61 Revisited* is a far cry from the joyous laughter of *Bringing It All Back Home*, recorded just six months earlier.

12

Hello, Vietnam

President Johnson doubles the draft call to thirty-five thousand men a month on July 28, two days before enacting Medicare and Medicaid.

President Lyndon Johnson was driving his special assistant Joseph A. Califano Jr. on his Texas ranch when, as Califano recalled, "We reached a steep incline at the edge of the lake, and the car started rolling rapidly toward the water. The president shouted, 'The brakes don't work! The brakes won't hold! We're going in! We're going under!'"[1]

Luckily, LBJ was playing a joke on his aide: he was driving an Amphicar, a vehicle that could be driven on a road or in a lake.

The months after Johnson's landslide victory in the 1964 presidential election were some of the most exciting in his life; it seemed all his dreams were within reach. When he lit the White House Christmas tree, he proclaimed, "These are the most hopeful times in all the years since Christ was born in Bethlehem." On January 8, in the first State of the Union address aired during prime time, Johnson announced his plans for the Great Society—government programs that together would create "abundance and liberty for all." His inauguration on January 20 drew the biggest crowds in Washington's history, until Barack Obama's in 2009.

In the late 1920s a young LBJ had taught poor Mexican-American kids in

Texas, and having seen poverty up close made him determined to end it. "If every person born could acquire all the education that their intelligence quotient would permit them to take, God only knows what our gross national product would be—and the strength we would add to our nation, militarily, diplomatically, economically, is too large even to imagine."[2]

President Franklin Roosevelt appointed Johnson the head of the National Youth Administration in Texas, where he helped disadvantaged kids. Then, in 1953, the forty-six-year-old Johnson became the youngest Senate majority leader in history. Thus when he became president after Kennedy's assassination, he knew how to work the political system. He framed many of his social programs as fulfilling Kennedy's ambitions, and he struck quickly, knowing that the honeymoon of his victory against Republican Barry Goldwater would not last long. He never read books or went to movies; his only interest was learning about the lives of his fellow politicians so he could better cajole, seduce, or threaten them with the famous "Johnson treatment."[3]

The Dow Jones stock market index had gone up 44 percent in the last two years, and everyone believed the future looked bright for continued economic expansion. Future economic rivals such as Germany and Japan had yet to challenge the dominance of the Detroit automakers. Unemployment was 4.1 percent, the gross national product had grown more than 5 percent in the last year, and Congress enjoyed a Democratic majority.

Thus Johnson pushed through a raft of social entitlements that would stand as the high-water mark for Big Government liberalism, despite congressional Republican George H. W. Bush and the American Medical Association denouncing new programs such as Medicare and Medicaid as "socialized medicine." Fellow congressmen Gerald Ford, Bob Dole, Strom Thurmond, and Donald Rumsfeld also opposed the programs.[4]

Medicare A taxed employers and employees a higher amount for Social Security, and then put the additional money into a trust fund for seniors to use for hospital bills and nursing home costs. Medicare B gave seniors the option to take some money out of their Social Security check to combine with government funds to pay for doctors, nurses, and tests. Medicaid was a mix of state and federal moneys that paid for the medical needs of families with children, low-income people on welfare, the disabled, and the elderly.

Johnson signed the bills into effect on July 30. Other Great Society bills established Head Start, public radio, public television, food stamps, the

Department of Housing and Urban Development, and the National Endowment for the Arts. Immigration reform addressed long-standing discrimination against southern and eastern Europeans and Asians. (Asian immigration in particular had been severely restricted.) Johnson also increased Social Security benefits and maternal-child health services, made it easier to qualify as disabled, added rehabilitation coverage, and lowered the age at which widows could begin receiving benefits. The Elementary and Secondary Education Act distributed federal money to schools.[5]

Simultaneously, the administration raced toward the moon. On March 18, Soviet Aleksei Leonov became the first man to walk in space, and the United States responded with a flurry of activity. From March to July, the unmanned lunar probe *Ranger 9* sent back live satellite pictures that were broadcast on TV. The United States put the first two-person crew and the first nuclear power reactor into Earth's orbit. On June 3, Edward Higgins White became the first American to walk in space. The *Mariner 4* sent the first pictures from Mars when it flew by the planet. On December 15, the U.S. *Gemini 6* and *7* accomplished the first rendezvous in orbit.

But across the Pacific, a nation a few thousand square miles larger than New Mexico was poised to end America's sense of omnipotence.

In 1858 France took over Vietnam, whose rubber, rice, and tin became some of the most valued commodities of the French empire. But the Vietnamese farmers received none of the profits from their exports, and the French taxed the peasants excessively. Protestors were beaten or killed. Ho Chi Minh (1890–1969) appealed to U.S. president Woodrow Wilson for help. But the U.S. administration ignored him, so he went to the Soviet Union instead, and adopted its Communist style of revolution to end colonial rule in his homeland.[6]

Ho Chi Minh's coalition, called the Viet Minh, went to war with France in 1946. The United States supported the French, fearing that if Vietnam went Communist, the other nations in the region would fall into the Soviet-Chinese bloc as well, a belief known as the Domino Theory.

France lost the war in 1954, and the Geneva Conference temporarily divided the country into North and South Vietnam, with the understanding that it would reunify in 1956 and have free elections. The Viet Minh ruled the north. From 1953 to 1956, they based their land-reform model on that of

China's Chairman Mao. The government took the land from the tiny percentage of people who owned it and executed approximately 50,000 to
175,000 "landlords," while many more starved.[7] More than a million fled from
North Vietnam to the south; two million more attempted but were prevented
from leaving by the Viet Minh.[8]

The United States moved to make the Republic of South Vietnam a permanent country, backing Ngo Dinh Diem in a fraudulent 1955 referendum.
Diem was a Catholic despite South Vietnam being 90 percent Buddhist. His
government was corrupt, and reformers were jailed or shot. South Vietnam
broke into civil war. The Viet Minh organized southern rebels into the National Liberation Front (NLF) to topple Diem and reunify with the north;
Diem's administration dubbed the NLF the Viet Cong (Vietnamese Communists). The Viet Minh aided them with arms and training.

In 1962 President Kennedy sent American advisers to train Diem's armies,
but the advisers could not tell the difference between neutral civilians and
Viet Cong so, per *The Pentagon Papers*, more than four million people, or
33 percent of South Vietnam's population, "were herded forcibly from their
homes" into "strategic hamlets," while their "old dwellings—and many of
their possessions—were burned behind them."[9] These strategic hamlets,
walled-in villages where armed guards prevented anyone from coming in
or going out, were run as labor camps.

South Vietnam was roiled by coups, but Johnson was not going to be the
first American president to lose a war. He told White House press secretary
Bill Moyers, "I'm not going to let Vietnam go the way of China. I told them
to go back and tell those generals in Saigon that Lyndon Johnson intends to
stand by our word, but by God, I want something for my money. I want 'em
to get off their butts and get out in those jungles and whip hell out of some
Communists. And then I want them to leave me alone, because I got some
bigger things to do right here at home."[10]

On March 2, Johnson ordered the Rolling Thunder bombing campaign,
and on March 8 the first combat troops, thirty-five hundred marines, landed
at China Beach to protect the air base in Da Nang. There were already
twenty-three thousand American military advisers training the South Vietnamese. Gen. William Westmoreland's strategy was attrition: kill as many
Viet Cong and North Vietnamese troops as possible until they give up.

Operation Rolling Thunder's mission was to bomb the North Vietnamese
until they stopped sending men, weapons, and supplies to the Viet Cong in

South Vietnam. It meant destroying their factories and their ability to transport aid to the south. But the North Vietnamese split their factories into smaller buildings and hid them in caves and villages. Some villages moved into tunnels up to a hundred feet underground, complete with kitchens, medical stations, wells, and rooms for families.[11] Small supply trains or truck convoys drove at night along the Ho Chi Minh Trail, which was covered by jungle foliage and not visible to bombers. Often, young girls helped conduct the traffic. When trucks were not available, men pushed supplies in wheelbarrows, with more strapped to their backs. When bridges were blown up, they were replaced with ferries or bamboo planks bound together, or pontoons made of boats tied to each other and camouflaged, or underwater bridges. During the first year of Rolling Thunder, ninety-seven thousand North Vietnamese volunteered to repair the destruction inflicted; a half million more citizens helped part time.[12]

The U.S. Air Force had designed its supersonic fighters and trained its pilots to drop nuclear bombs on the Soviet Union, so they were unprepared for dogfights when the North Vietnamese ambushed them with elderly subsonic Soviet fighter jets.[13] Often the Americans were forced to drop their bomb loads earlier than intended. (The Americans' need for a new air battle strategy eventually resulted in the Topgun and other pilot training programs.)[14] Meanwhile, the Soviet Union and China supplied North Vietnam with anti-aircraft weapons; 80 percent of American air losses came from these.[15]

On July 28, Johnson increased the number of troops from 75,000 to 125,000, which nearly doubled the men drafted per month, from 17,000 to 35,000. Within two years, the United States would have 500,000 men in South Vietnam, roughly the population of Fresno, California, today. Ultimately, the war would result in 58,286 American deaths. Estimates of Vietnamese deaths from the war from 1965 to 1975 range from 791,000 to 1,141,000.

On March 16, an eighty-two-year-old peace activist named Alice Herz immolated herself in Detroit to protest American involvement in the war.

Eight days later, on March 24 and 25, at the nearby University of Michigan, the Students for a Democratic Society (SDS) held the first large-scale "teach-in" about the Vietnam War, with talks, films, debates, and music about the conflict, drawing thirty-five hundred attendees. Two months later, on the other side of the country, at Berkeley, a thirty-six-hour teach-in attracted ten thousand to thirty thousand people on May 21–23. Pediatrician Dr. Benjamin Spock, Buddhist Alan Watts, comedian Dick Gregory, novelist Norman Mailer, and folk singer Phil Ochs were among the speakers and performers. President Johnson was hanged in effigy, and draft cards were burned. "Burn yourselves, not your cards," pro-war demonstrators retorted.[16]

During the Berkeley teach-in, socialist Paul Montauk and Jerry Rubin formed the Vietnam Day Committee (VDC). Rubin was a graduate student at Berkeley when the Free Speech Movement shut down the campus the year before, to fight for the right to fund-raise for the civil rights movement. That year he also joined a group of eighty-four students who visited Cuba illegally, later recalling, "As [Castro's second-in-command] Che [Guevara] rapped on for four hours, we fantasized taking up rifles. Growing beards. Going into the hills as guerrillas. Joining Che to create revolutions throughout Latin America. None of us looked forward to returning home to the political bullshit in the United States."[17] But he had returned, and now he announced that the VDC's "purpose was to create theatrical, disruptive events to make Vietnam an issue in people's lives."[18]

In the early 1950s, the so-called Silent Generation that preceded the baby boomers grimly acceded to the Korean draft. And during the early days of the Vietnam War, a vast majority of younger Americans showed support for military intervention. Thus, the rapid growth of the antiwar movement shocked even its own organizers. On April 17, fifteen thousand to twenty-five thousand demonstrated in Washington, DC, against the air campaign that had already dropped a thousand tons of bombs. By August 31, Johnson made burning draft cards a crime punishable by a five-year prison sentence and a thousand-dollar fine, though the first card burner arrested, David Miller, got twenty-two months for his act of defiance. On October 15 and 16, protestors demonstrated in forty American cities and in international cities including London and Rome. On November 2, a thirty-one-year-old Quaker named Norman Morrison immolated himself under the window of secretary of defense Robert McNamara's office at the Pentagon. On November 27, thirty-five thousand marched on the White House, chanting, "Hey, hey, LBJ, how many kids did you kill today?" SDS membership quadrupled by the end of the year, to forty-three hundred. In December, high school students in Des Moines wore black armbands to class to protest the war, and were suspended. Their case, *Tinker v. Des Moines Independent Community School District*, went all the way to the Supreme Court. (The students won in 1968.)

The Vietnam War occurred at a time when an unprecedented number of young people could afford to go to college and felt informed enough to question the government's decisions. And like the civil rights movement, the antiwar movement benefited from a new era in television coverage.

On August 5, *CBS Evening News with Walter Cronkite* aired a report by journalist Morley Safer in which he showed a search-and-destroy operation by American soldiers in the village of Cam Ne, believed to be a Viet Cong stronghold. As the cameras rolled, soldiers dragged women and children out of their ancestral huts and then set the structures on fire with Zippo lighters or flamethrowers. Elderly peasants begged for their homes to be spared, but 120 to 150 were leveled as women and children huddled together wailing. The report showed that the destruction of the village resulted in the capture of four men. Safer didn't mention that there had been marines killed in the village the previous month, or that at least one of the huts was connected to Viet Cong tunnels.[19] An enraged Johnson called CBS president Frank Stanton in the middle of the night. "Frank, are you trying to fuck me? Frank, this is your president and yesterday your boys shat on the American flag."[20] Johnson ordered a security check to see if Safer was a Communist; he wasn't, though he was Canadian.

A week later, on August 12, at a rally in Birmingham, Alabama, Martin Luther King Jr. gave his first statement on Vietnam. He called the conflict complex and ambiguous, and advised against looking backward to affix blame. He said war itself was the true enemy, and both sides were trapped in its vortex. To end the torment of the Vietnamese, he called on the United States to halt its bombings of the North and on Ho Chi Minh to stop demanding the withdrawal of American forces from the south. He said the first step toward peace would be rebuilding some of the villages that had been destroyed. His words went unheeded.

13

Folk-Rock Explosion, Part One

"I Got You Babe" is released on July 9, and "Eve of Destruction" gets leaked mid-July; the Byrds go on tour and Love takes over for them at Ciro's; and the Lovin' Spoonful debut with "Do You Believe in Magic" on July 20.

Salvatore Phillip "Sonny" Bono (born 1935) started out writing for Sam Cooke and served as Phil Spector's assistant. In the studio, he absorbed how Spector produced records and then promoted them to disc jockeys. He wrote "Needles and Pins" with Jack Nitzsche, and the cover by the Merseyside band the Searchers, with two heavily echoed six-string guitars, was a precursor to the folk-rock jangle.

Born 1946, Cherilyn "Cher" Sarkisian's parents married and divorced each other three times. Once, she was placed in an orphanage for several weeks because her mother was too destitute to care for her. She dropped out of school at sixteen to become a go-go dancer on the Sunset Strip, and lost her virginity to Warren Beatty after he cut her off in traffic one day.[1] Also when she was sixteen, she met Bono in a coffeehouse. Bono liked her friend, but her friend didn't dance, so Bono ended up dancing with Cher all night. He moved into an apartment next to the two girls, and became friends with Cher. When Cher lost her job, he said, "Well, you can live in my place and cook and clean."

"He had twin beds, and I lied to him about my age. I was a pretty fair housekeeper, but I couldn't cook at all. I was also real sickly, so Sonny ended up taking care of me all the time. I remember girls coming in and out of that house, like, by the thousands. The girls would say, 'Who's that?' And he'd go, 'Oh, that's just Cher.' We were just friends."[2]

Cher sang backup on some of Spector's hits, including "Be My Baby" and "You've Lost That Lovin' Feelin'," then lead on a novelty song Spector co-wrote called "Ringo, I Love You." It flopped because her deep voice led people to think a man was singing it. Then Bono was fired after he offered his boss some well-meant advice. After a deejay told Bono that Spector's latest Ronettes tune was out of fashion in the era of the British Invasion, Bono told Spector gently over the phone, "Phil, I think we need to change the sound." There was silence from the other end, and Bono realized he had inadvertently excommunicated himself.[3]

Now he had no choice but to make it, and he started to see Cher as the ticket. "I was like raw, aimless, untamed energy, and he saw a way to give it direction. He molded me. His dream was to push me into being a huge star."[4] He started writing songs for her, such as "Baby Don't Go," about a poor girl who leaves her hometown for the city to escape her sad past and become a lady. "Where Do You Go" returned to the theme of a lonely girl lost on the Sunset Strip.

Cher wanted Bono to perform onstage with her, to help with her stage fright. The Byrds were the hottest thing on the Strip, so Bono sneaked in a tape recorder to one of their gigs at Ciro's and then tried to beat them to the marketplace with Dylan's "All I Really Want to Do," complete with Byrds-style guitar. The two versions went head to head in May. Cher beat the Byrds in the United States (No. 15 to No. 40), though in the United Kingdom, the Byrds won (No. 4 to No. 9). The Byrds' McGuinn said, "What really got me most was Dylan coming up to me and saying, 'They beat you man,' and he lost faith in me. He was shattered. His material had been bastardized. There we were, the defenders and protectors of his music, and we'd let Sonny and Cher get away with it."[5]

Another song of Dylan's that was popular as a cover was the antilove song "It Ain't Me Babe." Bono turned it on its head, making it into a waltz for young hippie couples everywhere called "I Got You Babe." He and Cher recorded it backed by the Wrecking Crew, with producer Bono using everything he'd learned from Spector. After its release on July 9, it was No. 1 by August 14. The first folk-rock couple told everyone they had married in Tijuana in 1964, though they wouldn't officially wed until the birth of their daughter in 1969.

Per rock critic Richie Unterberger, the earliest-known use of the term *folk-rock* was in a *Billboard* cover story on June 12, "Folkswinging Wave On—Courtesy of Rock Groups," by Eliot Tiegel, who used the term to describe the Byrds, Sonny and Cher, the Lovin' Spoonful, the Rising Sons, Jackie DeShannon, and Billy J. Kramer.[6]

It was around that time that Dunhill Records owner Lou Adler gave a copy of Dylan's *Bringing It All Back Home* to one of his songwriters, P. F. Sloan, and told him to come up with a Dylanesque protest single for the Byrds. Between midnight and dawn, "Eve of Destruction" came to Sloan in a torrent.

He was nineteen, old enough to be sent to Vietnam but not old enough to vote yet (the voting age was twenty-one in all but four states), the same injustice Eddie Cochran sang about in 1958 in "Summertime Blues," except now there was a war on. Sloan was still haunted by the pounding martial drums from President Kennedy's funeral and worked those in, along with fears of nuclear apocalypse. He decried the hypocrisy of calling the Communists hateful while the Klan murdered in the South and congressmen dithered.

The Byrds rejected the song, though, so Sloan pitched it to Byrds imitators the Tyrtles (later, simply, Turtles) backstage at the Sunset Strip club the Crescendo (later the Trip). Howard Kaylan recalled, "Our jaws hit the ground. We all knew that it would be a monster hit, it was that powerful. But we also knew that whoever recorded this song was doomed to have only one record in their/his career. You couldn't make a statement like that and ever work again."[7]

But a growly singer named Barry McGuire was looking for work after leaving the New Christy Minstrels in January. Byrd Gene Clark had once been in the Christys, so he invited McGuire to come watch them play at Ciro's. After the Byrds' performance, McGuire led a conga line into the street. Dunhill's Lou Adler was there, and the two started talking about working together.

On Thursday, July 15, McGuire went into the studio with Sloan on six-string and harp, alongside two of LA's top session men, drummer Hal Blaine and bassist Larry Knechtel of the Wrecking Crew. McGuire recorded Sloan's "What Exactly's the Matter with Me" and needed a B side. They had ten minutes of studio time left, just enough to lay down one take of "Eve of Destruction." McGuire read the lyrics off the wrinkly paper on which Sloan had written them, building to a rage for the climax in which he bitterly reminds Selma, Alabama, not to forget to say grace while they bury their murdered black neighbors.

Sloan's writing-producing partner, Steve Barri, took a copy of the tape with him so he could listen to it in his office the next day. The president of Dunhill, Jay Lasker, heard it and took the tape to listen to it again himself. A few hours later, Lou Adler burst into the office, enraged. "Eve of Destruction" was playing on the radio, in what Adler believed was a completely unpolished form.[8]

Lasker had instructed a promo man to take the tape down to radio station KFWB to find out if it was too controversial to air. The program director was so exhilarated by the track that he played it on air immediately, and it became their most requested song since "I Want to Hold Your Hand." Adler initially thought McGuire needed to redo his vocals—after all, the singer had had trouble reading Sloan's handwriting—but in the end, Adler simply added a ghostly female background choir to make it sound less like a rough mix. Just as "Like a Rolling Stone" was doing that same July, the song had bypassed the gatekeepers. "Eve" would make it to No. 1 on September 25, as the kids across the country returned to school. Ironically, it would block its inspiration, Dylan, from rising above No. 2.

In October a group called the Spokesmen—comprised of a deejay and two of the songwriters responsible for "At the Hop," Lesley Gore's "You Don't Own Me, and "1-2-3," by Len Barry—issued "Dawn of Correction," their answer to "Eve of Destruction." The song made it to No. 36 on October 16, with lyrics affirming that Americans needed to keep the world free from Communists and that the A-bomb was ultimately good because it fostered negotiation. The song pointed to progress in voter registration, vaccination, the United Nations, and decolonization. (Luckily for the writers, these all rhymed.)

Sloan's reaction was "This is great! Maybe it's a dialogue happening: via the radio via musical recordings."[9] Sonny Bono sang in "The Revolution Kind" that men weren't necessarily radicals just because they spoke their minds (which he would prove when he became a Republican congressman in 1994). "It's Good News Week," by Hedgehoppers Anonymous, took the black comedy approach for their knockoff, in which nukes reanimate the rotting dead.

Now that Dylan had left topical protest behind, Phil Ochs stepped in with "Draft Dodger Rag." Ochs's "I Ain't Marching Anymore" was an epic account of the history of U.S. warfare in two minutes and thirty-five seconds, and he even tried his own electric version, though the acoustic original has more grace. Tom Paxton sang "Lyndon Johnson Told the Nation" and, in "We Didn't Know," equated the Americans who turned a blind eye to Jim Crow and Vietnam with "good Germans" ignoring the Holocaust during World War II. The Chad Mitchell Trio sang "Business Goes on as Usual," in which the economy booms while the singer's brother dies in a war he doesn't understand.

Both English folkie Donovan and Glen Campbell, the session guitarist struggling to become a country-pop star in his own right, covered Buffy St. Marie's "Universal Solider." (On the flip side, Donovan covered Mick Softley's "The War Drags On.") Campbell seems to have been caught unaware by the antiwar slant of the lyrics, and by October he was telling journalists, "The people who are advocating burning draft cards should be hung. If you don't have enough guts to fight for your country, you're not a man."[10] He was perhaps stung by the Jan and Dean answer song, "The Universal Coward."

On the country front, neither Loretta Lynn's "Dear Uncle Sam" or Willie Nelson's "Jimmy's Road" offered an opinion on the war itself. Rather, the songs focused on the death of a husband and a friend, respectively. However, Dave Dudley's "What We're Fighting For" and Johnnie Wright's "Hello Vietnam" were the pro-war anthems to be expected from the country and western genre. The latter song said that we had to learn to put out fires before they got too big, alluding to how the Allies had avoided going to war with Hitler for years, allowing him the time to grab more countries, implying we couldn't afford to do the same thing again with the Soviets and China. The writer of "Hello Vietnam," Tom T. Hall, also wrote a female version called "Good-Bye to Viet Nam," in which Kitty Hawkins sings how she just got news her man is coming back home to her.

Staff sergeant Barry Sadler of the Green Berets was a combat medic in Vietnam wounded by the booby trap stake called the Punji stick.[11] In the hospital, he wrote twelve verses of "The Ballad of the Green Berets." The author of a book called *The Green Berets*, Robin Moore, helped Sadler edit the song down. It was recorded late in the year, for the military, and was so popular that it leaked out, and RCA decided to release it. It sold a million copies in two weeks and topped the charts on March 5, becoming the No. 1 single of 1966.

A few weeks after "Eve of Destruction" itself leaked out, the Watts neighborhood of Los Angeles detonated into flames. Though it's impossible to say how many of its residents listened to the lyrics of a white folk-rock single, the song's rage at the state of race relations grew even more disturbing when the rioters began torching white-owned stores. LA disc jockey Bob Eubanks asked, "How do you think the enemy will feel with a tune like that No. 1 in America?"[12]

Sloan said that Dunhill Records received death threats. McGuire said, "'Eve of Destruction' was a scary song because it made it on its own; it had no 'payola,' no disc jockey manipulation. Phil [Sloan] told me later on that there was a letter that went out from *The Gavin Report* [the trade magazine for radio programmers] or something saying, 'No matter what McGuire puts out next, don't play it.' . . . Because their feeling was that I was like a loose cannon in the record industry, and they wanted to get me back in line."[13]

It was a shame, because McGuire's other Sloan-penned tracks are terrific. "What Exactly's the Matter with Me" mines the same ennui that the Mike Nichols film *The Graduate* would two years later. McGuire bemoans the futility of going to college just to get a job to buy a TV, but admits he can't march because he's too insecure. "Child of Our Times" expresses his worry for children being born into the "Eve of Destruction." Its B side, "Upon a Painted Ocean" is an invigorating mash-up of Dylan's "The Times They Are A-Changin'" and "When the Ship Comes In," its title borrowed from eighteenth-century British poet Samuel Taylor Coleridge's "The Rime of the Ancient Mariner."

In the wake of the success of "Eve of Destruction," P. F. Sloan got to release his own solo singles. "Sins of a Family" was another of the songs he wrote that night while listening to Dylan. It was certainly the catchiest folk-rock ditty to beg compassion for the daughter of a schizo hooker. But Sloan's pinnacle was "Halloween Mary," which uses all Dylan's tropes to sing the praises of a Sunset Strip scenester. (The title was itself probably inspired by a line in "She Belongs to Me.")

The Turtles made a passionate single out of Sloan's "Let Me Be," since, as lead singer Kaylan explained, it was "just the perfect level of rebellion . . .

haircuts and nonconformity. That was as far as we were willing to go."[14] Sloan also wrote hits for Johnny Rivers, Herman's Hermits, the Seekers, and the Grass Roots, but his career mysteriously faded after another year. Still, he could take solace in the fact that "Eve of Destruction" may have helped speed the passage of the Twenty-Sixth Amendment, which lowered the voting age from twenty-one to eighteen. Congressmen had attempted to lower the requirement during World War II, and President Eisenhower had backed a new constitutional amendment in 1953, but these efforts never passed. In 1969 the National Education Association began a new push with the help of the YMCA, the AFL-CIO, the NAACP, and U.S. congressmen, including Edward Kennedy. The Twenty-Sixth Amendment was ratified in 1971. Perhaps the fact that one of the biggest hits of the decade lamented being old enough to kill but not to vote was a crucial bit of agitprop that helped the campaign finally to succeed.

In May the Byrds had opened for the Rolling Stones for a week in cities up and down the state of California. In July, the Byrds took Vito Paulekas's freaky dance troupe with them in a sixty-passenger bus on their first tour outside the Golden State, to Colorado, South Dakota, Minnesota, Illinois, Iowa, Florida, Ohio, Missouri, and Kentucky. One of the dancers, Lizzie Donahue, recalled, "They thought we were from outer space. In Paris, Illinois, they actually threw us off the dance floor."

"We had to stick together because we were about the only thing that looked like us around the country," Michael Clarke said. "[In the South] they wouldn't serve us in restaurants. 'Hey, did your barber die?' 'Are you a boy or a girl?' "[15]

The Byrds' roadie was a friend of David Crosby's named Bryan MacLean, who lived above Paulekas's studio and looked like a cross between Michael Clarke and Chris Hillman. He'd grown up in Beverly Hills, among show business families. (He was friends with Dean Martin's son Dino and was Liza Minnelli's boyfriend when the two were little.) As a teen, he took up folk guitar, then was hit by the Beatles. "I walked out of *A Hard Day's Night* . . . different. I was never the same. I just immediately identified with that. I let my hair grow out and got kicked out of school, just immediately. That settled the whether-I-should-finish-high-school question right there."[16] He dated singer-songwriter Jackie DeShannon, whom the Byrds covered on their first album.

One night MacLean was hanging out at Ben Frank's (the diner on the Strip that the young hipsters went to when the clubs closed) when he got an offer from one of the most unusual musicians on the scene. Arthur Lee was a black singer in the R&B band LAGs (for "LA Group") with childhood buddy and lead guitarist Johnny Echols. For a long time they'd been looking for an angle to help them break out; Lee had even written his own surf songs.

Lee knew the Paulekas dancers would come see his band if MacLean were in it. So he invited MacLean to join, and the group became the Grass Roots—until they heard that songwriter P. F. Sloan ("Eve of Destruction") had created his own band with the same name. So they changed their name to Love, and quickly developed a following as the most iconoclastic folk-rock/proto-punk band in Hollywood (or anywhere), led by a black guy imitating a white guy (Mick Jagger) who imitated black guys. (They weren't the only interracial band in the middle of the decade, however. Rising Sons, with Taj Mahal and Ry Cooder; Booker T. and the M.G.s; the United Kingdom's Equals, with Eddy Grant; and the Mynah Byrds, with Rick James and Neil Young, could also claim that distinction.)

When the Byrds went on tour in July, Love took over their slot at Ciro's, alternating with Rising Sons and the Leaves. Soon they would be playing the Whisky a Go Go when it wasn't functioning as a disco. According to rock journalist Nik Cohn, "Discos were an early sixties development, an improvement on big, impersonal concert halls. The idea was that you had an intimate nightclub atmosphere and played mostly records, with only occasional live acts. First and last, discotheque records had to be dancing records."[17]

Discotheques originated in Paris. The first Whisky a Go Go opened there in 1947—go-go means "galore" in French—and then one followed in Chicago, in 1958. The Sunset Strip branch opened six years later. In July 1965 the club hired go-go dancers to dance in cages hanging from the ceiling. It was a concept borrowed from the TV music show *Hullabaloo*. Love would immortalize the Whisky in their song "Between Clark and Hillsdale (Maybe People Would Be the Times)," the title a reference to the club's street intersection.

Also in July, a new law allowed minors to dance in public eating places unaccompanied by parents, and the Strip was soon bursting with clubs and coffeehouses that catered to the baby boomers coming of age, such as Pandora's Box (where Brian Wilson had met his wife, Marilyn), Gazzarri's, the Sea Witch, the Fifth Estate, and the Trip.[18] Weekend traffic ground to a halt as kids cruised the streets and swarmed the sidewalks. Producers for a new TV pilot called *The Monkees* ran ads in September's *Variety* and the *Hollywood Reporter* reading, "Madness!! Auditions. Folk & Roll Musicians-Singers for acting roles in new TV series. Running Parts for 4 insane boys, age 17–21. Want spirited Ben Frank's-types. Have courage to work. Must come down for interview." Musician Stephen Stills arrived in town from New York and tried out. He was rejected because of his teeth and suggested the producers check out his friend Peter Tork. Meanwhile, one of Arthur Lee's biggest fans, Jim Morrison, prowled the Strip after Love's gigs. By the beginning of next year his band, the Doors, would start performing at the London Fog, a few buildings down from the Whisky. As the Byrds came chiming over the airwaves, the West Coast nights shimmered with limitless possibility.

✳

John Sebastian was the son of a classical harmonica player. He'd grown up in Greenwich Village around Woody Guthrie and Burl Ives and was the godson of Vivian Vance (Ethel on *I Love Lucy*). He played on numerous folk sessions, logged in and out of bands. With Zal Yanovsky, the son of a Toronto political cartoonist, he formed the Mugwumps with future Mamas and Papas members Denny Doherty and Cass Elliott in 1964. (Mugwump was originally the name given to a group of Republicans who switched allegiance to the Democrats in the 1800s. In his 1959 book *Naked Lunch*, William Burroughs appropriates the label for the sexually ambivalent creatures who eat candy with razor-sharp beaks and drip with addictive fluid.)

The Mugwumps recorded a few singles but broke up after eight months. Sebastian and Yanovsky kept playing their unique blend of jug band music, folk, country, blues, R&B, and honky-tonk, calling it simply "good-time music." In January they decided to go electric with a rhythm section, adding Joe Butler on drums and Steve Boone on bass. (Sebastian and Boone had played briefly on an unreleased *Bringing It All Back Home* session that month.[19]) Sebastian asked a friend what he should name his new band, describing the sound as "Mississippi John Hurt meets Chuck Berry." The friend suggested "The Lovin' Spoonful," a phrase from Hurt's song "Coffee Blues."

Yanovsky and Butler had an eight-by-ten room in the grubby Albert Hotel, and the assistant manager agreed to let them rehearse in the basement, where the ceiling was caving in. Butler said, "It inspired us, because it made us frightened of poverty."[20]

They gigged at the Night Owl Café, which was so small the drums didn't fit onstage and had to be on the floor in front of the rest of the band. Sebastian recalled,

> We were playing pretty steadily for the local people from Greenwich Village who were part of the jazz scene or part of the kind of downtown "in crowd." They were "finger poppers," guys who played chess, "beatniks." But there was this one particular night as we were playing, I looked out in the audience and saw this beautiful 16-year-old girl just dancing the night away. And I remember Zal and I just elbowed each other the entire night, because to us, that young girl symbolized the fact that our audience was changing, that maybe they had finally found us. I wrote "Do You Believe in Magic" the next day.[21]

Spector was interested, but the band didn't want to be dominated by Spector. Instead, they signed with the Kama Sutra record label and released "Magic" on July 20. (It was a good week for music: "Like a Rolling Stone," "Help!," and "Eve of Destruction" all came out within the same day or two.) Featuring Sebastian playing his signature autoharp, "Do You Believe in Magic," a celebration of young girls' souls and rock and roll setting you free, made it to No. 9, its euphoria serving as an innocent bookend to "Satisfaction." Now that the Beatles had moved on to melancholy singles, it was the Spoonful who bottled the exhilaration of going into the city to find girls to dance with all night. Two weeks before Dylan's metaphoric stoning at the Newport Folk Festival, the Spoonful exhorted the listener not to waste time choosing between jug band music or rhythm and blues: just get happy and blow your mind. "Magic" also used the word *groovy*, which had been around since the 1920s but was now beginning to gain critical mass with songs such as the Mindbenders' "A Groovy Kind of Love" and Simon and Garfunkel's alternatively spelled "We've Got a Groovey Thing Goin'."

On the Lovin' Spoonful's first album, *Do You Believe in Magic*, Sebastian continued to be haunted by the (not legal) girl who had inspired him with her dancing. Perhaps he was warning himself of the consequences of statutory rape when he refitted the guitar of "Prison Wall Blues," by Gus Cannon's Jug Stompers, for the gentle "Younger Girl," in which he moans that it is killing him to have to wait a few more years. Still, he was quickly distracted in their next single, "Did You Ever Have to Make Up Your Mind." Yanovsky's guitar wryly commiserates as a father of two girls tells Sebastian he has to go home and pick which daughter he wants. The song went to No. 2. The wailing "Night Owl Blues" let Sebastian show his chops as the son of a harp blower.

With "Daydream," Sebastian tried to rewrite the Supremes' "Baby Love" as a jug band song and wound up with another No. 2 hit on both sides of the Atlantic. The song inspired the Beatles and the Kinks to begin following their own music hall leanings with "Good Day Sunshine" and "Sunny Afternoon," respectively.

The band recorded the *Daydream* album from August to December. Boone cowrote (with Sebastian) two of the album's greatest tracks, "You Didn't Have to Be So Nice" and "Butchie's Tune." The disconsolate country guitar of "Butchie's Tune" sets the mood as the singer slips out on his woman for good, in the early dawn, before she wakes up. "Didn't Want to Have to Do It" is another sad ballad about breaking someone's heart. "It's Not Time" marries Bakersfield twang with wise lyrics about trying to be mature enough not to argue.

Brian Wilson later said that it was the Spoonful's "You Didn't Have to Be So Nice" that inspired him to write "God Only Knows," the centerpiece of *Pet Sounds*.[22] With its chiming guitar and warm humming vocals, "You Didn't Have to Be So Nice" made the Top 10 like all the Lovin' Spoonful's first seven singles. Woody Allen enlisted them for the soundtrack to *What's Up Tiger Lily?*, and Francis Ford Coppola grabbed them for *You're a Big Boy Now.* And soon John Lennon would even adopt Sebastian's circular wire-frame glasses, as distinctive as McGuinn's rectangular shades, for his own look.

The producers who created *The Monkees* TV show first considered hiring the Spoonful because they were playful clowns like the Beatles used to be, singing about old-time movies with their arms around one another, unconcerned with posing arrogantly aloof like the Stones or the Byrds. But the Spoonful didn't need a TV show; almost overnight they had catapulted into the big leagues, respected as formidable writers and performers.

Two members of their old band the Mugwumps, Mama Cass and Denny Doherty, were about to join them there.

14

Soulsville and the Godfather Challenge Hitsville to Get Raw

The Four Tops' "I Can't Help Myself" makes it to No. 1 twice, in June and July, and the Supremes debut at the Copacabana on July 29. At Stax Records, Wilson Pickett tops the R&B charts with the new beat of "In the Midnight Hour" on August 7, and Otis Redding releases "Respect" on August 15. That same week, James Brown tops the R&B charts with "Papa's Got a Brand New Bag," inventing funk.

Aside from their work with the Supremes, the writer-producer team of Holland-Dozier-Holland also transformed the Four Tops into a band that rivaled the Temptations for the position of Motown's most successful male group. The Tops started on Chess Records in 1956 and later moved to Columbia, but it wasn't until they joined Motown and HDH gave them "Baby I Need Your Loving," in 1964, that they made the Top 20. Then HDH retooled the Supremes' "Where Did Our Love Go" into "I Can't Help Myself (Sugar Pie Honey Bunch)" for the Tops, and the song went to No. 1 on June 19. After being interrupted for a week by "Mr. Tambourine Man," it returned to the top spot on July 3.

For the sequel, Dozier reversed the chords, and within twenty-four hours the team recorded, pressed, and distributed "It's the Same Old Song." It made No. 5 on the pop charts. The exercise epitomized their determination to suck every last drop of juice from a hit. But at the same time, the new lyrics were substantial: about how songs heard when we're in love return to haunt us after a breakup. "This Old Heart of Mine" recycles the melody again and mixes it with the bridge of the Supremes' "Back in My Arms Again." Realizing they would be pushing it to give it to the Tops, HDH gave the track to the Isley Brothers, and somehow "Heart" turned out the best of all (though it may just seem that way because it hasn't been as overplayed).

Frantically cranking out hits for the Tops, the Supremes, and Martha and the Vandellas, HDH didn't even cut demos. Dozier said, "I'd come up with an idea, Brian and I would finish it off and then run downstairs and cut the track with the band. A lot of times we didn't even have a title. Then we'd bring it back up and Eddie and I would sit there and bounce things around and (ask) what is this track saying?"[1]

Unfortunately July 16's "Nothing but Heartaches," released a week after "It's the Same Old Song," was a little too much of a retread and made it only to No. 11, ending the Supremes' streak of No. 1's after five. An irate Gordy quickly issued a memo: "We will release nothing less than top ten product on any artist; and because the Supremes' world-wide acceptance is greater than the other artists, on them we will only release number-one records."

Gordy was particularly irked because his plan to have the Supremes cross over into the supper clubs was finally coming to fruition: they debuted at the Copacabana on July 29. The club was owned by the Mob and featured a Brazilian theme with Copacabana Girls and, incongruously, Chinese food on the menu. To prepare, Gordy hired a charm school teacher to give the singers etiquette lessons, along with a fashion expert, makeup artist, and choreographer. All three Supremes had grown up in Detroit's Brewster-Douglass housing projects, and Ross said, "I think what stands out in my mind most about the Copa is the feeling of respect that we'll never forget from those audiences."[2] By playing the Copa, the Supremes paved the way for the Temptations, Marvin Gaye, and Martha and the Vandellas to play there as well, and once you played the Copa, you could play anywhere in the world. Soon Gordy would make the Artists Personal Development Department, a.k.a. the Motown Finishing School, a division of his empire.

The Copa was a turning point for Florence Ballard, who had been frustrated with her diminishing role in the trio. Barbra Streisand's "People" was

Ballard's showstopper in the Supremes' set, but a few days after their Copa debut, Ross was assigned the song for good. Mary Wilson wrote in her memoir, "From that moment on, Flo regarded what was in fact the highest achievement of our career as a disaster. She was sad and moody, and I could see the three of us being torn apart."[3]

Ballard was the one in the group who had initially been discovered, singing on her porch, by the manager of a doo-wop group called the Primes (later renamed the Temptations). He asked her if she had any friends who could also sing, and she brought in Wilson, who brought in Ross. Originally, they each took turns singing lead. But though Ballard had the stronger, more traditional R&B voice, Ross's higher-pitched, breathy vocals turned out to be ideally suited for the era's technology. Marvin Gaye said, "Motown understood the transistor radio. Back then, transistors were selling like hot cakes and Motown songs were mixed to sound good on transistors and car radios. Diana's voice was the perfect instrument to cut through those sound waves."[4]

As Gordy increasingly focused on Ross, Ballard protested the group's shift away from R&B and toward "whiter" pop—to little avail. When the band's success brought the singers the luxury of separate hotel rooms, she felt increasingly isolated. She turned to drink, gaining weight and missing performances.

She was haunted by a tragic event that happened shortly before signing with Motown. When she was sixteen, she had attended a sock hop with her brother but had gotten separated from him, so accepted a ride home from a boy she knew, future Detroit Pistons basketball player Reginald Harding.[5] He drove her to a darkened street and raped her at knifepoint. Following the assault, she stayed inside her house for weeks before confiding in Wilson and Ross. They were supportive, but no one back then knew how to deal with rape trauma syndrome. Wilson wrote, "Diane and I never discussed it again, not even between ourselves. I chalk that up to our youth."[6]

As for the Supreme caught in the middle, Wilson would later write that Ross was a diva and not very nice. She writes in her memoir that when she entreated Gordy to let her handle a lead, he said, "Oh, Mary. You know you can't sing!"[7] He said it jokingly, but it destroyed her confidence.

Despite the backstage tension, the trio was second only to the Beatles on the charts throughout the decade, with twelve No. 1 U.S. singles to the Beatles' twenty. Elvis had seventeen, but that included his work in the 1950s.

The Supremes were Gordy's main weapon in ending the era when a black single could rise only so high on the pop charts before a white performer appropriated it and had a bigger hit with it. Today, aside from the Beatles, Elvis, and Madonna, none of the artists with the most No. 1 hits is white—Mariah Carey (eighteen), Michael Jackson (thirteen), Whitney Houston (eleven), Janet Jackson (ten), and Stevie Wonder (ten). (And, of course, Michael Jackson and Wonder got their start at Motown.)

For soul purists, Stax Records, in Memphis, was considered more authentic than Motown because its shouters' vocals were grittier, its house band's guitars were more distorted, and it used bluesy horns and organs more than strings. For the best illustration of the difference, listen to the original "My Girl," by the Temptations (Motown), backed by the Funk Brothers and the Detroit Symphony Orchestra, and then Otis Redding's version (Stax), backed by Booker T. and the M.G.s, the Memphis Horns, and pianist Isaac Hayes.

The funny thing was, while people called Stax "blacker," it was owned by a white brother and sister, and its house band, Booker T. and the M.G.s, was integrated. Jim Stewart was a white banker who played country fiddle until being inspired, by the local success of Sam Phillips's Sun Records, to start his own label. His sister, Estelle Axton, who worked at a different bank, mortgaged her house to buy the one-track Ampex tape recorder for the bands to record on.[8] They couldn't overdub as Motown did, which gave Stax an earthier sound for its first six years, though in June the studio finally had a four-track installed. The label's moniker came from the siblings' names: "Stewart" plus "Axton."

They had their studio built in an old Memphis movie theater in the black ghetto, on 926 E. McLemore Avenue. (As an answer to the "Hitsville U.S.A" sign on the Motown house, they put "Soulsville U.S.A." on the theater marquee.) The slope of the original theater floor gave the room unique acoustics.[9] They transformed the theater's candy shop into the Satellite Record Shop—Satellite was the original name of their label. In their own version of Motown's quality-control tests, as soon as they recorded a song in the studio, Jim and Estelle would play the track in the record store, to check consumer reaction. If it was bad, they might rework it or drop it. Having a record store on site also let them keep close tabs on what was hot. Jerry Wexler, at Atlantic Records (the inventor of the term *R&B* for *Billboard* and the producer of both Ray Charles and the Drifters), arranged a deal for Atlantic to distribute Stax's records nationally.

Booker T. and the M.G.s played on almost all the Stax cuts by Otis Redding, Wilson Pickett, Sam and Dave, and Carla and Rufus Thomas. The band included two black guys, Booker T. Jones on organ and Al Jackson on drums, and two white guys, Steve Cropper on guitar and Donald "Duck" Dunn on bass (replacing Lewie Steinberg). Unlike Motown's Funk Brothers, Booker T. and the M.G.s had a No. 3 hit in their own name with "Green Onions." Cropper went for a dirtier guitar sound than other session axe men, while Jackson hit the skins as hard as Zeppelin's drummer John Bonham on tracks such as "In the Midnight Hour." The Memphis Horns filled out the sessions. Isaac Hayes often sat in when Booker T. was away studying music at Indiana University. Hayes would go on to stardom with the Oscar-winning "Shaft" in 1971.

Cropper wrote a lot of tracks with Otis Redding, starting with "Mr. Pitiful," which made it to No. 10 on the *Billboard* R&B chart in February. After Cropper heard a deejay say that Redding always sounded pitiful in his ballads, it occurred to him in the shower that the phrase might make a good song. He drove over and picked up Redding and, Cropper said, "We just wrote the song on the way to the studio, just slapping our hands on our legs. We wrote it in about ten minutes, went in, showed it to the guys, [Otis] hummed a horn line, boom we had it."[10] From then on, Redding would usually get an idea for a title, a lyric or two, a tempo, and an idea for horns, and then he would hum the horn arrangement to Cropper and the other players. Only two of his songs had background vocals; instead, horns were his call-and-response team.

Redding's songs were usually either slow ballads or stompers. Two of his finest ballads were "That's How Strong My Love Is," the B side of "Mr. Pitiful," and "I've Been Loving You Too Long," cowritten with the Impressions' Jerry Butler.

The archetypal stomper was "I Can't Turn You Loose," which probably started as a rip-off of the Four Tops' "I Can't Help Myself (Sugar Pie, Honey Bunch)" but ended up illustrating the difference between Redding and the Motown stable. Both he and James Brown had started out as Little Richard imitators, and both used lots of vocal interjections such as "Ha!" In terms of onstage physicality, Redding rocked circles around the Four Tops' Levi Stubbs and everyone else except Brown. He was almost as impassioned as Brown, though not as intricately graceful—more of a wild freight train shaking back and forth, manic and beaming ("Got to, got to keep a grip!"). Motown's lead singers, such as David Ruffin, by contrast, were cool, slick—farther removed from the black gospel tradition, in which the preacher hollered, rough and raspy; and more sedate for white consumption as per Berry Gordy's ambitions.

But as the 1960s progressed, the level of vocal distortion became the barometer of passion: the more the singer shredded his larynx, the more intensely soulful he was considered. Before the British Invasion, the Italian bel canto–style crooners (smooth and mellow) dominated white pop. But the Brits respected the "linen-ripping sound" of blues vocals, as Beatle producer George Martin called it.[11] All the great Motown singers of the era had it in them, including Ruffin, Stubbs, Gaye, and Wonder—but it was the rise of the Stax soul singers such as Redding, Wilson Pickett, and Sam and Dave that pushed them to get rawer. For example, compare the Four Tops' "I Can't Help Myself (Sugar Pie, Honey Bunch)" to their hit "Bernadette," released two years later.

These fierce soul belters were always pleading to their women, totally codependent, as Redding sings in "I'm Depending on You." Redding just asked for a little "Respect," the Four Tops couldn't help being weak, Don Covay begged his woman to have "Mercy, Mercy," the Temptations weren't "too proud to beg."

For *Otis Blue*, Redding's second album of the year (after *The Great Otis Redding Sings Soul Ballads*), Redding started recording on Saturday, July 9, at 10:00 a.m. He took a break from 8:00 p.m. to 2:00 a.m., to let Booker T. and the M.G.s play a gig, and then resumed recording until 2:00 p.m. Sunday. When Redding briefly left to take a physical for medical insurance, Cropper (who was also serving as producer) got the idea for him to cover the Stones' new single. "I went up to the front of the record shop, got a copy of the record, played it for the band and wrote down the lyrics. You notice on 'Satisfaction' that Otis said, 'fashion,' not 'faction.' I love it. That's what made him so unique. He'd just barrel right through that stuff, unaware of anything. He just didn't know the song. He hadn't heard it, as far as I know."[12] The Stones would later base their stage version on Redding's cover. The Stones' original version reached No. 19 on the R&B charts, while Redding took it to the R&B Top 5 and the pop Top 40.

The centerpiece of *Otis Blue*, "Respect," was written in a day, arranged in twenty minutes, and recorded in one take. Redding was complaining about the way his wife was treating him after he had returned from a tour, and M.G.s drummer Al Jackson said, "What are you griping about? You're on the road all the time. All you can look for is a little respect when you come home."[13] Redding had originally written the tune as a ballad for his road manager, Speedo Sims, and Sims's band, the Singing Demons, but after Jackson's comment, he was inspired to speed up the tempo and change the words. Sims's version didn't work out, so Redding gave it a shot. The singer comes home and complains to his woman that he's giving her all his money and just wants respect (and probably sex). Sims calls out, "Hey Hey Hey!" in the background.

"Respect" made it to No. 5 R&B. A week after it was released, the Los Angeles neighborhood of Watts blew up into one of the worst riots of the decade. But the track's force as a possible civil rights protest song seemed to be overshadowed by the more dominant conflict between the man and woman at the heart of the lyrics. However, that conflict was what the *women's* liberation movement was all about, so when Atlantic's Jerry Wexler produced Aretha Franklin's version two years later (in which she adds the "R-E-S-P-E-C-T" break and "sock it to me" repetitions), Redding's words became the ultimate feminist anthem. At the Monterey Pop Festival, Redding introduced the song by smiling and saying, "This is a song that a girl took away from me, a good friend of mine, this girl she just took this song, but I'm still gonna do it anyway."

"Coming to Stax literally changed my life," Jerry Wexler said. He had been burned out recording in New York, and the Memphis studio reinvigorated him. "The idea of coming to a place [like Stax] where four guys came to work like four cabinetmakers or four plumbers and hang up their coats and start playing music in the morning, and then the beautifully crafted records came out of this! God, can I get some of this, 'cause this is the way to go."[14]

Wexler brought Wilson Pickett to Stax in May, to cowrite with Steve Cropper. As they were coming up with "In the Midnight Hour," Wexler demonstrated a new dance the kids were doing up north called the Jerk. It inspired a new beat that would come to define all the Stax records to follow, in which Stax drummers would ever so subtly delay the backbeat—the *two* and the *four.*

Stax's beat, bass sound, and cowbell made the Beatles want to come there to record, but McCartney said Stax asked for too much money and "were obviously trying to take us for a ride, because we were the Beatles."[15]

More Pickett hits, such as "634-5789 (Soulsville, U.S.A.)" were recorded that year. To the casual listener, Pickett sounded very similar to Redding, especially since they used the same band, studio, and cowriter Steve Cropper. But live, clapping and swaying with his blindingly white smile, Pickett grooved a little less frantically than Redding did.

Sam Moore and Dave Prater met on the southern gospel circuit and teamed up as Sam and Dave. Sam was the tenor (higher pitched) and Dave the baritone (lower pitched), and they'd trade lines back and forth. Wexler found them in Miami and brought them to Stax, where they were paired with the songwriting team of Isaac Hayes and David Porter. Their hit "I Take What I Want" was inspired by the name of a story in *Bronze Thrills*, a confessional magazine,[16] and took the opposite approach of most pleading soul man stances: they were just going to pick up the girl and carry her away. Next, Hayes and Porter took the melody and opening lines from the gospel song "You Don't Know What the Lord Has Done for Me" to make "You Don't Know Like I Know," about what their woman has done for them. Hayes and Porter made Sam sing at the top of his range, which angered him, because it was hard to do; but he did it.[17] It was the same trick that Holland-Dozier-Holland used to get intense performances out of Levi Stubbs.

Porter studied Motown songs such as the Temptations' October release, "Don't Look Back," written by Smokey Robinson (and perhaps inspired by Dylan's line in "She Belongs to Me"). As Rob Bowman writes in *Soulsville, U.S.A.*, "He deduced that they all had an opening that laid out the scenario, followed that with a bit of action, and then some sort of denouement. All were in the first person, and none of them ended with a complete resolution. 'All of the songs followed that formula,' smiles Porter. 'I knew right then. I said, "Hey, we're gonna be some bad dudes in this music industry." That's when the thought processes really started working and an identity started taking place.'"[18]

Sam and Dave were the template for John Belushi and Dan Aykroyd's Blues Brothers duo. Cropper, Donald "Duck" Dunn, and Stax drummer Willie Hall joined the Blues Brothers' band, and Redding's "I Can't Turn You Loose" became their theme.

*

The year was a rich one for artists unaffiliated with big labels as well. In LA, Sonny Bono hooked Lawrence Darrow Brown up with a small label called Stripe Records, which renamed him Dobie Gray, after the title character in the TV show *The Many Loves of Dobie Gillis.* Gray's clubbing anthem, "The 'In' Crowd," was quickly followed by "See You at the Go-Go," in which he is backed by the Wrecking Crew.

St. Louis's Little Milton sang of life-and-death matters in "We're Gonna Make It," which topped the R&B charts in May and became a civil rights anthem. Milton sings to his woman that they may not be able to pay the rent or the heating bill amid the roaches, and they may have to go to the welfare line so they can afford beans, but they have each other, so they're gonna make it. Milton's protagonist even considers begging with a sign reading, "Help the deaf, dumb, and blind."

Chicago's Curtis Mayfield released his most explicit civil rights single yet, with "Meeting Over Yonder." With its rousing falsettos, it was in a long tradition of "meeting songs"—anything from a church meeting to a union meeting. On the pop side, the Impressions' exquisite "You're Cheatin'" took the riff of the Four Tops' "I Can't Help Myself" and transposed it to strings. "Woman's Got Soul" is a laid-back ode in the mode of the Temptations' "The Girl's Alright with Me."

And then there was the most independent of them all—Mr. Dynamite, Soul Brother No. 1, the Hardest Working Man in Show Business, the Godfather of Soul—James Brown.

Bob Dylan and the Animals may have sung about a gambling den/brothel in their versions of "The House of the Risin'/Rising Sun," but Brown was raised in one. In his autobiography, he writes of his aunt's roadhouse, "We were just trying to survive. That's what everything that went on in that house—gambling, bootlegging, prostitution—was about: survival. Some people call it crime, I call it survival. It's the same thing goes on right today in the ghetto."[19]

Born in 1933 of African, Chinese, and Apache descent, Brown was abandoned by both parents. As a child, he shined shoes and danced for the soldiers coming through town on their way to World War II; picked cotton; boxed. In the roadhouse, the bluesman Tampa Red taught him some guitar. From the preachers, Brown learned how to drop to his knees screaming.

If he had been a superhero, his origin scene might be when three white men tried to electrocute him. He was draining a ditch for them when an electric air compressor/pump fell into the water where he was working. They told him to turn it on:

> "Nosir," I said. "I don't want to."
>
> "Goddammit, boy, I said cut it on!"
>
> I stepped in the water and turned it on. When I did, it felt like a whole herd of horses was galloping over me. I couldn't let go of the tank; the electricity froze me to it. Junior [Brown's cousin] was jumping around and yelling, "Turn it off, turn it off!" But the men stood there, grinning. Junior ran into the filling station and got the man we were working for. He came running, and when he saw what was happening he pulled the plug. I collapsed, and Junior dragged me under a tree. When I came to, I just glared at the fella who'd told me to turn on the tank, but I didn't say anything. I didn't dare. The amazing thing is that when I recovered, we went back to work. I don't know why I wasn't killed, but I decided from that day on I'd never take any mess like that again. There were still a lot of lynchings around Georgia and South Carolina in those days[20] . . . Later, I used to walk down the street with my first wife in Toccoa, Georgia, and smile a crocodile grin and just *pray* that the white man didn't come up and mess with me like he messed with them other people. "Lord, don't let it happen," I'd say. Because if it did, I knew I was going to kill the man.[21]

He did time in juvenile detention and then prison for robbery. When he got out in 1952, he joined a gospel group and then rose to be one of Little Richard's greatest rivals. By the mid-1960s he was older than most of the soul singers but determined to top them all with his leopard's shriek and unparalleled footwork. His legs were always moving, gliding, sliding, shimmying, spinning, splitting—"boogying as if on an invisible Travelator (two decades before Michael Jackson's Moonwalk)," as journalist Philip Norman put it.

Brown's forty- to fifty-person revue and all its equipment traveled in one bus and one truck, and he worked five or six nights a week.[22] He would send his interior designer ahead to prep his hotel room for him. His pompadour was done in the morning, done again before the show, and then redone after the show. He thought hair and teeth were the most important things. "If your hair ain't right, something wrong with you. Gotta keep your hair right! Understand?"[23] His stage act was worked out down to the second. The band was fined a hundred dollars for missing cues or not shining their shoes properly. (Brown used to shine shoes, after all.)

The band would stretch songs out to ten minutes while Brown danced.[24] After the gigs, Brown would herd the group into the studio to record the improvised jams they'd come up with onstage that night. Local musicians would come by to party and network. Increasingly, Brown began to direct his musicians to pause a number of times inside the song, sometimes bringing everything to a complete halt, leaving just his voice unaccompanied. Music journalist Nelson George said, "All these kinds of stops and breaks—'cause he would literally make a sound, 'Uh,' and then, you know, slip-slide over, do a spin, come back, 'Uh'—would allow him to move around the stage, still be a vocal presence but not have to overdo the singing at a time when he's also dancing."[25]

On February 1, Brown and his band stopped by Arthur Smith Studios in Charlotte, North Carolina, en route to a show, and laid down "Papa's Got a Brand New Bag" in an hour. Brown made the rhythm even more staccato. Maceo Parker led the blasting horn section. New guitarist Jimmy Nolen rang out with the funky break Prince would reference in "Kiss" twenty-one years later. Music journalist Robert Palmer wrote that Nolen "choked his guitar strings against the instrument's neck so hard that his playing began to sound like a jagged tin can being scraped with a pocketknife."[26] Richard J. Ripani wrote, "The rhythms played by the horns, guitar, bass, and drum are all different yet complementary."[27]

They did it in one take. It was supposed to be a run-through, but despite the fact that Brown felt he messed up some lyrics, he knew he had to leave it as is—because everyone in the studio was dancing to the playback. He writes in his memoir that even though he was a soul singer, it was on this night that he started going off in his own unique direction.

"I had discovered that my strength was not in the horns, it was in the rhythm. I was hearing everything, even the guitars, like they were drums. I had found out how to make it happen. On playbacks, when I saw the speakers jumping, vibrating a certain way, I knew that was it: Deliverance . . . Later on they said it was the beginning of funk."[28] He'd been around as long as

Elvis Presley, but ten years into the game, still hungry at thirty-two, he burst out with the next evolution of popular music.

The song was seven minutes long, so Brown cut off the beginning, sped it up, and split it into part one on the A side and part two on the flip. He had to hold the single back for a few months until a dispute with his record label was resolved. Then he gave it to popular New York deejay Frankie Crocker, who hated it, but the phones lit up immediately with requests that the station play it again. Released in June, it went to No. 8 in pop and No. 1 in R&B for eight weeks, and was nominated for a Grammy.

Next came a redesigned version of Brown's song "I Got You (I Feel Good)." It started as a track named "I Found You," which he'd produced for his backup singer Yvonne Fair and then remade for himself as "I Got You" a year before. He performed it on *The T.A.M.I. Show, Shindig!,* and, most incongruously, the Frankie Avalon movie *Ski Party,* literally the whitest movie imaginable. But because of his court battle with his label, a judge blocked him from releasing that version. After his "Papa's" epiphany, he cut an updated version in Miami on May 6. More saber-tooth screaming, more sax, with the most pulsating, dive-bombing bass to cut through radio to date, courtesy of Bernard Odum. Released in October, "I Got You" made it to No. 3 on the *Billboard* pop chart and was No. 1 R&B for six weeks.

Brown finally wrested complete control from his label and began buying radio stations and restaurants, cutting out the middleman and working with record stores and disc jockeys directly to promote his records and concerts.[29] At the dawn of the Black Power movement, he was the model for black self-sufficiency, flying to the White House in his own Learjet to discuss the school dropout problem with Vice President Hubert Humphrey. After Malcolm X, no other black figure had the street credibility of James Brown.

The lyrics of "New Bag" are simple—just Brown trying to get a "new breed" babe to dance with him by showing he can do the Jerk, the Fly, the Monkey, the Mashed Potato, the Twist, and the Boomerang. But the phrase "new bag" came to symbolize the new Black Power approach many activists were embracing, along with a new way to deconstruct the blues for the next generation of musicians. With the song, as music critic Dave Marsh wrote, "Brown invented the rhythmic future we live in today."[30]

The word *funk* had been around for a while. Motown's house band was named the Funk Brothers; James Jamerson carved the word "Funk" into the neck of his bass. To be in a funk was like having the blues. But the term came to mean specifically James Brown's new style.

First, he stripped out all the melody and harmony so that the whole song was just about the rhythm. Every instrument became just another form of drum/percussion—guitars, keyboards, horns bursting just single notes.

Then, increasingly, as the decade progressed, he changed the rhythm itself. R&B's backbeat was "one *two* three *four*," but Brown switched the emphasis to the first beat, "*one* two three four."

Then he overlaid different rhythms simultaneously. The drums would be hitting the *one*, but the rhythm guitar would be playing on the *two* and *four*—syncopation.

"So I was able to hold that down on one and three, which nobody could play. . . . We just groove, people couldn't even get the sticks up."[31]

For comparison, check Otis Redding's version of "New Bag." He doesn't stop and start herky-jerky the way Brown does; he just plows ahead.

Funk evolved from soul and into the main black genre of the 1970s; then birthed disco and coexisted with it before being absorbed by hip-hop. The funk/disco beat was the first modern beat, the earliest one that kids today can relate to and dance to, the main strand of hip-hop's DNA. In the early 1980s, samplers were invented, and per hip-hop pioneer Afrika Bambaataa, James Brown was the most sampled artist, his tracks becoming the foundation of countless rap tunes.[32] Brown was outraged that he wasn't being paid for all this sampling, but it made him an icon with a reach unparalleled, the godfather of soul, funk, and hip-hop.

In the Heat of the Summer

Black fury at the slow pace of change erupts on August 11.

"Burn, Baby, Burn!"
—Los Angeles deejay Magnificent Montague

There had been a riot in Harlem the previous summer, so LBJ autho-rized Project Uplift, to create thousands of summer jobs for New York black youth, and the East Coast remained peaceful. No one seemed to be worried about the other side of the continent. National Guardsman Bob Hipolito later said the Watts neighborhood of Los Angeles wasn't like "the slums and ghettos of New York. Instead, the houses were all nice and tidy. It looked pretty affluent to me."[1] It was the opposite of Harlem: one- or two-story houses on wide streets lined with palm trees.

But the Great Migration of blacks from the South had turned Watts into the most densely populated part of the country, with scant employment for young people. And of approximately five thousand Los Angeles police offi-cers, only three hundred were black.[2] To many of the Watts residents, the LAPD was like an occupying force from another country.

On Wednesday, August 11, at 7:00 p.m., much of the neighborhood was outside, since it was ninety-four degrees and most homes in the neighborhood didn't have air-conditioning. A black driver told thirty-one-year-old California Highway Patrol officer Lee W. Minikus that a man driving around seemed to be drunk. Minikus saw the suspect make a wide turn, and he pulled the car over. Inside were brothers Marquette (twenty-two years old) and Robert (twenty-four) Frye.

Marquette, the driver, failed the sobriety test and was arrested without resisting. The brothers lived two blocks away, but the officer would not let older brother Robert take the wheel, instead calling for a tow truck. Robert went to get his mother. "Everything was going fine with the arrest until his mama got there," Minikus later recalled.[3] By then, a crowd of two hundred fifty had gathered.

Mrs. Frye started yelling at her son for drinking. According to the "Report by the Governor's Commission on the Los Angeles Riots," Marquette Frye,

who until then had been peaceful and cooperative, pushed her away and moved toward the crowd, cursing and shouting at the officers that they would have to kill him to take him to jail. The patrolman pursued Marquette, and he resisted. The watching crowd became hostile, and one of the patrolmen radioed for more help. Within minutes, three more highway patrolmen arrived. Minikus and his partner were now struggling with both Frye brothers. Mrs. Frye, now belligerent, jumped on the back of one of the officers and ripped his shirt. In an attempt to subdue Marquette, one officer swung at his shoulder with a night stick, missed, and struck him on the forehead, inflicting a minor cut.[4]

A witness named Lacine Holland recalled that the police threw Marquette "in the car like a bag of laundry and kicked his feet in and slammed the door . . . A policeman walked by, and someone spit at him. The crowd got very upset. When the person spat, the policeman grabbed a woman so strong[ly] that her hair rollers fell out. She looked pregnant because of the smock, but I think she was actually a barber. She wasn't the one who spit on them."[5]

By 7:23 p.m., all three Fryes were handcuffed, and by 7:30 p.m. they were all at the police substation.

Motorcycle cops rode onto the sidewalks to disperse the crowd. Tommy Jacquette, a twenty-one-year-old who had grown up with Marquette, said, "The crowd would retreat, but then when the police left, they could come back again. About the second or third time they came back, bottles and bricks began to fly. At that point, it sort of like turned into a full-fledged confrontation with the police. A police car was left at Imperial and Avalon, and it was set on fire. The rest was history . . . I was throwing as many bricks, bottles and rocks as anybody. My focus was not on burning buildings and looting. My focus was on the police."[6]

It was just six months since the TV news had televised the police brutality of Bloody Sunday, and now the Watts rioters yelled, "Just like Selma!"

"Long live Malcolm X!"

"This is the end for you, Whitey!"[7]

By 12:20 a.m., fifty to seventy-five people, 70 percent of them kids, were throwing bricks, rocks, chunks of concrete, wood, and wine and whiskey bottles at the windshields of cars driven by whites. One man stood at an intersection and signaled which of the approaching cars should be targeted with stones. Soon, the rioters were pulling white motorists out of their cars and beating them.

Twenty-nine people were arrested that night, but the crowd continued to grow, reaching one thousand. At 2:00 a.m., the first business, a market, was looted. It took five hundred officers until 4:00 a.m. Thursday to restore order.

That day, government and police officials met with black community leaders, but the officials rejected the community leaders' proposal that white police in Watts be replaced with black officers. Meanwhile, on the street, young men on corners called at the cops, "Wait until night, whitey, we gonna get you."[8]

Lerone Bennett Jr., in *Before the Mayflower*, writes,

When the sun went down the lid came off Watts. Old people poured out of the houses and apartment buildings and joined young people, who were determined to settle old accounts with the police. Pawnshops, hardware stores and war surplus houses were raided, stripped of guns and set on fire. The streets were barricaded with bus benches, and pitched battles were fought with policemen. Some policemen were mobbed and had to club their way to safety. Taunting rebels tried to pull other police out of their squad cars; still others were lured into traps with false reports and ambushed.[9]

The family who ran Nat Diamond Empire Furniture fled just as someone lobbed a Molotov cocktail on the curb in front of their door. Stan Diamond recalled, "On television, we were seeing pictures of our store and people walking out with ranges and sofas and TVs . . . We called the police, and they said, 'Well, if you value your life, you'll stay away.' . . . Years ago, my dad was one of the few people that would give credit to a lot of the black people in the area . . . We were appreciated in the community for so many years. We didn't deserve what we got."[10]

Betty Pleasant was a high school journalist who saw people walking out of Nat's with sofas before setting the place on fire with cries of "Burn, baby, burn!" The looters continued, going to a department store, where they broke the windows and heaved goods onto the street. When the place was emptied, they threw Molotov cocktails inside and burned it down. Pleasant asked a man why he'd thrown one, and he said to "get back at whitey." Next, rioters hit a supermarket. "The problem, as far as the residents were concerned, is that they were white-owned stores selling substandard stuff for high prices . . . [the supermarket] was notorious for selling awful food. Several months before, I covered a demonstration there where people were trying to get them to sell better meat, better baked goods, better produce. They burned it to a fare-thee-well. Burned it down. I don't think they even bothered to loot that sucker."[11]

Author Bennett wrote, "Eyewitnesses reported a 'carnival gaiety' among participants."[12] Motown anthems like "Dancing in the Streets," "Nowhere to Run," and "Shotgun" blared and took on whole new meanings. For the most part, homes, schools, libraries, and churches were left alone, though one church was set aflame at 1:28 a.m. late Thursday night/early Friday morning. Rioters threw bottles and rocks at firefighters, so after 1:57 a.m., sheriff's deputies stopped allowing firemen into the area.

After a lull, the authorities left at 5 a.m., so Friday the thirteenth's looting, per *After the Mayflower,* "was leisurely and orderly. Some looters went through the stock to find the right size; others hired rental trailers to haul away refrigerators, stoves and air-conditioners . . . Unharmed, for the most part, were black-owned establishments with hand-lettered signs in the window: 'Blood

Brother,' 'Negro-owned,' 'We Own This One' . . . One band of rebels went from store to store smashing windows and taking what they wanted. All of the men were armed with pistols and rifles, and the group was led by a black woman armed with two bricks."

Deejay Magnificent Montague had been shouting his catchphrase "Burn, baby, burn!" for two years, whenever he played a record he thought was great. But as it became the slogan of the rioters, the mayor and police chief pressured the station's general manager to get Montague to stop saying it, claiming it was inciting the crowds. In his 2003 autobiography *Burn, Baby! Burn*, Montague recounted his soul-searching for the first few days of the disturbance. He didn't want to be "an Uncle Tom" and continued using the phrase. "But it was a white-owned station, managed by whites, under pressure from the government, under pressure from the FCC. I didn't own the license, and they would have put me off the air—I knew it."[13] After his Friday shift he signed off for the weekend, unsure what he would say Monday morning.

At 5 p.m. Friday, twenty-three hundred National Guardsmen arrived and started digging foxholes and setting up machine guns at intersections. Guardsman Hipolito said, "People that we talked to were innocent civilians that were just terrified. They were happy we were there."[14]

At 6:30 p.m. Friday, local resident Leon Posey and his friend Emerson Lashley went to a barbershop. While Lashley watched from the barber's chair, Posey stepped outside to see what was going on down the street. Lashley recalled, "The next thing I knew, then I heard some shots. Then I just saw him fall."[15] Posey's was the first death. A crowd had been throwing rocks at the LAPD, believing the police had orders not to shoot, and the police had panicked. Charles Fizer, a member of the R&B group the Olympics, which had recently released the original "Good Lovin'," was shot to death on his way to rehearsal. Using guns stolen from gun shops, rioters shot sniper-style at officers and helicopters.

Comedian and civil rights activist Dick Gregory wrote in his memoir *Callus on My Soul* that he

> decided to head up to Watts and try to help in any way I could. The first thing I saw when I got there was a little Black boy standing over a body, crying. As I got closer to the scene, I found out that the little boy was crying over the headless body of his father . . . I don't know exactly how

it happened, but at some point I found myself right between riot-helmeted police and a group of very angry, armed Black men. This confrontation was happening in a housing project; clearly, innocent people were going to die in this standoff if someone did not stop them. I walked between the two groups and tried to calm things down, but after I'd walked about one hundred feet, bullets started to fly. I kept walking, even when I felt a burning pain in my leg. It took me a few more minutes to realize that I had been shot. I couldn't believe it! After all the marching I'd done in the South, after all the times I'd been arrested by redneck deputies in the past four years, here I was shot by a Black man in California! But the face of that little boy crying over his father's corpse, and the faces of all the little children of Watts who were in the line of fire, overshadowed any physical pain. I kept walking. Either side could have easily killed me, but I think the brothers were as shocked as I was that I'd been hit. When I yelled at them, "Alright, goddamn it. You shot me, now go home!" they turned and started going back into their homes.[16]

At 12:55 a.m. Friday night/Saturday morning, a car drove into the Guardsmen, at which point they were instructed to load their weapons and affix bayonets to their rifles. Looters were now shot, and the cases against the Guardsmen later ruled as justifiable homicide. A hundred fire engine companies entered the area. By 3:00 a.m., the Guardsmen numbered more than three thousand, but the bedlam continued. The riot had spread to fifty square miles.

By 11:30 p.m. Saturday night, there were 13,900 National Guardsmen present. On Sunday, August 15, the Guardsmen, LAPD, and Sheriff's Office secured the area. That day, Governor Pat Brown walked through the neighborhood rubble. On Monday morning Magnificent Montague switched his catchphrase to "Have mercy, baby!"

Over the course of six days, thirty-one thousand to thirty-five thousand adults had, at some point, engaged in the riots. Thirty-four people were dead, twenty-five of them black. A thousand were hospitalized and four thousand arrested. Six hundred buildings were damaged or destroyed, the equivalent of more than forty million dollars in property damage. The governor's McCone Commission report said the causes of the riots had included high unemployment, bad schools, poverty, inequality, bad housing, housing discrimination, and "a deep and longstanding schism between a substantial portion of the Negro community and the Police Department."[17]

Watching the riot on TV, Frank Zappa wrote "Trouble Every Day," in which he sings that it happened because all Watts residents could hope for was to grow up to be a janitor. Phil Ochs sings in "In the Heat of the Summer" that anger, greed, drink, and police brutality all played a part, and the community had been down so long that they had to make somebody listen.

Watts resident Tommy Jacquette said,

People keep calling it a riot, but we call it a revolt because it had a legitimate purpose. It was a response to police brutality and social exploitation of a community and of a people . . . People said that we burned down our community. No, we didn't. We had a revolt in our community against those people who were in here trying to exploit and oppress us. We did not own this community. We did not own the businesses in this community. We did not own the majority of the housing in this community. Some people want to know if I think it was really worth it. I think any time people stand up for their rights, it's worth it.[18]

Victoria Brown Davis, an eighteen-year-old Watts resident at the time, said, "The mood of the people after the riots? Some of them were still angry, wondering what was it all for. Because now they didn't have the stores they had frequented or the facilities they needed."[19]

On his ranch in Texas, a stunned and demoralized LBJ didn't answer the phone for the first two days of the riots. "How is it possible? After all we've accomplished? How can it be?" he said to aide Joseph Califano.[20] He told another aide, "I have moved the Negro from D+ to C−. He's still nowhere. He knows it. And that's why he's out on the streets. Hell, I'd be there, too."[21] To Martin Luther King Jr., Johnson said, "There's no use giving lectures on the law as long as you've got rats eating on people's children and unemployed and no roof over their head and no job to go to and maybe with a dope needle in one side and the cancer in the other."[22]

The following September, Johnson made the U.S. Department of Housing and Urban Development (HUD) a Cabinet-level agency, but he knew his Great Society had been dealt a devastating blow. About two weeks before the riots, on July 30, he had signed the Medicare bill; and the following week, on August 6, MLK was there with him when he signed the Voting Rights Act, which finally ensured black electoral power in the South. But within the very same week that the most powerful civil rights legislation in the country's history had been enacted, the riots frightened many white voters and sent them in droves out of the Democratic Party and into the Republican camp for the next generation. The many riots that followed over the rest of the decade would transform numerous inner cities into burned-out war zones that would never recover.

16

Help!

Lennon records his theme song for the Beatles' second film, released July 29, and the group has two very different visits, with the Byrds and Elvis, in Los Angeles, on August 24 and 27.

The Beatles held their place at the "toppermost of the poppermost," as they called it, by maintaining the same staggering output they had the year before—another two albums, another movie, more huge tours, a second book of short humor pieces by Lennon. Lennon-McCartney's songwriting company, Northern Songs, was floated on the British stock exchange. "Let's write a swimming pool today," they'd say.[1] "I always liken songwriting to a conjurer pulling a rabbit out of a hat," McCartney later commented. "We'd be amazed to see what kind of rabbit we'd pulled out that day."[2] Their self-titled Saturday morning cartoon debuted, and while the Beatles initially detested it—Starr was painted as a big-nosed buffoon—it would drum their music into the heads of subsequent generations through syndication over the next couple of decades.

On their tours, police barricades had to be set up at the hotels the band was staying in, to keep the throngs at bay; some kids tried to climb the sides of the buildings. The hotels were besieged with fan mail; sheets and doorknobs were stolen as mementos. Evenings might start with a helicopter ride descending into a sea of exploding flashbulbs. After the concert was the daily escape in delivery truck, armored car, or ambulance. Then, after the flight to a new city, perhaps they'd take it easy by playing Monopoly or watching TV. Or maybe it'd be time for "Satyricon," as Lennon would later dub their escapades, referencing Fellini's surreal film about debauchery in ancient Rome.[3]

A Hard Day's Night contains just the barest hint of what went on backstage. Lennon offhandedly sniffs a bottle of Coca-Cola on a train, a gag presumably no Beatlemaniac of the era understood. When McCartney berates Starr for allowing his grandfather to go to a gambling casino, he rues, "He's probably in the middle of some orgy by now!" to which the other Beatles cry, "Orgy? Oh yeah!" and run out the door. In real life, Ronnie Spector, lead singer of the Ronettes, relates in her memoir the night Lennon brought her into the back of the group's hotel suite, where a crowd had gathered around a member of the Beatles' entourage having sex with a woman on a bed. "This was 1964, when you couldn't even get films with that stuff in them—and here was an actual girl having naked sex in every different position!" When the innocent Spector gasped "Oh my God" in a mixture of disgust and fascination, Lennon quickly escorted her out.[4] Whenever reporters witnessed improprieties, the Beatles kept them quiet by giving them exclusives—or free hookers, as they did one time in Atlantic City.[5]

But as success became commonplace it lost its thrill, leaving just the exhaustion of relentless touring and record deadlines. Fame also prompted the return of Lennon's father, who had disappeared on him when he was five. Freddie Lennon looked a lot like his son, if his son had lived sixty years with one foot in the gutter and had lost his teeth. On June 24, Lennon released his second volume of writing, *A Spaniard in the Works*, which includes the poem "Our Dad," in which Lennon throws his father out, calling him a clown and a ponce, and his father in turn calls John's mother a whore. On December 31, Freddie tried to make some money by issuing a single on Pye Records (the Kinks' label) called "That's My Life (My Love and My Home)," perhaps in response to Lennon's "In My Life." Freddie's B side seemed to be a reprimand to his boy: "The Next Time You Feel Important" asserted that kings come and go and glory fades away, but only God remains.

Beyond his father, the daily crush of people Lennon had to navigate was maddening, from government officials who threatened to leak Beatles scandals to the press unless they met with the officials' kids, to darker sycophants lurking in the wings. Richard Lester recalled, "I saw it happen to Paul McCartney once—the most beautiful girl I've ever seen, trying to persuade him to take heroin. It was an absolutely chilling exercise in controlled evil."[6]

Former groupie-author Pamela Des Barres writes in her memoir about seeing Lennon that year, when she was a teenage Beatlemaniac. "We had to get past the Beatle Barricade and onto someone's personal property so we could prowl the Bel Air [Calif.] hills and FIND THE BEATLES!!! . . . On the way down the hill, a limousine passed by, and I saw John Lennon for an instant. He was wearing his John Lennon cap, and he looked right at me. If I close my eyes this minute, I can still see the look he had on his face. It was full of sorrow and contempt. The other girls were pooling tears in their eyes and didn't notice, but that look on John Lennon's face stopped my heart, and I never said a word . . . The look on John's face made me grow up a little, and I worked hard in school and decided to get a part-time job."[7]

In the Beatles' second movie, the sacrificial ring from a bloodthirsty cult lands on Starr's finger, and the sect resolves to kill him. Most of the screen time features the boys trying to escape the villains in what was intended as a parody of the James Bond series. Originally the film was to be entitled *Eight Arms to Hold You*, a pun both on the number of Beatle arms and the arms of Kali, the Hindu goddess. But while many Beatlemaniacs may not have minded being held by all four Beatles simultaneously, some wise soul came up with the less creepy title *Help!* The release of "Help Me, Rhonda" on March 8 may have subliminally contributed. Another "help" song, "I Can't Help Myself (Sugar Pie, Honey Bunch)," was released on April 23.

John banged out the theme in one night that April, just as he had written the theme to *A Hard Day's Night* in one evening a year earlier. At the time, Lennon didn't think much about it. But a comparison of the two tracks shows him feeling galvanized in the earlier song and desperate twelve months later.

Journalist Maureen Cleave, with whom Lennon was having an affair, asked him why he never used words with more than one syllable, so he included "insecure," "independence," "self-assured," and "appreciate" in the lyrics.[8] She still wasn't impressed, which was probably one reason he liked her.

Lennon sings that when he was younger he never needed help, but now he's changed his mind and opened up the doors. The part about being younger may have been inspired by the chorus of Dylan's "My Back Pages."

And as for the "doors," they could have been inspired by Aldous Huxley's 1954 book *The Doors of Perception*, about his experiences with hallucinogens. The book takes its title from the line by poet William Blake "If the doors of perception were cleansed, everything would appear to man as it is, infinite. For man has closed himself up, till he sees all things through narrow chinks of his cavern." Lennon wrote the song two weeks after his first acid trip. Perhaps when Lennon and Harrison recounted their LSD experience to friends, someone told them to check out Huxley's book. While psychedelics and the literature about them were still largely unknown, McCartney's good friend Barry Miles worked at Better Books, one of London's countercultural hubs, where Ginsberg read that spring.

The group recorded "Help!" in a four-hour session at Abbey Road on April 13. The other Beatles encouraged Lennon to speed it up to make it more pop. McCartney added a countermelody; he and Harrison sang the lyrics a half beat before Lennon did. On the twelfth take, Harrison added the lead guitar arpeggios, and then overdubbed the descending guitar notes in the vein of Nashville's Chet Atkins.[9]

Rolling Stone later rated it the twenty-ninth greatest song of all time. It was a precursor to the stark honesty of Lennon's solo album *Plastic Ono Band*. When Lennon recorded that album, in the midst of undergoing "primal scream" psychotherapy, he remarked that the lyric of "Help!" was still "as good now as it was then. It is no different, and it makes me feel secure to know that I was aware of myself then."[10]

The genius of the group was that, at the height of Beatlemania, when they were the most successful band on earth, they let us in on their insecurities. While the lyrics were simple, they were no longer adolescent. Their music was now adult; they acted their age.

The song was so strangely confessional for its time that it's surprising that it became one of the top five worldwide best sellers of the year. But it resonated because it mirrored the insecurity of the culture at large. To parents who had survived the Depression and World War II, America's rampant consumerism represented security, but it left many of their children feeling empty as they began to question age-old assumptions about sex, patriotism, race, religion, and drugs. Soon the baby boomers would begin seeking out new cures to their anomie. "Help!" served as both Lennon's and his generation's theme song as they journeyed through the many self-help options the new global village offered, from pharmacology to psychotherapy, religion, meditation, and activist politics.

"Help!" resonated, too, because of the camaraderie implicit in the group's performance. Wrote critic Dave Marsh, Lennon "sounds triumphant, because he's found a group of kindred spirits who are offering the very spiritual assistance and emotional support for which he's begging. Paul's echoing harmonies, Ringo's jaunty drums, the boom of George's guitar speak to the heart of Lennon's passion, and though they can't cure the wound, at least they add a note of reassurance that he's not alone with his pain. You can make some great music on that basis. And they did."[11]

***Help!* cost twice** as much to make as *A Hard Day's Night*, and critics had high hopes for the film. *Night* had bowled them over, and the movie that director Richard Lester made afterward had just won the Cannes Palme d'Or, the grand prize at the world's premiere film festival.

The Knack . . . And How to Get It (released June 3) was far more honest about Beatlemania than *A Hard Day's Night* could afford to be, since the Beatles movies needed to uphold a wholesome image for the group's young fans. *The Knack*, on the other hand, opens with a neurotic nerd (Michael Crawford) watching in awe as an endless stream of women wait to enter the apartment of the domineering rock star (Ray Brooks) who lives upstairs. Whenever a young lady leaves the rocker's room after a tryst, he solemnly places a medallion around her neck and gives her a stamp for her stamp book, Lester's metaphor for how "bagging a Beatle" was the ultimate validation for the proto-groupies.

The nerd asks the rock star to teach him "the knack" of seducing women—until they become rivals for the affections of a young lady (Rita Tushingham) just arrived in London from the hinterlands. The film was Lester's take on the sexual revolution, symbolized by a surreal set piece in which the characters push a giant iron bed through the city while a Greek chorus of elders voices its disapproval.

With stunning black-and-white photography by David Watkins (who would go on to shoot *Help!* in color), haunting score by Bond composer John Barry, silent gags and frenzied Pop Art editing, it was a hit with the *New York Times*, *Newsweek*, and most reviewers, though the rock star's misogyny dates it today for some. Ironically, it was based on a play written by a woman, Ann Jellicoe.

Unfortunately, such zest was not to be found in *Help!* because, as Lennon later explained, "We were smoking marijuana for breakfast . . . and nobody could communicate with us, because we were just all glazed eyes, giggling all the time. In our own world."[12]

The screenplay that Charles Wood and Marc Behm came up with was not as witty as *A Hard Day's Night*'s Oscar-nominated script by Alun Owen, and as weed replaced speed, the boys were not inspired to match the barrage of one-liners and asides that delighted in the first film. Now they were bored with the filming process, running off to sneak hits as often as possible. In fact, *Help!*'s quirky humor often arises from how the deadpan foursome can't even be bothered to act. So while Bob Dylan's gift of pot revolutionized the group's music, it seems that pills were better for making classic films.

Richard Lester was thus forced to pad out the movie with the antics of other comedians. As Lennon commented, "It was like putting clams in a movie about frogs."[13] There are nice touches, such as the Beatles' fantasy pad, in which each Beatle has his own section of a large one-room apartment in a different color. Harrison's has grass on the floor, which a landscaper mows with a pair of chattering teeth. Starr's has vending machines. Lennon's bed is one of the more interesting ones in cinema: a sunken pit in the floor with steps leading down and a mini bookcase. The film inspired *The Monkees* TV show, which would later be credited with making hippies safe to parents. Lester's zany Technicolor style was also emulated by the TV show *Batman* and the next generation of advertising.

A Hard Day's Night's subtext is the generation gap, with McCartney's jealous grandfather trying to sabotage the group. The second film (however unconsciously) heralds the hippies' immersion in Indian culture. On the surface, its racist caricatures of Hindus as human sacrificers is pure xenophobia. The leader of the cult is even played by a white Australian, Leo McKern. But, as noted, it is the shoot that whetted Harrison's interest in the sitar. And while the group filmed in the Bahamas, on Harrison's twenty-second birthday a local swami named Vishnudevananda appeared and gave the Beatles copies of *The Complete Illustrated Book of Yoga*. Perhaps the yogi saw the giant statue of the Hindu goddess Kali rising out of the ocean while all the characters fought on the beach in the ridiculous climax.

The yoga book would later inform the lyrics of Harrison's "Within You, Without You": "When man realizes that nothing is outside and everything is within himself, then he will be able to transcend the limitations of space and time. In Yoga, this stage is known as self-realization or God realization, where there is no difference between the knower, knowledge, and the known; and where the past and the future merge with the present—the eternal 'now' of the Hindus."[14] Eastern philosophy would become the tool Harrison relied on to help him cope with Beatlemania.

✳

After the Byrds' jaunt through the states in the second half of July, they flew to England for a string of dates on August 3–21. One of the Beatles' old publicists, Derek Taylor, had taken on the job of breaking the Byrds in the United Kingdom after "Mr. Tambourine Man" made No. 1 there. He almost destroyed them when he dared hype them as "America's answer to the Beatles," because the Byrds were not tight musically and could not withstand the scrutiny; Michael Clarke had been drumming for only a year. They got a bad reception, but the Beatles befriended them.

A year before, Roger McGuinn had been inspired to start playing Beatles songs to the folkies because he believed the Fabs were consciously "doing their version of the '50s rock 'n' roll rockabilly sound and the folk thing combined," using folk harmonies and chord changes. But now he learned that "They didn't know how to fingerpick and they didn't play banjos or mandolins or anything. They weren't coming from where I was coming from at all, which I'd given them credit for. I thought they knew all that stuff and were just being real slick about it. But it was just kind of an accident. It was a great accident."[15]

On August 13 the Beatles flew to New York for their third American tour. They taped their final *Ed Sullivan* appearance on the fourteenth, and then played the first rock concert in a sports arena, on Sunday, August 15, at Shea Stadium in Queens, home to the New York Mets baseball team and the New York Jets football team.

Opening for them were soul saxophonist great King Curtis (who would play on Lennon's solo *Imagine* album), Motown singer Brenda Holloway (who Dick Clark claimed had the most fantastic voice he'd ever heard),[16] Cannibal and the Headhunters (an East LA Mexican American band whose hit "Land of a Thousand Dances" was later covered by Wilson Pickett), and the instrumental group Sounds Incorporated, whom the Beatles knew from their Hamburg days.

The Beatles kicked in with "Twist and Shout," and for the length of their twelve-song, thirty-minute set were unable to hear one another over the audience pandemonium, despite the hundred-watt amplifiers Vox had designed for the event. "Can you hear me?" Lennon called before "Dizzy Miss Lizzy." "Hello?!"

McCartney bounced up and down even more than Herman's Hermits' Peter Noone for "Can't Buy Me Love," and shrieked "I'm Down," while Lennon cracked Harrison up by playing the keyboard with his elbow. Jagger, Richards, and their manager, Oldham, watched from behind the dugout as guards chased fans across the field. Also in attendance were McCartney's and Starr's future spouses, Linda Eastman and Barbara Bach, before they knew them. The sound quality was poor, so for the subsequent concert film, the Beatles secretly played some of the numbers live in the studio to overdub onto the footage.

The $304,000 gross was the biggest in music history up until that time. The Beatles took $160,000 for themselves. The show's sold out crowd of 55,600 would stand as the concert attendance record for eight years. Even at the end of the decade, the Stones and Led Zeppelin would play to arenas with only 18,000 capacities. It wouldn't be until 1973 that Zeppelin broke the Beatles' record, at Tampa Stadium with 56,800, at which point the era of stadium rock began. The promoter who organized the Shea event, Sid Bernstein, later claimed that Lennon told him in the 1970s, misty-eyed, "Sid, at Shea Stadium, I saw the top of the mountain." Whether Lennon really did say that, it *was* the peak for the Beatles' live career. Next year, when they returned to Shea on August 23, eleven thousand seats went unsold, perhaps due to the backlash over Lennon's comment that the Beatles were "more popular than Jesus." After 1966 the Beatles would cease touring permanently.

The Beatles had a five-day break in the Byrds' hometown Los Angeles on August 23–27, during which time they rented Zsa Zsa Gabor's home at 2850 Benedict Canyon Drive, a horseshoe-shaped mansion on stilts off Mulholland Drive. Joan Baez and the actresses Eleanor Bron (*Help!*) and Peggy Lipton (later on the TV show *The Mod Squad*) hung out there. Women tried to climb up the canyon to get in. When some fans rented a helicopter and circled above at three hundred feet, Beatles manager Epstein requested a no-fly zone over the house.

Harrison recalled, "John and I had decided that Paul and Ringo had to have acid, because we couldn't relate to them any more . . . It was such a mammoth experience that it was unexplainable: it was something that had to be experienced, because you could spend the rest of your life trying to explain what it made you feel and think."[17]

In New York they had scored some acid-dosed sugar cubes wrapped in tinfoil. On August 24, Starr did one with Lennon and Harrison, but McCartney declined. Lennon said, "Paul felt very out of it 'cause we were all a bit cruel. It's like, 'We're taking it and you're not.' . . . I think George was pretty heavy on it. We were probably both the most cracked. I think Paul's a bit more stable than George and I. I don't know about straight. Stable."[18]

The Byrds had just returned to town, so the Beatles invited them over to drop acid with them; McGuinn and Crosby were the only ones who came. McGuinn said, "It was like going to see the president or something. You had to go down in a limousine, and there were screaming girls on either side. Then the guards would open the gates, and you'd drive in to the estate and they'd close again, and everybody would be pressed up against the fence."

Girls who had managed to sneak in hid under tables and in the cupboards. One climbed in through the window while a tripping Starr tried to shoot pool with the wrong end of his pool cue. "Wrong end? So what fuckin' difference does it make?"[19]

The Beatles and the Byrds went into the master bathroom and sat in a large, sunken tub, passing around a guitar and playing each other their favorite songs. Both Lennon and McGuire picked "Be-Bop-a-Lula" as their favorite '50s rocker.[20] Crosby talked about how he had watched some of Indian virtuoso Ravi Shankar's sessions at World Pacific Studios, where the Byrds' manager had been an engineer.

Then actor Peter Fonda, future star of the LSD movie *The Trip*, arrived. McGuinn and Fonda had become friends three years earlier when McGuinn was playing guitar for Bobby Darin in Vegas. It was trendy to talk about death on acid because of Leary's conflation of the drug with the Tibetan Book of the Dead, so Fonda mentioned, "I know what it's like to be dead." On his eleventh birthday he'd shot himself in the stomach but survived; a year earlier his mother had killed herself by slitting her own throat in a sanitarium.

Lennon recalled, "We didn't want to hear about that! We were on an acid trip, and the sun was shining and the girls were dancing (some from *Playboy*, I believe), and the whole thing was really beautiful and 'Sixties.' And this guy—who I really didn't know, he hadn't made *Easy Rider* or anything—kept coming over, wearing shades, saying 'I know what it's like to be dead,' and we kept leaving him because he was so boring. It was scary, when you're flying high: 'Don't tell me about it. I don't want to know what it's like to be dead!' "[21]

Harrison said, "He was showing us his bullet wound. He was very uncool."[22]

On a cheerier note, McGuinn told Harrison how he discovered the Byrds' signature twelve-string sound after seeing Harrison play the Rickenbacker in *A Hard Day's Night*. Harrison was touched by the respect accorded to him by the LA group, as he was used to being in his bandmates' shadow. The jangle pop style that the Beatles and the Byrds were developing together would be an integral part of the Beatles' next album.

On the Beatles' first *Ed Sullivan* appearance, Sullivan read a telegram that Colonel Tom Parker, Elvis's manager, had sent in Presley's name congratulating them. But Presley put off meeting them for over a year. McCartney said, "We didn't feel brushed off; we felt we deserved to be brushed off. After all, he was Elvis, and who were we to dare to want to meet him?"[23]

Actually, Presley didn't want to meet them because he knew he was in a slump. Though not even he realized it, he produced an album or two worth of good-to-classic songs every year through 1964. The problem was, the great songs were mixed in with crappy throwaways from his movies and slapped together with no rhyme or reason on weak soundtrack albums. The Beatles and Dylan were just now bringing cohesion to the album as an art form; Presley's discography was the epitome of what *not* to do.

Meanwhile, when he tried acting in an ambitious movie such as *Wild in the Country*, the film didn't do well at the box office, whereas mindless fluff movies made him 1964's highest-paid actor in Hollywood. So he tuned out on uppers and downers and phoned it in for three flicks a year. He became more interested in buying motorcycles or horses to ride with his entourage, the Memphis Mafia. Sometimes he'd send them out to buy every flashbulb in town so they could dump them into the swimming pool and shoot them with BB guns.

The Beatles pose as a marching band while filming their second feature film, *Help!*, in Obertauern, Austria, in March. *From left:* Paul McCartney, Ringo Starr, John Lennon, and George Harrison. *(Courtesy of United Artists/Photofest)*

Bob Dylan and Joan Baez in Embankment Gardens, London, on April 27. Dylan's tour of England would be captured in the documentary feature *Don't Look Back*, directed by D. A. Pennebaker. *(Courtesy of Bettmann/Corbis/Associated Press)*

James Brown warms up for the Los Angeles syndicated TV show *Shivaree* on June 26, three weeks after the release of "Papa's Got a Brand New Bag." *(Courtesy of Photofest)*

Andy Warhol, taboo-bursting artist, filmmaker, and manager of the Velvet Underground, with model/actress Edie Sedgwick, muse to Bob Dylan and Lou Reed. *(Courtesy of the Associated Press)*

Stevie Wonder (*foreground*) with the Motown musicians known as the Funk Brothers: producer Clarence Paul (*behind Wonder*); *back row, from left:* Joe Hunter on piano, Larry Veeder on guitar, Benny Benjamin on drums, James Jamerson on bass, and Mike Terry on sax. *(Courtesy of Photofest)*

Folk singer–turned-pop star Marianne Faithfull enjoyed a string of Top 10 U.K. hits throughout the year and was perhaps one of the inspirations for Dylan's "Like a Rolling Stone." *(Courtesy of London Records/Photofest)*

The Rolling Stones perform in Münster, Germany, on September 11, four days after recording "Get Off My Cloud" in Hollywood. *From left:* Charlie Watts on drums, Brian Jones on guitar, and Mick Jagger. *(Courtesy of the Associated Press/Schroer)*

A bondsman and a U.S. Marshal escort Johnny Cash from El Paso County Jail to the federal courthouse on October 5 after his arrest for crossing the Mexican border with 688 Dexedrine speed capsules and 475 Equanil downers. *(Courtesy of the Associated Press)*

The Grateful Dead (at the time named the Warlocks) imitate the Beatles' *Help!* album cover, wearing Beatle boots. On December 4 they changed their name when they began performing for Ken Kesey's Acid Tests. *From left:* Jerry Garcia, Bill Kreutzmann, Bob Weir, Phil Lesh, and Ron "Pigpen" McKernan. *(Courtesy of Photofest)*

The Byrds in New York for their December 12 appearance on *The Ed Sullivan Show. From left:* Chris Hillman, David Crosby, Jim McGuinn, Michael Clarke, and Gene Clark. *(Courtesy of Photofest)*

He finally let the Colonel talk him into inviting the Fab Four to his mansion in Bel Air on August 27. It's interesting to note the protocol of Beatle meetings in '64 and '65: Dylan and the Byrds came to them, but the Beatles called on Presley.

En route, the Beatles got high in the backseat of their limo and started cracking up. At 11:00 p.m., they pulled up past the fans gathered at Presley's gates and parked next to the King's Rollses and Cadillacs. One of them reminded the others that they were going to see Presley, and they all piled out of the car laughing, trying to pretend they weren't baked.

Presley was just back in the States from shooting *Paradise, Hawaiian Style*, tan in his red shirt, black windbreaker, and gray pants. "Oh, there you are!" Lennon joked nonchalantly. Presley smiled and shook everyone's hand and led them into his huge living room with thick white carpet, two pool tables, and a bar.

Lennon and McCartney sat on Presley's right on a crescent white couch, Harrison and Starr on his left. The managers and the Memphis Mafia watched in the background. The jukebox played "Mohair Sam," Charlie Rich's Elvis-style hit, along with singles by Cilla Black, Muddy Waters, Presley, and the Beatles. Elvis played along on bass, the amplifier next to his huge color TV. Presley had the first remote control the Beatles had ever seen.

Lennon said in his Peter Sellers/Dr. Strangelove voice, "Zo, zis ees the famous Elvis." Later, he admitted he was nervous as hell, as were all the Beatles, staring in silence at the man who'd inspired them to become musicians. Ten years before, after Presley was discovered by Howlin' Wolf's producer Sam Phillips, his "morally insane" pelvis had hammered away at puritan repression. When Lennon first heard "Heartbreak Hotel," he didn't understand the words, but it made his hair stand on end. Harrison was thirteen and riding his bike when he heard the song come out a window, giving him a "rock and roll epiphany."[24] For McCartney, Presley was the first guy who not only sounded rock and roll but also looked it.

Finally, Presley said, "If you damn guys are gonna sit here and stare at me all night I'm gonna go to bed."

That broke the ice, and Presley asked them about the recent Shea Stadium concert and how many hits they'd written. Lennon asked him if he was working on his next film, and Presley said, "Ah sure am. Ah play a country boy with a guitar who meets a few gals along the way, and ah sing a few songs."[25] The Beatles glanced at each other, and then Presley and his manager cackled and explained that any time they varied from that formula they lost money.

But Lennon started into rough waters when he asked why Presley didn't do rock anymore, like his old Sun records. Presley said his movie schedule was to blame, but that maybe he'd do another one.

"Then we'll buy it," Lennon said tactlessly.

Lennon noticed a lamp from last year's presidential election that read "All the Way with LBJ." According to journalist Chris Hutchins, who was there as a friend of both Presley's and the Beatles', Lennon started making some antiwar comments that annoyed Presley, who had served in the army.

Priscilla came in, and Lennon started making eyes at her. Hutchins wrote, "Lennon was distracted by Priscilla's shapely legs as she walked to the bar where I was savoring an orange juice. As far as I can recall, nobody drank alcohol that night. 'You've made a big hit with Mr. Lennon,' I told her. 'Then that's his first mistake,' she replied. 'Elvis is very jealous.'"[26]

Presley quickly had his Mafia escort Priscilla out. McCartney later said, "I can't blame him, although I don't think any of us would have made a pass at her. That was definitely not on—Elvis' wife, you know! That was unthinkable."[27]

Still, it was starting to seem like Lennon had some sort of Oedipal desire to kill (or at least seriously piss off) his rock-and-roll father. Always the diplomat, McCartney asked if they could play some music. Presley produced guitars for a jam session, apologizing to Starr for not having drums. Starr beat on the furniture as the group sang "I Feel Fine."

"Coming along quite promising on bass, Elvis," McCartney said.

Starr played pool with some of the Mafia. The Colonel and Beatles manager Epstein gambled at the roulette table. Harrison tried to find out if anyone had pot, but the Mafia were amphetamine-and-booze southerners, though Presley's New Age hairdresser, Larry Geller, may have shared a joint with him out by the pool.

There was some talk of the Beatles singing in Presley's upcoming movie *Paradise, Hawaiian Style.* Then the group invited Presley to visit them the next day. Presley was politely noncommittal. On his way out, Lennon cried, "Long live the King!"[28] The artists' respective fans massed outside the gates chanted, "Elvis!" and "Beatles!" at each other.

Presley didn't show up at the Beatles' place the next day, though some of his entourage visited. Perhaps regretting his gracelessness of the day before,

Lennon asked them to tell Presley that "if it hadn't been for him, I would have been nothing."[29] He said Presley was the only American they had wanted to meet. "Not that he wanted to meet us!"[30] Lennon said Frank Sinatra and Dean Martin only tried to hang out with them because of the women.

When the Mafia relayed Lennon's message to Presley, he just smiled. Presley was notably more welcoming when singer Tom Jones visited him on his movie set. Presley told Jones he knew every song on Jones's album and even sang them to him.[31]

Ironically, the Beatles and Presley shared more interests than they knew. Urged on by his hairdresser Geller, for the last year and a half Presley had been devouring a whole raft of spiritual books, including the Tibetan Book of the Dead, *Cosmic Consciousness, The Infinite Way, Beyond the Himalayas, The Life and Teachings of the Masters of the Far East, The Prophet*, and *The Impersonal Life*.

On March 5, driving back from Graceland to Hollywood to shoot possibly his worst movie, *Harum Scarum,* he expressed frustration to Geller in Amarillo that he had been studying for a year but had not had a religious experience. Then, outside Flagstaff, as Presley stared out the windshield in awe, he saw the clouds form the face of Soviet dictator Joseph Stalin. "Why Stalin? Why Stalin? Of all people, what's he doing up there?"

He pulled the car over and ran out into the desert, followed by Geller. When Geller caught up to him, Presley was crying, "It's God!" He hugged Geller joyfully. "I saw the face of Stalin and I thought to myself, Why Stalin? Is it a projection of something that's inside of me? Is God trying to show me what he thinks of me? And then it happened! The face of Stalin turned right into the face of Jesus, and he smiled at me, and every fiber of my being felt it."[32]

One of Presley's favorite books was Paramahansa Yogananda's *Autobiography of a Yogi*, and during the filming of *Harum Scarum*, on March 17, he went to the Pacific Palisades, California, ashram of one of Yogananda's disciples, Sri Daya Mata (originally Faye Wright). He joined her Self-Realization Fellowship and would often go there to read and meditate.

He also read *The Doors of Perception* and made all the Memphis Mafia read Leary's *Psychedelic Experience*. He tried LSD on December 28, with Priscilla, Geller, and entourage member Jerry Schilling. At one point, Priscilla sobbed and told Presley he didn't really love her. But most of the trip was beautiful, as they looked at his tropical fish and the drops of dew on the lawn, though they never tried it again.[33]

Presley's Memphis Mafia did not respect his spiritual studies, and behind his back called Geller "the swami" or "Rasputin." Presley tried to get Priscilla to read *Autobiography of a Yogi*, but it put her to sleep, in contrast to Harrison's future wife, Pattie Boyd, who took him to his first Maharishi lecture. As Harrison delved deeper into Indian mysticism, his band members supported his exploration and eventually joined him on his trek to India three years later. It's sad to think of how much more Presley and the Beatles could have had to talk about, had they only known they were both interested in spirituality.

In fact, it was a gospel song that kept Presley at the top of the charts that year. His five-year-old cover of "Crying in the Chapel" was released as a single for Easter and surprised everyone by becoming a No. 3 hit in the United States and No. 1 in the United Kingdom. Presley began to think it was time to start seriously recording again. Next spring he would record the classic gospel album *How Great Thou Art* and, during the sessions, cover Dylan's "Tomorrow Is a Long Time." With Dylan covers being all the rage, it could have been the most notable one of all; Dylan later called it "the one recording I treasure most."[34] Naturally, Presley's clueless manager buried it on a lame soundtrack album. Still, the King was on his way back.

IV *

AUTUMN

Next Day You Turn Around
and It's Fall

Frank Sinatra begins his comeback with *September of My Years*, the
Beatles' "Yesterday" hits No. 1 on October 9 and becomes the most covered song of the decade, and the Rolling Stones rush to record their
own song with strings on October 26.

*

Frank Sinatra, a.k.a. the Chairman of the Board, was trying to figure
out how to push his way back into "Beatle land." At the moment, he was
firmly ensconced in easy listening, which was as much its own alternate di-
mension as country.

In the 1950s, many radio stations wanted to play popular songs without
the rock beat. *Billboard* started listing such songs on a chart separate from
pop, R&B, and country. It changed the name a number of times (pop-standard
singles, middle-road singles) until finally settling on easy listening in 1965.[1]
It became the most popular FM format nationwide (rebranded "adult contemporary" in 1979). Like Muzak and elevator music, it was safe for doctors'
offices and supermarkets, generally the modern version of big band music.

Nat King Cole, who passed away in February, was one of easy listening's
mainstays. Sinatra gave Tony Bennett a huge boost when he told *Life* that

Bennett was the best singer in the business. Bennett's version of "The Shadow of Your Smile" beat out "Yesterday," Sinatra's "September of My Years," and "King of the Road" for Grammy Song of the Year. The song was the theme to Liz Taylor's movie about Big Sur bohemians, called *The Sandpiper*, and won the Oscar for Best Original Song as well. Everybody in easy listening covered it: Barbra Streisand, Shirley "Goldfinger" Bassey, Perry Como, Andy Williams (who had the top-rated NBC variety show), Herb Alpert, Trini Lopez, Johnny Mathis, Bobby Darin, and even Marvin Gaye, his desire to be an old-school crooner still going strong.

The Righteous Brothers and Phil Spector had returned in July with "Unchained Melody." Another group of "brothers" with resounding baritones—the Walker Brothers—scored in August with "Make It Easy on Yourself," a track written by the easy listening kings Burt Bacharach (music) and Hal David (lyrics), a powerhouse team from the Brill Building. Other Bacharach-David hits included Jackie DeShannon's "What the World Needs Now Is Love," Manfred Mann's "My Little Red Book" (covered by Love), and Tom Jones's "It's Not Unusual" and "What's New Pussycat?"

The most indelible easy listening *image* of the year was the album jacket of Herb Alpert and the Tijuana Brass's *Whipped Cream & Other Delights*, featuring model Dolores Erickson. She was three months pregnant when they photographed her, and was no doubt responsible for many of the six million copies sold. (She was actually covered in *shaving* cream, because it didn't melt under the lights.) "Sorry, we can't play the cover for you," Alpert would tell audiences. The album's instrumental version of "A Taste of Honey" made it to No. 7 and won four Grammys, including Record of the Year (which was different from Song of the Year).

Sinatra's Rat Pack itself was the embodiment of the old-school image of masculinity that the "Beatle land" proto-hippies were upending: in tuxedos, with Jack on the rocks in hand instead of a joint, hair short and neatly coiffed. Sinatra and Dean Martin sang in the bel canto ("fine singing") style of eighteenth- to nineteenth-century Italy—conversational, relaxed, with clear diction. (In marked contrast to the likes of Mick Jagger, who followed Fats Domino's dictum that one shouldn't sing the words too clearly.) The Pack was perhaps the last hurrah of vaudeville, with Martin prat-falling in mock drunkenness and Sammy Davis Jr. defying gravity as perhaps the greatest tap dancer on earth.

But in one way they were more progressive than the rockers, the first interracial supergroup. Italians had long suffered their own version of discrimination in the United States, so Sinatra would insist that Davis be allowed to stay in the hotels they played, and he and Martin would accompany Davis to MLK rallies.

That didn't stop them from joking about race. Onstage at the Sands Hotel in Vegas, Martin would pick Davis up and say, "I'd like to thank the NAACP for this wonderful trophy."[2] Sinatra would throw the tablecloth from a dinner tray over Davis with "Put on your sheets and we'll start the meeting," prompting Davis to cry, "Oh come on!" and storm offstage in mock-disgust. When Davis danced, they'd say, "I think it's the African Queen, folks."[3]

"Did you ever see a Jew Jitsu?" Sinatra asked Davis, who had converted to Judaism.

"Did you ever see a WOPsicle?" Davis shot back.

"Shut up, Sam, and sit in the back of the bus!"

"Jewish people don't sit in the back of the bus."

"Jewish people own the bus!"[4]

"He sho' sing good for a white fella, don't he?"

When they weren't sticking tongues out at one another, Davis would try to grab Martin's ass. When Martin rebuffed him, Davis pouted and said, "You weren't like that last night."[5]

You could almost make the case that Sinatra enabled the creation of Medicare and Medicaid. When Rat Pack member Peter Lawford's brother-in-law Jack Kennedy was running for president, Sinatra got his mobster friend Paul "Skinny" D'Amato (a.k.a. Mr. Atlantic City) to make sure Kennedy won the West Virginia primary. Kennedy's father, Joe, then asked Sinatra to ask the head of the Chicago Mafia, Sam Giancana, to help deliver Illinois in the presidential election.[6] (Democratic mayor Richard Daley helped rig it as well.) Kennedy beat Nixon by the smallest margin in history; his assassination gave Johnson the opportunity to push through his social programs.

The Rat Pack gave its last show for twenty-three years on June 20. It was broadcast live to movie houses across the country, a fund-raiser for a St. Louis halfway house for ex-convicts, the favorite charity of Sinatra's good friend Teamster vice president Harold Gibbons. The Pack had run its course after countless "summits" at Vegas casinos and in movies such as *Ocean's Eleven*, *Sergeants 3*, and *Robin and the 7 Hoods*.

Martin had parlayed a number of big hits the previous year into the new *Dean Martin Show*, which began its nine-year run on NBC in September.

But though Sinatra had released two essential singles last year, "My Kind of Town" and "Softly, as I Leave You," he hadn't managed a Top 20 pop hit since "Witchcraft" a decade before, except for "Me and My Shadow," with Sammy, in 1962. His song with Tommy Dorsey's band, "I'll Never Smile Again," had been the very first No. 1 on the first *Billboard* chart back in 1940. He'd earned seven more since, and wanted another. But he was turning fifty in December. Was it too late?

Sinatra had already been washed up once, in the 1950s, and had recreated himself as a serious actor with *From Here to Eternity*. He got serious again and looked mortality in the face with one of his strongest albums, *September of My Years*, released September 25. In the title track he wonders what happened to his youth, but children's laughter on a carousel helps him come to terms with aging as the bittersweet orchestral arrangements of Gordon Jenkins bathe him like an autumn breeze.

Driving in his car, Sinatra had heard the Kingston Trio's "It was a Very Good Year" on the radio and decided to cover it for the album, as it echoed the same theme. In it, he looks back on the women from different eras in his life—small-town girls at seventeen, city girls who live upstairs at twenty-one, blue-blooded ladies in limos at thirty-five. The song might have inspired Lennon's "In My Life," which the Beatles recorded a few weeks later, on October 18. "Good Year" went to No. 1 on easy listening and won the Grammy for Best Male Vocal Performance and Arranger. The LP took home Album of the Year.

Sinatra's comeback continued with the TV special *Frank Sinatra: A Man and His Music*. The press release read that it was for people who were "tired of kid singers wearing mops of hair thick enough to hide a crate of melons." During the show, Sinatra gives thanks to all the deejays who still played him in "Beatle land." The special was shot on tape right when TV switched over to color full time, aired November 24, and won an Emmy and a Peabody Award.

There was an accompanying double album, though only three new songs were recorded for it. (And those were new versions of old hits: "Come Fly with Me," "Love and Marriage," and "I'll Never Smile Again.") When Sinatra started his own label five years before, he rerecorded many of his hits from the 1940s and '50s, and the best of them were compiled onto *A Man and His Music*. Many Sinatra purists insist on the originals, but some like his redos better. The originals are more sensitive, tentative, halting, but the older

Sinatra swaggers and swings more, rocks a little faster (probably because he just wanted to bang them out and get out of the studio), more in the cocky *Swingers* lounge style that he came to symbolize for later generations. *A Man and His Music* is a lively contrast to the somber *September of My Years*, and won the Grammy Album of the Year for 1966. What is mysterious is that records today indicate that *A Man and His Music* was released in November 1965, which would seem to make it ineligible for the 1966 Grammies. The win is also a surprising achievement for a greatest hits retrospective comprised of rerecorded songs. All this would lead one to believe that Sinatra seized on some sort of technicality and put the fix in with the Grammy voters—were the album not packed wall to wall with classics such as "Fly Me to the Moon," "Luck Be a Lady," "I've Got You under My Skin," and "In the Wee Small Hours."

Sinatra would take breaks from a film shoot to fly to Vegas for a gig, wired on speed, and then get back on the plane and return to the shoot, often doing only one take per scene, and getting dangerous if asked to do more. During the filming for *Von Ryan's Express* (the No. 10 movie of the year), he met twenty-one-year-old Mia Farrow, a star on the soap opera *Peyton Place*. In August, he took her on a chartered 168-foot yacht with twenty-three crew members; maybe it was there she lost her virginity to him.

Their May-December romance was echoed among many couples across the country. As youth began to revel in the sexual revolution, middle-aged marrieds looked out, haunted, from their windows, wondering if they'd played it too safe with their lives. By decade's end, the archetype of the older man bewitched by the flighty hippie girl would be prevalent in films such as *Cactus Flower* and a whole mini-genre starring Peter Sellers: *I Love You, Alice B. Toklas!*; *There's a Girl in My Soup*; *Hoffman*; and *The Bobo*.

At Sinatra's pad, Farrow's friends from India would come over and hand him a flower. "That made him feel square for the first time in his life," Farrow said.[7] When Sinatra's daughter Nancy threw him a huge fiftieth birthday party in December, he didn't bring Farrow because he knew his ex-wife (Nancy's mother) would be there. That night, stewing by herself, Farrow took scissors to her waist-length hair. "I chopped my silly hair off because I was bored with me," she told Sinatra when he returned.

"It's terrific. Now you can go out for Little League like the rest of the boys!"[8]

Sinatra's ex Ava Gardner later quipped, "Ha! I always knew Frank would end up in bed with a little boy."

After Farrow had Vidal Sassoon clean up her handiwork, her example ushered in the new pixie cut, as the model Twiggy did as well.

The following year, Sinatra married Farrow and knocked the Beatles' "Paperback Writer" out of the No. 1 spot with "Strangers in the Night," and then returned to No. 1 the next year with "Something Stupid," a duet with his daughter. That was the same year the Sands casino cut him off for running up a five-hundred-thousand-dollar debt. When he got belligerent, shouting atop a table, the manager knocked his teeth out, so Sinatra drove a golf cart through the casino's plate-glass window. "This place was sand when they built it, and it'll be sand when I'm fucking done with it!"[9] Swinging through his midlife crisis His Way.

Though he was perhaps the world's most eligible bachelor, Paul McCartney actually lived with the family of his girlfriend, Jane Asher, during the first few years of Beatlemania. When he wasn't on tour, he stayed in the garret of the Ashers' eighteenth-century five-story townhouse on Wimpole Street in London, enjoying warm dinners with Jane; her brother, Peter (of the pop duo Peter and Gordon); her mother, Margaret; and father, Richard, the head of the psychiatric department at the Central Middlesex Hospital. McCartney's room was next to Peter's, which was why he ended up writing four songs for Peter and Gordon (including "A World without Love" and "Woman").

Often fans would loiter around the front door, so McCartney would climb out his window (four stories up), enter the apartment of the retired colonel next door, and then head down to the basement apartment, where the tenants would let him exit into the back alley.[10]

Mrs. Asher was a classical music instructor—she taught Beatles producer George Martin the oboe—and McCartney and Lennon composed a number of tracks in her music room in the basement, including "I Want to Hold Your Hand." McCartney's exposure to the classics through Mrs. Asher no doubt abetted his growth into baroque pop. While living with the Ashers, he took piano lessons at the Guildhall School of Music and Drama, which George Martin had also attended.

While sleeping at the Ashers' in early 1964, McCartney had the melody for his most successful song come to him in a dream. Upon waking, he rushed to the piano before he forgot it. Because the melody was heavier than the Beatles' regular material, he was afraid he had subconsciously plagiarized it. Over the course of a year, he played it for everyone from his music publisher to the Yardbirds, to see if anybody recognized it, all the while trying to come up with better lyrics than the placeholders, "Scrambled Eggs / Oh baby, I love your legs." (Decades later, some would claim the song bore a slight resemblance to Nat King Cole's "Answer Me, My Love," from 1953.)

Lennon said, "Every time we got together to write songs for a recording session, this one would come up. We almost had it finished . . . We made up our minds that only a one-word title would suit, we just couldn't find the right one. Then one morning McCartney woke up and the song and the title were both there, completed. I was sorry in a way, we'd had so many laughs about it."[11]

It was while McCartney was in Portugal on vacation in May that the lyrics for "Yesterday," as the song was to be called, came to him. Decades later, he would muse that they were perhaps subconsciously inspired by his mother's death from breast cancer when he was fifteen. When he learned of her death, he asked aloud, "What will we do without her money?" and later felt ashamed, which many have speculated inspired the line about saying something wrong. Lennon's mother was killed two years after Paul's, when she was struck by a car driven by an off-duty policeman. McCartney later wrote, "Now we were both in this; both losing our mothers. This was a bond for us, something of ours, a special thing."[12]

The songs for their film *Help!* had been locked back in February, so "Yesterday" was finished too late to make the soundtrack. Compared to Lennon's four classics in the film, McCartney's "The Night Before" and "Another Girl" were enjoyable but slight. But while there were only seven songs performed in the movie, the *Help!* album needed fourteen tracks. So McCartney banged out three cuts on June 14, each far superior to the songs of his that made the feature, and each about as different from the others as possible.

Capitol Records was so taken with the chugging acoustic bliss of "I've Just Seen a Face" that they held it back to make it the opening song on the American version of *Rubber Soul*, in order to make that album seem more folk-rock. (It was one of McCartney's many "seeing" songs throughout the year: "Tell Me What You See," "You Won't See Me," "I'm Looking through You.") "I'm Down" was his own version of the Little Richard shriekers that were his forte.

He did two takes of "Yesterday" with just himself on guitar; none of the other Beatles could think of anything to add to the track. But producer George Martin, who had worked in the BBC's classical music department and then recorded classical music and show tunes as the head of EMI's Parlophone division, asked McCartney to let him add a string quartet.

The year before, McCartney and Lennon had written a jazzy waltz for Cilla Black named "It's for You" that featured George Martin's orchestra. McCartney thought it turned out to be one of their best compositions, so he hesitantly acquiesced, but insisted, "No vibrato, I don't want any vibrato!"[13] He associated violins with vibrato with Montovani, a best-selling easy listening orchestra conductor who seemed corny to the group.

McCartney didn't want to look like he was trying to be a solo artist, so "Yesterday" was not released as a single in the United Kingdom. In fact, it was buried as the second-to-last song on the U.K. *Help!* album. But it was released as a single in the States on August 6, held the top spot for four weeks in October, and became the most covered song of the decade, with more than twenty-five hundred versions recorded to date. Though they didn't actually win any Grammys, the Beatles were nominated for ten that year, six of which were for "Yesterday," including Song of the Year. *Rolling Stone* would later rate it the thirteenth greatest song of all time.

Its aching desolation further propelled the group away from its adolescent image. As the chaotic upheaval of the 1960s intensified, for many it reflected a mourning for the stability of 1950s culture and tradition, the flip side to the era's dazzling change. In McCartney's own life as well, unimaginable success came with grueling complications, and at times he yearned for simpler days—but knew there was no going back.

On October 26, Queen Elizabeth II made the Beatles Members of the Order of the British Empire in honor of the huge revenues they generated for the United Kingdom when they opened the U.S. market to English bands and helped popularize all things British, from fashion to cars such as the Jaguar and Mini Cooper—for being "Super salesmen for Britain," McCartney later called it. Prime minister Harold Wilson had submitted them for consideration, as he was a fellow Liverpudlian, and many felt it was a bid by him to look good to younger voters. Some older soldiers sent back their medals in protest.

The group arrived at Buckingham Palace in Lennon's Rolls-Royce, waving to the masses held back by the police, some kids clambering onto the gates and lampposts for a better look. In the Great Throne Room their names were called out, and they each separately walked forward and bowed. The Queen shook each of their hands. "It's a pleasure to present you with this."

"Thank you."

After the ceremony, she asked them, "Have you been together long?"

"Yes, many years," McCartney said.

"Forty years and it don't seem a day too much," said Starr.

He later recalled, "She had this strange, quizzical look on her face, like either she wanted to laugh or she was thinking, 'Off with their heads!'"[14]

The not-so-secret story of the Beatles is the competition between the two primary composers. Lennon was the leader of the band back in 1957 but realized McCartney was talented and brought him in. When Martin agreed to produce the Beatles, he had to decide whether Lennon or McCartney would be the front man. At the time, all groups had a leader, à la Buddy Holly and the Crickets. Martin found Lennon's voice slightly stronger, but McCartney's looks appealed more to female fans. Then, in the first of many ways in which Martin thought outside the box, it suddenly occurred to him that there didn't need to be one front man. Thus the band was freed to evolve in its naturally dual-powered way.

Nineteen sixty-three was the heyday for Lennon-McCartney writing songs together, both for themselves and for other artists. In that year and the following, they gave away sixteen compositions to their manager's other clients and groups such as the Rolling Stones.

All their songs were credited to Lennon-McCartney until the end of the decade, but by 1964, Lennon and McCartney would usually write the initial drafts of songs separately. Whoever initiated the song would usually sing lead. Then they'd get together and help each other polish off the compositions. For instance, Lennon mostly wrote "Ticket to Ride," but McCartney came up with the idea for the unusual drums, and played lead guitar.

Martin said Lennon's forte was words and McCartney's was music. Lennon penned lyrics and then had to come up with the music, while McCartney came up with melodies and then needed words. Each envied the other's gift.[15] McCartney was the son of a bandleader, and Lennon benefited from his musical embellishments. Lennon in turn would mercilessly bash any weak lyrics, challenging McCartney to push himself.

After "Please Please Me," their next three singles were joint efforts, but then "Can't Buy Me Love," which was primarily McCartney's, went to No. 1. At this point, Lennon stopped writing songs for other artists and focused on generating twice as many Beatle cuts as McCartney, and the next five A sides were his. McCartney was actually writing as many songs as Lennon in 1964, but they were given to Peter and Gordon, Cilla Black, and Billy J. Kramer, either because they weren't as strong or because he'd agreed to take the assignment.

Playboy asked Lennon, "Was there resentment from McCartney at first?"

"No, it wasn't resentment, but it *was* competitive . . . up to that period it was mainly my domination of the record scene. Although I *never* dominated the fan worship because the kids . . . the girls always went for him. Mine was a male following more than a female following."[16] Lennon's desire to wrest the attention away from the heartthrob McCartney pushed him to write the hits and be the wittiest Beatle in press conferences and films.

But "Yesterday" marked the beginning of a shift in balance between the two. Henceforth, McCartney would give away only one song a year to other artists and catch up with Lennon in his number of Beatle cuts per album, even surpassing him two years later. After "Yesterday," almost all the Beatles' A sides would be McCartney's, as Lennon dived into the rabbit hole of his psychedelicized mind.

Almost every Rolling Stones song was tough, if not outright mean. But sporadically throughout their career they'd surprise listeners with their vulnerable side—though typically, the motivation was cash. "Yesterday" topped the American charts for the entire month of October, so on October 26 (the day the Beatles were honored by the Queen), Jagger and Richards went into the studio with the Mike Leander Orchestra to do their own version of a song they'd written for Marianne Faithfull a year before. After Oldham discovered the seventeen-year old, he told his songwriters, "She's from a convent. I want a song with brick walls all round it, high windows, and no sex."[17] The duo penned the ultimate Rapunzel anthem for her in "As Tears Go By," about a rich young lady crying while watching children play outside her window. Jagger wrote the words, Richards came up with the melody.

"Well, it was already a hit, so, you know," Jagger laughed about the Stones remake, "and Andrew was a very simple, commercial kind of guy. A lot of this stuff is done for commercial reasons."[18] Still, they had tapped into a softer side of themselves, opening the door for future gentle classics.

Faithfull said, "It's a great fusion of dissimilar ingredients: 'The Lady of Shalott' to the tune of 'These Foolish Things.' The image that comes to mind for me is the Lady of Shalott looking into the mirror and watching life go by. It's an absolutely astonishing thing for a boy of 20 to have written: A song about a woman looking back nostalgically on her life. The uncanny thing is that Mick should have written those words so long before everything happened. It's almost as if our whole relationship was prefigured in that song."[19]

The Stones' version went to No. 6 on the U.S. pop charts—and No. 10 on easy listening.

Folk-Rock Explosion, Part Two

The electrified "Sound of Silence" is released in September, Dylan clones fill the charts in autumn, the Mamas and the Papas record "California Dreaming," Goffin and King meet Dylan on October 1 and vow to catch up, while Dylan takes on the hecklers and rebuffs the activists.

Reporter: How many people who major in the same musical vineyard in which you toil, how many are protest singers?

Bob Dylan: Um . . . how many?

Reporter: Yes. How many?

Bob Dylan: Uh, I think there's about, uh, 136.

Reporter: You say about 136, or you mean exactly 136?

Bob Dylan: Uh, it's either 136 or 142.[1]

Dylan's "Like a Rolling Stone" *almost* topped the charts in September, blocked from the No. 1 position only by Lennon's "Help!" and then, gallingly, by "Eve of Destruction"—stymied by his own imitation!

His post-Newport string of concerts began at Forest Hills on August 28, where they booed the electric portion of his set and someone yelled "You scumbag!"[2] Dylan told the band to keep playing "Ballad of a Thin Man" until they quieted down. The crowd sang along with Dylan for "Like a Rolling Stone," then resumed their booing. But his skin was growing thicker now. After the gig, Dylan hugged the band. "It was fantastic," he said, "a real carnival and fantastic."[3]

During his San Francisco press conference on December 3, he acknowledged that people booed him "just about all over" the country, but he seemed unfazed. "I mean they must be pretty rich to be able to go someplace and boo. I couldn't afford it if I were in their shoes."[4]

The Byrds released "Turn! Turn! Turn!" on October 1, and it would become their second U.S. No. 1. Along with "I Got You Babe" and "Eve of Destruction," it made folk-rock the third most popular genre at the top of the American charts for the year, with four hits, behind Britpop (thirteen) and Motown (six), and ahead of the Brill Building (three) and the Beach Boys (one). There was another folk-rock single released in September that would also eventually hit No. 1, though it would take three months to get there. But three months was nothing for two friends who had been struggling to make it for a decade.

Paul Simon met Artie Garfunkel during a production of *Alice in Wonderland* in the sixth grade. They started practicing Everly Brothers two-part harmony, and in 1957, before they were out of high school, they sang their first single, "Hey, Schoolgirl," on *American Bandstand* as the duo Tom and Jerry, right after Jerry Lee Lewis performed "Great Balls of Fire." But their next singles didn't do anything, and when Garfunkel found out that Simon had cut a song on his own, they went their separate ways for a few years.[5] Simon worked on some compositions with Queens College friend Carole King, then pushed some of his own songs to Dylan producer Tom Wilson. Wilson recalled, "He came to me to sell tunes, and he sold me! He's a very, very intelligent being."[6]

Wilson was especially taken with "He Was My Brother." Inspired by the topical songs on *The Freewheelin' Bob Dylan*, it concerns a civil rights activist who gets shot. Wilson agreed to produce him, and Simon asked if he could include a friend at Columbia University with whom he used to sing. Simon had a strong voice, was a skilled guitarist, and wrote the songs, but Garfunkel's tenor brought an indelible angelic harmony—"I love a song with a high, pole-vault peak," Garfunkel would say[7]—and his blond afro was striking.

Wilson convinced them they could use their real names, and the team re-corded *Wednesday Morning, 3 AM* in March 1964. Wilson's regular session guys played on the album, including Bill Lee on stand-up bass. The eerie thing was, the following June, a student Simon knew from Queens College, Andrew Goodman, went down to Mississippi to join the civil rights move-ment in Freedom Summer and was one of the three civil rights workers murdered by the Klan. Hearing the news made Simon ill. He revised "He Was My Brother" to reflect Goodman's death when he and Garfunkel per-formed it live.[8]

Simon had come up with the music to "The Sounds of Silence" in Febru-ary 1964, in a mood haunted by Kennedy's assassination the previous No-vember. (Originally "Sounds" was plural, though later it would be changed to "Sound.") The tiles of his bathroom made a good echo, and he'd often play guitar without the lights on, hence the song's opening lines in which he greets his old friend darkness. "A Hard Rain's A-Gonna Fall" has a verse about ten thousand people whispering and nobody listening. "Blowin' in the Wind" asks how many ears one man has to have before he hears people cry. So Simon sings of people who talked but didn't speak and people who heard but didn't listen. Maybe there is something of *Howl*'s Moloch in the image of people bowing and praying to the neon gods they made.

"The Sound of Silence" became one of the era's most eloquent warnings against silent complicity in the face of murder—in the South and, later, in Vietnam. Perhaps both Simon's and Dylan's protest songs were informed by the Holocaust, as well, as both writers were Jews born in America while the genocide was in progress overseas. But unlike the other civil rights songs on *Wednesday Morning, 3 AM*, "Silence" is vague enough to be timeless, allow-ing *The Graduate* to revive it three years later to express a young suburban-ite's ennui.

Unfortunately, silence was what greeted the album's release. Disheartened, Garfunkel went back to Columbia. Simon heard that London was ravenous for folk, so he went there to busk. He wrote "Red Rubber Ball" with Bruce Woodley of the Seekers for a hundred pounds; the song defiantly proclaims his resilience in the face of bitter disappointment. He wrote "Someday One Day" for the Seekers as well.

In the wake of British Dylan mania after his May tour, Simon was given the chance to record his own solo LP in June and July. Since it was released only in the United Kingdom, Simon and Garfunkel would later redo a number of the tracks, and thus *The Paul Simon Songbook* is like an unplugged version of the next two Simon and Garfunkel albums, minus Garfunkel, which allows one to see how much the blond singer added to the mix.

Songbook is almost a concept album of Simon's battle with depression. (Understandable—he and his buddy finally made an album after seven years with his hero's producer and it flopped.) In "I Am a Rock," Simon tries to convince himself that he's happy living a life of isolation, but in "A Most Peculiar Man," he turns on the oven and gasses himself like Sylvia Plath. Even in his ode to his English girlfriend, Kathy Chitty ("Kathy's Song"), the raindrops are dying. À la *Freewheelin'*, Simon put Chitty on the cover with him, sitting on "Sound of Silence" cobblestones.

"April Come She Will" takes its structure from the English rhyme "Cuckoo, Cuckoo, What Do You Do?" Love rests in Simon's arms in the spring and then prowls the night and flies away. Other seasonal songs include "Leaves That Are Green," in which he watches the leaves wither after his girlfriend has vanished. Its "hello goodbye" verse perhaps inspired the Beatles' hit two years later. Simon was already cornering the market on intoxicating folk-pop you feared to listen to lest it stab you in the heart with gorgeous grief. The Simon and Garfunkel version of "Flowers Never Bend with the Rainfall," recorded the following year, boasts a guitar almost as cheerful as the Beatles' "I've Just Seen a Face"—until you remember it is about death.

Wilson had forgotten about *Wednesday Morning, 3 AM* because it sold only about a thousand copies. But one day, a promotions guy told him that the album was selling in Florida. "He said, according to our guy in Miami it was 'Sound of Silence' they liked, but they wanted a beat put to it. So I took Dylan's backing band and went and overdubbed it, everything, on my own, 'cause they [Simon and Garfunkel] weren't around."[9]

"Mr. Tambourine Man" was a week away from being the No. 1 record when Dylan and Wilson recorded "Like a Rolling Stone" on June 15. After Dylan left, on the same day, Wilson gathered a different set of musicians for the "Silence" overdub: guitarists Al Gorgoni (who plays on *Bringing It All Back Home*) and Vinnie Bell, bassist Joe Mack, and drummer Buddy Salzman.

Gorgoni recalled, "I remember listening to Paul's acoustic guitar part through the headphones and basically just copping it. I had this Epiphone

Casino, which had the right sound. People used to think it was a twelve-string electric like the Byrds; it's not, it's just me and Vinnie playing together, mixed together onto the same track. And Vinnie added a few bluesy fills that you can hear in there as well. It took us a couple hours, and it was done."[10] Since the Byrds had used an echo, engineer Roy Halee put an echo on the "Silence" track.

Wilson said, "In fact, the single was held up from July to late September or October, by which time I'd left for MGM—more money."[11] Before Wilson left, he did the same folk-rock trick with doo-wop icon Dion "The Wanderer" DiMucci, capturing magnificent covers of "It's All Over Now, Baby Blue" and Tom Paxton's "I Can't Help but Wonder Where I'm Bound," along with Dion originals such as the aching "Knowing I Won't Go Back There."

Garfunkel wasn't too impressed when he heard the new version of "Silence." "It's cute. They've drowned out the strength of the lyric and they've made it more of a fashion kind of production. And you never know. I was mildly amused and detached with the certainty that it was not a hit. I don't have hits."[12]

But then it started its slow but inexorable climb. Simon returned to the States to regroup with Garfunkel. When they played *Hullabaloo*, the show's guitarist was Vinnie Bell, who plays on the record. But Simon didn't know him and told the musical director he wanted to show the musician how to play the guitar part. The director said he already knew, but Simon said, "No, I did a special thing on the record that I want him to do with the sound."

Simon introduced himself to Bell and then said, "I'd like to show you, if you don't mind, how I did this thing on the record."

Bell assured him he knew just what to play.

"No, here, just watch my fingers."

"Paul, I did the record."

Bell recalled, "And of course there was this silence. And he said, 'Well . . . okay . . . Are you sure you did the record?' I said, 'Yeah. It's *this*, right?' And I played [sings part]. And he said, 'Yeah, that's it.' And I said, 'Okay, you'll get that. Don't worry.' "[13]

At Columbia, Bob Johnston took over as Simon and Garfunkel's producer just as he had for Dylan. They cranked out the *Sounds of Silence* LP in December and released it in January to cash in. LA's Wrecking Crew performs on some of it: Larry Knechtel on keyboards, Glen Campbell on guitar, and Hal Blaine on drums. Some of the music tracks were recorded in Johnston's home base, Nashville. The only new songs were "We've Got a Groovey Thing Goin'" and "Blessed," the latter featuring Simon in his favorite pose of brooding through the dark streets among the meth drinkers, pot dealers, hookers, and thieves, wondering why the Lord has forsaken him.

"This is probably my most neurotic song," Simon would say to introduce "I Am a Rock."[14] It was rerecorded on December 14. It was touching to see the duo harmonize when they performed the song live, belying the singer's insistence that he has no need for friendship. It reached No. 3.

Just in case one suicide song ("A Most Peculiar Man") wasn't enough, Simon updated "Richard Cory," a poem by Edwin Arlington Robinson about a factory worker who can't understand why the town's richest man just shot himself. They also recorded a hit that would be held off for their next album, "Homeward Bound," written when Simon was missing his girlfriend, Kathy. On January 1, the sepulchral "Sound of Silence" was the No. 1 record, ringing in the New Year with a distinct air of foreboding. After eight years, the two kids from Queens had finally made it.

The folk-rock boom snowballed into the trend du jour with albums such as *Jan and Dean Folk 'n Roll*, *Johnny Rivers Rocks the Folk*, and even *Waylon Jennings Folk-Country*. It's ironic that the era's most iconoclastic writer birthed the most successfully cloned template embraced by the LA producers in the second half of the year. Mix Dylan lyrics (or at least anti-establishment lyrics) with Beatles/Byrds jangle, harmonies and drums, and—presto!—a hip new single.

The Turtles approached their cover of "It Ain't Me Babe" as if they were the Zombies, and made it to No. 8. In September, Manfred Mann took Dylan's "If You Gotta Go, Go Now" to No. 2 in the United Kingdom, and also covered "With God on Our Side." Another group that rose out of the Troubadour's hootenanny scene, the Association, made its debut in October with Dylan's "One Too Many Mornings." P. F. Sloan and Steve Barri dubbed themselves the Grass Roots and covered "Mr. Jones (Ballad of a Thin Man)" in the studio, before turning the band over to other musicians to tour. The Four Seasons covered "Don't Think Twice" under the name the Wonder Who? The Leaves did "Love Minus Zero/No Limit," the Daily Flash did "Queen Jane Approximately." The Myddle Class bravely took on "Gates of Eden." Even the Beach Boys recorded "The Times They Are A-Changin'." Odetta released a full album of *Odetta Sings Dylan.* Eventually, Dylan's label would take out ads reading, "Nobody Sings Dylan Like Dylan." Though perhaps that should have been amended to "Except for Mouse and the Traps," a Texas garage band fronted by Ronnie Weiss whose "A Public Execution" was the most hilarious spot-on Dylan imitation of the decade.

When Donovan first met Dylan in London in May, they sat around playing each other songs. Donovan played a song he'd written about "darling tangerine eyes" based on a melody he'd heard at a festival—and the song was Dylan's "Mr. Tambourine Man." "You know," Dylan said, "I haven't always been accused of writing my own songs. But *that's* one I did write."[15] Still, Dylan liked Donovan's "Catch the Wind," and the two became friends. Dylan introduced Donovan to the Beatles, with whom he became tight. Donovan also became friendly with Joan Baez, whose romance with Dylan was reaching its painful end. Dylan had passive-aggressively invited her to accompany him during his spring tour of England, but then pointedly declined to invite her onstage to perform with him. Dylan still kept his blossoming affair with Sara Lownds hidden from Baez, but grew increasingly cold to her. Baez took some solace in Donovan's arms and he accompanied her to Vietnam War protests.[16]

The Kinks didn't cover Dylan, but on September 17 they released a folky four-song collection called *Kwyet Kinks,* with Ray Davies's first stab at social commentary, "A Well Respected Man," inspired by his stay at a resort where he felt the rich guests acted snobby toward him. He painted a picture of an always-punctual stockbroker, healthy in body and mind; even his sweat smells better than everyone else's. But despite his smug, conservative image, behind the scenes he can't wait to inherit his dad's money, and his dad fools around with the maid. His mom dissuades him from marrying the girl next door because he just lusts for her; meanwhile she herself gives the eye to young men. The song's success encouraged Ray to continue down the path of finely observed satires of British culture.

It was also the year Dylan's manager Albert Grossman broke Canadian Gordon Lightfoot internationally. Lightfoot had a Dylanesque way with bittersweet melodicism, and fellow Grossman act Peter, Paul and Mary covered both the piercing "Early Morning Rain" and cynical "For Lovin' Me." The Grateful Dead also recorded the former in a November demo, while Nico proved herself the equal to any of the folk divas with "I'm Not Sayin'." On

June 19, Marty Robbins topped the country charts with Lightfoot's "Ribbon of Darkness."

Judy Collins's *Fifth Album* has "Early Morning Rain" alongside three Dylan tracks and Phil Ochs's song about the Watts riots, "In the Heat of the Summer." The same month, her rival Joan Baez went electric with the help of Bruce "Mr. Tambourine Man" Langhorne on *Farewell, Angelina*, which includes four Dylan covers, a Donovan tune, and her U.K. No. 8 rendition of Phil Ochs's "There but for Fortune."

For Marianne Faithfull's three albums of the year, she stayed away from those writers but did cover another up-and-coming singer-songwriter named Tom Paxton with "The Last Thing on My Mind." Her singles were an enchanting mix of folk and pop: "Come and Stay with Me," "This Little Bird," "Summer Nights," and "Go Away from My World." Manager Andrew Oldham tried to recreate the success he had with Faithfull by pairing Vashti Bunyan with Jagger/Richards's "Some Things Just Stick in Your Minds," in which they tried to combine "As Tears Go By" with "Blowin' in the Wind."

Both Jagger and Dylan yearned for Faithfull, and they both also considered Françoise Hardy the ideal woman. She recorded *Françoise Hardy in English* and performed its songs in an English special, *The Piccadilly Show*. The winsome beauty of "Ce Petit Coeur" and the epic orchestration of "Non, Ce n'est Pas un Rêve" are stirring even if you can't understand French. In November she had a part in French New Wave director Jean-Luc Godard's *Masculin Féminin*, which concerns the relationship between a tempestuous radical and a pop singer. Godard had the actors improvise based on notes he wrote each night before the shoot, in order to capture his vision of "The Children of Marx and Coca-Cola."

And in a bumper crop year for folk chanteuses, one of the most bewitching had just made her way to Los Angeles.

In the early 1960s, John Phillips was in a folk band called the Journeymen with his good friend Scott McKenzie. On the road, Phillips met sixteen-year-old model Michelle Gilliam (born 1944) and, in December 1962, left his wife and two kids to marry her. Their nine-year age gap was just two years short of Sonny and Cher's.

On tour, Phillips also met folkie Denny Doherty, and after the Journeymen split, Phillips tried to form the New Journeymen in spring 1965 with Michelle and Doherty. Doherty pushed for Cass Elliot to be in the group. One night, when the others were on acid, Doherty had her come by and introduce herself. Phillips thought Elliot's voice was too low and that she wasn't attractive enough.

That summer, Phillips, Michelle, Doherty, and Phillips's five-year-old daughter Mackenzie went to the Virgin Islands on American Express cards. They lived in tents, and the adults took acid every day and hung out at a bar called Creeque Alley, owned by Hugh Duffy, later mythologized in the Mamas and Papas song "Creeque Alley."[17] Cass followed them down, pestering Phillips to be allowed to join, and he finally relented.

Suddenly, their old friend Barry McGuire was jetting up the charts with "Eve of Destruction." A couple of years earlier, when Phillips lived at the Earl Hotel, McGuire would come by and jam with him and Roger McGuinn. Cass knew him, too, and called him up and asked him if he needed backing vocalists. They went to see him in LA and played him songs such as "California Dreamin'," which Phillips had written two years earlier in New York, in the dead of winter, waking Michelle up to help him finish it. McGuire wanted to record it with them backing him.

Mogul Lou Adler heard them and quickly decided to become their manager-producer. Originally they were going to release "Go Where You Wanna Go" as their first single. But as the group worked out their vocal counterpart for McGuire's version of "California Dreamin'," Adler realized he had struck gold and told them that *that* had to be their single. Apologetically, they asked McGuire for it back. He was bummed, but understood. Producer Adler replaced McGuire's vocal track with Doherty's on top of the Wrecking Crew's instrumentation and added a flute. Now they needed a name, and the foursome picked theirs after they heard that the Hells Angels called their ladies Mamas.

The single was the first of Phillips's West Coast anthems, and after its release in December, it inspired countless to pack up and follow their freedom. But just as "California Dreamin'" was becoming a reality, Michelle and Doherty almost blew the whole thing apart. During Cass's birthday celebration, Phillips and Cass passed out. Wordlessly, Doherty led Michelle into the apartment next door, where they made love. The Monday after, the foursome signed the deal with Adler's company, Dunhill. That Wednesday, Phillips caught his bandmate and wife in flagrante delicto.[18]

Somehow the band kept going. Phillips and Michelle moved to a different part of town. But Doherty said, "Michelle had found a little independence and could go out and have a fling with whoever she wished at that point, because her husband had just condoned the fact that she was having a dalliance with me, for reasons known only to himself. So she started seeing other people, and now she's got two guys, me and John, going, [heartbreaking moan] 'Ahh, ohh . . . ' She's seeing other people, and he can't really get into it with her. I can't really get into it with her because of the group thing, and they're husband and wife. Meanwhile, I'm standing back, and Cass is going, 'You son of a bitch . . . ' It was a rather *touchy* time."[19]

Another day, Phillips tried to sneak up on Michelle and Doherty and catch them, but Michelle spied him approaching and ran off. When she sneaked back, she heard Phillips saying, "I understand, Denny. I understand what a little *temptress* she is." Michelle recalled, "I thought, '*Wait* a minute. Now it's all my fault?' They were talking very manfully, like buddies."[20]

Cass, meanwhile, had long carried an unrequited torch for Doherty and was furious with Michelle, though she eventually forgave her. Cass proposed to Denny, but he declined. Doherty wrote the melody to "I Saw Her Again Last Night," and then Phillips penned lyrics about Doherty and Michelle's infidelity, Doherty said, "Because [John] wanted me to sing it onstage every night. 'Here you are—sing about it!' "[21] Even Fleetwood Mac twelve years later would have trouble matching the Mamas and the Papas' twisted interband dynamics. And Michelle hadn't even started her affair with Byrd cofounder Gene Clark yet. By that time, "California Dreamin'" would be tied with "The Ballad of the Green Berets" for top-selling song of 1966.

"Folk-rock" implied anticommercial authenticity, so it was ironic that much of the music was performed by the West Coast's slick studio pros, the Wrecking Crew. They played on the tracks of Barry McGuire, Simon and Garfunkel, the Mamas and the Papas, Sonny and Cher, and the Byrds' first single—not to mention the Beach Boys, Elvis Presley, Frank and Nancy Sinatra, Dean Martin, Johnny Rivers, and the Righteous Brothers.

Bassist Carol Kaye was just about the only female in the male-dominated scene. Brian Wilson called her the greatest bass player he'd ever met. Though Wilson started out as the Beach Boys' bassist, in 1964 he'd started delegating that task on records. The Beach Boys bass had a profound effect on Paul

McCartney: "It set me off on a period I had then for a couple of years of nearly always writing quite melodic bass lines."[22] Still, Kaye has always been quick to credit, "those were 99 percent [Wilson's] notes."[23] Along with pop songs, Kaye also played bass on TV theme songs such as *The Addams Family*.

In May through July, the U.S. No. 1 chart bounced from tracks played by the Crew ("Help Me, Rhonda") to tracks played by Motown's session team, the Funk Brothers ("Back in My Arms Again," "I Can't Help Myself") to the Wrecking Crew again ("Mr. Tambourine Man"). Ultimately, of the twenty-seven U.S. No. 1 hits of the year, the Crew and the Brothers tied, with six No. 1s each. (The other Crew songs were "You've Lost That Lovin' Feelin'," "This Diamond Ring," "Eve of Destruction," and "I Got You Babe.")

But while the session musicians could still flourish in the new era, Bob Dylan's anti-authority, increasingly surreal lyrics made the straightforward material of the hit factory the Brill Building seem old-fashioned. And Dylan's rise proved you didn't need to be a heartthrob to perform your own material. His and the Beatles' examples undermined the old-school producer's job of picking a pretty face to sing someone else's song.

The Saturday Evening Post assigned Al Aronowitz, the reporter who'd introduced the Beatles to Dylan, a story on girl groups. During the course of writing it, he became friends with the Brill's songwriters Gerry Goffin and Carole King. The Beatles had wanted to meet the husband-and-wife team, so in mid-August, when Aronowitz, en route to a party in the Beatles' suite at New York's Warwick Hotel, saw King on the street, he invited her along. King's introduction to the Fabs didn't go as smoothly as Dylan's.

She arrived at the crowded party knowing, as she wrote in her memoir, *A Natural Woman*, that "early in their career Paul and John reportedly had said that they hoped to become the Goffin and King of the United Kingdom. I had taken this to mean not that they hoped to marry each other and live in New Jersey but that they aspired to be successful songwriters."[24]

When she introduced herself to McCartney, he warmly listed off all the songs by her and her husband that the Beatles respected. But when King found Lennon, in a different section of the suite, stoned, and surrounded by women, he made "a remark so disrespectful that I cannot remember what he said, but I remember how I felt. I had proffered a face of friendship, and he had responded with a figurative slap. Had I been mature enough to realize that pushing the edge of decorum was a reflex for John at that stage of his life, I might not have taken it so personally. But I was very young, and I took it very personally."[25] She left the party. Goffin later characterized it as "John made come-ons to Carole, but in a kidding way."[26]

When King met Lennon again eleven years later she asked why he'd been so rude. "D'you really want to know?" he said after a pause. "It's because I was intimidated. You and Gerry were sooch [*sic*] great songwriters."[27]

It didn't go well with Dylan, either, when the couple went backstage to meet him after his Carnegie Hall show on October 1. Goffin told Dylan, "You've got a right to be very proud of yourself."

Dylan replied enigmatically, "I do?"[28]

His road manager, Bobby Neuwirth, later snidely asked King, "You're the chick who writes songs for bubblegum wrappers, right?"[29]

Goffin said Dylan's lyrics made him feel "like a dwarf."[30] The latest songs the couple had been trying to sell now seemed out of date, so they gathered up the acetates of the demos they had made for them and snapped them in half, vowing to catch up to the new folk-rock style. They also began to manage a New Jersey group with Aronowitz called the Myddle Class. (The success of the Byrds saw a mini-boom in bands with "y" in their names, such as the Cyrkle and, initially, the Tyrtles.) Goffin and King wrote "Free as the Wind" for their clients, a wistful anthem to newly liberated young ladies "running wild and riding high," released in December. Aronowitz also briefly managed the Velvet Underground with Lou Reed at that time, and on December 11, the Underground opened for the Myddle Class at New Jersey's Summit High School.

Just as Dylan got the Beatles into weed, Aronowitz got Goffin into it—and then LSD. Goffin, a former chemist, began making his own and soon had Spectoresque ambitions of producing sessions with dozens of musicians. His fellow Brill composer friends Mann and Weil began to worry about his increased drug intake and wrote "Kicks" as a plea for him to straighten out. (The Animals turned down the song because it was antidrug, leaving it for Paul Revere and the Raiders to release the next year, in February.)

Goffin painted "Love Your Brother" on the side of his house, and one night he started raving so strangely that a scared King called Mann-Weil. Brill mogul Don Kirshner lived near Goffin-King, so Mann-Weil asked him to check on them. Kirshner arrived to find Goffin on the roof planning to "hurt himself."[31] Kirshner talked him down, saying, "There's too much to lose." Kirshner contacted a doctor, and Goffin was taken to the psychiatric ward. "How could you do this to me?" Goffin asked Mann and Weil.[32]

He was first diagnosed as schizophrenic, then manic (now called bipolar), for which he was prescribed Thorazine. When the Thorazine made him depressed, the doctors gave him electroshock therapy and, eventually, lithium. Amazingly, Goffin and King still proceeded to write the very anticonformist anthems they'd intended to, such as "Pleasant Valley Sunday," "Wasn't Born to Follow," "Goin' Back," "Porpoise Song," and perhaps greatest of all, "You Make Me Feel Like a Natural Woman," for artists such as the Byrds, the Monkees, Dusty Springfield, and Aretha Franklin, before King divorced Goffin and became one of the era's most successful singer-songwriters with *Tapestry.*

✳

Along with the hecklers at Dylan's concerts, there was another group constantly calling to him: the idealists, such as Joan Baez, asking him to become a leader in the antiwar movement. Phil Ochs wanted him for the Sing-in for Peace, the Vietnam Day Committee wanted him for its November march—everybody wanted him to use his power to stop the war.

When Dylan was a teen, his father ran a furniture store and sent Dylan out on some repossession runs, to take back appliances from families who couldn't pay.[33] Dylan didn't like it, and he sang about the plight of the poor on his early albums. He turned down *The Ed Sullivan Show* because they wouldn't let him sing "Talkin' John Birch Paranoid Blues." He wrote songs that inspired a lot of people. But now he was getting ready to downshift.

On November 19 he secretly married Sara Lownds; their first son, Jesse Byron (named for the controversial Romantic poet), was born January 6. Three more children would follow. Over the next few years, their home in Woodstock was constantly invaded by strange hippies who believed Dylan to be their guru. To distance himself from the counterculture, he moved away from rock and into country music. He didn't want to be the spokesman for his generation or a messiah. The ones who did, such as King and, later, Lennon, got shot.

"All I'd ever done was sing songs that were dead straight and expressed powerful new realities," he writes in his memoir. "I was more a cowpuncher than a Pied Piper."[34]

Johnny Cash recorded "The One on the Right Is on the Left" in November as a spoof of the folk craze that had engulfed the pop charts thanks to his buddy Dylan. (After a correspondence, the two met when they both performed at the Newport Festival the year before Dylan went electric.) In the song, a folk group implodes due to differing political convictions. On stage, the one on the right, the one on the left, and the one in the middle descend into a violent fistfight, while the one in the rear incompetently burns his driver's license before getting drafted. The song predicted the chaotic divisions that would erupt across the country for the rest of the decade. Cash advises artists to keep their opinions to themselves and work on performing songs well. About the only person who would heed his advice, ironically, would be Dylan, whose lyrics grew ever more inscrutable. He wasn't going to lead a revolution. But he did lead a lot of people to think for themselves.

19

It Came from the Garage

The McCoys hit No. 1 with "Hang on Sloopy," on October 2; the forefathers of punk grapple with the British Invasion; and the original garage rockers, the Beach Boys, miss with an experimental single but hit with "Barbara Ann."

Throughout September and October, the songs that held the American top spot were heavy: "Help!", "Eve of Destruction," and "Yesterday." But there was a brief respite for one week only when, on October 2, "Hang on Sloopy" went to No. 1.

The song was by the Brill Building's Bert Berns and Wes Farrell, a rewrite of Berns's own "Twist and Shout." However, while the writers were seasoned pros, the band that recorded the song, the McCoys, were teenagers from Union City, Indiana. They had been discovered by the Strangeloves, which was the name the songwriting team Feldman-Goldstein-Gottehrer came up with for themselves after writing "I Want Candy" with Berns. They sang the song backed by session musicians, and when the single made it to No. 11 in August, the songwriters (sans Berns) put on wigs and told the press they were Australian sheep farmers. They got an actor to help them with their fake accents, said they used the Masai drums of the Aborigines (really a tympani), and opened for the Beach Boys. While they toured the Midwest, they discovered Rick and the Raiders, led by eighteen-year-old guitarist Rick Derringer, and told Berns about them. Berns renamed the Raiders the McCoys, they quickly cranked out "Sloopy," and it became one of the most enduring rock hits of the era.

Elsewhere in American pop/rock, the Four Seasons and the Vogues ("Five o'Clock World") were still hanging on to their cleanly parted hair, turtlenecks, and sweaters. But in the wake of the British Invasion, many American bands had adopted English-sounding names and costumes. The Beau Brummels took their name from the ultimate British dandy. Paul Revere and the Raiders took the opposite tack, claiming the name of the man who warned the American colonists of the approaching Redcoats, with band members dressing in Revolutionary War–style uniforms. Underneath the goofy garb, they were hardcore Seattle rockers who scored with their November release "Just Like Me." With "Lies," the Knickerbockers did the most precise Beatles imitation, as the band had both Lennon and McCartney sound-alikes. Almost as bad as the Byrds' original name, the Beefeaters, was the Little Lord Fauntleroy outfit the Young Rascals wore: rounded collars, skinny ties, knickers, and knee socks. But their first single, November's "I Ain't Gonna Eat Out My Heart Anymore," is bluesier than their image would have led one to expect.

The blue-eyed soul dance master of the year was Mitch Ryder, backed by the Detroit Wheels. Their live shows in Michigan were so explosive that black Motown acts opened for *them*. Ryder figured "Jenny Take a Ride" (a medley of Chuck Willis's "C.C. Rider" and Little Richard's "Jenny Jenny") was just a B side, but Keith Richards and Brian Jones visited the studio and predicted it would be a hit. Indeed, it made it to No. 10.

The Sir Douglas Quintet were another group trying to fool people they were British, even though they were from San Antonio, Texas, and had two Hispanic members, which was why their first album cover just showed the group in shadow. The album was also named *The Best of the Sir Douglas Quintet*, even though it was their first. But the group would endure for nine years and become one of Dylan's favorites. Their first hit, "She's about a Mover," mixed front man Douglas Sahm's Ray Charles–like vocals with Augie Meyers' Farfisa organ in the Tex-Mex style, rock with a Latin influence from south of the border.

Another Tex-Mex band was Sam the Sham and the Pharaohs. Instead of British costumes, Domingo "Sam" Zamudio wore an Arabic turban and tunic and drove a hearse with velvet curtains. In June, he released his three-chord ode to his cat, "Wooly Bully." Even though it stalled at No. 2, *Billboard* declared it the best-selling song of the year.

Perhaps the most exhilarating Texas band was the Bobby Fuller Four, whose rolling electric guitar and crashing drums sounded like an updated Buddy Holly. (Richie Valens's producer, Bobby Keane, produced the band, and the Crickets' lead guitarist, Sonny Curtis, wrote its hit "I Fought the Law.") "Another Sad and Lonely Night" and "Love's Made a Fool of You" are rousing tracks, and December's "I Fought the Law" would go on to be the theme song for many counterculture heroes. (Fourteen members of Ken Kesey's entourage, the Merry Pranksters, were arrested for pot in April, and Timothy Leary was given thirty years for trying to drive into Mexico with marijuana in the car on December 23. Others who wound up with jail sentences before the decade was over included Mick Jagger, Keith Richards, Jerry Rubin, Abbie Hoffman, Tom Hayden, the Black Panthers, and Jim Morrison—not that they all served.)

As with Holly, Fuller's potential was snuffed out far too soon. He died at age twenty-three the next July, in circumstances still shrouded in mystery. The Los Angeles County Coroner's Office's autopsy stated that he was found facedown in the front seat of his car next to a partially filled gas can. The cause of death is listed as "inhalation of gasoline." His demise was originally declared a suicide, but rumors that he was drenched in gasoline and that his finger was broken led to speculation that he was murdered, perhaps by the Mob.

The groups most beloved by contemporary hipsters were the most unpolished of the lot, the proto-punk garage rockers. The genre was so named because the borderline-competent bands often practiced in their parents' garages, sometimes barely making it much farther into the outside world.

Most of the garage bands did not even become one-hit wonders, but they were immortalized in the influential 1972 collection *Nuggets: Original Artyfacts from the First Psychedelic Era*, compiled by Lenny Kaye, the future guitarist of the Patti Smith Group, and Elektra Records' Jac Holzman. The liner notes refer to the music as "punk," apparently unaware that since the nineteenth century, the term referred to a man who is raped in prison. Kaye may have been inspired by influential rock critic Dave Marsh, who in *Creem* magazine in 1971 referred to a Hispanic American band from Michigan called ? and the Mysterians as "punk rock."[1] In 1965 they recorded "96 Tears," with its distinctive continental Vox organ sound, for a local label; when the national Cameo-Parkway label rereleased it the following February, it made it all the way to No. 1 on the *Billboard* pop chart.

The *Nuggets* bands, the Velvet Underground, the Motor City 5, and the Stooges (with Iggy Pop)—these were not big sellers in the 1960s, but they inspired punk bands of the 1970s such as the Ramones. As Iggy Pop said of the Velvet Underground's self-titled first album, "That record became very key for me, not just for what it said and how great it was, but also because I heard other people who could make good music without being any good at music. It gave me hope. It was the same thing the first time I heard Mick Jagger sing. He can only sing one note, there's no tone, and he just goes, 'Hey, well baby, baby, I can be oeweoww . . .' Every song is the same monotone, and it's just this kid rapping. It was the same with the Velvets. The sound was so cheap and yet so good."[2] It was more empowering hearing a band that sounded exciting and cool without being technically good—perhaps even sounding technically incompetent—than hearing a virtuoso band, because it made you believe you could go out and do it yourself.

Garage rockers often emulated the glowering poses of the Rolling Stones on their album covers, along with Jagger's harsh vocals. Sometimes they tried to cop his accent: American white kids imitating a British white kid imitating an American black guy. There was a lot of sneering, such as in the Lyrics' "So What!!" in which the vocalist vociferously establishes that he's unimpressed by the rich girl. Most of the songs expressed bitterness toward the fairer sex, maybe because the writers were still nerds in high school, or had lost the girl to the winner of the local Battle of the Bands.

Tripping on LSD also gained popularity as a theme, in such tracks as "Out of Our Tree" by the Wailers, from Tacoma, Washington (not the identically named Jamaican group or Waylon Jennings's group) and in "Strychnine" (alluding to the rumor that street LSD was laced with rat poison), by fellow Tacoma band the Sonics.

Musically, the bands might employ the trebly folk-rock guitar of the Byrds, but more frequently they copped the Stones or the Yardbirds copping black blues, complete with wailing harmonica. "Primitive," by the Groupies (before the word gained currency as a term for party girls), reworked Howlin' Wolf's "Smokestack Lightning" and summed up the whole aesthetic. After the Stones unleashed "(I Can't Get No) Satisfaction," by the end of the year all the Gibson Maestro Fuzz-Tone boxes were sold out as countless garage bands integrated distortion into their assault in songs such as Count Five's "Psychotic Reaction."

The other quality that bound most garage bands together was one they didn't want: low-budget production values. Ironically, future indie rockers such as the White Stripes and the Strokes deliberately attempted to capture the distorted, two-dimensional sound. Kurt Cobain said, "The Sonics recorded very, very cheaply on a two-track, you know, and they just used one microphone over the drums, and they got the most amazing drum sound I've ever heard. Still to this day, it's still my favorite drum sound. It sounds like he's hitting harder than anyone I've ever known."[3]

The song every garage band had to know was "Gloria," by Them. In it, Van Morrison yawps like a seriously irate alligator with perhaps the most ripped-up British blues vocals of them all, while über–session guitarist Jimmy Page stings and rings, influencing everybody years before Zeppelin—before anyone even knew it was Page playing. But the song was banned in many parts of the United States because Morrison sings of the titular female coming upstairs to his room. Chicago's Shadows of Knights changed the words and released their own version in December, scoring the American Top 10 hit.

In November, LA folk-rock band the Leaves released the first version of the "murdered-my-girlfriend" tune "Hey Joe," which would soon rival "Gloria" as the go-to garage anthem. Everyone from Love to the Byrds covered it, until Jimi Hendrix slowed it down the following year and annihilated all previous comers, backed by the unearthly Breakaways trio moaning like the ghost of the slain girlfriend. Another November release by an LA group, the Standells' "Dirty Water," was a favorite due to its lyrics about frustrated college girls who had to be back in their dorms by midnight.

Probably the most archetypal proto-punk band was LA's the Seeds. (As with the Leaves, by the end of 1965, band names that referenced drugs were taking over from misspelled animal names; fruits and vegetables would be next.) Their first single, "Can't Seem to Make You Mine," came out in March. As Sky Saxon's goofy vocals demonstrate, bands still didn't take themselves seriously, though acid and politics would solemnize them in a year or two. Saxon wrote the seminal "Pushin' Too Hard" (released in November) after a fight with his girlfriend. Though the singer is yelling at a girl in the song, with the draft now breathing down young men's necks, many heard the lyrics (lines about just wanting to be free to live his life the way he wants) as antiestablishment. The song had the fuzz tone and the reverb, along with a new trend: minor keys on an electric keyboard. The Turtles' Mark Volman said that originally the Sunset Strip was dominated by the folk-rock sound of the Byrds and the Turtles, but that it was soon overtaken by darker, minor-key bands such as the Seeds, the Chocolate Watchband, and the Doors.[4] Both the Seeds and Love had residencies at the Hollywood club Bito Lito's; the Doors would open for the Seeds there.

In cape and bad Prince Valiant haircut, Saxon frugged to the electric piano like an uninhibited (if slightly clueless) Mick Jagger, cool because he was so free, influencing the smart-moron ethos of Iggy Pop and the Ramones. Decades later Saxon opined, "Garage music is not bad, because Christ was born in a manger, which was probably like a garage of that time."

Probably the most successful garage band of all time was the Beach Boys. When the Wilson brothers were small, their father, Murry, turned the garage into a music room, where he and his wife, Audree, played the Hammond B-3 organ and piano while singing with the boys. Later, Brian Wilson slept there.[5] One day, Dennis came home from the beach and told Brian he should write a song about surfing because it had gotten really popular. When their folks went on vacation, they used the food money their parents had left them to buy instruments, and came up with their first hit, "Surfin'."

Now, four years later, thinking July's *Summer Days (and Summer Nights!!)* had temporarily satiated his label, Capitol, Wilson believed himself free to write an album that could make use of all the experimentation he had been doing in the studios with orchestras. To give himself the proper beach-oriented writing space, he had a wooden box built four feet off the ground in his dining room, put a grand piano in it, and then filled it with two feet of sand. But then Capitol started pressuring him to deliver his *third* album of the year, in time for Christmas sales.

Wilson wanted to get back to writing his baroque opus as soon as possible, so he decided the band would bang out a bunch of covers of songs by the likes of the Beatles, Dion, and even Bob Dylan—Jardine leads them through "The Times They Are A-Changin'"—and then overdub sounds as if there were a party going on in the studio, and call it *Beach Boys' Party!* The resultant album *would* stand today as a nice unplugged-style album if the annoying crowd sounds could be stripped out.

The group was recording in the studio next door to Jan and Dean, LA's other big surf group. William Jan Berry and Dean Ormsby Torrence started out as the Barons, a group that had rehearsed endlessly in Berry's garage while they were in high school. On September 23, after the duo had a fight, a drunken Dean stalked over to the Beach Boys and ended up singing lead on their album's cover of "Barbara Ann."

With *Party!* in the can, Wilson returned to his ambitious music. The arrangement of November's "The Little Girl I Once Knew" was groundbreaking in that the song comes to a complete stop at a number of points during the track. Lennon raved to *Melody Maker*, "This is the greatest! Turn it up, turn it right up. It's *got* to be a hit. It's the greatest record I've heard for weeks. It's fantastic. I hope it will be a hit. It's all Brian Wilson. He just uses the voices as instruments. He never tours or does anything. He just sits at home thinking up fantastic arrangements out of his head. Doesn't even read music. You keep waiting for the fabulous breaks. Great arrangement. It goes on and on with all different things. I hope it's a hit so I can hear it all the time."[6] But the pauses were too avant-garde for the radio. Programmers feared listeners would change the station if they heard silence, and the song went only to No. 20.

Ironically, the ragged song the Boys tossed off with Dean singing lead, "Barbara Ann," went to No. 2 on both sides of the Atlantic, becoming the fifth-highest charting hit of their career, and the sing-along for drunken frat boys everywhere.

20

Anarchy and Androgyny, British Style

In mid-October the Who struggle to channel their rage into the *My Generation* album instead of at one another. On November 6, "Get Off My Cloud" becomes the Stones' second U.S. No. 1 as they push the envelope with drugs and bad behavior.

In the beginning the Who was vocalist Roger Daltrey's group, but when Keith Moon joined the band, the maniacal drummer synched with fellow speed freaks Townshend and Entwistle to form a musical combo of such ferocious energy that they threatened to lift off and leave Daltrey in their dust.

Daltrey felt that amphetamines impeded his singing ability. "Once I got off the pill thing, I realized how much the band deteriorated through playing on speed. Musically, it really took a downturn." He thought drugs were turning the music into noise without tempo. So the pugnacious singer stalked offstage one night in September in Denmark, grabbed the others' stash of pills, and flushed them down the toilet. Moon freaked out and attacked Daltrey with a tambourine. Daltrey flattened him, gave him a bloody nose—and was thrown out of the band.

Townshend said, "Roger puts this band together then finds the three dwarves that he's brought in to support him suddenly sort of leaving him behind . . . Moon was a genius, Entwistle was a genius, I was maybe getting in the vicinity, and Daltrey was just a singer."[1]

Daltrey reflected, "It was the first time in my life that I realized I loved something else other than myself . . . [If I was being] thrown out for being like I was, then I have to change, because the band was more important to me than anything[2] . . . I thought if I lost the band I was dead. If I didn't stick with the Who, I would be a sheet metal worker for the rest of my life."[3] They brought him back on probation, warning that, with one more outburst, he would be dismissed for good. He worked on not raising his voice again off-stage.

Despite Townshend's remark that Daltrey was "just a singer," if it had been Townshend singing the lyrics he wrote, the Who's front man would have been a high-pitched neurotic instead of a hard-punching, working-class Everyman in cutting-edge clothes and shades. Journalist Nik Cohn wrote that Townshend "used one recurrent framework, he always has done: he cast himself as one teenage boy and this boy was the archetypal Shepherd's Bush [west London] Mod, a bit dumb, a bit aggressive, a bit baffled . . . Townshend wasn't like this Mod hero at all, of course, but Roger Daltrey was. I mean, Daltrey wasn't stupid but he was no theorizer, he was interested mostly in girls and cars, he wasn't too articulate, and Townshend used him like a mouthpiece."[4] The duo was a modern version of Cyrano de Bergerac (Townshend) and Christian de Neuvillette (Daltrey), working together to win the Roxanne of fame and validation.

"My Generation" was originally inspired by blues and folk songs such as "Young Man Blues," by Mose Allison, and "Talkin' New York," by Bob Dylan. Daltrey stuttered the first time he tried it, because he hadn't rehearsed it, but the band had him recreate the stutter for the final version because they thought it evoked the image of a jittery mod on pills, and because John Lee Hooker had a song called "Stuttering Blues."

The group's previous single, "Anyway, Anyhow, Anywhere," had allowed Townshend and Moon the chance to show their chops. On "My Generation," Entwistle uncorks one of the few bass solos to make pop radio, working to keep pace with James Brown's bassist Bernard Odum. Daltrey snarls that since the things that the older generation does look cold, he hopes he dies before he gets old (perhaps influenced by Berkeley Free Speech activist Jack

Weinberg's sound bite to the *San Francisco Chronicle*, "We have a saying in the movement that we don't trust anybody over 30."[5]) Then the track explodes into the anarchy of the band's stage show climaxes.

The Who Sings My Generation was recorded October 11–15 and released December 3 (the same day as *Rubber Soul*), the finest long-playing debut of the year. Its low-budget, echoey sound actually gives the songs more heft, starting with the atmospheric feedback opening of "Out in the Street."

"The Kids Are Alright" is an archetypal teen scenario that Townshend's hero Brian Wilson might have come up with. Other guys are dancing with the singer's girl, but he tells himself he doesn't mind; he just needs to get outside. He had some plans for himself and his girl, but she told him her folks wouldn't let her. Who can say if that's true or if she just wants to dance with the other guys—all he knows is he has to leave her behind before he goes out of his mind. The lengthy instrumental section was inspired by English baroque composer Henry Purcell's chamber suite *The Gordian Knot Untied*.[6]

"Circles (Instant Party)" tells of what happens to the singer after he leaves the dance. He gets wasted to forget his girl and tries to walk home, but he's so drunk he keeps walking in circles. The song was the embryo of the plot of the Who's movie about the mod movement, *Quadrophenia*, set in 1965 and shot in 1979.

Townshend writes in his memoirs that while the other three band members carried on rock star love lives after the gigs, he was insecure, afraid of being rejected, and would usually just go home and record demos, behavior that prompted rumors that he was gay.[7] Part of him liked the rumors, as he felt the point of mod was creating a new male, nonmacho archetype, the "elegant, disciplined, well-to-do, sharply dressed and sexually indeterminate and dangerously androgynous yobbo"[8] [thug]. In fact, a sizable percentage of mods were rent boys (prostitutes), and would often dance by themselves or with other guys instead of girls. Still, the album's "La-La-La Lies" and "It's Not True" both take pains to deny the rumors about him and assert that he has a woman who loves him.

The album is rounded out by some James Brown and Bo Diddley covers, plus the insane instrumental barnstormer "The Ox"—like "Wipe Out" on PCP. Moon's rampage on that track created the gold standard for all subsequent barbarian drummers, from Mitch Mitchell and Ginger Baker to John Bonham. Certainly no other band combined James Brown, sonic innovation, gender confusion, fashion, Pop Art pretension, and pure mayhem like the Who—though another British group reconfigured the same ingredients in its own inimitable fashion.

*

One night, the Stones' manager, Andrew Oldham, was stoned in his bathtub reading Anthony Burgess's novella about murderous hooligans, *A Clockwork Orange*. He began to think of ways he could sell the Stones as the *anti*-Beatles. When Oldham was growing up, Elvis Presley was sold as the dirty rebel alternative to the squeaky-clean Pat Boone. Perhaps the Stones could capture the teen demographic that didn't like the Beatles because their parents accepted them. For those who felt too cool for McCartney's elfin bobble head, there could be surly Jagger, glowering bug-eyed like a mod vampire in the shadows. "Would You Let Your Sister Go with a Rolling Stone?"—Oldham would later recall that he saw the phrase in front of him like a movie graphic designed by Saul Bass. *Melody Maker* ran it. *The Evening Standard* revised it to "But Would You Let Your Daughter Marry One?" Oldham began planting newspaper stories of kids being suspended for having dirty Stones hair instead of clean, neat Beatles hair. "Are you Beatles or are you Stones?" kids began asking each other. "The Stones are more than just a group, they are a way of life," ran one of Oldham's liner notes.

For the back of February's *The Rolling Stones, Now!* Oldham went into full *Clockwork Orange* mode. "Cast deep in your pockets for the loot to buy this disc of groovies and fancy words. If you don't have the bread, see that blind man knock him on the head, steal his wallet and lo and behold you have the loot, if you put in the boot, good, another one sold!" Then writer Tom Wolfe out-Oldhamed Oldham with "The Beatles want to hold your hand, but the Stones want to burn your town."

On March 18, the Stones' limo pulled up to a filling station in a London borough, and bassist Wyman asked if he could use the bathroom. The attendant said there wasn't one. Jagger, Jones, and another in their entourage joined Wyman to ask again. The attendant yelled, "Get off my forecourt!" so Jones made faces and danced around singing, "Get off my foreskin!" The group went down a side street ten yards away and pissed against a wall. Oldham made sure the press knew about it, embellishing that Jagger had sneered, "We piss anywhere, man!" The case went to court, and on July 22,

Jagger, Jones, and Wyman were fined five pounds for "behavior not becoming young gentlemen."

The most rebellious activity the musicians could boast was doing drugs, since it was illegal. Thus the airwaves became rife with young white musicians striving to outdo one another by getting on the charts the most blatant references to being high. Aside from the moral arguments, there are numerous theories as to why marijuana was outlawed in the U.S. in 1937. After the repeal of Prohibition in 1933, federal agencies that fought alcohol were downsized and needed new targets to justify their funding. Industrial giants such as DuPont and Hearst feared hemp as a competitor to their fabric, paper, and oil industries, and lobbied against it. Pot's illegality could be used against its main consumers at the time: blacks and Mexican farmworkers.

The interracial Beat/jazz/folkie scenes and civil rights movements were some of the main places marijuana was disseminated to whites, though even in the early 1960s in Greenwich Village it was scarce. Producer Erik Jacobsen said, "To buy pot then in the Village you had to go to a junkie, to a dealer. John (Sebastian) and I went many times to some incredible tenement building on the Lower East Side which was like dead people on the street. There were junkies, but there were no white potheads—very few. It was before that all happened."[9]

Keith Richards writes in his memoir that at the beginning of the year he was mystified how the black musicians on the tour circuit always looked so sharp, while Richards was always so exhausted and ratty looking. A black musician reached into his coat pocket, produced a Benzedrine pill and a joint, and said, "You take one of these, you smoke one of those. But keep it dark!" Richards writes, "I felt like I'd just been let into a secret society. Is it all right if I tell the other guys?"[10] It was, but he was told to keep it to themselves. That didn't last long.

Before 1965, none of the bands had drug songs—except, ironically, Peter, Paul and Mary. *Newsweek* ran an article in 1964 about how the children's song "Puff the Magic Dragon" could be about marijuana. *Puff* and *drag*—get it? The dragon and his friend Jackie Paper play in the mist with sealing wax, perhaps a reference to the strip of glue on rolling paper. (The heroine of the Stones' "19th Nervous Breakdown" would have a father who made sealing wax.)

Then, after "Mr. Tambourine Man," the top bands all sang about tripping—in "Day Tripper," "19th Nervous Breakdown," and "Sloop John B." In "Candy Man," Donovan comes right out and says that he is bummed his dealer has gone to Morocco and can't get him high anymore.

Breaking the law made people feel edgy and glamorous, the way the Lost Generation had when they drank during Prohibition in the 1920s. More important, many baby boomers came to prefer a mellow high to getting tanked. And drugs gave the bands a new well of inspiration, now that they had all pretty much cleaned out the cupboard of R&B and folk covers. They felt that drugs helped them look outside the box they'd been programmed into by an uptight society. So, just as Romantic poet Samuel Coleridge wrote about his opium trip in "Kubla Khan" 150 years earlier, the '60s musicians began to erect countless odes to hallucination.

While idealists argued over whether music really could change the world, both liberals and conservatives agreed that the Pied Pipers greatly contributed to increased drug use. In 1966/67, 21 percent of college students had smoked weed, and 6 percent had tried acid. In 1967/68 that number shot to 57 percent for weed and 17 percent for acid.[11]

Most listeners assumed that the "cloud" in "Get Off of My Cloud" came from a joint. The song is a prime example of how to remake your smash hit the same but different. The "hey-hey" hook from "Satisfaction" was recycled for crowd sing-alongs, and Watts's instantly recognizable drumbeat set the kids dancing to the proto-Hustle of the Chez Vous Walk (also known as the Marvin Gaye Walk). Richards's distorted guitar snarls, as if in aggravation at being hounded by the record label to top "Satisfaction" just eight weeks later. Jones simplifies the "Last Time" riff into the stoned shrug of "What, me worry?" Recorded September 6 and released September 25, "Cloud" topped both the U.S. and U.K. pop charts on November 6.

In the song, Jagger just wants to chill, but a guy starts banging on the door trying to sell him detergent—a riff on a recent series of commercials in which a man knocks on housewives' doors to see if they have his brand. Then Jagger's neighbor yells at him to turn down the stereo, just as every kid's parents did. Irate, Jagger drives off and takes a nap in his car, only to wake up with a parking ticket on the windshield—a nod to Dylan's "Subterranean Homesick Blues," in which he warns listeners to watch their parking meter. The song's title could have been inspired by Solomon Burke's hit that year, "Got to Get You Off My Mind," or by Jones's gas station incident crack, "Get off my foreskin!"

Jagger's songs tell stories, unlike most of the Beatles', and his stories are also decipherable, unlike Dylan's. As with Dylan, Jagger's unconventional voice and looks pushed him to become a high-concept lyricist in order to compensate. Jagger also compensated by becoming the heir to Elvis as the most electrifying white performer.

Rolling Stone magazine asked him decades later, "What did you think was going on inside you at 15 years old that you wanted to go out and roll around on a stage?"

"I didn't have any inhibitions. I saw Elvis and Gene Vincent, and I thought, 'Well, I can do this.' And I liked doing it. It's a real buzz, even in front of 20 people, to make a complete fool of yourself. But people seemed to like it. And the thing is, if people started throwing tomatoes at me, I wouldn't have gone on with it. But they all liked it, and it always seemed to be a success, and people were shocked. I could see it in their faces."

"Shocked by you?"

"Yeah. They could see it was a bit wild for what was going on at the time in these little places in the suburbs."[12]

Of all the English front men, Jagger was already the most animated on-stage. Then he was nuked and mutated by James Brown's radioactive waves when both were filming *The T.A.M.I. Show*. Brown was peeved that the new-comer Stones had been chosen to close the show over him, just because they were young white teen idols, and he vowed to make them wish they'd never left England. The Stones wisely wanted to change their slot, but were denied.

Brown writes in his memoir that he didn't think he'd ever danced so hard in his life, and the audience kept calling him back for encores. "At one point during the encores I sat down underneath a monitor and just kind of hung my head, then looked up and smiled. For a second, I didn't really know where I was . . . By that time I don't think Mick wanted to go on the stage at all. Mick had been watching me do that thing where I shimmy on one leg, and when the Stones finally got out there, he tried it a couple of times. He danced a lot that day. Until then I think he used to stand still when he sang, but after that he really started moving around."[13]

When one compares Jagger's performances on TV shows before and after *T.A.M.I.*, it becomes clear how direct (and skillful) his copying of Brown was, from the way he held the microphone stand to the undulating knees to the clapping, jumping up, and doing the half splits. After Ike and Tina Turner opened for the Stones, Jagger would absorb Tina's style in the same fashion.

The success of "Satisfaction" also drove Jagger to new levels of exhilaration. On *Shindig!* on May 20 (before the song's release), Jagger pumps his knee and does a few flamenco claps over his head, but he's rather subdued. By the fall, he's gliding, legs flying out to either side; bobbing his head like a chicken and pointing; slapping an imaginary face with upraised hand like a haughty baron; jack-knifing over with the mike and then flipping the stand upside down above his head. For the "satisfaction" bit, he alternately glares or licks his lips.

He began jumping around more than even Brown, and then started adding in-your-face pansexuality. Promoting "Get Off of My Cloud" on TV, he tossed his hair and stared with big, wide Diana Ross eyes while draping his mic cord over his shoulder, pouting with delicate waves of a limpish wrist, and sticking his butt out with the flamenco claps.

He'd gone through a big camp phase when he first moved out of his folks' house and was living with Richards and Jones in a squalid two-bedroom flat in Chelsea, before the band made it. Jagger would put on pancake makeup, lipstick, mascara, a powder-blue linen housecoat, a lavender hairnet, stockings, and high heels and, Richards recalled, would be "wavin' his hands everywhere—'Oh! Don't!'—a real King's Road queen for about six months. Brian and I immediately went enormously butch, sort of laughing at Mick."[14] Because they had no heat, in the winter they all slept in the same bed together, and Richards's former partner Anita Pallenberg said Jagger and Jones had a brief fling, though both were extreme womanizers.[15] (Jagger even seduced the mother of one of Jones's illegitimate children.) Later, Jagger would periodically share a bed with manager Oldham.

It took more balls for Jagger to act gay than it did to act black. In the early days, people in the audience would shout "Queer!" and "Homo!" People spat at him in New York. Yet later bios claimed that by 2010 he had slept with more than four thousand women, including Carla Bruni, Angelina Jolie, Uma Thurman, Farrah Fawcett, and Carly Simon.[16]

Back in the mid-1960s, he was at a King's Road restaurant with gay interior designer Nick Haslam when a snide older man asked Jagger, "Are you a man or a woman?" Jagger glared at him for a beat and then rose, unfastened his trousers, and let it all hang out.[17]

He was the forefather of the glam rock era of David Bowie and *Rocky Horror*'s "Sweet Transvestite" from Transylvania. In *Sexing the Groove: Popular Music and Gender*, Sheila Whiteley writes that Jagger "opened up definitions of gendered masculinity and so laid the foundations for self-invention and sexual plasticity which are now an integral part of contemporary youth culture."[18] He absorbed both gay and black culture to smash through repression and liberate a lot of white men, gay or straight, showing you could dance free and still rock—and even do the funky chicken if you wanted.

But the Stones wouldn't have sustained without the Jagger/Richards songwriting partnership. By the middle of the year, their pop and R&B sensibilities had entwined. Had the best of their originals been collected on one coherent album, it would have equaled Dylan's and the Beatles' releases: "Satisfaction," "Get Off of My Cloud," "The Last Time," "Play with Fire," "Heart of Stone," "I'm Free," "The Spider and the Fly," "19th Nervous Breakdown," "Mother's Little Helper," "Ride on Baby," "Sitting on a Fence," and "As Tears Go By."

On December 3–5, the Stones played Sacramento, San Jose, San Diego, and LA, and then went into RCA Studios in Hollywood to record through December 8. *Rubber Soul* and *The Who Sings My Generation* were released on the third of the month, the Byrds' *Turn! Turn! Turn!* album released on the sixth. Ken Kesey had given Richards and Jones acid after their San Jose gig. Some girls whom the band knew from Phoenix showed up, and Wyman encouraged them to walk into the studio naked to surprise the band. Oldham took one into the control room and had sex with her in front of everyone.[19]

The track "19th Nervous Breakdown" was a further rewrite of "Play with Fire" mixed with "Like a Rolling Stone." A socialite whose mother owes a million dollars in taxes has been emotionally damaged by her ex. But when Jagger tries to help her on an acid trip, he realizes she's actually disarranging his mind.

"Mother's Little Helper" was a preemptive reply to the charge that the Stones were leading kids to drug abuse, a portrait of a stressed-out housewife addicted to Valium. In it, Jagger warns the frazzled mother that she'll get an overdose if she doesn't dial it back with the pills—one of the few times the Stones advocated just saying no. Richards imitates the sitar of "Norwegian Wood" with his electric twelve-string.

Other tracks reflect Jagger's deep antipathy to marriage, not least because his two-year relationship with Chrissie Shrimpton (model Jean Shrimpton's sister) often degenerated into screaming matches. Once, she even kicked him down the stairs.[20] Shrimpton was one of a number of his girlfriends who would attempt or succeed in suicide. In "Sitting on a Fence," Jagger watches his friends from school settle down and get a mortgage because they can't think of anything else to do. Then they realize the choice wasn't right and they go out at night and don't come back. Richards accompanies him in the Appalachian style of folk guitarist Bert Jansch. Jones joins in on harpsichord at the end.

Jones plays the harpsichord in "Ride on Baby" as well, a breakthrough to the Stones' next formula: Jagger savaging women with misogynistic lyrics while Jones plays catchy pop on a cornucopia of exotic instruments. A young lady walks up to Jagger and, despite her bloodshot eyes, tries to act shy, but Jagger's already seen her before, in a "trashy magazine." When they get together, she smiles vacantly but looks through him. He kicks her out and condenses "Like a Rolling Stone" into one line, saying she'll look sixty-five when she turns thirty and won't have any friends left. In the New Year, Jagger would turn his venom on Chrissie Shrimpton with songs such as "Stupid Girl," "Under My Thumb," and "Out of Time."

When the Stones were in the studio a few months earlier, Jones had been frustrated. Closed out of the songwriting partnership, he felt he'd lost hold of what had once been his band. He could be the most handsome and striking Stone, but his life of excess and cruelty was catching up to him, and he sometimes appeared to be in a trance, with bags under his eyes like a degenerate Morlock.

But then, on September 14 in Munich, he met the darkly alluring model Anita Pallenberg. "I got backstage with a photographer," Pallenberg remembered. "I told [Brian] I just wanted to meet him. I had some Amyl Nitrate and a piece of hash. I asked Brian if he wanted a joint, and he said yes, so he asked me back to his hotel, and he cried all night. He was so upset about Mick and Keith still, saying they had teamed up on him. I felt so sorry for him."[21]

The support of a hip and intelligent beauty revitalized Jones. To "Ride on Baby" he piled on the marimbas, Autoharp, congas, twelve-string Rickenbacker, and koto, and began his quest to fuse Delta blues with Elizabethan lute music.

Since the group had recorded "Play with Fire" the January before, chamber pop had gathered steam: in the Beatles' "Yesterday" and "In My Life"; the Beach Boys' *Today* album; the Yardbirds' Gregorian chants in "Still I'm Sad" and Spanish scales in "Evil Hearted You"; the Henry Purcell influence on the Who's "The Kids Are Alright"; the flute solo in "California Dreamin'";

the harpsichord in Simon and Garfunkel's "Leaves That Are Green." The Zombies' minor-key electric piano in "Tell Her No" inspired five New York teens to form the Left Banke. The group began recording their first album *Walk Away Renée/Pretty Ballerina* in December; the title track features both harpsichord and string quartet. With the Stones, Jones would be one of the major forces in baroque pop. Even if he wasn't writing the songs, they would be unimaginable without his instrumental embellishments. Playing unusual instruments also earned him more camera time. Briefly, Jones was back.

Oldham originally wanted to call the Stones' next album *Could You Walk on the Water*, with a shot of the band members up to their necks in a reservoir. The label put the kibosh on that, and it was eventually titled *Aftermath*. But no doubt the Stones were floating a little in their minds the day Jagger, Oldham, and publicist Tony Calder cruised along the Pacific Coast Highway in a red Ford Mustang. Each time they hit the radio button to change the station, "Satisfaction" was playing.[22] They must have felt like "I'm Free," the B side of "Get Off of My Cloud." In the song, Richards's tremolo'd guitar grooved with Jones's organ and the group's harmonies, halcyon like the cloudless blue.

Got to Keep on Moving

MLK takes on Chicago while Stokely Carmichael and the SNCC introduce the Black Panthers. Nina Simone embodies "Black Is Beautiful," and Coltrane flies into the free jazz stratosphere. Ska lays the foundation for hip-hop.

Thanks to the Civil Rights and Voting Rights Acts, Martin Luther King Jr. believed that "Old man Segregation is on his deathbed," so he changed his focus to poverty. "What good does it do to be able to eat at a lunch counter if you can't buy a hamburger?"[1] After a "People to People" tour of northern cities, in September he announced the Chicago Freedom Movement, which would focus most of its energy on ending housing discrimination that prevented blacks from moving out of the slums and into the suburbs. At the end of the year he moved his family into a tenement in the West Side ghetto. But while northerners professed to abhor the bigotry of the South, they also feared for the property value of their nest eggs, and in the months to come the demonstrations would be swarmed by angry white folks as twisted with rage as the rednecks. During one Chicago march, someone threw a brick at King's head and knocked him down. "I have seen many demonstrations in the South, but I have never seen anything so hostile and so hateful as I've seen here today," he said.[2]

As the struggle shifted from the ability to vote to issues such as housing discrimination, busing, and affirmative action, consensus on the best course of action began to splinter. At the same time, many blacks became impatient with King's nonviolent ethos. The leader who would first articulate the new era's defiance was Stokely Carmichael of the Student Nonviolent Coordinating Committee (SNCC). Singer Nina Simone called him the most handsome man in America.[3] He had been a Freedom Rider, and then worked to register black voters in Alabama. In March, when King marched through Lowndes County on the way from Selma to Montgomery, Carmichael approached all the blacks who came out to see MLK and got their contact information to register them.

Despite (or because of) the passage of the Voting Rights Act on August 6, Alabama was as dangerous as ever. On August 13, twenty-nine civil rights activists protested a whites-only store and were jailed. When they were released on August 20, a white Episcopalian named Jonathan Myrick Daniels, who had come down from Harvard with his wife to help, attempted to enter Varner's grocery store with a seventeen-year-old black girl to buy a soft drink. An engineer for the state highway department named Thomas Coleman was working as a special deputy at the door and pointed a shotgun at the girl. Daniels pushed her down and took the blast. Another civil rights worker tried to flee with Daniels's wife, and the deputy shot him as well. The jury accepted the deputy's claim that he had acted in self-defense, and he was acquitted.

Alabama was basically a one-party state, and the flag of the state's Democratic Party had the words "white supremacy" written on it. So Carmichael and the SNCC knew they needed their own independent political party, and in December they announced the formation of the Lowndes County Freedom Organization.[4] They started holding voter drives and political classes for the residents, 80 percent of whom lived under the poverty line. For their symbol, they picked a leaping black panther, claws bared. Even if the voter couldn't read, he could see the symbol and know which way he should vote.[5]

By the end of the year, Carmichael had decided that whites could no longer occupy leadership positions in the SNCC and began formulating his concept of Black Power. "It is a call for black people in this country to unite, to recognize their heritage . . . We have to do what every group in the country did—we gotta take over the community where we outnumber people so we can have decent jobs."[6] Instead of integration, many Black Power advocates wanted black-controlled institutions; some even called for an independent black state.

The following year, the Lowndes party logo and Carmichael's call for Black Power inspired Huey Newton and Bobby Seale to found the Black Panther Party in Oakland, California. They also drew on the example of the Deacons for Defense and Justice, a group of black veterans from World War II and Korea who formed twenty-one chapters throughout Alabama, Mississippi, and Louisiana to protect civil rights workers from the Klan with guns. Founded in November 1964, they settled on their name the following January and incorporated as a non-profit in March.

The voter drive finally succeeded, because August 6's Voting Rights Act outlawed literacy tests and sent federal examiners into the South to monitor elections. The act became one of the most successful pieces of legislation in history, vastly increasing blacks' presence in elections. Within months, more than two hundred fifty thousand new black voters were enfranchised. In 1964, 6 percent of Mississippi voters were black, but five years later that number was 59 percent.[7] The number of black elected officials rose over the next twenty years from a hundred to seventy-two hundred.[8] Even Lowndes County had a black sheriff by 1970.

In general, black entertainers were not yet referring to the struggle in their performances. Bill Cosby enjoyed a series of Grammy-winning comedy albums and got some flak for not talking about civil rights issues in his comedy act, but he maintained, "A white person listens to my act and he laughs and he thinks, 'Yeah, that's the way I see it, too.' Okay. He's white. I'm Negro. And we both see things the same way. That must mean that we are alike. Right? So I figure this way I'm doing as much for good race relations as the next guy."[9] That lack of controversy enabled him to become the first black person to star in a TV drama, with Robert Culp in *I Spy*. When it premiered on September 15, four stations in Georgia, Florida, and Alabama wouldn't run it, but it became one of the year's biggest hits.

Black artists left the job of making protest songs to whites such as Phil Ochs ("Here's to the State of Mississippi") and even the Yardbirds ("You're a Better Man Than I"). It was easy for whites to rake southern states over the coals from inside a coffeehouse in Greenwich Village, but blacks had to tread lightly—or face the repercussions. Up through the early 1960s, blacks were often allowed to play only black clubs in the South, East, and even Midwest; such venues became known as the "Chitlin' Circuit." Even during their most recent summer American tour, the Beatles had to stipulate in their contracts that they would not play segregated venues, to make sure they didn't find themselves inadvertently supporting racists. Though the ropes that had once blocked off the black sections of dance halls from the white ones had come down, most black artists were hesitant to appear confrontational, because they didn't want to be closed out of the new venues and record markets that had just opened up to them. In 1968, when James Brown proclaimed, "Say It Loud, I'm Black and I'm Proud," he was shut out of white radio.

Nina Simone, however, dared to tackle racial themes head-on in tracks such as her cover of Billie Holiday's lynching song, "Strange Fruit," which was why Carmichael called Simone the true singer of the civil rights movement. She wrote in her autobiography, "I realized that what we were really fighting for was the creation of a new society. When I had started out in the movement, all I wanted were my rights under the Constitution. But the more I thought about it, the more I realized that no matter what the President or the Supreme Court might say, the only way we could get true equality was if America changed completely, top to bottom. And this change had to start with my own people, with black revolution."[10]

The change had to start with her own view of herself. Simone recorded her composition "Four Women" in autumn.

The women in the song are black, but their skin tones range from light to dark, and their ideas of beauty and their own importance are deeply influenced by that. All the song did was to tell what entered the minds of most black women in America when they thought about themselves: their complexions, their hair—straight, kinky, natural, which?—and what other women thought of them. Black women didn't know what the hell they wanted, because they were defined by things they didn't control. And until they had the confidence to define themselves, they'd be stuck in the same mess forever. That was the point the song made . . . The song told a truth that many people in the USA—especially black men—simply weren't ready to acknowledge at that time.[11]

The "Black Is Beautiful" cultural movement was gathering steam in its fight against internalized self-hatred. The phrase was perhaps first introduced in 1962, when the African Jazz-Art Society and Studios put on a fashion event in Harlem called the Grandessa Models Naturally—"The Original African

Coiffure and Fashion Extravaganza Designed to Restore Our Racial Pride & Standards."[12] The movement celebrated dark skin, African facial features, and natural, unstraightened hair. Simone replaced her wig and gown with an Afro, African dresses, turbans, and hoop earrings.

Diana Ross's favorite wig, on the other hand, was modeled on Annette Funicello's coif. Motown's mogul Gordy even secured a deal with a Lansing, Michigan, company to produce the Supremes Special Formula White Bread, with the group's image on the package.[13]

After the trio's previous single, "Nothing but Heartaches," missed the Top 10, Holland-Dozier-Holland regrouped, came up with lyrics about tears of joy and a thousand violins, gave Ross a more challenging vocal, and made the orchestra bigger—and for two weeks, starting November 20, the Supremes were back on top with "I Hear a Symphony." They followed it up with their most ambitious single yet, "My World Is Empty without You," in a foreboding minor key with harpsichord and organ. It made only No. 5, but when the Stones retooled it for "Paint It Black" they'd take it all the way to No. 1 the following year.

Aside from the Supremes, the only other female to top the R&B charts that year was Fontella Bass of Chess Studios, for almost the entire month of November. "Rescue Me" was often misattributed to Aretha Franklin, because the two artists sounded similar—Bass's mother toured in a gospel group with Franklin's dad, who was a preacher—but at the time, Franklin's label, Columbia, was pushing her to focus on jazz and standards. It would be two more years before she found her full strength by tapping into her gospel background with Atlantic Records producer Jerry Wexler's help at FAME Studios in Muscle Shoals, Alabama.

Wexler had left Stax for FAME because Stax's musicians didn't get along with Wilson Pickett. For its part, Stax was starting to feel that Wexler was bringing his artists down to Stax to dip into its special soul recipe, but not giving the studio a fair piece of the long-term big-picture money. One of the songs that sold Wexler on FAME came about because construction worker Percy Sledge was laid off in Muscle Shoals at the end of the year, prompting Sledge's girlfriend to dump him just as she was becoming a model. Sledge poured his heartbreak into "When a Man Loves a Woman."[14]

Joe Tex also recorded at FAME. He was the man James Brown considered his main rival, and for three weeks in October he had the R&B No. 1 with "I Want to Do (Everything For You)." Other hits from Tex included "Don't

Make Your Children Pay (for Your Mistakes)." Between Sledge and Tex, Wexler figured FAME in Muscle Shoals could be his new Stax.

Motown's assembly line was humming along, though Smokey Robinson was having trouble matching the success of last spring's "My Girl" for the Temptations. The next four singles he cowrote and produced for them—"It's Growing," "Since I Lost My Baby," "Don't Look Back," "My Baby"—were gems, but none cracked the pop Top 10, and Gordy warned that if the next single didn't, he'd give an up-and-coming producer named Norman Whitfield a shot at the Temps.

In December, Robinson decided to make the next one a dance record and switched up the lead singers, giving "Get Ready" back to Eddie Kendricks to sing. The track was a euphoric dynamo (and probably the only song to use "fee-fi-fo-fum" in its lyrics), but it inexplicably stalled in the Top 30, so the Temps were given to Whitfield, who brought Ruffin back up front to rip into "Ain't Too Proud to Beg" the first week of the new year.

Robinson's own group, the Miracles, was doing well; one of their most enduring classics made the Top 20 in August, "The Tracks of My Tears." Echoing the lyrics of Lennon's "I'm a Loser," the singer laughs in public and wears the mask of a clown, but inside, his tears are falling. In turn, the Beatles took inspiration from the song's twelve-string guitar intro by Marv Tarplin for Lennon's "In My Life" on *Rubber Soul*. Robinson would revisit the theme in "Tears of a Clown" the next year.

Go-go discotheques were growing in popularity. Never ones to miss out on a dance craze, the Miracles captured the thrill of hitting the clubs with the booming tom-toms of "Going to a Go-Go." These singles, along with "Ooo Baby Baby," "Choosey Beggar," and "My Girl Has Gone" (the latter a reworking of "The Tracks of My Tears"), were compiled on one of the year's most hit-packed albums, November's *Going to a Go-Go*. (It was their first to be credited to Smokey Robinson and the Miracles instead of just the Miracles, which was the precedent that made Diana Ross and David Ruffin want to do the same with their own groups.) All the tracks were originals except "My Baby Changes Like the Weather," and seven of the twelve were cowritten by Pete Moore. It would be their only album to make the pop Top 10—strange, considering what seminal artists they were.

Also that November, Marvin Gaye made it to No. 8 on the pop charts with "Ain't That Peculiar," written by Robinson, Moore, Tarplin, and White. The lyrics are dark—Gaye's woman continually does things designed to hurt him, and his tears won't sway her—but the music is ebullient. Gaye's "ah ah ah!"s with Motown's session backup singers the Andantes picks up where his hero Ray Charles and the Raelettes left off, as Gaye swings effortlessly through the instrumental break before swerving back out with an agile "Ooooooo!"

Gaye was one artist who was troubled by the lack of social commentary in his music.

> I remember I was listening to a tune of mine playing on the radio, "Pretty Little Baby," when the announcer interrupted with news about the Watts riots. My stomach got real tight, and my heart started beating like crazy. I wanted to throw the radio down and burn all the bullshit songs I'd been singing and get out there and kick ass with the rest of the brothers. I knew they were going about it wrong, I knew they weren't thinking, but I understood anger that builds up over years—shit, over centuries—and I felt myself exploding. Why didn't our music have anything to do with this? Wasn't music supposed to express feelings? No, according to BG [Berry Gordy], music's supposed to sell. That's his trip. And it was mine.[15]

Thus the year's most militant call to arms would come not from a musician but from Beat poet LeRoi Jones (who later renamed himself Amiri Baraka). He'd already crossed the line in last year's spoken-word piece "Black Dada Nihilism," backed by the jazz of the New York Art Quartet, in which he calmly exhorts the listener to rape white girls and their fathers, and cut their mothers' throats.

"When Malcolm was murdered," Jones said, "I began to hold all white people responsible, even though in some part of my mind I knew better. But it was this heinous act . . . that made me pack up and move to Harlem and sever all ties with most of the white people I knew, many of whom were my close friends."[16] That included Jones's Jewish wife and two daughters.

He opened the Black Arts Repertory Theatre/School in April with federal funding from Project Uplift. Apparently, the government wasn't scrutinizing his poetry. In his manifesto "Black Art" he roars that poems are bullshit unless they have teeth, can shoot guns, assassinate. He wanted poems like fists and daggers that beat "niggers," stabbed "owner-jews," pulled out the tongues of cops and killed them in the alleys, and set fire to "Whities ass." He wanted a black poem and a black world, he concluded.

The Black Arts movement pushed for black studies in universities and celebrated soul food and African-style clothes. Jazz composer Sun Ra's Arkestra performed at Black Arts events that summer, and Baraka called Sun Ra the resident philosopher.

It was Sun Ra, along with fellow avant-garde musicians such as Ornette Coleman and Archie Shepp, whom John Coltrane followed into the LSD-inspired reaches of free jazz. Coltrane chose to get inaccessible to the masses on the eve of his greatest mainstream success with last winter's *A Love Supreme*. The musicians investigated dissonance, overblowing, and screeching at the highest registers of their instruments. Bebop had once been incomprehensibly insane to an older generation, but now had become the new status quo, so the vanguard had to keep pushing farther out.

The albums of Sun Ra (born Herman Poule Blount in 1914) seemed ready-made for the acid enthusiasts who loved to gaze at the psychedelic dreamscapes of Marvel comics such as *The Fantastic Four* and *Dr. Strange*. *The Heliocentric Worlds of Sun Ra, Volume One* holds cuts such as "The Cosmos," "Other Worlds," "Nebulae," and "Dancing in the Sun." His next album, *The Magic City*, was recorded live in the loft of famed Nigerian drummer Olatunji. Sun Ra's concerts would last five to six hours, and eventually the Sun Ra Arkestra formed its own commune.

Sun Ra's saxman, Farrell "Pharoah" Sanders, joined Coltrane for his next album, *Ascension*. Recorded in June with ten other musicians, it was one forty-minute piece—not something you could put on in the background like *A Love Supreme*. Its frantic, atonal *squonks* left many mystified but a devoted contingent mesmerized. In October, on his album *Om*, Coltrane chants the Hindu Bhagavad Gita and, with Pharoah, the Buddhist Tibetan Book of the Dead; there is debate in the jazz community whether Coltrane and his band were tripping when they recorded it.

Increasingly, Coltrane incorporated elements of African and Eastern music. In August he named one of his sons after sitar player Ravi Shankar, with whom he was planning to study before his untimely death two years later, at age forty, from liver cancer.

Jones/Baraka writes,

Trane carried the deepness in us thru Bird and Diz [bebop founders Charlie Parker and Dizzy Gillespie], and them, and back to us. He reclaimed the Bop Fire, the Africa, Polyrhythmic, Improvisational, Blue, Spirituality of us. The starter of one thing yet the anchor of something before . . . Trane, carrying Bird-Diz bop revolution, and its opposing force to the death force of slavery and corporate co-optation, went through his various changes, in life, in music. He carried the Southern black church music, and blues and rhythm and blues, as way stations of his personal development, not just theory or abstract history. He played in all these musics, and was all these persons. His apprenticeship was extensive, and deep, the changes a revealed continuity.[17]

*

The rage in Baraka's poetry prefigured the anger that hip-hop would give voice to two decades later in its political and gangsta phases. Meanwhile, the forerunner of the rapping technique, toasting, was in full bloom in Jamaica as part of ska culture.

Ska was created the same way American music was: through African forms mixing with European forms. It sprang from Jamaican folk music, called mento. Mento coalesced when Nigerian and Ghanaian slaves mixed the music they had brought with them with the music that Spanish and British plantation masters forced them to play.

Calypso was from a different Caribbean pair of islands, Trinidad and Tobago. It formed when music from the Nigerian and Kongolese slaves mixed with French music that stretched back to the troubadour days.

Americans were stationed in Jamaica during and after World War II, and the islanders began to mix mento and calypso with American rhythm and blues and jazz.

Mento and calypso both used the upstroke (hitting the guitar strings up toward the ceiling) instead of the more traditional downstroke. Then ska turned the R&B shuffle beat backward to highlight the offbeat. Hitting the guitar with an upstroke on the offbeat was called the skank, and the horns and other lead instruments would follow the skank.

Dancing to ska was called skanking. The style looked like running in place while you hooked your elbows while kicking out one foot and then the other.

"Sound systems" were trucks with turntables, huge speakers, and a generator. The deejay would take his truck into the Kingston ghetto and have a street party, blasting music and selling food and booze. Thousands of people would show up.

Prince Buster, one of the originators of ska, said the first ska songs were by African American sax player Willis Jackson, instrumentals such as "Later for the Gator," "Oh Carolina," and "Hey Hey Mr. Berry."[18] But when American labels begun diluting R&B with white pop and country to appeal to white American kids, Jamaican sound system entrepreneurs started making their own records, mixing R&B with their own island's genres. Nobody had any money, but everyone would work on everyone else's sessions.

Sound system owner Clement "Coxsone" Dodd had visited the states and heard the wild American disk jockeys and encouraged his deejays to emulate them. In proto-rap style, they began chanting over instrumental tracks by bands such as the Skatalites, going "ska-ska-ska," "ch-ch, ch-ch, ch-ch," or grunting.[19] Historian Clinton Hutton says, "[The deejay] could cover the weaknesses in a selection with live jive, with toasting, with scatting, with bawl out."[20] Count Machuki started beatboxing "peps" over parts of records he thought were boring.[21]

The Orange Street corridor in downtown Kingston was the ska epicenter, with clubs and record stores like Coxsone's Muzik City and Prince Buster's Record Shack. The Motown of the scene was Beverley's Restaurant and Ice Cream Parlour (also a record shop).[22] Four years earlier a thirteen-year-old Jimmy Cliff had convinced Beverley's owner, Chinese Jamaican Leslie Kong, to produce his song "Hurricane Hattie." Kong started his own label, Beverly's, and soon Desmond Dekker joined the roster. Dekker worked at a welding plant with Bob Marley, and Cliff helped record Marley's first singles, "Terror" and "One Cup of Coffee"/"Judge Not" for Beverly's.

Dekker's current singles included "Generosity," "Get Up Edina," "This Woman," and "Mount Zion." Regarding the last tune, Rastafarians believed that their leader, Ethiopian emperor Haile Selassie, descended from King Solomon and the Queen of Sheba, making them all descendants of Israel. They believed Haile Selassie would lead them back to paradise in Zion.

The Maytals had sung backing vocals on one of Dekker's singles from a year before, "King of Ska." Their lead singer was Frederick "Toots" Hibbert, a raspy Otis Redding type who grew up singing gospel in Jamaica. In 1965 Toots and the Maytals released their debut album, *The Sensational Maytals*. The Maytals' backing group was the Skatalites, the house band at Coxsone's recording facility/label, Studio One.

Prince Buster had one of the top ska hits of the year with "Ten Commandments." (The title of his hit "Madness," from two years earlier, would be taken as the name for the English ska band that would reach the Top 10 in 1982 with "Our House.") Alton and the Flames released one of the major anthems, "Dance Crasher," imploring "rude boys" to be gentlemen and not break up the parties. Rude boys were ghetto delinquents who tried to look like American movie gangsters or jazz musicians by wearing sharp suits, thin ties, and pork pie or trilby hats. Sound system owners would pay rude boys to start fights at rival parties, hence their nickname "dance-hall crashers."

Ska made enough inroads into the United Kingdom that the Beatles attempted to imitate it in "I Call Your Name," though it's doubtful anyone would recognize the song as ska today. Mods became fans of ska tracks such as the Skatalites' "Guns of Navarone" and Prince Buster's "One Step Beyond." The U.K. label Blue Beat released a lot of Jamaican singles, and gradually the term *blue beat* became generic for ska among the mods.[23] Many mods shared neighborhoods with Jamaican and West Indian immigrants and adopted the look of the rude boys. The mod movie *Quadrophenia* features them as part of the scene.

While representing Jamaica at the World's Fair in New York City, Jimmy Cliff met Chris Blackwell, an English producer who was making a name for himself releasing Jamaican music in the United Kingdom. (Later, Blackwell's label, Island, would be the home of Bob Marley and U2.) Blackwell had already convinced one of the stars of the late 1950s Jamaican scene, Jackie Edwards ("the Nat King Cole of Jamaica"), to move to England and write songs for him. Blackwell agreed to manage Cliff, and Cliff arrived in London in the fall, just as one of Jackie Edwards's songs, "Keep on Running," was recorded by a white band that Blackwell managed, the Spencer Davis Group, with Stevie Winwood.[24] Edwards's version on his own album, *Come On Home*, is terrific, a mix of Motown with intimations of the reggae sounds of Cliff, Johnny Nash, and Bob Marley to come. Edwards wrote the Spencer Davis Group's next two hits, too, "Somebody Help Me" and "When I Come Home."

Cliff's in the background of "Keep on Running," pumping up the band in the intro with "Yeah! All right! Okay!"[25] He toured with them in autumn, and with the Who and Jimi Hendrix the following year. But his journey got rough; landlords told him to move out of their buildings because of the color of his skin. Snow was hard for a Jamaican to deal with as well.[26] His later anthems, such as "Hard Road to Travel," "Sitting in Limbo," and "Many Rivers to Cross" sprang from this trying period. One of the few people Cliff could relate to was Eddy Grant, a bleach-blond Guyanese. Grant formed a band in North London that year with another black guy and two white twin brothers—hence their name, the Equals.

Bob Marley's father was a plantation overseer of Welsh descent who married an eighteen-year-old Afro-Jamaican when he was sixty-one. The two separated after Bob was born in 1945. The father paid child support but didn't see his son, and died when Marley was ten.

Marley's mother lived with the father of Neville Livingston, who would later change his name to Bunny Wailer. Their parents had a daughter together named Pearl. Marley and Bunny were tight, and in 1957 they started listening to the American R&B coming over the airwaves from distant U.S. radio stations—doo-wop groups such as Frankie Lymon and the Teenagers, the Platters, and the Drifters. Lennon and McCartney were doing the same thing in Britain at the time.

When Peter Tosh (born Winston Hubert McIntosh) met Marley and Bunny, the fact that Tosh had taught himself to play guitar and keyboards inspired them to learn how to play instruments as well. Tosh popularized the "chik, chik" guitar sound of reggae. (He later had a son with Bunny's sister.)[27]

The three formed a vocal harmony trio and sang on the corners of Trench Town, in Kingston, coached by a popular singer named Joe Higgs, who gave free lessons. First they called themselves the Teenagers, but since Frankie Lymon's band was already called that, they soon became the Wailing Rude Boys, then the Wailing Wailers—"wailing" to express the angst of living in the ghetto.[28]

In 1962 they sold seventy thousand copies of the eminently danceable "Simmer Down," a message to the rude boys to control their temper and stop turning to crime. They released seventeen singles in 1965 alone, including "Rude Boy," where their doo-wop roots fuse with reggae skank. Their output that year included numerous Beatle covers such as "I Should Have Known Better," "And I Love Her," and "Ringo's Theme," the instrumental version of "This Boy" from the American *A Hard Day's Night* soundtrack album.

Jamaica did not have the same copyright laws as the United States, so the group took the Impressions' "People Get Ready" and turned it into an early version of "One Love." When Marley redid it in 1977, he slowed it down—comparing the two versions illustrates the difference between ska and the later form, reggae—and renamed it "One Love/People Get Ready," crediting Curtis Mayfield. The Wailers also did a version of "Like a Rolling Stone," with very different lyrics.

By the end of the year, ska had started evolving into rock steady, the link between ska and reggae. In rock steady, the beat slowed down and the piano and bass took over for the trombone. The lyrics became more political as well. A ten-year-old boy named Clive Campbell was there at the dance halls, absorbing how the deejays did it. After his family moved to the Bronx two years later, he changed his name to DJ Kool Herc, got his own sound system with two turntables, and started toasting for free at block parties, helping to ignite the hip-hop revolution.

Warhol Meets the Velvet Underground and Nico

Their partnership paves the way for an assault on homophobia, repression—and sanity.

Andy Warhol and his director, Paul Morrissey, wanted to make more movies, but they needed cash. A businessman had offered to pay Warhol for the right to use his name in association with a nightclub that was set to open soon, and Warhol and Morrissey started thinking that managing a band to play in the nightclub might be a good way to raise money.[1]

They first considered approaching the Fugs, along with a folk duo who often played with the Fugs called the Holy Modal Rounders. Velvet Underground guitarist-bassist Sterling Morrison called the two groups "the only authentic Lower East Side bands."[2] The Fugs' Ed Sanders owned the Peace Eye Bookstore and published *Fuck You: A Magazine of the Arts*. The band's Tuli Kupferberg was a poet who had been immortalized in Ginsberg's *Howl* for jumping off the Brooklyn Bridge (though it was actually the Manhattan Bridge, and the jump necessitated a body cast for his spinal injuries). Kupferberg had named the group the Fugs because Norman Mailer had used the term in his book about World War II soldiers, *The Naked and the Dead*, as a euphemism for "fuck." *The Fugs First Album* was recorded in June and featured the eerily gorgeous "Carpe Diem" about the Angel of Death, "I Couldn't Get High," "Boobs a Lot," "Slum Goddess," and a cover of Romantic poet William Blake's "Ah! Sunflower, Weary of Time."

Both bands were filmed playing at the Factory. But Warhol and Morrissey had a sense that they would be too difficult to deal with. They kept looking for a group to manage.

Christa Päffgen was a German model who renamed herself Nico and had a supporting role in Federico Fellini's masterpiece of decadent pop society, *La Dolce Vita*. She met Dylan in Paris in the spring of 1964. He had sung the praises of *La Dolce Vita*'s Anita Ekberg in "I Shall Be Free No. 10" and was no doubt happy to meet another starlet from the film. Nico accompanied him to Germany and Athens while he wrote much of his fourth album, *Another Side of Bob Dylan*. The track "Motorpsycho Nitemare" features a woman who looks like she stepped out of *La Dolce Vita*. Nico later claimed Dylan wrote "I'll Keep It with Mine" for her, but then again, both Joan Baez and Judy Collins claimed that, too.

A year later, Nico hooked up with the Rolling Stones' Brian Jones. The Stones' manager, Andrew Oldham, took her on as a client and decided to give her the same treatment that had launched Marianne Faithfull's career. In late May he produced her cover of folk singer Gordon Lightfoot's "I'm Not Sayin'," with Jones and Jimmy Page on guitar. Oldham and Page wrote the atmospheric B side "The Last Mile," which mourns lost childhood like the singles by Oldham's other chanteuses Faithfull and Vashti.

That month, when Nico was in Paris, she met Warhol, Edie Sedgwick, and Warhol's assistant, Gerard Malanga, at the nightclub Chez Castel, where *What's New, Pussycat?* had been filmed. The film's stars, Peter Sellers, Woody Allen, and Ursula Andress, were hanging out that night as well. Malanga gave Nico the number of the Factory and told her to visit the next time she was in New York.[3]

Around that time, Dylan's (and Lightfoot's) manager, Albert Grossman, heard Nico's single, along with a demo she'd made with Dylan, singing "I'll Keep It with Mine," and offered to manage her if she came to the States. So she flew to New York and went to the Factory with Brian Jones. Morrissey

thought she was "the most beautiful creature that ever lived."[4] He and Warhol wanted to use her in movies and maybe something musical.

According to Morrissey, "Grossman would come to the Factory to listen
to Nico practice, but he got more interested in Edie."[5] Grossman began to
speculate that Sedgwick might have a future as a Hollywood star, so he,
Dylan, and Bobby Neuwirth began discouraging her from making more films
with Warhol. Sedgwick began to resent that Warhol had never paid her for
her appearances. His films didn't make any money—he had to sell paintings
to fund them—but that didn't appease her.[6] By the end of the year, their
relationship had grown tense. Warhol superstar Viva said, "When Edie left
with Grossman and Dylan, that was betrayal, and he was furious."[7]

One of her last Warhol films was shot in December and released in 1966.
In *Lupe*, Sedgwick plays the real-life Mexican actress Lupe Vélez, who was
found dead with her head in the toilet after overdosing on barbiturates.
After the shoot, she hung out with Dylan at the Kettle of Fish. When Warhol
showed up later, he mused to one of his Factory acolytes, "I wonder if Edie
will commit suicide. I hope she lets me know so I can film it."[8]

Shortly thereafter, Dylan came by the Factory for a "screen test," allow-
ing Warhol to film him for fifteen minutes while he sat completely still. As
payment, Dylan took one of Warhol's silk screens of Elvis Presley, driving
off with it tied to the top of his station wagon. Warhol wrote in his memoirs,
"Later on, though, I got paranoid when I heard rumors that he had used the
Elvis as a dart board up in the country. When I'd ask, 'Why did he do that?'
I'd invariably get hearsay answers like 'I hear he feels you destroyed Edie,' or
'Listen to "Like a Rolling Stone"—I think you're the "diplomat on the chrome
horse," man.' I didn't know exactly what they meant by that—I never listened much to the words of songs—but I got the tenor of what people were
saying—that Dylan didn't like me, that he blamed me for Edie's drugs."[9] Dylan
eventually traded the Elvis painting to Grossman for a couch. But the joke
was on Dylan: in 2012, Warhol's *Double Elvis (Ferus Type)* sold for more than
thirty-seven million dollars.[10]

✳

When Brooklyn native Lou Reed was seventeen, his folks were alarmed by
his bisexual tendencies. A psychiatrist recommended shock therapy three
times a week at Rockland State Hospital. Reed said later, "I resent it. It was

a very big drag. From 12 on I could have been having a ball and not even thought about this shit. What a waste of time. If the forbidden thing is love, then you spend most of your time playing with hate. Who needs that? I feel I was gypped."[11]

At twenty-three, the future poet laureate of depravity got a job as a staff songwriter at budget label Pickwick Records, which put out imitation surf-rock and Merseybeat (the pop/rock style of bands from cities along England's River Mersey such as Liverpool). "There were four of us literally locked in a room writing songs. They would say 'Write ten California songs, ten Detroit songs,' then we'd go down into the studio for an hour or two and cut three or four albums really quickly, which came in handy later because I knew my way around a studio."[12]

Reed needed a band to play his dance-craze spoof "The Ostrich," which actually didn't sound that far removed from later Velvet Underground classics like "Sweet Jane." To back him he found the Primitives. Their bassist, John Cale, also played atonal viola for the composer La Monte Young, whose minimalist "drone music" was inspired by Indian and Japanese music—as well as the hum of the transformers on telephone poles. Cale did performance art, too, such as *Plant Piece*, in which he tried to kill a plant by screaming at it.

Throughout the spring and summer of his twelfth year, Cale was molested by his organ tutor at church. "Like so many boys who lack a close relationship with their fathers, I was extremely insecure and susceptible to this kind of predator. There was a second guy I became involved with around the same time who was also into molestation," he writes in his memoir. "I'd stop and visit this man. It happened a couple of times, then I quit out of self-disgust. I remember feeling there was something wrong somewhere, and I remember consequently being cruel to a cat, strangling it with a fascination to see how far I could go without killing. Obviously I saw myself in the cat, and I had to come to terms with male relationships, to calm that aspect down . . . Anyway, I never came to terms with the problem. It always haunted me . . . It was there when I fought the school bully during lunch break. It was there when I laid my first sweetheart in the mud and grass behind the stones."[13]

Reed and Cale formed their own group, the Warlocks, the same name the Grateful Dead were using that year. They rechristened themselves the Velvet Underground after a paperback that sensationally reported on all the sexual activity secretly going on beyond the bounds of heterosexual intercourse.

Lou Reed got Sterling Morrison, a friend from Syracuse University, to play guitar or bass, depending on whether Cale was playing the bass, viola, or keyboards. A friend of Morrison's had a sister who was a drummer—Maureen Tucker. She was influenced by African drummer Olatunji and Bo Diddley. She didn't play the bass drum with her foot, as most drummers did, but instead tipped the drum up like a tom-tom, and she rarely used cymbals. She was one of the first female rock drummers.

In July, at their loft on Ludlow Street in Manhattan, they recorded six demos of songs that they would rerecord a year later for their debut album. The demo of Reed's ode to "Heroin" was close to the final version. Perhaps Reed had been encouraged to write the groundbreaking song after *Life* ran one of its most controversial photo spreads in February, on New York's "Needle Park," actually named Sherman Square, where heroin addicts congregated. The article follows a real-life couple, Karen and John, as John gets locked up and then overdoses. "To get money, Karen prostitutes [herself] and pushes, John loots cabs."[14] The *Life* portrait inspired the 1971 feature film *Panic in Needle Park*. Junkies figure as characters also in the play *Balm in Gilead*, which premiered in January, the first full-length Off-Off-Broadway production.

Reed's "I'm Waiting for the Man" relays in journalistic detail his protocol for going into Harlem and scoring heroin. "Run Run Run" is another song about addicts selling their soul for a fix, overdosing, and turning blue. "There She Goes Again" lifts the hook of Marvin Gaye's "Hitch Hike." In the song, Reed's ex has left him, and when he sees her on the street back down on her knees, he decides he'd better hit her.

"Venus in Furs" was inspired by the 1870 novel of the same name by Leopold von Sacher-Masoch, from whose name the term *masochism* is derived. Sacher-Masoch was the great-great-uncle of folk-pop star Marianne Faithfull, so John Cale managed to get the Velvet Underground's demo to her. Faithfull never responded when the group tried to follow up.[15]

In 1967, Faithfull's friends the Beatles would win raves for an innovation that echoed that demo. "Heroin" features guitar and viola rising to a shrieking crescendo, imitating a drug rush. On "A Day in the Life," the Beatles instructed an orchestra to play their instruments from the lowest to highest notes in a cacophony before Lennon sings of "four thousand holes," which some Beatle fans believed to be an allusion to the mark left by a needle.

Certainly the Beatles always had their ear to the ground, but whether the Velvets truly influenced them is unknown.

Al Aronowitz, the journalist who introduced the Beatles to Dylan, started managing the band in November and got the Velvets a gig opening for the Myddle Class, the group he managed with Carole King and Gerry Goffin, at Summit High School in New Jersey. On December 11, they played "There She Goes Again," "Heroin," and "Venus in Furs," and promptly drove all the kids out of the auditorium.

On December 15, Morrissey saw the Velvets playing at New York City's Café Bizarre and convinced Andy Warhol to manage them. Aronowitz was a pretty well-connected manager himself; he brought Brian Jones to Lou Reed's pad to score some acid for Jones and Dylan the night of the Great Northeast Blackout (November 9). But the Velvets jumped ship for Warhol, and within two weeks were spotlighted on the *CBS Evening News with Walter Cronkite*, in a piece called "The Making of an Underground Film." The segment focused on Morrissey making a short film about the Velvets' song "Venus in Furs."

Part of the group's appeal to the Warhol crowd was their androgynous female drummer—and Warhol and Reed would become good friends. Reed wrote "All Tomorrow's Parties" about the Factory scene, and it became Warhol's favorite song. Warhol loved to annoy his audience, so tracks such as "The Black Angel's Death Song," with screeching viola and feedback, was just his cup of meat. He even wanted the Velvet Underground's album to have a skip built into "I'll Be Your Mirror," so it would repeat the title infinitely.

Still, at the time, Warhol and Morrissey did not find Reed a completely compelling front man, and paired the band with Nico to alternate with Reed as lead singer. Reed was annoyed at sharing the spotlight, though Nico would hook up with both him and Cale. Morrissey projected film onto the Velvets while they played, accompanied by a series of multimedia events (whip-twirling dancers, Edie Sedgwick frugging, and strobe lights) called the "Exploding Plastic Inevitable," thus creating the East Coast version of the Acid Tests. The Doors caught their show at the Trip in LA, and seeing dancer Gerard Malanga's black leather pants, Jim Morrison was inspired to get his own. "He stole my look!" Malanga later screamed.[16]

Their first album would be produced by Dylan's old producer Tom Wilson, who must surely rank as one of the hippest producers of all time, with a resume that includes Sun Ra, Cecil Taylor, John Coltrane, Dylan, Simon and Garfunkel, Dion, the Velvet Underground, and Frank Zappa's Mothers of Invention (he was convinced to handle Zappa after hearing his song about the Watts riots, "Trouble Every Day"). Wilson pushed Lou Reed to write "Sunday Morning" for Nico for the single.

Warhol asked Reed to write "Femme Fatale" for Sedgwick, just before she left his scene altogether. After her tragic OD in 1971, her legacy consists of numerous photographs, a few hours of celluloid, and a few Dylan songs that may or may not be about her on *Highway 61* and *Blonde on Blonde.* But she continues to fascinate later generations as the archetypal party girl raging past the edge of decorum in a futile effort to forget her troubled past, in the tradition of Zelda Fitzgerald, Brett Ashley, and Holly Golightly.

Though their commercial success in the '60s was limited, the Velvet Underground went on to become one of the most groundbreaking and influential bands of all time. And as Warhol's movies grew (relatively) more sophisticated and were co-opted by mainstream films like *Midnight Cowboy*, he became, with Ginsberg, the premier outlaw of gay liberation. In an era when gay men like the Beatles' manager Brian Epstein were blackmailed by hustlers who demanded exorbitant amounts to keep their secrets, Warhol took everything he'd been told to hide and shoved it back in society's face.

Acid Oz

LSD permeates both coasts thanks to the CIA and Timothy Leary. In the San Francisco Bay area, Hunter Thompson introduces Merry Prankster Ken Kesey to the Hells Angels. The Angels attack anti-war protestors on October 16, prompting Allen Ginsberg to invent Flower Power. The same evening, the Jefferson Airplane play _The Tribute to Dr. Strange_ and the Haight-Ashbury begins to percolate. The Grateful Dead play their first Acid Test on December 4.

*

Dr. Albert Hofmann was a chemist at Sandoz Laboratories in Basel, Switzerland. He was experimenting with ergot, a fungus that grows on rye bread, to see if it could improve blood circulation. He synthesized lysergic acid diethylamide (LSD-25) on November 16, 1938, but put it on a shelf and forgot about it until he accidentally touched some on April 19, 1943, and had his first accidental acid trip while riding home on his bike.

He wrote in _LSD, My Problem Child,_ "This condition of cosmic consciousness, which under favorable conditions can be evoked by LSD or by another hallucinogen from the group of Mexican sacred drugs, is analogous to spontaneous religious enlightenment, with the _unio mystica._ In both conditions, which often last only for a timeless moment, a reality is experienced that exposes a gleam of the transcendental reality, in which universe and self, sender and receiver, are one."[1]

Neuroscientist Marc Lewis wrote in *Newsweek* that LSD "goes to work in the brain by blocking serotonin receptors. Serotonin's job is to reduce the firing rate of neurons that get too excited because of the volume or intensity of incoming information. Serotonin filters out unwanted noise, and normal brains rely on that. So by blocking serotonin, LSD allows information to flow through the brain unchecked. It opens up the floodgates—what author Aldous Huxley called *The Doors of Perception*."[2]

Sandoz Laboratories marketed the drug to the psychiatric community for therapeutic use. Psychiatrists experimented to see if the drug could treat alcoholism or mental disorders such as schizophrenia. LSD was legal, and Sandoz distributed it for free to anyone with proof that they were conducting medical research, as long as they shared whatever results they found.

The CIA thought LSD could be used to make the enemy disoriented and vulnerable, and perhaps serve as a tool for interrogation and brainwashing. To explore its efficacy as a truth serum, the CIA's Project MKUltra set up brothels in San Francisco and Greenwich Village, where prostitutes paid by the government served drinks dosed with LSD to unsuspecting johns while CIA agents watched from behind two-way mirrors and recorded the results.[3] The CIA devised the setup in part because it believed the men would be too embarrassed to talk about where they had been. These "safe houses" operated for over a decade.[4]

But by the end of the year, as the hippie counterculture's experiments with LSD began to make headlines, the CIA decided to close down operations in San Francisco. Officials became concerned that their reputation would be tarnished if word leaked out, since the subjects of their experiment had not given informed consent.[5] The New York safe house was closed the following year. By this time, the Agency had determined that LSD's effects were too unpredictable to serve as a reliable truth serum. The CIA's program was revealed in 1974, in the hearings held by Vice President Nelson Rockefeller to investigate past CIA activity. Senator Edward Kennedy's subcommittee focused on MKUltra.

The most famous acid proselytizers were two former Harvard professors named Timothy Leary and Richard Alpert (who would later change his name to Ram Dass and, in 1971, publish *Be Here Now*, a book on spirituality and yoga). Leary and Alpert believed that LSD shared the ability to induce religious experiences, along with the mescaline in the peyote cactuses used in Native American sweat lodge rituals, the DMT in the ayahuasca brew drunk by Amazonian shamans, and the psilocybin found in two hundred kinds of mushrooms. Their entourage was based in Millbrook, New York, in the sixty-four-room estate owned by William Mellon Hitchcock, the grandson of the founder of Gulf Oil. In Millbrook, Leary introduced the drug to visiting artists and politicians, believing that if society's elite were enlightened, humanity could be steered toward Eden. They took LSD in the morning and tripped until late afternoon, often playing Indian music and meditating.

Sometimes their trips threatened to become bad ones, and in those instances Leary turned to *The Doors of Perception* for advice. Huxley wrote that he could be calmed from panic if someone was there to remind him of the Clear Light referenced in the Tibetan Book of the Dead. Leary, Alpert, and psychologist Ralph Metzner developed the practice into a guide for LSD users they called *The Psychedelic Experience: A Manual Based on the Tibetan Book of the Dead,* dedicated to Huxley. The word *psychedelic* itself was invented by Huxley (with the help of psychiatrist Humphry Osmond) to describe the acid experience. The word is derived by combining the Greek words for "mind" (*psyche*) and "to reveal, make visible" (*deloun*).

On the West Coast, Stanford creative writing student Ken Kesey had taken part in an experiment that, unbeknownst to him, was funded by MKUltra. A psychology grad student told him that the Menlo Park Veterans Hospital was paying volunteers seventy-five dollars a day to take drugs that mimicked psychosis in order to study their effects. Kesey took part, and he liked the drugs so much that he started sneaking them out and sharing them with his friends. He got a job as a night aide at the hospital's psychiatric ward and wrote *One Flew Over the Cuckoo's Nest* based on his experiences there.

He used his profits to buy a school bus, which he and his gang, called the Merry Pranksters, painted like a Day-Glo Jackson Pollock explosion. They cut out a hole so they could sit on the roof, wired the bus for sound, painted "FURTHUR" (*sic*) above the windshield, and took off on a cross-country trip. The bus driver was Kesey's friend Neal Cassady, the real-life hero of Kerouac's *On the Road*, thus turning the trip into a Technicolor sequel to the Beat classic, with the Pranksters the missing link between the beatniks and the hippies. Their bus ride inspired the Beatles' "Magical Mystery Tour," the Doors' "The End," and the Who's "Magic Bus." Tom Wolfe immortalized the Pranksters in the non-fiction book *The Electric Kool-Aid Acid Test*.

Kesey bought property in the redwood forest of La Honda, California, forty-five miles south of San Francisco, and it was there the Pranksters spent

much of 1965 trying to assemble a movie out of the sixteen-millimeter footage they had shot during their trip, but it would remain unfinished until docu-
mentarians used it in 2011 for the feature *Magic Trip*. Mainly, they hosted a
series of Saturday night acid parties, frequented by counterculture luminaries such as Cassady's close friend Allen Ginsberg. Ginsberg himself had been
given acid at Stanford, in experiments funded by the CIA in 1959. He, in
turn, gave the drug to bebop musicians Dizzy Gillespie and Thelonious Monk.[6]

The woods around Kesey's place were filled with trees painted fluores-
cent colors and strung with black lights. Spotlights were placed two hundred feet up in redwoods, and artwork such as random glued-together doll
parts and a hanged man sculpture swayed from the branches. Speakers
blasted music and weird sound effects. A metal sculpture of nude figures,
called *Boise's Thunder Machine*, was mic'd to create a deafening echo if you
hit it. It was the Burning Man Festival twenty-one years ahead of time.

"The most bizarre [party] was when we invited Kenneth Anger and the
San Francisco diabolists out for Mother's Day," Kesey recalled. Prankster Page
Browning got a hen and "put its head on the stump and chopped the head
off. Page threw the chicken, still alive and flopping, right into the audience.
Feathers and blood and squawking and people jumping and screaming and
all these diabolists and Kenneth Anger got up and left. They didn't think it
was funny at all. We thought we were paying them the sort of honor they
would expect. We out-eviled them. It all had that acid edge to it of 'This is
something that might count.' We might conjure up some 80-foot demon that
roared around. As Stewart Brand said, 'There was always a whiff of danger
to it.'"[7]

It was journalist Hunter S. Thompson who was indirectly responsible
for the arrival of the world's most notorious bikers at La Honda. At the time,
Thompson was writing *Hell's Angels: The Strange and Terrible Saga of the
Outlaw Motorcycle Gangs*, having formed an edgy relationship with them.
Some of them admired his chutzpah and shared his love of guns and flooring motorbikes down the Pacific Coast Highway at 3:00 a.m. They thought
he'd offer a corrective to what they perceived as slanderous media coverage
of them (especially stories of rape). Most important, he kept them plied with
free beer.

Thompson looked up to the already famous Kesey, whom he'd met at a
TV roundtable show for writers in San Francisco that summer. They went
for beer afterward, and then Thompson said he had to go meet the Angels,

and invited Kesey along. Kesey in turn invited the Wild Ones to La Honda, though Thompson didn't think it was necessarily a good idea. They arrived on August 7 amid the dancing beatniks, writers, intellectuals, and grad students. The stereo blasted the Beatles, the Stones, and Ray Charles, as Ginsberg wrote in his poem "First Party at Ken Kesey's with Hell's Angels."[8] Cop cars were parked at the edge of the property. Kesey and fourteen other Pranksters had been busted for pot in April. LSD was legal, though, and the cops couldn't enter Kesey's home, because they didn't have a warrant, but they would search everyone as soon as they left the premises.

One of the most infamous moments in counterculture history happened at that weekend's party, alluded to obliquely in both Wolfe and Thompson's books in a way that implied that Cassady's girlfriend, Anne Murphy, was gang-raped by the Hells Angels. But both she and the biography *Neal Cassady: The Fast Life of a Beat Hero*, by David Sandison and Graham Vickers, gave a more nuanced recount. Murphy lived a wild life: struggled with thoughts of suicide, shot methamphetamine, and participated in Hollywood orgies with as many as thirty participants. She was desperately in love with Cassady, but he saw other women concurrently. Wrote Sandison and Vickers, "Her bitter response was to slip into an ambient state of drugs and sexual promiscuity while still seeing Neal from time to time. He called her Superslut. 'I kind of liked that, I recall,' she later admitted."[9]

At La Honda, Cassady was seeing two other women besides Anne, so when the Angels arrived, she slipped off to be, as she put it, "joyously" gangbanged by many of them.[10] They brought in Cassady, and he participated as well. Afterward, they handed her a card that read, "You have just been assisted by a member of the Hells Angels, Oakland Chapter." Cassady staggered out, naked, to curse at the police while being fellated by a new woman before leaving on a road trip the next day. At Kesey's parties, the line between ecstasy and madness was nonexistent. One Prankster, Cathy "Stark Naked" Casamo, was institutionalized after her time "on the bus," and another, Sandy Lehmann-Haupt, also needed psychiatric treatment.

The Haight-Ashbury hippie scene had its roots in the Cabale Creamery, a beatnik/folk music coffeehouse in Berkeley cofounded by Chandler A. Laughlin III. For the last two years, Laughlin and about fifty of his friends had been emulating Native American peyote ceremonies. On June 29 he opened the Red Dog Saloon in the mining town of Virginia City, Nevada, four hours northeast of San Francisco—out in the middle of nowhere, so they could do what they wanted. The era's first psychedelic rock poster, by George Hunter and Mark Ferguson, promised the evening would be "The Limit of the Marvelous."

Hunter and Ferguson, who played in the Red Dog's house band, the Charlatans, wanted to embrace a uniquely American style, in rebellion against the British Invasion. They dressed in nineteenth-century Victorian clothing from old Westerns, garb that fit with the saloon. They also carried guns, not just because of the Wild West pose but for self-defense; after all, they were longhairs far away from San Francisco.[11] The Charlatans played blues, country, and folk, extending their pieces into long jams. Chemist Owsley Stanley provided the LSD; later he would become the Grateful Dead's benefactor and soundman. Bill Ham projected a primitive version of the liquid light show he was developing. Over the next weeks, a couple hundred people made the trek to the saloon.

Back in San Francisco, the music scene was just starting to pick up. The Beau Brummels had some proto-folk-rock hits even before the Byrds (produced by Sylvester Stewart of Sly and the Family Stone, no less), but they were away touring most of the year and missed their city's transformation to psychedelia. We Five reached No. 3 with "You Were on My Mind."

Perhaps We Five's co-ed template was on folkie Marty Balin's mind when he invited female Signe Toly Anderson to be co-lead singer of his new group, the Jefferson Airplane. Balin had played the character Action in a San Francisco production of *West Side Story*, painted, and sculpted, and then decided he wanted to go folk-rock after hearing the Byrds. He formed the Airplane to play at his new club, the Matrix (a former pizza parlor), and they made their debut on August 13.

They in turn inspired the formation of another group, the Great Society, which featured the powerful contralto of Grace Slick. The Great Society made its debut at North Beach's Coffee Gallery on October 15, the day of massive Vietnam Day Committee protests. Eventually, Slick replaced Anderson in the Airplane, bringing with her two compositions that would become the Airplane's biggest hits, "Somebody to Love" (written by her bandmate brother-in-law Darby Slick) and "White Rabbit," Grace's uncanny homage to the hallucinogens of Lewis Carroll's *Alice in Wonderland*.

Meanwhile, some of the regulars from "Red Dog Summer" formed a

concert production collective called the Family Dog and lived in a commune called the Dog House, a large Victorian at 2125 Pine Street. To keep
the Red Dog spirit going, they hosted the "Tribute to Doctor Strange" dance
party on October 16 at the Longshoreman's Union Hall at Fisherman's Wharf.
Dr. Strange was Marvel Comics' mystic magician who, with the help of
the Book of Vishanti, traveled through trippy dimensions and defeated
flame-headed demons such as the dread Dormammu. Fellow Marvel superheroes such as the Fantastic Four and Thor were also favorites of the hippies, due to their way-out cosmic landscapes.

Ginsberg wore his white Indian gown, while the hippies dressed as pirates or cowboys with painted faces, or in green velvet granny dresses and
lace, their lively colors in marked contrast to the black-clad beatniks of yesterday. "They all joined in a snake dance," wrote Barry Miles, "weaving circles and figure eights through the hall" to the sounds of the Jefferson Airplane,
the Charlatans, and the Marbles. Bathed in the swirling lightshow, Grace Slick
howled at the revelers to feed their heads. Berkeley student Jann Wenner was
a friend of one of the Pranksters, and Slick introduced him to jazz columnist
Ralph Gleason, who would later help Wenner found *Rolling Stone* magazine.[12]

Poster artist Victor Moscoso recalled, "I dug what was going on. I dug
the scene. In fact, all I wanted to do at that point was event posters, as if I
understood intuitively that this was a historical opportunity . . . I knew these
were historical events, and they've got the dates on them, so you can line
them up and see the progression. That's what I wanted to do. I stopped painting. I turned on, tuned in, and dropped out."[13] Moscoso's posters for the
Family Dog would pioneer the use of photographic collage and vibrating
colors. Another poster artist, Wes Wilson, would soon create a psychedelic
font that looked as if it were moving and melting. Rick Griffin, Alton Kelley,
and Stanley Mouse were other pioneers of the emerging form.

The Family Dog returned the following weekend, on October 24, with
"A Tribute to Sparkle Plenty." (Sparkle Plenty was a character in the *Dick
Tracy* comic strip, a baby of extraordinary beauty.) The Lovin' Spoonful head-
lined the gig. The Grateful Dead's Jerry Garcia recalled,

> The first time that music and LSD interacted in a way that came to life
> for us as a band was one day when we went out and got extremely high
> and went that night to a concert by the Lovin' Spoonful . . . We ended

up going into that rock and roll dance and it was just really fine to see that whole scene—there was just nobody there but heads and this strange rock and roll music playing in this weird building. It was just what we wanted to see . . . We began to see that vision of a truly fantastic thing. It became clear to us that playing in bars was not going to allow us to expand into this new idea.[14]

The Dead's Phil Lesh told Ellen Harmon of the Family Dog, "Lady, what this little séance needs is us."[15]

In the parks, the San Francisco Mime Troupe was performing its satirical guerrilla theater. In August, Parks and Recreation determined that the shows were not in good taste, but the troupe continued performing anyway, so director Ronnie Davis was busted for obscenity and for not having a permit.

The troupe's manager, Bill Graham, was a German Jew who fled the Holocaust, arriving in New York at age ten, parentless. He became a mambo champion and then moved to San Francisco to be near his sister. He was the office manager of a truck manufacturer until he met the troupe at a free concert in Golden Gate Park. On November 6, Graham arranged for the Airplane, the Fugs, and poet Lawrence Ferlinghetti to perform at a benefit for Davis's legal fees at the Calliope Ballroom. Experimental films were projected on bedsheets, colored light shows on the walls. Ginsberg was there, of course—and the line went around the block. When the police tried to shut it down, Graham told them Sinatra and Liberace were en route, so they let the show continue. Graham began to realize there was money to be made in the scene. A second Mime Troupe benefit followed, on December 10. Then Graham took the Airplane on as clients. In a year he would open the Fillmore ballroom and become the most famous rock promoter of all time.

North Beach had been the scene for the beatniks when Ginsberg debuted *Howl* in 1955, but the new cheap neighborhood for students and bohemians was Haight-Ashbury. Gary Duncan, the guitarist of the Quicksilver Messenger Service, said,

What was really going on in San Francisco in the early sixties was a whole other thing most people don't know about. The underground scene was really a lot heavier than what was publicized and what people think happened, you know, hippies playing music with flowers in their hair, all that crap . . . I first started hanging out there back when there were no hippies. There were beatniks, and crash pads, poets and painters, every kind of drug imaginable and every kind of crazy motherfucker in the world. It was kind of cool to be in on something that nobody else knew about. Early on, there was a big scene that was totally invisible. If you knew the right address and knocked on the door, you could walk through that door into a whole other world. You'd go to, say, 1090 Page Street, open up the door, and there'd be a fourteen-bedroom Victorian house with something different going on in every room: painters in one room talking to each other, musicians in another room. It was really cool, and to all outward appearances there was nothing happening. It was like a secret society.[16]

Ten-Ninety Page Street was a Victorian rooming house owned by the parents of one of the members of the band Big Brother and the Holding Company. There was a ballroom in the basement, so Big Brother manager Chet Helms began charging fifty cents for bands to hold Wednesday night jam sessions there, which grew into weekend parties where admission was charged to raise money for rent. Big Brother and the Quicksilver Messenger Service formed there, and Helms's friend from Austin, Texas, Janis Joplin, visited periodically and sat in, before permanently joining Big Brother in the spring of 1966.

At the Blue Unicorn coffeehouse, you could wash dishes for food.[17] Chet Helms organized meetings there for the group LEMAR ("Legalize Marijuana"). The Sexual Freedom League met to fight censorship; legalize nudity, abortion, and prostitution; establish sex education in schools; lower the age of consent to sixteen; and give lectures on "Sex and Civil Rights," "How to Be Queer and Like It," and "Sex in the Mental Hospital"—and of course organize nude parties/orgies. In August, the group received national press with its "Nude Wade-in."[18]

At the Open Theatre, mixed media were projected onto nude bodies. The Magic Theatre for Madmen Only, its name derived from a locale in Herman Hesse's *Steppenwolf*, sold antiques along with pipes, bongs, and posters. In March, Edward Craven-Walker patented his invention the lava lamp, and Chicago's Lava Manufacturing Corporation had begun manufacturing Lava Lites. The Psychedelic Shop, generally regarded as the first head shop, opened on Haight Street on January 3, 1966.

*

The birth of the hippie counterculture coincided with the anti-war movement. But if the dedicated radicals who emerged from Berkeley's Free Speech Movement were hopeful that hippies would swell their ranks, they found that many of them were more interested in dropping out of society than they were in changing it.

The first indication that the drug culture might disrupt the coherence of the movement came when Ken Kesey was invited to speak at the October 15 Vietnam Day Committee rally in Berkeley. When it was his turn to address the throng, he said,

> You know, you're not gonna stop this war with this rally, by marching . . .
> They've been having wars for ten thousand years . . . I was just looking at
> the speaker before me . . . and you know who I saw and who I heard? . . .
> Mussolini . . . That's the cry of the ego, and that's the cry of this rally! . . .
> Me! Me! Me! Me! . . . And that's why wars get fought . . . ego . . . because
> enough people want to scream, "Pay attention to me!" . . . There's only one
> thing's gonna do any good at all . . . And that's everybody just look at it,
> look at the war, and turn your backs and say . . . Fuck it.

He then played an off-key rendition of "Home on the Range" on his harmonica.

Despite his strange speech, the following day, two thousand to five thousand marched to Oakland to demonstrate at an army induction center. The crowd sang "Help!" and Country Joe and the Fish jug band played their "I-Feel-Like-I'm-Fixin'-to-Die Rag" on a flatbed truck while the Merry Pranksters' Day-Glo school bus, "Furthur," followed—until the parade was stopped at the county line by four hundred cops, with the Hells Angels biker gang looming behind them. Allen Ginsberg tried to cool the rising tension by chanting "Hare Krishna," but suddenly an Angel snatched a sign and roared "Cowards! Go back to Russia, you fucking Communists!" The Angels lunged at the protestors, and the cops in turn began fighting with the Angels; one officer received a broken arm, and some Angels got their heads split by police clubs.

The pro-war Angels vowed to disrupt the protest scheduled for November 20 as well, and to beat up the "filthy Commies." Upon hearing this, Ken Kesey and Allen Ginsberg went to head Angel Sonny Barger's house to talk them out of it. The Angels and Kesey's Pranksters had been partying together since August. Everyone took LSD, played Dylan and Joan Baez records, and Ginsberg even got the Angels to chant the Buddhist Prajnaparamita sutra. According to Kesey, Ginsberg went "right into the lion's mouth with his little cymbals. Ching, ching, ching. And he just kept talking and being his usual absorbing self. Finally they said, 'OK, OK. We're not going to beat up the protesters.' When he left, one of the Angels, Terry the Tramp, says, 'That queer little kike ought to ride a bike.' From then on, he [Ginsberg] had a pass around the Angels. They had let all the other Angels know, 'He's a dude worth helping out.' They were absolutely impressed by him and his courage."[19]

Still, the Free Speech Movement asked Ginsberg for suggestions on what to do if the Hells Angels changed their minds and marauded again. On November 19 the *Berkeley Barb* published his essay, "Demonstration or Spectacle as Example, as Communication or How to Make a March/Spectacle": "Masses of flowers—a visual spectacle—especially concentrated in the front lines. Can be used to set up barricades, to present to Hells Angels, police, politicians, and press and spectators whenever needed or at parade's end . . . Marchers should bring crosses, to be held up in front in case of violence; like in the movies dealing with Dracula."[20]

Ginsberg also recommended bringing flags, musical instruments, children's toys, and candy bars for the Angels and police, and the Constitution, little paper halos, white flags, and movie cameras. If the scene grew tense, marchers could sit or do mass calisthenics and chant the Lord's Prayer, Om, or "The Star-Spangled Banner." And if violence threatened to erupt, he advised that a sound system blast the Beatles' "I Want to Hold Your Hand" and the marchers burst into dance. He proposed floats of Christ with Scared Heart and Cross, Buddha in meditation, and Thoreau behind bars. Also, he said that in advance of the march, the rumor should be spread that women would pull down the pants of anyone who opposed them.

The same day the *Berkeley Barb* published Ginsberg's piece, the Angels called a press conference and said that although they considered the demonstration a "despicable un-American activity," in the interest of public safety, they would not attend, as their patriotism could inspire them to violence. They also sent a telegram to LBJ offering to go to Vietnam as "a crack group of trained gorillas [*sic*]."[21] The next day, between 6,000 and 10,000 people marched unharmed.

Ginsberg's "Demonstration or Spectacle as Example" manifesto may have been partially inspired by Dylan. When Jerry Rubin asked the singer to participate in the VDC march, Ginsberg recalled that Dylan agreed but added, in typically enigmatic fashion, "Except we ought to have it in San Francisco right on Nob Hill where I have my concert, and I'll get a whole bunch of trucks and picket signs—some of the signs will be bland, and some of them have lemons painted on them, and some of them are watermelon pictures, bananas, others will have the word 'Orange' or 'Automobile' or the words 'Venetian Blind.' I'll pay for the trucks, and I'll get it all together and I'll be there, and we'll have a little march for the peace demonstration."[22]

Ginsberg said, "I think Dylan offered it somewhat ironically, but I think he would have gone through with it . . . I think that was the beginning of our realization that national politics was theatre on a vast scale, with scripts, timing, sound systems. Whose theatre would attract the most customers, whose was a theatre of ideas that could be gotten across?"[23] Still, the VDC declined to take Dylan up on his offer.

Ginsberg's vision of using masses of flowers in antiwar protest was perhaps his most influential meme, though the phrase "flower power" itself does not appear in his essay. One of the earliest-known appearances of the actual term would be the Flower Power Day rally organized in May 1967 by Abbie Hoffman, the activist who cofounded, with Jerry Rubin, the radical street theater group the Yippies. Hoffman may have been combining Ginsberg's flower concept with the phrase "Black Power," which Stokely Carmichael popularized in 1966. (Hoffman had worked in the Student Nonviolent Coordinating Committee, which Carmichael chaired.) Rubin never hesitated to give props to Ginsberg: "If you want to see the birth of Yippie, [Ginsberg] came out and he gave a speech about how to march again with the Hells Angels attacking."[24] Whoever came up with the term, by the time of Hoffman's May 1967 rally, flowers and hippies were inextricably linked. That same month, the Mamas and the Papas' leader, John Phillips, wrote and produced Scott McKenzie's hippie anthem, "San Francisco (Be Sure to Wear Flowers in Your Hair)." Flower power's most iconic moment came in October 1967, when an eighteen-year-old actor named George Harris surprised National Guardsmen at the Pentagon by sticking carnations in the barrels of their rifles.

One autumn night in La Honda, the Pranksters all did DMT, the ayahuasca (yagé) brew that the Amazonian natives drank. Kesey walked outside onto Route 84. As Tom Wolfe recounted in *The Electric Kool-Aid Acid Test*, Kesey stood in the middle of the road, his mind alternating between the thought that he was God and the thought that he was just high. A car came at him going fifty miles an hour. Kesey balanced on the center line and gestured. The car slowed and went around him. "And he knows with absolute certainty he has . . . all the power in the world and can do what we wants . . . the Power and the Call, and this movie is big enough to include the world, a cast of millions, the castoff billions . . . Control Tower to Orbiter One. CONTROL."[25]

"When you've got something like we've got, you can't just sit on it," Kesey said. "You've got to move off of it and give it to other people. It only works if you bring other people into it."[26]

Kesey loved comics and believed he was the real-life equivalent of Captain America, a man transformed into a superhero when government scientists give him a super serum. Kesey felt he was his own *Cuckoo's Nest* protagonist, Randle McMurphy, inspiring beaten-down people to escape their mental prisons. "The purpose of psychedelia is to learn the conditioned responses of people and then to prank them. That's the only way to get people to ask questions, and until they ask questions they're going to remain conditioned robots."[27] Kesey and Ginsberg saw acid as a tool that could help the masses sweep away dysfunctional programming and determine what they really wanted, and thus recreate a healthier society.

The Pranksters advertised their first official Acid Test with a poster hung at the Hip Pocket Bookstore of Santa Cruz. They held the test at one of the Pranksters' homes on November 27 and charged a dollar admission. It was an unstructured performance art happening, with Owsley's LSD, a slide show by Stewart Brand on the Native Americans' way of life, Ginsberg chanting mantras, Cassady rapping while juggling a sledgehammer, and Kesey playing his eerie flute. But if they were going to start charging, they needed something extra.

✳

The Warlocks jug band played their first gig on May 5 at Magoo's Pizza in the Menlo Park suburb. Guitarist Jerry Garcia's first wife, Sara Ruppenthal Garcia, said, "What we'd been doing before was very organic and elemental. Although we might not have spoken of it that way, there was this deeply spiritual aspect to it for us. When we took acid, we started listening to the Beatles. Dylan's first electric album came out right about then, too. We had been putting him down. But taking acid and listening to that album was incredible. So the resistance to amplified music waned. And there wasn't a huge market for jug bands."[28]

After seeing the Lovin' Spoonful, a jug band that had gone electric, the Warlocks decided to follow suit. They recorded their first electric session at Golden Gate Studios on November 3, covering songs such as Gordon Lightfoot's "Early Morning Rain," in which they contrasted the downbeat lyrics with peppy organ. They already had the elastic, percolating, bittersweet sound that would still be present twenty years later on tracks such as "Touch of Grey." The Farfisa organ of "Mindbender (Confusion's Prince)" sounded like a more foreboding "Incense and Peppermints," by the Strawberry Alarm Clock.

But there was another group called the Warlocks, who had a recording deal—not to mention a third group of Warlocks who would soon rename themselves the Velvet Underground. ("Warlocks" was tied with "Wailers" for most popular name of the year.) So they had to pick a new name. They took DMT. Then, as bassist Phil Lesh recalled, Garcia picked up an old *Britannica World Language Dictionary* and the pages fell open. "The words 'grateful' and 'dead' appeared straight opposite each other across the crack between the pages in unrelated text . . . In that silvery elf voice he said to me, 'Hey, man, how about the Grateful Dead?' " It was a folklore term common to many mythologies—describing a spirit who is thankful that someone has arranged his burial.

Leary's *Psychedelic Experience: A Manual Based on the Tibetan Book of the Dead* advocates ego death in an acid trip. Perhaps the band's name referenced that, just as Huxley's *The Doors of Perception* was the inspiration for the name for the Doors. Garcia also enjoyed EC (Entertaining) horror comics, with their crypt keeper and attendant ghouls.[29] Perhaps the new name also had something to do with a car crash Garcia was in four years before. His friend was driving ninety miles per hour and flipped the car, sending Garcia through the windshield and his other three friends out of the car as well. The automobile landed on one of them, killing him. Garcia said the tragedy was "where my life began. Before then I was always living at less than capacity. I was idling. That was the slingshot for the rest of my life."[30]

Merry Prankster Page Browning, a friend of Phil Lesh's, told Lesh and Garcia stories about the Pranksters' cross-country bus trip. Garcia had been at some of Kesey's parties back when Kesey was at Stanford. Browning came to one of the group's gigs, and then told Kesey they'd be good for the Acid Tests.

The band's first show as the Grateful Dead was on Saturday, December 4, in San Jose, at the second Acid Test, after a Rolling Stones gig at the San Jose Civic Auditorium. The Pranksters gave out flyers to concertgoers leaving the show. The handbills featured a picture of Uncle Sam saying, "Can You Pass the Acid Test?" along with the address. Up to four hundred people came.[31] Per Stones bassist Bill Wyman, Keith Richards and Brian Jones attended, and within a few days the band recorded "19th Nervous Breakdown," in which Jagger sings about his first trip.

The Prankster named Mountain Girl (a.k.a. Carolyn Elizabeth Adams Garcia, who would become Garcia's second wife) recalled that the Dead at first "were almost voyeuristic. They would come through, perform, and take off again."[32]

Sara Ruppenthal Garcia said, "The new thing was, 'Can You Pass the Acid Test?' Do you have the resources to open up your nervous system to anything? I wasn't sure I could . . . It meant a lot to him [Garcia], and it was hard for him to figure out. He was amazed by it."[33]

Garcia's brother Clifford said,

Actually, Jerry didn't love that scene up there at Kesey's right away. It took him a while to fit into it. He was always telling me, "These people are up in the woods getting ripped and doing this . . ." like it was beneath him to do that. I said, "Jerry, people do that all over. What's the big deal? If you want to play with these guys, that's what you have to do." I'd lay that kind of trip on him whenever I talked to him about it. I said, "Don't feel bad about doing that shit." He didn't think they were too stable of a group and he knew they were party animals. He wasn't into it. It was a wild scene.[34]

But gradually, Garcia realized that the band had the freedom to play at the Acid Tests if they wanted to and the freedom *not* to play if it got too strange. They ended up performing at, by guitarist Bob Weir's estimation, every Acid Test except one, in Mexico. Weir said,

No one had ever even imagined that stuff like that could possibly happen until it did. It was actually better than realizing my dreams . . . You would walk by a microphone, for instance, and maybe say something, and then a couple minutes later you'd hear your own self in some other part of the room coming back at you through several layers of echo. The liquid light shows began there. I think it was the first time anyone saw them. People were rather gaily adorned: dyed hair, colorful clothing and stuff like that. And everybody was loaded to the gills on LSD. There was a lot of straight-ahead telepathy that went on during those sessions. We learned during those sessions to trust our intuitions, because that was about all we had to go on. When you learn to trust your intuitions, you're going to be more given to try things, to experiment. And you're going to be more given to extemporaneous assaults of one sort or another. We learned to start improvising on just about anything. We were participants, and so were they. We were all just making waves, as big and bold as we could, and seeing where they rippled against each other and what kind of shimmers that all caused.[35]

The Dead started to do long extended improvisations, a jazz-like approach with a rock beat.

The third Acid Test, on December 10, was in a log cabin, the first one with a strobe light. Along with the Dead, the poster advertised "Cassady and Anne Murphy vaudeville." Each Test was bigger than the one before, and established the template for the rock concerts and raves to follow, with the light show's pulsating amoeba river-skies projected over the group and the dancers. On December 17, at Muir Beach, the organizers showed some of the bus movie. When cops showed up in the parking lot, Garcia headed them off and somehow convinced them there was no reason for them to go inside. As the police walked away, Garcia touched his hat to them with the words "The trips, Captain." From then on he was Captain Trips.[36]

December 18's Test was in Palo Alto, Christmas Eve's in Portland, Oregon. Over the next few weeks, Acid Tests would be held on the Sunset Strip and even in Watts, before a return to San Francisco for the Trips Festival of January 21–23. The Dead and Big Brother and the Holding Company played for ten thousand attendees. A thousand people were turned away each night.

Quicksilver Messenger Service's Gary Duncan said, "Things like that have to exist secretly. That's why, when they brought it into the public eye, it sort of went away. That early side of San Francisco was never really publicized. There was a while when the place was just totally free. You could go anywhere, do anything you wanted, and nobody hassled you. The spotlight wasn't on everybody. As soon as the spotlight came on and there was money to be made, then it went the way of all things."[37]

The Acid Tests were the epicenter of the trilogy of books that together encapsulated the trajectory of the counterculture. Neal Cassady and Allen Ginsberg are protagonists in *On the Road,* the book that ignited the Beat movement; *The Electric Kool-Aid Acid Test* captures the hippie era's idealistic peak; and Hunter S. Thompson's *Fear and Loathing in Las Vegas* portrays the burnout of the morning after. But one justly famous passage from Thompson's book recounts the euphoria of San Francisco nights before people knew the dream was doomed to crash. Flooring his motorcycle across the Bay Bridge, Thompson was "absolutely certain that no matter which way I went I would come to a place where people were just as high and wild as I was . . . There was madness in any direction, at any hour . . . There was a fantastic universal sense that whatever we were doing was right, that we were winning . . . We had all the momentum; we were riding the crest of a high and beautiful wave."[38]

24

Rubber Soul

The Beatles release their synthesis of folk, rock, soul, baroque, proto-psychedelia, and the sitar on December 3.

Dylan hung out with the Beatles a couple of times at the Warwick Hotel when they were in New York on August 13–17 for *The Ed Sullivan Show* and the Shea Stadium gig. Whenever he visited the Beatles, he brought a copy of his new record to play for them. "Hey, John, listen to the lyrics, man."

But Lennon was getting high and drunk on wine. "Forget the lyrics!" Lennon recalled, "You know, we're all out of our minds; are we supposed to be listening to lyrics? No, we're just listening to the rhythm and how he does it."[1]

But whether or not he was aware of it, Lennon continued to borrow words from Dylan songs. For *Help!*'s "You've Got to Hide Your Love Away," he took the image of "facing the wall" from Dylan's "I Don't Believe You (She Acts Like We Never Have Met)." In an attempt to make it less Dylanesque, he replaced the harmonica with a flute. In fact, Lennon stopped playing harmonica entirely, which he had done on eleven earlier Beatle songs.

The Beatles returned to London on September 1 and entered the studio on October 12 to record their new album. That day, they did the first take of "This Bird Has Flown," the working title of "Norwegian Wood." The guitar sounded close to some of Dylan's riffs: slightly reminiscent of "It's Alright Ma (I'm Only Bleeding)" and another, as yet unrecorded, song that Dylan played for the Beatles when they were hanging out. The track needed something to set it apart.

Along with copies of Ravi Shankar's albums *Portrait of Genius* and *Sound of the Sitar*, Harrison had recently bought a sitar. His conversations with David Crosby about Shankar while they were tripping last August had inspired him. Also, when the Beatles arrived back in Britain from the States, the Kinks were at No. 10 on the charts with the Indian-influenced "See My Friends." When the Kinks toured Australia and Asia at the beginning of the year, they had a stopover in Bombay. Ray Davies said, "I remember getting up, going to the beach and seeing all these fishermen coming along. I heard chanting to start with, and gradually the chanting came a bit closer, and I could see it was fishermen carrying their nets out."[2] Author/jazz musician Barry Ernest Fantoni recalled socializing with the Beatles one night when they heard the Kinks' song. Realizing Davies's guitar sounded like a sitar—the Kinks' song has no Indian instruments, but the guitar imitates a tambura, while Ray's vocal whine and drone lend his voice an Indian quality—they discussed getting one for their next record.[3]

Lennon asked Harrison if he could add the instrument to "Norwegian Wood." "He was not sure whether he could play it yet because he hadn't done much on the sitar, but he was willing to have a go."[4]

Harrison's sitar flourishes, as rudimentary as they were, kicked the nascent Indian craze into high gear. Soon Donovan, Them, the Moody Blues, the Pretty Things, Paul Butterfield, the Doors, and Traffic all employed "raga rock," as the Byrds' publicist coined it for the release of *their* sitar-inspired "Eight Miles High," in 1966. Even the Velvet Underground appropriated the Indian drone. Next year, Harrison would travel to India to study with Shankar, the beginning of a life-long friendship. Just as Harrison's twelve-string arpeggio at the end of "A Hard Day's Night" birthed the sound of folk-rock, his growing fascination with Indian instruments would soon expose millions of Beatles record buyers to world music. When his India trip led him to pursue Transcendental Meditation with the Maharishi, it also encouraged countless baby boomers to look into Eastern philosophy.

Still, despite the sitar, Dylan knew Lennon had borrowed from him again. Three months after *Rubber Soul*'s release, he mocked both the waltz time and storyline of "Norwegian Wood" in "4th Time Around," then ended the song with an appeal not to ask for his crutch. Al Kooper recalled, "I asked him about it—I said, it sounds so much like 'Norwegian Wood,' and he said, 'Well actually, "Norwegian Wood" sounds a lot like this. I'm afraid they took it from me, and I feel that I have to, y'know, record it.' Evidently, he'd played it for them, and they'd nicked it. I said, 'Aren't you worried about getting sued by The Beatles?' and he said, 'They couldn't sue me!'"[5]

Dylan played "4th Time Around" for Lennon in a hotel and asked the Beatle what he thought about it. Lennon said he didn't like it. Still, Dylan played it to all of London at the Royal Albert Hall the final night of his '66 world tour. Lennon later admitted to interviewers that it made him very paranoid,[6] and he ceased writing Dylan-inspired songs. It seemed ironic for Dylan to complain, considering he had appropriated melodies from other sources for "Blowin' in the Wind," "Hard Rain," "Don't Think Twice," "The Times They Are A-Changin'," "It Ain't Me Babe," and "She Belongs to Me," to name just a few.

On the surface, Lennon's short and abstract lyrics were the antithesis of Dylan's, but the American had freed him up to express alienation and ennui in a way that hadn't been done before. And Dylan convinced him he didn't need to separate the part of his brain that composed pop songs from the one that wrote the subversive wordplay of his books, and the two sides began to meld.

"Norwegian Wood" itself concerns an extramarital affair in the apartment of a young lady who owns nothing on which the singer can sit, just the '60s version of Ikea, the "Norwegian wood" of the title. Peter Asher, who lived down the hall from McCartney in the Asher household, "had his room done out in wood; a lot of people were decorating their places in wood . . . But it's not as good a title, Cheap Pine, baby," McCartney said.[7]

In the song, the woman tells the singer she has to go to work in the morning. He ends up sleeping in the bathtub. Then, when he wakes up, she's gone, so he lights a fire. McCartney elaborated that the female in the song "led him on, then said, 'You'd better sleep in the bath.' In our world the guy had to have some sort of revenge. It could have meant I lit a fire to keep myself warm, and wasn't the decor of her house wonderful? But it didn't, it meant I burned the fucking place down."[8]

Back in June, when McCartney recorded "I'm Down," he wrapped a take by uttering, "Plastic soul, man, plastic soul," which is what the band had heard

black guys call Mick Jagger. The phrase became the album title, twisted into
a pun on tennis shoes. They recorded a blues track called "12 Bar Original"
that recalled Tommy Tucker's "Hi-Heel Sneakers," ultimately held off the album. The LP's soulful opening track almost never survived, either.

McCartney arrived at a writing session at Lennon's with an idea about
"Golden Rings," but it was a nonstarter. One of them wanted to throw in the
towel, but the other kept pushing, "No, we can do it." It fell into place when
they changed the title to "Drive My Car," a blues term for having sex. It turned
into a little story about an actress who tells a guy he can be her limo driver.
Proudly, he counters that he can do better than being her chauffeur, but she's
so sexy she talks him into it. Then, in the last verse, she admits that she
doesn't have a car.

The key was getting a deep bass sound. Harrison listened to Otis Redding's "Respect" and suggested that he and McCartney play something similar on bass and guitar at the same time.[9] But Abbey Road Studios couldn't
get a bass sound as loud or as full as the black labels. Next time, the Beatles
fumed, they'd record at Stax.

"It needs cowbell," Lennon said, like "In the Midnight Hour." It was the
first Beatles session to go past midnight, wrapping at 12:15 a.m.

"Satisfaction" had challenged the Beatles' supremacy—Stones manager
Oldham called it "The National Anthem"[10]—by sweeping the masses onto
the dance floor with its lyrics of sexual frustration. So Lennon fought back
in "Day Tripper," with his own dance riff about a "prick teaser," and then
gave the line to McCartney to sing as "big teaser." Lennon joins in for the
chorus, and they remake "Twist and Shout" for the instrumental break. The
main riff itself was inspired by Bobby Parker's "Watch Your Step,"[11] just as it
had been for "I Feel Fine," recorded almost exactly a year earlier. Critic Dave
Marsh said "Day Tripper" was the closest the Beatles had ever come to making a soul record, and Otis Redding put it in his set.

Many of the Beatles' songs chronicle the old-fashioned male's frustrations
with the modern, independent woman. McCartney wanted Jane Asher by
his side constantly. Unfortunately for him, she was determined to pursue her
acting career. Thus many of McCartney's finest mid-'60s tracks rose out of
their arguments. "[Songwriting] is often a good way to talk to someone or to
work your own thoughts out. It saves you going to a psychiatrist, you allow
yourself to say what you might not say in person."[12]

After he broke up with Asher, McCartney found a woman who truly would accompany him here, there, and everywhere, even onstage, Linda Eastman—and angst largely disappeared from his work in the 1970s.

"You Won't See Me" was written in the Asher house while she was out of town doing a play. "I'm Looking through You" was a disillusioned reprimand, as if McCartney weren't himself fooling around on tour—he felt that as long as he wasn't married, it wasn't cheating. Except for "Yesterday," McCartney's songs of the era seldom take responsibility for the conflict.

Still, the band needed more material, always more material. Racking his brain, Lennon remembered a melody McCartney used to play back in the old days. When Lennon was in art school, existentialists were trendy. When McCartney went to one of the art school parties, he saw a bohemian with goatee and striped shirt singing a French song. McCartney developed a parody where he would mumble words as if he were French, trying to be mysterious for the ladies. Lennon suggested McCartney put some words to that melody. So McCartney hired a friend to help him with the French lyrics, and for the phrasing in the bridge, he imitated Nina Simone in her recent cover of "I Put a Spell on You," again per Lennon's suggestion. "Michelle" won the Grammy for Song of the Year and was the forty-second most played song of the century, per BMI, even though it was never released as a single by the Beatles.

Rubber Soul **was** the last time Lennon's persona on record was "normal" for many years. The next album would see him plunging into the lysergic vortex, followed by reinventions as a mystic, peace guru, radical, and junkie before staggering back toward the middle of the road circa 1973. But on October 18, he offered "In My Life," which would go on to be a wedding (and funeral) standard.

Remembering journalist Kenneth Alsop's encouragement to write something like his books, Lennon imagined a bus trip from his old house into town. "I had Penny Lane, Strawberry Fields, Tram Sheds—and it was the most boring sort of 'What I Did On My Holidays Bus Trip' song and it wasn't working at all. I can*not* do this! I cannot do this! But then I laid back and these lyrics started coming to me about the places I remember . . . And it was, I think, my first real major piece of work. Up till then it had all been sort of glib and throwaway. And that was the first time I consciously put my literary part of myself into the lyric."[13]

McCartney adapted Marv Tarplin's guitar intro from "The Tracks of My Tears" for the beginning. They knew they needed something special for the instrumental, but didn't know what, so they left an empty space when they recorded the rhythm track. Then producer George Martin had an inspiration. He overdubbed a keyboard part, as he had on many Beatles tracks, but this time he played it slower than normal, then sped up the recording to make it sound like a harpsichord. The group's next phase of studio experimentation was beginning.

Lennon's "Girl" sings of a relationship with S/M overtures, with an aloof, dominating woman who believes pain leads to pleasure. "There is no such thing as the girl; she was a dream . . . It was about that girl—that turned out to be Yoko, in the end—the one that a lot of us were looking for."[14] Lennon made sharp intakes of breath into the mike to sound like he was either taking a hit from a joint or having sex. McCartney added a Zorba-like bit he had heard played on a bouzouki during a holiday in Greece.

The band liked the "la la la"s the Beach Boys sing in "You're So Good to Me" on the *Summer Days (and Summer Nights!!)* album. So, for backing vocals, they had the idea to sing "dit dit dit"s, which soon morphed into "tit tit tit"s. They had already gotten "prick teaser" past Martin. This time, during the playback, Martin asked, "Was that 'dit dit' or 'tit tit' you were singing?"

"Oh, 'dit dit,' George, but it does sound a bit like that, doesn't it?"

In the car, the Beatles broke down laughing. Martin had done comedy records for *The Goon Show* with Peter Sellers and Spike Milligan, so he probably knew anyway.

"Run for Your Life" is the flip side of "Girl." Now Lennon is the sadist, recycling the lyric from Presley's "Baby Let's Play House," that he'd rather see his woman dead than with another man. Beyond the hypocrisy of an epic womanizer being jealous, there is the threatening tone already apparent in earlier tracks such as "No Reply" and "You Can't Do That." His book *In His Own Write* makes some jokes about domestic abuse: "Not even his wife's battered face could raise a smile on poor Frank's head . . . A few swift blows had clubbed her mercifully to the ground, dead."[15] Some years later, after Yoko Ono's influence turned him into a feminist, Lennon proclaimed "Run for Your Life" his least favorite Beatles song and said he regretted writing it.

✻

The meeting with the Byrds the August before had inspired Harrison to write his first classic, "If I Needed Someone." He was heading toward marriage with Pattie Boyd, so the lyrics addressed all the women of the world, saying that had he met them earlier, it might have worked out, but now he was too much in love (but give me your number just in case). The band got down the rhythm track, highlighted by McCartney's "drastically arpeggiated"[16] bass, in one take, and then overdubbed the soaring harmonies and tambourine. Harrison sent an advance copy to the Byrds through publicist Derek Taylor, with a note: "This is for Jim [McGuinn]," Harrison told Taylor. "Tell Jim and David that 'If I Needed Someone' is the riff from 'The Bells of Rhymney' and the drumming from 'She Don't Care about Time,' or my impression of it."[17] The sound was so transcendent that Lennon adopted it for his own "Nowhere Man," recorded a week later.

The latter song had its roots in Lennon's restlessness living in the suburb of Weybridge, outside London. "[It] won't do at all. I'm just stopping at it, like a bus stop. Bankers and stockbrokers live there; they can add figures, and Weybridge is what they live in, and they think it's the end, they really do. I think of it every day—me in my Hansel and Gretel house. I'll take my time; I'll get my real house when I know what I want. You see, there's something else I'm going to do, something I must do, only I don't know what it is. That's why I go 'round painting and taping and drawing and writing and that, because it may be one of them. All I know is, this isn't it for me."[18]

In his Hansel and Gretel house, Lennon spent five hours one morning trying to write a "song that was meaningful and good."[19] The deadline to get *Rubber Soul* out in time for Christmas sales was upon them. "Nothing would come. I was cheesed off and went for a lie-down, having given up." Soon McCartney would be coming around to lend a hand. "Then I thought of myself as Nowhere Man sitting in his nowhere land."[20] The song "came, words and music, the *whole* damn thing, as I lay down . . . So letting it *go* is what the whole game is. You put your finger on it, it slips away, right? You know, you turn the lights on, and the cockroaches run away; you can never grasp them."

The Byrds' McGuinn said that Dylan had shocked Lennon by pointing out that he had nothing to say. Lennon said, "For years on Beatles tours, Brian Epstein had stopped us from saying anything about Vietnam or the war. He wouldn't allow questions about it."[21] The blindness of "Nowhere Man" echoes the deaf masses of "Blowin' in the Wind" and "The Sound of Silence."

(Also, Lennon really was practically blind without his glasses.) But unlike those fatalistic songs, Lennon exhorts the Nowhere Man to get out there and see what he's been missing—the world is at his command, if he just realizes his power.

Just as the Beatles chased more bass for their soul tracks, they tried to out-treble the Byrds for the folk-rock tracks "Nowhere Man" and "If I Needed Someone." "They're among the most treble-y guitars I've ever heard on record," McCartney boasted.

> The engineer said, "Alright, I'll put full treble on it," and we said, "That's not enough." He said, "But that's all I've got." And we replied, "Well, put that through another lot of faders and put full treble up on that. And if that's not enough we'll go through another lot of faders." They said, "We don't do that," and we would say, "Just try it . . . if it sounds crappy we'll lose it, but it might just sound good." You'd then find, "Oh, it worked," and they were secretly glad because they had been the engineer who put three times the allowed value of treble on a song. I think they were quietly proud of those things.[22]

Harrison and Lennon play in unison, as they did a year before on "I Feel Fine," on their Sonic Blue Stratocasters. McCartney and Starr lock into one of their most supple drum and bass grooves. The instrumental climaxes with the sound of a bell, like an epiphany.

"In the beginning was the Word," begins the Gospel of John in the New Testament. In Lennon and McCartney's "The Word," they sing that they have seen the light, and their mission is to spread love and sunshine. But there is an eerie, almost discordant edge to the church organ, as if they sense that messianic ambitions don't come without risk. Lennon and Harrison's future spiritual songs, "Imagine" and "My Sweet Lord," would disturb psychotic Beatle stalkers Mark David Chapman and Michael Abram, turning the movie *Help!* tragically real.

The band had been singing about love for years, but this was a new kind of love, agape, the nonromantic form that embraced all humanity, the precursor to "All You Need Is Love" and Lennon's peace anthems. In a few years, Lennon would determine that being an antiwar activist was the best use of his power, moving in the opposite trajectory of Dylan, who escaped into seclusion with his family.

For "The Word," McCartney said, "we smoked a bit of pot, then we wrote out a multicolored lyric sheet, the first time we'd ever done that. We normally didn't smoke when we were working. It got in the way of songwriting, because it would just cloud your mind up—'Oh, shit, what are we doing?' It's better to be straight. But we did this multicolor thing."[23]

A year later, Yoko Ono came by McCartney's house asking for song lyrics she could give to avant-garde composer John Cage, who collected manuscripts. McCartney didn't have any, but he sent her on to Lennon, who gave her the colorful lyric sheet of the "The Word." In a few years, she would become his partner in his antiwar efforts.

When interviewers asked Lennon about LSD in August, he said he didn't know much about it. But by October he was trumpeting it in the title of "Day Tripper," which he wanted to be the next single. The title was a pun on day-trippers who journey somewhere but come home the same night, in the sense both of a girl who wouldn't commit full time to him in a relationship and of "weekend hippies," people who maybe partied with psychedelics a little on the weekend but then went back to their conventional lives. Ten months after Dylan sang about the drug-centric counterculture in "Subterranean Homesick Blues," the lifestyle was now established enough for Lennon to critique a woman's commitment to it.

But the other band members believed "We Can Work It Out" was a more commercial choice for the single. That song would stand as one of the last Beatles compositions to feature different parts written by each member of the songwriting team. It was predominantly McCartney's piece, but Lennon wrote the bridge about life being too short to waste time fighting. Recording the piece took eleven hours, the longest time spent on a track to date. Harrison had the idea to do it like a German waltz. Lennon used a Salvation Army harmonium in his endless quest for new colors.

Still, Lennon argued vehemently that "Day Tripper" be the A side. They compromised with a double-A-side single, though, as the others predicted, McCartney's effort was more popular, making it to No. 1 in the United States while "Day Tripper" made No. 5. "We Can Work It Out" turned out to be the group's fastest-selling hit since McCartney's previous A side, "Can't Buy Me

Love." It was also the last of the Beatles' streak of six U.S. No. 1 singles in a row.

"We Can Work It Out" was inspired by McCartney's fights with Asher, with the singer imploring a woman to see it his way (though not offering to compromise), and it resonated with troubled couples everywhere. But the song was broad enough to hold numerous meanings. Some listeners applied it to the U.S. racial divide, some to the hope that the war in Vietnam could be averted.

Now the band just needed an album cover. Robert Freedman photographed them at Lennon's house in brown suede jackets, then later regrouped with the band so they could pick which shot to use. McCartney recalled, "Whilst projecting the slides on to an album-sized piece of white cardboard, Bob inadvertently tilted the card backwards. The effect was to stretch the perspective and elongate the faces. We excitedly asked him if it was possible to print the photo in this way."[24] Like the fish-eye lens cover of June's *Mr. Tambourine Man*, the photo, stretching as it does like The Ad Lib's table during Lennon and Harrison's first acid trip, announced the onset of psychedelia, adding another layer to the pun of the album's title.

Christmas Time Is Here

A Charlie Brown Christmas brings a new honesty about psychotherapy while decrying consumerism; the Byrds hit No. 1 with words from *Ecclesiastes*; *Rubber Soul* inspires Brian Wilson to create the greatest rock album ever; Johnny Cash tangles with the Klan; and Stevie Wonder comes of age.

As the cultural shifts in race relations, sexual mores, drug use, and patriotism shook the windows and rattled the walls, a heightened sense of mass anxiety was only natural. And as a new candor began to unfold, neurosis became the common denominator in everything from John Lennon's angst-ridden confessionals such as "I'm a Loser" and "Help!" to the troubled superheroes of Marvel Comics.

In the April 1 edition of the *Village Voice*, Sally Kempton wrote that the "maladjusted adolescent Spider-Man" was "the only overtly neurotic superhero I have ever come across. Spider-Man has a terrible identity problem, a marked inferiority complex, and a fear of women. He is antisocial, castration-ridden, racked with Oedipal guilt, and accident-prone."[1] Spider-Man went to a psychiatrist—though, unfortunately, the shrink turned out to be the villain Mysterio in disguise.

Freudian theories, such as subliminal effects on the subconscious, the

Oedipus complex, and compensation, began making their way into the culture in the 1920s, through intellectuals and artists. By 1957, up to 14 percent of Americans had undergone some form of psychotherapy, particularly as it was used to try to help soldiers integrate back into civilian life.[2] Many still feared that going to a "head shrinker" implied that one was crazy, but between 1950 and 1975, the number of psychologists increased eightfold.[3]

Eternal patient Woody Allen made his screenwriting and acting debut in *What's New Pussycat?* It was the eighth-highest-grossing film of the year, featuring Peter Sellers as a psychotic psychiatrist who boasts, "My father was Vienna's most renowned gynecologist. He was a brilliant pervert . . . I use all kinds of unorthodox therapies. For example, I've had the greatest success shutting people in dark closets."[4]

Like Allen, Charlie Brown was also a frequent visitor to his psychiatrist, Lucy, as he was plagued by pantophobia, "the fear of everything." In the 1960s, half the United States read Charles Schulz's *Peanuts* newspaper comic strip every morning, and on April 9, 1965, the characters appeared on *Time*'s cover.

The inspiration for Lucy was Schulz's wife, Joyce.[5] They ultimately divorced in 1972, but although she was a hard-ass, she also pushed the shy Schulz and made him ambitious enough to create a multimedia and merchandising empire out of his drawing studio that earned him thirty to forty million dollars a year, all by drawing a strip a day for fifty years, without an assistant.

Schulz's alter egos were, alternately, the beleaguered Charlie Brown, the thoughtful Linus (who needed his security blanket despite his wisdom), the consumed Schroeder (his piano a stand-in for Schulz's drawing board), and the confident, whimsical Snoopy.

In 1963, producer Lee Mendelson approached Schulz to make a documentary on him.

We've just done a show on the world's greatest baseball player . . . why not do one on the world's worst baseball player, Charlie Brown? . . . He was very cordial but . . . he just wanted to focus on doing the comic strip at that time. I asked him if he happened to have seen the Willie Mays special on NBC-TV, and he said he had. "I really liked the show. Willie is a hero of mine. Why do you ask?" I told him I had produced the show and wanted to do something similar with him. There was a long pause, and then he said: "Well maybe we should at least meet. If Willie can trust you with his life, maybe I can do the same. But I can't promise anything."[6]

They made the documentary and called it *A Boy Named Charlie Brown*. (The title was later recycled, at the end of the decade, for the first Charlie Brown feature film.) Once it was in the can, Mendelson needed music. He was driving across the Golden Gate Bridge when he heard the bossa nova–style "Cast Your Fate to the Wind" on the radio. Mendelson called *San Francisco Chronicle* jazz writer Ralph Gleason and asked him who had done the song. Gleason referred him to the song's composer, Vince Guaraldi, a.k.a. "Dr. Funk." The song had been a cut on his album *Jazz Impressions of Black Orpheus*, a collection of songs inspired by the classic feature film about the Orpheus myth set in Rio de Janeiro during Carnival. "Cast Your Fate to the Wind" won the Grammy for Best Original Jazz Composition, and then Sounds Orchestral covered it and scored a Top 20 pop hit. Mendelson and Guaraldi spoke; then Guaraldi called him back two weeks later to play him a musical idea over the phone. Mendelson didn't want to hear it that way, but Guaraldi insisted he had to play it or he'd forget it. "Linus and Lucy" became the Peanuts theme song—and a jazz standard.

In May, Mendelson convinced Coca-Cola to sponsor *A Charlie Brown Christmas* special, and CBS gave it the green light. Schulz wasn't a fan of jazz, but he agreed that Guaraldi's music worked, so they brought him back. To animate the special, Schulz wanted to use Bill Melendez, who had worked on Disney films going back to *Pinocchio*, *Fantasia*, *Dumbo*, and *Bambi*, as well as many *Bugs Bunny/Looney Toons* cartoons. Melendez had already brought the *Peanuts* characters to life when Schulz licensed them to Ford commercials from 1959 to 1965. (Though Schulz decried commercialism, he also licensed his characters to Dolly Madison and Met Life.) Schulz trusted Melendez because he rendered the characters just as they were in the strip, though the ads are disconcerting when viewed today because Linus has a Brooklyn accent.

The previous year's *Rudolph the Red-Nosed Reindeer* showed that holiday specials could break the mold, with its story about misfits (including an elf who doesn't want to make toys but would rather be a dentist) who stop the abominable snow monster and save Christmas. A fable about the value of nonconformity, it is narrated by Burl Ives, who was blacklisted for being "Red," a Communist sympathizer.

Though Schulz's hero was known for being "wishy-washy," the 2008 biography *Schulz and Peanuts* reveals that, when it came to his art, his creator was not. In a meeting with Schulz, Mendelson pushed for a laugh track on the Peanuts special, since, he said, all comedy shows had them:

> "Well, this one won't. Let the people at home enjoy the show at their
>   own speed, in their own way."
> Then [Schulz] rose and walked out, closing the door behind him.
> Mendelson, shocked, turned to Melendez. "What was that all about?"
> "I guess," replied Melendez, "that means we're not having a laugh track!"[7]

If the lack of a laugh track was upsetting, Schulz dropped a bomb when he informed the producers that Linus would recite the Gospel for one minute. Schulz said, "We can't avoid it; we have to get the passage of St. Luke in there somehow. Bill, if we don't do it, who will?"

Even though he hadn't attended church regularly for the last seven years, Schulz taught a Methodist Sunday school for adults and drew a single strip panel about teenagers called *Young Pillars* for the *Church of God* magazine. He tried to avoid the issue, but if asked about church by the press, he said, "I don't know where to go. Besides, I don't think God wants to be worshipped. I think the only pure worship of God is by loving one another, and I think all other forms of worship become a substitute for the love that we should show one another." In his Sunday school classes, he would raise a topic but just listen to people discuss it and not offer his opinion.[8]

Mendelson made one last push to cut the biblical recitation for the sake of entertainment, but Schulz "just smiled, patted me on the head, and left the room."

At the beginning of *A Charlie Brown Christmas*, the bags around Charlie's eyes indicate that he is heavily stressed out. "I think there must be something wrong with me, Linus. Christmas is coming, but I'm not happy. I don't feel the way I'm supposed to feel. I just don't understand Christmas, I guess. I might be getting presents and sending Christmas cards and decorating trees and all that, but I'm still not happy. I always end up feeling depressed."

He is also disturbed by the over-the-top Christmas decorations on his dog's house, his little sister's unbridled greed, and the commercialization of the sacred holiday, echoing the folkies who booed Dylan at Newport. (Wisely, an opening sequence with Snoopy catapulting Linus into a Coca-Cola sign was cut.⁹)

Psychiatrist Lucy encourages Charlie to direct the school Christmas play to "feel involved" with the holiday, and then instructs him to buy a tree for the show—preferably a pink aluminum one. Instead, Charlie picks out a sickly little natural one, just as Jesus, champion of the weak, would have done. The kids all denounce Charlie for not having picked a good tree.

"Isn't there anyone who knows what Christmas is all about?" he howls.

"Sure, Charlie Brown, I can tell you what Christmas is all about." Linus recites the Gospel of Luke, chapter 2, verses 8–14, which announces Jesus' birth. "Glory to God in the highest, and on earth peace and goodwill towards men. That's what Christmas is all about, Charlie Brown."

Inspired, Charlie tries to decorate the tree on his own, but the heavy ornaments appear to kill it. Then the rest of the gang uses the decorations from Snoopy's house and turn Charlie's wilted sapling into a beautiful tree. Charlie joins them in singing "Hark! The Herald Angels Sing" in the snow under the sparkling stars.

Compared to the gentle standards of today's children's programming on *Disney Jr.* and *Nickelodeon*, the kids' cruelty to Charlie and his depression are pretty severe. The CBS executives didn't like the special; they thought the music was weak and that the kids who performed the voices sounded amateurish. Indeed, most of them were real little kids, not pros, who had to be recorded reading one sentence at a time, with their lines edited together later. But the show was already listed in *TV Guide*, so CBS honored its commitment to run it. The network just wouldn't be ordering any sequels.

The special aired on December 9. The execs of little faith were stunned the morning after to see that it brought in a 49 share of the Nielson ratings, meaning half the TVs in the country had tuned in. It was the second-most-watched show that week, behind *Bonanza*, and the highest-rated Christmas special in history. *Variety* called it "Fascinating and haunting," and it won an Emmy and a Peabody.¹⁰

"Charlie Brown is not used to winning, so we thank you," Schulz said when accepting the Emmy.

Schulz vetoed the idea of polishing the amateur voices and low-budget animation for future rebroadcasts, as these made the show as real and endearing as the little tree. Guaraldi's *Charlie Brown* soundtrack would go on to be one of the best-selling holiday albums of all time. The perennial airing of *A Charlie Brown Christmas* became a unifying bastion of tradition in the face of the culture wars that lay ahead.

As equally unorthodox as a cartoon character with a security blanket reciting the Bible was a rock band reaching No. 1 with lyrics from the Book of Ecclesiastes, the same week the *Peanuts* TV special aired.

In the late 1950s, Pete Seeger's publisher told him he couldn't sell his protest songs. Angry, Seeger decided to turn some verses from the Bible into a song, and created "Turn! Turn! Turn!" in just fifteen minutes.[11] His only original contributions were the title and six words at the end about peace.

That song the publisher easily sold, to the Limeliters and Marlene Dietrich. At the time, Jim McGuinn was in the Limeliters' backing band, and he arranged the song for Judy Collins to sing on *Judy Collins 3*.

On the Byrds' tour bus, when they weren't playing tapes of Ravi Shankar and John Coltrane, McGuinn's future wife, Dolores, asked him to play the song on his acoustic, and he jazzed it up with a rock-and-samba beat.[12] It took the band seventy-eight takes to get it right[13]—cracking that snare at the perfect moment would have been tricky even if drummer Clarke hadn't been a newbie—but at last it was molded into the ultimate single for the holidays.

***Rubber Soul* hit stores** December 3. The Beatles' label mate Brian Wilson and some friends listened to it while sitting at a table sharing a joint. Wilson said,

> It blew me fucking out. The album blew my mind, because it was a whole album with all good stuff. It was definitely a challenge for me. I saw that every cut was very artistically interesting and stimulating . . . I suddenly realized that the recording industry was getting so free and intelligent. We could go into new things—string quartets, auto harps, and instruments from another culture. I decided right then: I'm gonna try that, where a whole album becomes a gas. I'm gonna make the greatest rock 'n' roll album ever made! So I went to the piano thinking, *"Goddamn, I feel competitive now"* . . . I said, "Come on. We gotta beat the Beatles." That was the spirit I had, you know? Carl and I had another prayer session, and

we prayed for an album that would be better than *Rubber Soul*. It was a prayer, but there was also some ego there. We intertwined prayer with a competitive spirit. It worked, and the next album [*Pet Sounds*] happened immediately.[14]

Wilson's usual lyricist, Mike Love, was on tour, so on December 6, Wilson contacted a jingle writer named Tony Asher (born 1938), whom his friend Loren Schwartz knew. Wilson played Asher *Rubber Soul* and said they had to write material to top it. Asher took a three-week break from his ad agency. Wilson and Asher would talk about their love affairs, then Wilson would tape record brief musical ideas he called "feels," which he'd play on the piano. "Once they're out of my head and into the open air, I can see them and touch them firmly. They're not 'feels' anymore."[15] At the end of the day, Asher would take the tapes home and write lyrics for them.

On December 22, a year after his nervous breakdown on the plane to Texas, Wilson was back in the studio working on a song about the "worst trip" he'd ever been on, "Sloop John B." It was a West Indian folk song about a shipwreck that the Kingston Trio had covered. Jardine had played it for Wilson earlier in the year, trying to convince him that the Beach Boys should cover it. They did, but Wilson didn't let him sing lead on it. Wilson took the first and third verse for himself and gave the second verse to Love, because he thought Love's voice was more "commercial." Hal Blaine slammed the drums as hard as anyone in a year of hard-slamming drummers, and then locked in with Carol Kaye's bass. To make it folk-rock, Wilson had an electric twelve-string delivered to the studio for Wrecking Crew session guitarist Billy Strange to play; afterward Wilson gave it to him along with an amp and five hundred dollars in cash.[16] The sax and flutes melded with the clarinet and organ until all the instruments fell away except the Boys' vocal polyphony, so you could hear Wilson's arrangement in all its resplendent glory.

On December 7, the Supreme Court of Massachusetts finally decided the case of Georgie Porgie, a.k.a. George Leonard Jr., the musician who was suspended indefinitely from Attleboro High School because he wouldn't cut his hair.

The Court decreed, "We are of the opinion that the unusual hair style of the plaintiff could disrupt and impede the maintenance of a proper classroom atmosphere or decorum. This is an aspect of personal appearance and hence akin to matters of dress. Thus as with any unusual, immodest or exaggerated mode of dress, conspicuous departures from accepted customs in the matter of haircuts could result in the distraction of other pupils." If schools didn't have the right to enforce their code, the Court said, they would not be able to handle "unpredictable activities of large groups of children."[17]

The ACLU took on a similar long hair high school case in Dallas the following year, and lost as well.[18] Leonard never did go back to high school, but continued on as a professional musician.

Johnny Cash also was in court that month. He returned to El Paso on December 28 and pleaded guilty to crossing the Mexican border with 1,143 pills in his luggage. Eventually he'd get off with a thirty-day suspended sentence and a thousand-dollar fine. But the December trip started a new chapter of drama for Cash when a photo taken of him and his wife, Vivian, on the courthouse steps was put to nefarious use by the National States' Rights Party. They were white supremacists, quasi-Nazis, complete with armbands, and part of the Ku Klux Klan. Their national chairman had served three years for bombing the Bethel Baptist Church in Birmingham, Alabama. In the South, three years was all you got for terrorism if you were white. The party's newspaper, the *Thunderbolt*, ran the picture of the Cashes in their January issue with the headline "Arrest Exposes Johnny Cash's Negro Wife." The article railed, "Money from the sale of Cash's records goes to scum like Johnny Cash to keep them supplied with dope and Negro women." It also called Cash's children "mongrelized." When Cash toured the South, the Klan ran newspaper ads reading, "FOR CASH, CALL THIS NUMBER." The phone number led to a recording that told callers to boycott Cash concerts because the singer was married to a black woman.[19]

"If there's a mongrel in the crowd, it's me, because I'm Irish and one-quarter Cherokee Indian," Cash snarled.[20] Vivian just wanted to ignore the issue, but Cash's manager, Saul Israel Holiff, worried that the racist southern market would cancel shows, and felt they needed to address the accusation. Holiff sent the *Thunderbolt* documentation of Vivian's genealogy, stating that she was Italian, Dutch, and English.[21]

"How long? Not long!" Martin Luther King Jr. had roared nine months earlier, but the *Thunderbolt* brouhaha was just one of countless examples showing how far the country still had to go to achieve his dream of racial harmony. The Christmas before, when President Johnson lit the White House tree, he had declared the times to be the most hopeful since Christ was born. For a moment, when King gave his victory speech in Montgomery in March, maybe it was—until Johnson increased the draft call to thirty-five thousand a month in July, and Watts rioted in August. From then on, war and riots cast their pall over the rest of the decade. As the calendar flipped to January 1, 1966, the song at the top of the charts began with an eerie greeting to Darkness, the singer's old friend.

But in the next spot below Simon and Garfunkel's "The Sound of Silence," the Beatles sang that we could work it out. At No. 3, James Brown yowled that he felt good. At No. 4, the Byrds sang that it was not too late for peace.

And there was a new song making its way toward the Top 20, from the fifteen-year-old kid at Motown, Stevie Wonder. They'd told him at the school for the blind that all he'd be able to do in life was make potholders, but he got signed for his harmonica playing, even though Berry Gordy wasn't too sold on him.[22] The live chart-topper "Fingertips (Part 1 and II)" had him touring nonstop for two years. "How are we supposed to follow him?" everyone else on the Motown Revue cursed. The young Wonder was the mascot at the Motown house, fooling people with his perfect imitation of Gordy over the intercom, getting away with pinching butts, joking he was going to take a car out for a drive.[23] He was a permanent fixture in the Snake Pit, where the Funk Brothers recorded. Sometimes he'd burst in while they were taping because he couldn't see that the red "Recording" light was on, but they wouldn't have the heart to tell him. He picked up everything he could learn from them, and gave drummer Benny Benjamin the nickname Papa Zita.

But Wonder's voice had begun to change, and Gordy was thinking it might be time to let him go. He hadn't had a hit since "Fingertips," two and a half years before.

Wonder had an idea for a song, something with a beat like "Satisfaction" (in which drummer Charlie Watts imitates Benjamin). Maybe Wonder got the phrase "Uptight" from the line in Brown's "Papa's Got a Brand New Bag." Writer/producers Sylvia Moy and Henry Cosby helped Wonder with the lyrics—about a poor kid who is "Uptight" because his girlfriend is rich; but "Everything's Alright" because she loves him anyway. When they recorded it, they didn't have the lyrics in Braille, so Moy whispered each line into Wonder's ear a beat before he sang it.[24]

James Jamerson plucked with his right index finger, a.k.a. the Hook, infusing the bass with the same attitude he had when a mugger tried to rob him—Jamerson yanked out his gun from his waistband, pistol-whipped the thief, and took *his* money.[25] Benjamin brought it home for the kid like he was beating "on a bloody *tree*," as Lennon had it.[26] Things would get a lot more uptight in the next couple of years, but with artists such as Wonder and the Stones trading beats back and forth, there would also be moments that were pure outta sight.

EPILOGUE

Strike Another Match,
Go Start Anew

By the end of the year, many parents had caught on to the fact that long-haired musicians were singing to their children about drugs, pre-marital sex, and questioning authority. With ever-growing frequency, mothers and fathers looked on in horror as their children began emulating their heroes and experimenting with mind-altering chemicals, which sparked innumerable parent-child fights and led to a surge in addiction. Many would later maintain that the arrival of the Beatles and the Stones marked the moment when Western civilization began declining. Evangelical writer David A. Noebel stated in his 1965 pamphlet *Communism, Hypnotism, and the Beatles* that folk-rock was devised by the Soviets to brainwash teens, and then followed it up with the book *Rhythm, Riots, and Revolution*. LSD was made illegal in California on October 1, 1966.

The backlash came down hard on the musicians who served as the most prominent PR men for cultural change. Dylan continued to be booed nightly for going electric, was denounced as Judas. He tried to make a joke out of it with the chorus to "Rainy Day Women #12 and 35," lamenting that everyone must get stoned, both with pot and with rocks, as was done to sinners in biblical times. But it wasn't a joke in May when a knife-wielding Glasgow hotel waiter denounced Dylan as a traitor to folk music. Dylan's bodyguard/chauffeur forced the man out of the room, but was scarred in the process.

When Lennon's paramour Maureen Cleave interviewed him for a March 1966 newspaper profile, he made an offhand comment that the Beatles were more popular than Jesus. The remark was reprinted in a U.S. teen magazine in August, and in one fell swoop, the Beatles managed to enrage more people than the Rolling Stones could ever hope to. Reactionaries who had been largely silent for the first two years of global Beatlemania snapped. Cities in the South banned the group's music, and a Texas radio station organized a Beatle bonfire, recalling both the Nazi book burnings and the Ray Bradbury book *Fahrenheit 451*, whose movie adaptation was released that fall. The pun of the Beatles' recent album title, *Revolver*, stopped being funny when the KKK issued death threats, as did Japanese conservatives angered when the group played the Budokan martial arts hall built on sacred ground, near the Yasukuni Shrine. Also that summer, the Beatles issued an American compilation album, *Yesterday and Today*, with a cover featuring decapitated baby dolls and slabs of meat. Lennon commented that the cover was "as relevant as Vietnam," which further alienated many conservatives. The Beatles and Dylan both stopped touring for the rest of the decade.

According to journalist Philip Norman, the FBI and Britain's MI5 conspired to bust the Stones.[1] After the 1967 police raid at Richards's residence, Jagger was given three months for a single speed tablet, while Richards was given a year in prison for allowing marijuana to be smoked in his home. This backfired when public outcry over the severity of the band members' sentences led to their early release and enshrined them as rock's ultimate bad boys.

Conversely, the Lovin' Spoonful were undone when guitarist Zal Yanovsky gave the authorities the name of his dealer, to avoid deportation after he and bassist Steve Boone were arrested for possession of pot in San Francisco. To the rock community, such an act was as treacherous as when film director Elia Kazan named names before the House Un-American Activities Committee. Yanovsky quit the group and went back to Canada.

Donovan was also busted for pot, and fined two hundred fifty British pounds. The Byrds were not busted, but their song "Eight Miles High" was called out as a drug song by the trade publication *The Gavin Report*,[2] resulting in a ban by many radio stations, and bringing to an end the group's time as a major commercial force.

The marijuana that the bands had celebrated had become their Achilles' heel, allowing authorities to persecute them in ways they couldn't have had the musicians just been politically outspoken. But the musicians didn't need the government to destroy them; they could do it themselves. Many rapidly progressed from pot and LSD to coke and heroin, just like the educational films had warned. The musicians' realization that they had the heroin monkey on their back, along with the police busts and acid casualties, turned the music dark and downbeat in the last two years of the decade. Four of the scene's biggest luminaries would self-destruct by age twenty-seven: Jimi Hendrix, Janis Joplin, Jim Morrison, and Brian Jones.

Media overhype and the John Phillips–penned anthem "San Francisco (Be Sure to Wear Some Flowers in Your Hair)" drove countless young people and tourists to Haight-Ashbury, and as a consequence, runaways, hustlers, and pimps overwhelmed the neighborhood. Speed and heroin replaced pot and acid. Rape, ODs, and crime escalated, despite the best efforts of community groups such as the Diggers to provide free food and crash pads. A schism developed between the Beautiful People/"trust fund hippies" and the "ghastly drop-outs, bums and spotty youths, all out of their brains," as George Harrison's wife, Pattie, called the kids she met in the Haight. After the 1969 murder spree by Charles Manson's "family," rich LA hipsters quickly walled themselves off from the street, just as the Stones did after one of the Hells Angels fatally stabbed a black man in front of their stage at Altamont.

Minds opened by drugs made many receptive to the growing number of cults. The Process Church of the Final Judgment broke off from Scientology in 1965 and was an early influence on Manson, with its embrace of both God and the Devil. The same year saw the release of a movie about the drug addiction program Synanon, which would soon declare itself a church where women had to shave their heads, married couples had to sleep with other cult members, and men had to have vasectomies. These cults were just the tip of the iceberg as the consciousness movement of the next decade saw an explosion in new organizations, some benign and some abusive.

Beyond the counterculture, the dark side of the sexual revolution would manifest in skyrocketing divorce rates and the return of sexually transmitted diseases. As the availability of the Pill allowed women to forestall pregnancy and their financial independence increased, divorce for all Americans doubled from 10.6 per 1,000 in 1965 to 22.8 per 1,000 in 1979. For baby boomers specifically, the divorce rate tripled in the 1970s. Since the 1960s, the number of families with just one parent in the household tripled.[3]

Per the Centers for Disease Control, gonorrhea shot up from 259,000 cases in 1960 to 600,000 cases in 1970, though syphilis shrank from 122,000 reported cases in 1960 to 91,000 in 1970.[4] There was also an increase in the annual number of outpatient visits for genital herpes in the United States, rising from 20,000 in the late 1960s to 150,000 in the mid-1990s. By 1982, more than 20 million Americans had acquired herpes II in a population of 232 million.[5]

✳

At the height of American prosperity, President Johnson and Martin Luther King Jr. believed the United States had a chance to win the War on Poverty and eradicate slums. But Johnson's Great Society was put to the side almost immediately as Vietnam continued to eat up more of the federal government's tax dollars.

The civil rights coalition split between those who believed in nonviolence and a militant faction that initially found its spokesman in the SNCC's Stokely Carmichael. Carmichael began using the term *Black Power* during the March Against Fear in June 1966, and released his manifesto *The Basis of Black Power* that year. After the SNCC's Lowndes County Freedom Organization adopted the black panther as its symbol, Huey Newton and Bobby Seale formed the Black Panther Party in Oakland, California, in October 1966. Briefly, SNCC and the Panthers worked together, but the FBI's undercover COINTELPRO program sowed division between the two groups, leading Newton to accuse Carmichael of being a CIA agent. Carmichael moved from the United States to Guinea in 1968.

Meanwhile, the long hair and incendiary proclamations of many in the antiwar movement alienated middle-of-the-road citizens who might have been more receptive to the message had it come from people who dressed and acted more conventionally. Beyond appearances, drugs compromised the mental clarity of many radicals, who believed that a socialist American Revolution was imminent. The Weather Underground (named after a line in Dylan's "Subterranean Homesick Blues") began a campaign of bombing government buildings and banks affiliated with the war effort in Vietnam. They warned the people in the buildings before the bombs went off, but one of their bank robberies resulted in the death of three people. The excesses of the Underground were easy for conservatives to vilify, scaring the mainstream white majority toward the Republican Party of Nixon and Reagan.

Still, perhaps the radicals would not have been able to succeed even if they had dressed as conservatively as Martin Luther King Jr. In the spring of 1968, King announced plans to build an encampment in Washington, DC, for his Poor People's Campaign. The idea behind the campaign was that it would bring the city to a halt through civil disobedience and force Congress to pass an Economic Bill of Rights for the poor, which would guarantee jobs at a living wage or adequate income for those unable to find jobs. With the campaign scheduled to begin on May 2, King was assassinated on April 4.

Meanwhile, riots became an annual urban event for the latter half of the decade. In cities such as Detroit and Newark, most whites quickly moved away, but black capitalists were not able to replace the white businesses with their own on the scale necessary to generate the tax base needed for quality schools and police. Crime and the heroin epidemic swamped the inner cities of the 1970s, to be replaced by the crack wars of the 1980s. South Central Los Angeles rioted again in 1992. By then, Detroit was long a ghost town.

In 1968, Richard Nixon branded Americans who loathed the hippies, activists, and radicals the Silent Majority, but it was Ronald Reagan who most effectively mobilized this majority to end the era of progressivism.

Reagan began as a Roosevelt liberal in his youth, but his politics began to shift once he became president of the Screen Actors Guild in the early 1950s. During his tenure he worked secretly with the FBI, alerting them to Communists in the film industry. After his term as SAG president ended, he became spokesman for *General Electric Theater*, a CBS anthology show that ran from 1953 through 1962. He also performed many speaking duties for GE, then the largest corporation on the planet. He increasingly espoused the need to shrink the growing federal government and, in particular, lower taxes. Reagan denounced Medicare as socialism and warned that if it weren't stopped, "one of these days you and I are going to spend our sunset years telling our children and our children's children what it once was like in America when men were free."[6]

His 1964 speech made in support of presidential candidate Barry Goldwater, "A Time For Choosing," put Reagan on the map as a serious political contender. In 1965 he wrapped his final job as an actor, hosting the TV series *Death Valley Days*, and published his autobiography *Where's the Rest of Me?* He toured the state of California to see if he could successfully run for governor there, and spoke out against the Fair Housing Act, saying that "if an individual wants to discriminate against Negroes or others in selling or renting his house, it is his right to do so."[7] He vowed "to send the welfare bums back to work" and "clean up the mess"[8] at Berkeley by investigating "charges of Communism and blatant sexual misbehavior on the Berkeley campus." These included "sexual orgies so vile I cannot describe them to you,"[9] not to mention Vietnam Day Committee dances in which underage kids reveled while psychedelic movies featuring nude torsos were projected.

Reagan branded antiwar demonstrations "the fruit of appeasement,"[10] and didn't need to say much about the Watts riots—he just sat back and let the white vote oust liberal governor Pat Brown and sweep him into power.

In 1980 he chose Philadelphia, Mississippi, as the place to announce his campaign for president, using it as an opportunity to speak out on his belief in states' rights. The city was most famous for being the place where the Klan murdered three civil rights workers in 1964.

After LBJ, Republicans controlled the White House for twenty of the next twenty-four years, followed by a Clinton administration that was accommodating to business. The end of liberal consensus meant that there was little political opposition to globalization, as corporations escaped the American unions into the developing world with the help of technology, outsourcing, and automation. CEOs continued to live in the United States, but employed workers elsewhere at subsistence wages, then sold the goods back to Americans. Well-paying manufacturing jobs declined as nonsustaining service-sector jobs increased. The weakening of organized labor, loss of the industrial sector to globalization, return of Germany and Japan as economic competitors, the rise of China—plus the added competition as women and minorities rose in the U.S. workforce—resulted in the stagnation of middle-class wages for half a century (when adjusted for inflation).

In some ways, it was as if the yin and yang had flipped. In the early 1960s, the country had been repressed and unequal, but offered economic security for many. Now the country was culturally free, but the middle class was shrinking.

Neuroscientist Marc Lewis wrote in *Newsweek*,

The serotonin drugs we favor today shift human experience in the opposite direction from LSD. SSRIs (selective serotonin reuptake inhibitors) like paroxetine (Paxil) and fluoxetine (Prozac) are the most prescribed pills in the U.S., used to treat depression, anxiety, PTSD, OCD, and undefined feelings of ickiness. Instead of getting rid of serotonin, these drugs block the reabsorption process so that serotonin keeps piling up in the synapses. The result: an extra-thick blanket of serotonin that filters out the intrusions of anguish and anxiety, making our inner worlds more secure. Instead of turning on, tuning in, and dropping out, they help us turn off, tune out, and drop in—into a solipsistic safety zone, protected from too much reality. What do these newer drugs tell us about our culture and how we perceive our world? Apparently, now is not a time of exuberant exploration but a time to hunker down and play it safe. Instead of letting the world in, with all its uncertainties, we try to keep it out. And a barricade of serotonin makes that possible. The drugs we create, the drugs we take, the drugs we abuse—they offer an idealized antidote to the cravings of our times. LSD was born from our craving for freedom. SSRIs reflect our need for security.[11]

But if the utopian goals of ending poverty and war did not succeed, the efforts still produced results. For those who opposed the war, the peace movement provided a community in which to take refuge. Political activist Frank Bardacke said in the film *Berkeley in the Sixties,*

> The whole national mythology was that Vietnam was a consensus war, was bipartisan foreign policy. All significant sectors of the American public accepted the war, and the people who opposed it were marginalized freaks, kooks, you know, unimportant people. It was a real statement for a person to say, "Yes, I am willing to march out against the war." And when thousands of people did that, it broke that consensus . . . After the Tet Offensive, when [General] Westmoreland came to Johnson and said in order to continue the land war in Vietnam we are going to need a million men, Johnson was told by J. Edgar Hoover that if we tried to get a million men out of this country, he could not ensure the domestic security of this country. And that was one of the questions, one of the considerations that he made when he decided . . . to end the land war and resign . . . We did put limits on America's ability to wage the war in Vietnam.[12]

Since the draft ended in 1973, it has not been reinstituted. While equally tragic, the 5,281 American deaths in the Iraq and Afghanistan wars were significantly fewer than the 47,424 American combat deaths in Vietnam.[13]

As more people experimented with psychedelics, and then afterward tried to hold on to the feelings of serenity and wonder through natural means, there was a boom in the exploration of alternative forms of spirituality. The Beats had promoted Buddhism since the 1950s, but it was George Harrison's songs espousing Hindu philosophy and featuring Indian musicians, and the Beatles' study of Transcendental Meditation, that truly kick-started the human potential movement of the 1970s (rebranded New Age in the 1980s). In this way, the musicians helped expand the freedom of religion that the United States was founded on to encompass options outside the Judeo-Christian tradition. At the same time, the hippie "Jesus freaks" contributed to the rise of "born-again" evangelical Christianity at the dawn of the '70s.

With the prevalence of the Pill and other contraceptives such as IUDs and spermicides, there was a sharp increase in the number of women who both attended and graduated college. Only 8 percent of pre-baby boom women graduated from institutes of higher learning; 20 percent of boomer women did.[14] In 1966 the National Organization for Women (NOW) took up the struggle for the Equal Rights Amendment (ERA) and the fight to end the wage gap between men and women. The ERA would not be achieved, but legalized abortion (*Roe v. Wade*) would, as would a gradual cultural reeducation on issues ranging from sexism, domestic violence, date rape, and the new lifestyle choices available to women. By the end of the 1960s, the civil rights movement had also paved the way for movements for gays, Native Americans, Chicanos, environmentalists, and others.

Today, freedom of speech in politics and art is largely secure in the United States, as is the right to criticize government and demand increased transparency. As of this writing, more than thirty states allow gay marriage. At some point in the 1970s, even white working-class southerners grew their hair long.

Originally, musicians seemed to be having more fun than anyone else and inspired others to emulate their freedom in thought and appearance. They ended up becoming walking science experiments for the wholesale reconsideration of values in Western society: which limits were worth breaking (racism, sexual repression, homophobia) and which perhaps made sense (restrictions against harder drugs). In the end, most baby boomers reaffirmed the consumer lifestyle, and "Satisfaction" was used for a 1990 *Snickers* commercial. But now people were free to pursue the way of living that suited them, economically, spiritually, and sexually.

In 1965, the combined forces of mass media, the Pill, and hallucinogens took the Western world on a roller-coaster ride that was both exhilarating and fearsome, which was why the paradoxical "Like a Rolling Stone" was the anthem of the year, as it captured both extremes in the same chorus. Those forces stirred demands that the musicians gave voice to on a flood of records—"Respect," "Let Me Be," "It's My Life," "People Get Ready," "A Change Is Gonna Come," "Think for Yourself," "Go Where You Wanna Go," "Anyway, Anyhow, Anywhere," "Freedom Highway," "I'm Free"—that chronicled and propelled a social reformation as the old world forged its uneasy synthesis with the new.

Notes

Citations without page numbers are from the e-book version of the book.

INTRODUCTION

1. Braunstein, Carpenter, and Edmonds, *The Sixties Chronicle*, 263.
2. "African-American Population," U.S. Census Bureau, 1993, http://www.infoplease .com/ipa/A0922246.html#ixzz35PrOevQM.
3. Leonard J. Leff, "Hollywood and the Holocaust: Remembering The Pawnbroker," *American Jewish History*, 1996.
4. Doug Linder, "The Trials of Lenny Bruce," *Famous Trials*, http://law2.umkc.edu /faculty/projects/ftrials/bruce/bruceaccount.html.
5. McClelland, *Nothin' but Blue Skies*, 73.
6. Quoted in Unterberger, *Turn! Turn! Turn!*, 162.
7. E. Glenn Schellenberg and Christian von Scheve, "Emotional Cues in American Popular Music: Five Decades of the Top 40," *Psychology of Aesthetics Creativity and the Arts* (August 2012), http://www.researchgate.net/230745983_Emotional_cues _in_American_popular_music_Five_decades_of_the_Top_40.
8. Fiona Macrae, "Help! Pop Music Really Is Slower and Sadder Than When the Beatles and Abba Ruled the Charts," *Daily Mail*, Sept. 12, 2012, http://www.dailymail.co .uk/sciencetech/article-2209527/Help-Pop-music-slower-sadder-Beatles-heydey -researchers-say-Lady-Gaga-exception.html.

PROLOGUE

1. Pete Hamill, "The Death and Life of John Lennon," *New York Magazine,* December 20, 1980.
2. Ibid.
3. Ibid.
4. Hajdu, *Positively 4th Street*, 197.

5. Ibid., 197.

6. *Rolling Stone Magazine, The Rolling Stone Illustrated History of Rock & Roll,* 212.

7. Dave Rybaczewski, "'I'm a Loser' History," Beatles Book, http://www.beatlesebooks .com/im-a-loser.

8. The Beatles, *The Beatles Anthology,* 160.

9. Spitz, *Dylan,* 273.

10. Unterberger, *Turn! Turn! Turn!,* 108.

11. Melody Rousseau, "The Price of Fame," *Saga,* http://www.saga.co.uk/lifestyle/peo ple/celebrities/alan-price.aspx/.

12. Brown and Gaines, *The Love You Make.*

13. Cherri Gilham, "Joint Accounts," *The Guardian,* Sept. 10, 2000, at http://www.the guardian.com/theobserver/2000/sep/10/featuresreview.review.

14. Miles, *Paul McCartney,* 188.

15. The Beatles, *The Beatles Anthology,* 158.

16. Miles, *Paul McCartney,* 189.

17. Sheff, *All We Are Saying,* 174.

18. Phil Alexander, "Ray Davies: The Kinks v the Beatles," mojo4music.com, November 6, 2013, at http://www.mojo4music.com/8571/ray-davies-kinks-v-beatles/.

19. Unterberger, *Turn! Turn! Turn!,* 109.

20. Heylin, *Bob Dylan,* 34.

1. I GOT A HEAD FULL OF IDEAS

1. Ian McPherson, "Jagger/Richards: Songwriters, Part I," http://www.timeisonourside .com/songwriting.html.

2. Ibid.

3. Andersen, *Mick.*

4. Jann Wenner, "Jagger Remembers," *Rolling Stone,* December 14, 1995, http://www .jannswenner.com/Archives/Jagger_Remembers.aspx.

5. McPherson, "Jagger/Richards: Songwriters, Part I."

6. Richards and Fox, *Life,* 84.

7. Hajdu, *Positively 4th Street,* 236.

8. Brown, *Bob Dylan: American Troubadour,* 16.

9. Wyman, *Stone Alone,* 314.

10. Sean Willinz, "Bob Dylan, the Beat Generation, and Allen Ginsberg's America," *The New Yorker,* Aug. 16, 2010.

11. Unterberger, *Turn! Turn! Turn!,* 104.

12. Scoppa, *The Byrds,* 18.

13. Weller, *Girls Like Us,* 184.

14. Dillon, *Fifty Sides of the Beach Boys,* 31.

15. Kubernik, *Canyon of Dreams,* 70.

2. HITSVILLE USA AND THE SOVEREIGNS OF SOUL

1. Moon, *Untold Tales, Unsung Heroes*, 241.
2. Smith, *Dancing in the Street*, 14.
3. Echols, *Hot Stuff*, 14.
4. Ibid., 13.
5. Ken Sharp, "Holland-Dozier-Holland on Some of the Hits," *Metro Times*, Nov. 21, 2007.
6. "Berry Gordy On Diana Ross: Motown Founder Describes Fateful Moment With Supremes Singer," huffingtonpost.com, June 15, 2013.
7. Hillary Crosley, "Berry Gordy Talks 1st Time with Diana Ross," The Root, Feb. 13, 2013, http://www.theroot.com/articles/culture/2013/02/berry_gordy_and_diana_ross_he_talks_first_time.html.
8. Posner, *Motown*, 88.
9. Ibid., 121.
10. Cohn, *Awopbopaloobop Alopbamboom*, 117.
11. Scott Warmuth, "Bob Dylan and the Lie about America's Greatest Living Poet, Good Talk," swarmuth.blogspot.com, August 2012.
12. Robinson, *Smokey*.
13. Elizabeth Blair, "My Girl," npr.org, June 4, 2000.
14. Ritz, *Divided Soul*, 78.
15. Ibid., 110.
16. Ibid., 114.
17. Ibid., 100.
18. Ibid., 109.
19. "The Death of Sam Cooke: Conspiracy Theories Still Abound 42 Years Later," Pan-African News Wire, Dec. 11, 2006, http://panafricannews.blogspot.com/2006/12/death-of-sam-cooke-conspiracy-theories.html.
20. Kot, *I'll Take You There*, 40.
21. Ibid., 42.
22. Ibid., 81.
23. Ibid., 88.
24. Graham Rockingham, "Mavis Staples Recalls Her Lost Love," *The Hamilton Spectator*, http://www.thespec.com/whatson-story/2149883-mavis-staples-recalls-her-lost-love/.
25. Kot, *I'll Take You There*, 88.
26. Ibid., 89.

3. THE BRILL AND THE BEACH BOYS FIGHT BACK

1. Weller, *Girls Like Us*, 105–8.
2. Ibid., 119.
3. Marc Myers, "The Song That Conquered Radio," *Wall Street Journal*, July 12, 2012, http://online.wsj.com/news/articles/SB10001424052702303343404577519042622092010.

4. Ibid.

5. Myers, "The Song That Conquered Radio."

6. Lambert, *Inside the Music of Brian Wilson*, 147.

7. Badman, *The Beach Boys*, 73.

8. Ibid., 75.

9. Ibid., 83.

10. Ibid., 102.

11. "Dennis Wilson: The Real Beach Boy," directed by Matt O'Casey, episode on *Legends* (BBC, 2010), DVD.

12. Dillon, *Fifty Sides of the Beach Boys*, 49.

13. Badman, *The Beach Boys*, 10.

14. "The Beach Boys/Murry Wilson: Help Me Rhonda (Full Audio Session)," on You-Tube, http://www.youtube.com/watch?v=_bxfR-Vuo8Y.

4. RESOLUTION: *A LOVE SUPREME*, MALCOLM X, AND THE MARCH FROM SELMA TO MONTGOMERY

1. Kahn, *A Love Supreme*.

2. Ibid.

3. Ibid.

4. Eric Westervelt, "The Story of 'A Love Supreme,'" *All Things Considered*, NPR, March 7, 2012, http://www.npr.org/2000/10/23/148148986/a-love-supreme.

5. Kahn, *A Love Supreme*.

6. "The Making of 'A Love Supreme,'" public radio program, Joyride Media, 2002.

7. *Eyes on the Prize: The Time Has Come (1964–66)*, directed by James A. DeVinney and Madison D. Lacy (PBS, 1987), DVD.

8. Ibid.

9. Evanzz, *The Judas Factor*, 301.

10. *Eyes on the Prize: Bridge to Freedom (1965)*, directed by Callie Crossley and James A. DeVinney (PBS, 1987) DVD.

11. Ibid.

12. Ibid.

13. Adelle M. Banks, "Favorite Songs Carried MLK through Troubled Times," *Huffington Post*, Jan. 11, 2012, http://www.huffingtonpost.com/2012/01/11/mlk-favorite-songs_n_1200393.html.

14. King Jr., "Southern Christian Leadership Conference Annual Report, 1965."

15. Michael T. Kaufman, "Gary T. Rowe Jr., 64, Who Informed on Klan in Civil Rights Killing, Is Dead," *New York Times*, October 4, 1998; John Blake, "The Voting Rights Martyr Who Divided America," CNN.com, Feb. 28, 2013; Stanton, *From Selma to Sorrow*.

16. McGonigal, *Well Down Freedom Highway*.

17. Kot, *I'll Take You There*, 108.

5. NASHVILLE VERSUS BAKERSFIELD

1. Rich Keinzle and Lenny Kaye, *Nashville Rebel* box set book, 8.
2. Hyatt, *The Billboard Book of Number One Adult Contemporary Hits*.
3. Alan Cackett, "Buck Owens Biography," *Americana, Roots, Country, and Bluegrass Music* (blog), http://www.alancackett.com/buck-owens-biography.
4. Dana Spiardi, "Happy Birthday, Buck Owens: A Natural Class Act," *No Depression* (blog), August 12, 2012, http://www.nodepression.com/profiles/blogs/happy-birthday-buck-owens-a-natural-class-act.
5. Sisk, *Buck Owens*, 97.
6. Cackett, "Buck Owens Biography."
7. William Michael Smith, "How Willie Nelson & Charley Pride Integrated East Texas," *Houston Press*, Jan. 27, 2011, http://blogs.houstonpress.com/rocks/2011/01/willie_nelson_charley_pride.php.
8. Nelson and Shrake, *Willie*, 160.
9. Jennings and Kaye, *Waylon*.
10. Ibid.
11. Hilburn, *Johnny Cash*.
12. Brett Johnson, "Johnny Cash's First Wife Tells of Romance, Heartbreak," *Ventura County Star*, Nov. 18, 2007, http://www.vcstar.com/news/2007/nov/18/they-walked-the-line.

6. WEST COAST NIGHTS

1. April 2014 interview with Erick Trickey, re: McGuinn show, August 9, 2008, at Cain Park in Cleveland Heights, Ohio.
2. Burke and Griffin, *The Blue Moon Boys*, 41.
3. Unterberger, *Turn! Turn! Turn!*, 81.
4. Joe Bosso, "David Crosby on the Impact of the Beatles: They Changed My Life," *Music Radar*, Feb. 8, 2014, http://www.musicradar.com/us/news/guitars/david-crosby-on-the-impact-of-the-beatles-they-changed-my-life-593827.
5. Vincent Flanders, "Interview with Roger McGuinn of the Byrds—February 1970," http://www.vincentflanders.com/roger-mcguinn-interview.html.
6. Unterberger, *Turn! Turn! Turn!*, 107.
7. Miles, *Hippie*, 60.
8. Priore, *Riot on Sunset Strip*, 76.
9. Weller, *Girls Like Us*, 185.
10. Hjort, *So You Want to Be a Rock 'n' Roll Star*, 31.
11. Kubernik, *Canyon of Dreams*, 74.
12. Ibid., 70.
13. Gaines, *Heroes and Villains: The True Story of the Beach Boys*, 134.
14. Gillian Friedman, "Brian Wilson—A Powerful Interview," *Ability*, n.d. 2006.

7. ENGLAND SWINGS

1. Beatles, *The Beatles Anthology*, 194.
2. Pattie Boyd, "The Dentist Who Spiked My Coffee with LSD," *Daily Mail*, August 2007, http://www.dailymail.co.uk/tvshowbiz/article-473207/Patti-Boyd-The-dentist-spiked-coffee-LSD.html.
3. Jann S. Wenner, "The Rolling Stone Interview: John Lennon, Part I," Jan. 21, 1971, http://www.jannswenner.com/Archives/John_Lennon_Part1.aspx.
4. Beatles, *The Beatles Anthology*, 177.
5. Norman, *Shout!*, 273.
6. Ibid., 273.
7. Beatles, *The Beatles Anthology*, 177.
8. Ibid., 179.
9. Ibid., 177.
10. Wenner, "The Rolling Stone Interview: John Lennon, Part I."
11. Beatles, *The Beatles Anthology*, 179.
12. Badman, *The Beatles*.
13. Davies, *The Beatles*, xxxiv.
14. di Perna, *Guitar Masters*.
15. Hayward, *Tin Pan Alley*, 122.
16. Cohn, *Awopbopaloobop Alopbamboom*, 186.
17. Schaffner, *The British Invasion*, 116.
18. Ibid., 116.
19. Townshend, *Who I Am*.
20. Ibid.
21. Ibid.
22. Ibid.
23. Schaffner, *The British Invasion*, 119.
24. Davies, *Americana*.
25. Ibid.
26. Ibid.

8. SATISFACTION

1. Anderson, *Mick*, 70.
2. Wyman, *Stone Alone*, 315–16.
3. Ibid., 318.
4. Booth, *Keith*.
5. Beatles, *The Beatles Anthology*, 196.
6. Booth, *Keith*.
7. Lydia Hutchinson, "The Rolling Stones' (I Can't Get No) Satisfaction," July 26, 2013, Performing Songwriter Be Heard, http://performingsongwriter.com/rolling-stones-satisfaction/.

8. Ian McPherson, *(I Can't Get No) Satisfaction*, timeisonourside.com, http://www
.timeisonourside.com/SOSatisfaction.html.

9. Ibid.

10. Crystal Bell, "The Rolling Stones, '(I Can't Get No) Satisfaction': The Story Behind
The Music," huffingtonpost.com, June 6, 2012, http://www.huffingtonpost.com
/2012/06/06/the-rolling-stones-i-cant-get-no-satisfaction_n_1573493.html.

9. LONG HAIR AND THE PILL ON TRIAL

1. Patterson, *Eve of Destruction*.

2. Wyman, *Stone Alone*, 314.

3. Norman, *Mick Jagger*, 133.

4. Jason Horowitz, "Mitt Romney's Prep School Classmates Recall Pranks, but Also
Troubling Incidents," *Washington Post*, May 10, 2012, http://www.washingtonpost
.com/politics/mitt-romneys-prep-school-classmates-recall-pranks-but-also-
troubling-incidents/2012/05/10/gIQA3WOKFU_print.html.

5. Philip Rucker, "Mitt Romney Apologizes for High School Pranks That 'Might Have
Gone Too Far,'" *WashingtonPost*, May 10, 2012, http://www.washingtonpost.com/
politics/mitt-romney-apologizes-for-high-school-pranks-that-might-have-gone-
too-far/2012/05/10/gIQAC3JhFU_story.html?hpid=z2%E2%80%83.

6. Mikhail Safanov, "Confessions of a Soviet Moptop," *The Guardian*, August 7, 2003,
http://www.theguardian.com/music/2003/aug/08/thebeatles.

7. Gottlieb, *Do You Believe in Magic?*, 135.

8. Knowles, "The Birth Control Pill—A History."

9. Gabriella Doob, "In 1965, Brown Physician Sparked Furor over the Pill," Feb. 5,
2007, *Brown Daily Herald*, http://www.browndailyherald.com/2007/02/05/in-1965-
brown-physician-sparked-furor-over-the-pill/.

10. Ibid.

11. "Morals: Sex & the Pembroke Girl," *Time*, Friday, Oct. 8, 1965, http://content.time
.com/time/magazine/article/0,9171,842199,00.html.

12. Farber, *The Columbia Guide to America in the 1960s*, 334.

13. Gottlieb, *Do You Believe in Magic?*, 141.

14. Associated Press, "Premarital Sex Trends," *New York Times*, April 17, 1985.

15. Gottlieb, *Do You Believe in Magic?*.

16. Polan and Tredre, *The Great Fashion Designers*, 103–4; "Quant: From the King's
Road to the International Market," *The Miniskirt Revolution* (blog), http://themini
skirtrevolution.wordpress.com/2010/05/11/quant-from-the-kings-road-to-the-
international-market/.

17. Cody Bay, "They Sold Kittenish Teenage Clothing as 'Self-Sufficient as James
Bond,'" *On This Day in Fashion* (blog), June 4, 2010, http://onthisdayinfashion
.com/?p=744.

18. Shrimpton, *Jean Shrimpton*, 107.

19. Patterson, *Eve of Destruction*.

20. Delix Contreras, "Lee Hazlewood: Writer Gave Music Biz the 'Boots,'" *All Things Considered*, Aug. 06, 2007, http://www.npr.org/templates/story/story.php?storyId=12537578.

21. Weller, *Girls Like Us*, 186.

22. Ibid., 187.

23. Gottlieb, *Do You Believe in Magic?*.

24. Ibid.

10. THE KING OF POP ART AND THE GIRL OF THE YEAR

1. Prather, *Regarding Warhol*, 281.

2. Marc Stein, "The First Gay Sit-In," History News Network, May 9, 2005, http://hnn.us/article/11652.

3. Jacki Lyden, "'Baby Jane' Holzer's Flight From High Society To Warhol Superstar," npr.org, March 15, 2014.

4. Wolfe, *The Kandy-Kolored Tangerine-Flake Streamline Baby*.

5. Stein and Plimpton, *Edie*.

6. Ibid.

7. Ibid.

8. Ibid.

9. Marilyn Bender, "Edie Pops Up as Newest Superstar," *New York Times*, July 26, 1965.

11. MASTERPIECE HIGHS AND THE BOOS OF NEWPORT

1. *Breakfast at Tiffany's*, directed by Blake Edwards (Paramount, 1961), DVD.

2. Eric Norden, "Truman Capote Playboy Interview," *Playboy*, March 1968.

3. Boylan, J. Gabriel, "The Q&A: Greil Marcus, Critic, Scholar," *More Intelligent Life*, April 20, 2010, http://www.moreintelligentlife.com/blog/j-gabriel-boylan/qa-greil-marcus-critic-scholar.

4. Wyman, *Rolling with the Stones*, 147.

5. Faithfull, *Faithfull*, 45.

6. Nat Hentoff, "Bob Dylan Playboy Interview," *Playboy*, 1966.

7. Marcus, *Like a Rolling Stone*, 70.

8. Polizzotti, *Bob Dylan's Highway 61 Revisited*, 32–33.

9. Kooper, *Backstage Passes and Backstabbing Bastards*.

10. Shaun Considine, "The Hit We Almost Missed," *New York Times*, Dec. 3, 2004.

11. "Bruce Springsteen on Dylan," Rock & Roll Hall of Fame, http://rockhall.com/inductees/bob-dylan/transcript/bruce-springsteen-on-dylan/.

12. Dylan, *Chronicles*, 115.

13. *No Direction Home: Bob Dylan*, directed by Martin Scorsese (PBS, 2005), DVD.

14. Ibid.

15. David Kupfer, "Longtime Passing: An Interview with Pete Seeger," *Whole Earth*, Spring 2001.

16. Gleason, *The Rolling Stone Interviews*, 18.

17. Kooper, *Backstage Passes and Backstabbing Bastards*.

18. Shelton, *No Direction Home*, 40.

19. *No Direction Home: Bob Dylan*.

20. Hajdu, *Positively 4th Street*, 262.

21. Hentoff, "Bob Dylan Playboy Interview," 1966.

22. Michael Watts, "The Man Who Put Electricity into Dylan," *Melody Maker*, January 31, 1976.

23. Marsh, with Swenson, *The Rolling Stone Record Guide*, 114.

24. Jeffrey Jones, "The Ballad of Mister Jones . . . by Mister Jones," *Rolling Stone*, Dec. 18, 1975.

25. Gottlieb, *Do You Believe in Magic?*, 39.

26. Kooper, *Backstage Passes and Backstabbing Bastards*.

27. *No Direction Home: Bob Dylan*.

28. Mick Jagger, "The 100 Greatest Dylan Songs," *Rolling Stone*, May 16, 2013.

29. Polizzotti, *Bob Dylan's Highway 61 Revisited*, 133.

30. Nelson Algren, "His Ice-Cream Cone Runneth Over," *New York Herald Tribune*, May 16, 1965.

12. HELLO, VIETNAM

1. Rebecca Onion, "When LBJ Drove on Water," *The Vault* (blog), Slate.com, n.d., http://www.slate.com/blogs/the_vault/2013/03/06/photo_lyndon_johnson_drives_in_a_lake_in_his_amphicar.html.

2. Patterson, *Eve of Destruction*.

3. Ibid.

4. Ibid.

5. Ibid.

6. "Ho Chi Minh: Vietnam's Enigma," *Biography*, produced by Gary Tarpinian (A&E, 2000), DVD.

7. Bissell, *The Father of All Things*; and Dang Phong, *The History of the Vietnamese Economy*.

8. "The State of the World's Refugees 2000—Chapter 4: Flight from Indochina," *United Nations High Commissioner for Refugees*, http://www.unhcr.org/publ/PUBL/3ebf9bad0.pdf.

9. *The Pentagon Papers*, "Counterinsurgency: Strategic Hamlet Program, 1961–63," *New York Times*, n.d., 28, http://www.documentcloud.org/documents/205512-pentagon-papers-part-iv-b-2.html.

10. Dallek, *Flawed Giant*, 100.

11. "Vịnh Mốc Tunnels," wikipedia.com, http://en.wikipedia.org/wiki/V%E1%BB%8Bnh_M%E1%BB%91c_tunnels.

12. Morocco, *Thunder from Above*, 56.

13. Tilford, *Setup*.

14. Ibid.

15. Thompson, *To Hanoi and Back*.

16. Branch, *At Canaan's Edge*, 361.

17. Rubin, *DO IT!*.

18. Sloman, *Steal This Dream*, 59.

19. Smyth, *Freedom of the Press and National Security in Four Wars*, 86–87.

20. Michelle Ferrari, *Reporting America at War: An Oral History*, PBS.org, http://www
.pbs.org/weta/reportingamericaatwar/reporters/safer/camne.html.

13. FOLK-ROCK EXPLOSION, PART ONE

1. Coplon, *The First Time*.

2. Dotson Rader, "Cher: 'It Takes a Very Strange Man to Be the Right Man for Me,'"
Parade, http://parade.condenast.com/40362/dotsonrader/1112-cher-extras/.

3. Hartman, *The Wrecking Crew*, 91.

4. Rader, "Cher."

5. Rogan, *The Byrds*, 81–83, 182.

6. Unterberger, *Turn! Turn! Turn!*, 134.

7. Ibid., 170–71.

8. Hartman, *The Wrecking Crew*, 120–22.

9. "P. F. Sloan in His Own Words: The Stories behind the Songs," http://www2.gol
.com/users/davidr/sloan/aboutsongs.html.

10. Rose Marie Walker, "Singer Thinks Draft Card Burners Should Be Hung," *Albuquerque Tribune*, Oct. 22, 1965.

11. "Staff Sergeant Barry Sadler Hits #1 with 'Ballad of the Green Berets,'" history
.com, http://www.history.com/this-day-in-history/staff-sergeant-barry-sadler-hits-1-
with-quotballad-of-the-green-beretsquot.

12. White, *The American Century*.

13. Greenwald, *Go Where You Wanna Go*.

14. Unterberger, *Turn! Turn! Turn!*, 171.

15. Einarson, *Mr. Tambourine Man*.

16. Phil Nee, "The Last Interview," Perfect Sound Forever.com, http://www.furious
.com/perfect/bryanmaclean.html.

17. Cohn, *Awopbopaloobop Alopbamboom*, 106.

18. Priore, *Riot on Sunset Strip*, 86.

19. Unterberger, *Turn! Turn! Turn!*, 110.

20. Lillian Roxon, "The Lovin' Spoonful: Do You Believe in Magic," *Eye Magazine*,
May 1968, in Albert Hotel website, at http://thehotelalbert.com/rock_roll/lovin
_spoonful.html.

21. Signed D.C., "Give a Hoot," *It's All The Streets You Crossed Not So Long Ago* (blog),
http://streetsyoucrossed.blogspot.com/2005/08/give-hoot.html.

22. David J. Criblez, "Beach Boys: Our Top 50 Hits," Newsday, June 22, 2012, http://

www.newsday.com/entertainment/music/beach-boys-our-top-50-hits-1 .3794840.

14. SOULSVILLE AND THE GODFATHER CHALLENGE
HITSVILLE TO GET RAW

1. Bronson, *The Billboard Book of Number 1 Hits*, 163.
2. Ibid., 176.
3. Wilson, *Dreamgirl and Supreme Faith*, 173.
4. Adrahtas, *Diana Ross: The American Dream Girl: A Lifetime to Get Here*, 24.
5. Benjaminson, *The Lost Supreme*, 22.
6. Wilson, *Dreamgirl and Supreme Faith*, 64–66.
7. Ibid., 173.
8. Bowman, *Soulsville, U.S.A.*, 21.
9. Ibid.
10. Ibid., 56.
11. Beatles, *The Beatles Anthology*, 93.
12. Bowman, *Soulsville, U.S.A.*, 57.
13. Black, *Classic Tracks Back to Back: Singles and Albums*, 71.
14. Bowman, *Soulsville, U.S.A.*, 61.
15. Badman, *The Beatles*.
16. Bowman, *Soulsville, U.S.A.*
17. Ibid., 88.
18. Ibid., n.p.
19. Brown, with Tucker, *James Brown*, 16.
20. Ibid., 24.
21. Ibid., 25.
22. George, *The Death of Rhythm and Blues*.
23. "James Brown: Soul Survivor," directed by Jeremy Marre, *American Masters* (PBS, 2003), DVD.
24. George, *The Death of Rhythm and Blues*.
25. Dan Bindert, "Papa's Got a Brand New Bag," *All Things Considered*, NPR, July 29, 2000, http://www.npr.org/2000/07/29/1080113/npr-100-papas-got-a-brand-new-bag.
26. George and Leeds, eds., *The James Brown Reader*.
27. Sullivan, *Encyclopedia of Great Popular Song Recordings, Volume 2*, 223.
28. Brown, with Tucker, *James Brown*, 158.
29. George, *The Death of Rhythm and Blues*.
30. Marsh, *The Heart of Rock & Soul*, 5.
31. "James Brown: Soul Survivor."
32. Ibid.

15. IN THE HEAT OF THE SUMMER

1. Valerie Reitman and Mitchell Landsberg, "Watts Riots, 40 Years Later," *Los Angeles Times*, Aug. 11, 2005, http://articles.latimes.com/2005/aug/11/local/la-me-watts 11aug11.
2. Ibid.
3. Ibid.
4. John Alex McCone, "Violence in the City—An End or a Beginning? A Report by the Governor's Commission on the Los Angeles Riots, 1965," Dec. 2, 1965, http://www .usc.edu/libraries/archives/instress/mccone/contents.html, accessed June 25, 2014.
5. Reitman and Landsberg, "Watts Riots, 40 Years Later."
6. Ibid.
7. Bennett, *Before the Mayflower*, 418.
8. Ibid., 419.
9. Ibid., 419.
10. Reitman and Landsberg, "Watts Riots, 40 Years Later."
11. Ibid.
12. Bennett, *Before the Mayflower*, 419.
13. Montague, *Burn, Baby! Burn!: The Autobiography of Magnificent Montague,* 134.
14. Reitman and Landsberg, "Watts Riots, 40 Years Later."
15. Holloway, *Passed On*, 76.
16. Gregory, *Callus on My Soul*, 110–11.
17. McCone, "Violence in the City."
18. Reitman and Landsberg, "Watts Riots, 40 Years Later."
19. Ibid.
20. Patterson, *Eve of Destruction*, 182.
21. Ibid., 186.
22. "Lyndon Johnson, Martin Luther King Jr. Friday, August 20, 1965—5:10 pm–5:24 pm," Presidential Recordings Program, Miller Center, University of Virginia, http:// whitehousetapes.net/transcript/johnson/wh6508-07-8578.

16. HELP!

1. Joan Goodman, "Paul McCartney Playboy Interview," December 1984, The Ultimate Experience Beatle Interview Database, http://www.beatlesinterviews.org /db1984.pmpb.beatles.html.
2. Miles, *Paul McCartney*, 163.
3. Jann S. Wenner, "January 1971 Rolling Stone Interview," www.jannswenner.com /Archives/John_Lennon_Part1.aspx.
4. Ronnie Spector, *Be My Baby.*
5. Kane, *Ticket to Ride*, 77–79.
6. Norman, *Shout!*, 273.
7. Des Barres, *I'm with the Band*, 28–29.

8. Beatles, *The Beatles Anthology*, 173.

9. Lewisohn, *The Complete Beatles Recording Sessions*, 58.

10. Wenner, "January 1971 Rolling Stone Interview."

11. Marsh, *The Heart of Rock & Soul*, 185.

12. David Sheff, "Playboy Interview with John Lennon and Yoko Ono," *Playboy*, January 1981, www.john-lennon.com/playboyinterviewwithjohnlennonandyokoono.htm.

13. Rodriguez and Shea, *Fab Four FAQ: Everything Left to Know about the Beatles . . . and More!*

14. Swami Vishnudevananda, *The Complete Illustrated Book of Yoga.*

15. Ted Myers, liner notes of box set *Four Decades of Folk Rock*, Time Life Entertainment, 2007.

16. *American Bandstand,* September 12, 1964, youtube.com, https://www.youtube .com/watch?v=30HmJSDvkG0.

17. Beatles, *The Beatles Anthology*, 191.

18. Wenner, "January 1971 Rolling Stone Interview."

19. Brown and Gaines, *The Love You Make.*

20. "The Beatles Take LSD in Los Angeles with the Byrds and Peter Fonda," The Beatles Bible, Aug. 24, 1965, http://www.beatlesbible.com/1965/08/24/lsd-los-angeles-byrds-peter-fonda/.

21. Sheff, *All We Are Saying*, 179–80.

22. Beatles, *The Beatles Anthology*, 191.

23. Ibid.

24. Ibid., 27.

25. Norman, *John Lennon.*

26. Chris Hutchins, "Book Review: Elvis Meets the Beatles, by Chris Hutchins and Peter Thompson," *Sunday Express*, Oct. 8, 2011, http://www.express.co.uk/entertainment/books/276232/Book-review-Elvis-Meets-The-Beatles-by-Chris-Hutchins-and-Peter-Thompson.

27. Beatles, *The Beatles Anthology*, 191.

28. Norman, *John Lennon.*

29. Ibid.

30. Goldman, *Elvis*, 450.

31. Guralnick, *Careless Love*, 212.

32. Ibid., 195.

33. Ibid., 217–18.

34. Jann S. Wenner, "The Rolling Stone Interview: Bob Dylan," Nov. 29, 1969, http://www.jannswenner.com/Archives/Bob_Dylan.aspx.

17. NEXT DAY YOU TURN AROUND AND IT'S FALL

1. Sterling, *The Concise Encyclopedia of American Radio*, 244–45.

2. *Live and Swingin': The Ultimate Rat Pack Collection*, produced by Paul Atkinson, Jimmy Edwards, and Robin Hurley (Bristol Productions, 2003), DVD.

3. *Rat Pack: The True Stories of the Original Kings of Cool*, directed by Carole Langer (A&E, 2001), DVD.

4. *Frank Sinatra, Dean Martin, Sammy Davis Jr. at Villa Venice, Chicago—Live 1962*, Vols. I & II, Jazz Hour Compact Classics, 1993.

5. *Rat Pack: The True Stories of the Original Kings of Cool*.

6. Ibid.

7. Kelley, *His Way*, 422.

8. Ibid., 391.

9. Nicholas Köhler, "The Rat Pack's Inside Man," Maclean's, April 4, 2013, http://www .macleans.ca/society/life/the-inside-man/.

10. Miles, *Paul McCartney*, 116–17.

11. Beatles, *The Beatles Anthology*, 175.

12. Miles, *Paul McCartney*, 49.

13. Lewisohn, *The Complete Beatles Recording Sessions*, 59.

14. Beatles, *The Beatles Anthology*, 183.

15. *Produced by George Martin*, directed by Francis Hanly (Eagle Rock Entertainment, 2011), DVD.

16. Sheff, *All We Are Saying*.

17. Norman, *Mick Jagger*.

18. Jann S. Wenner, "The Rolling Stone Interview: Jagger Remembers," Dec. 14, 1995, http://www.jannswenner.com/Archives/Jagger_Remembers.aspx.

19. Faithfull, *Faithfull*, 24–25.

18. FOLK-ROCK EXPLOSION, PART TWO

1. *No Direction Home: Bob Dylan*.

2. Kooper, *Backstage Passes and Backstabbing Bastards*, 44.

3. Ibid.

4. Jonathan Cott, *Dylan on Dylan*, 73.

5. Browne, *Fire and Rain*, 32.

6. Watts, *Melody Maker*.

7. "100 Greatest Singers," *Rolling Stone*, http://www.rollingstone.com/music/lists/100-greatest-singers-of-all-time-19691231/art-garfunkel-20101202.

8. Jackson, *Paul Simon*, 61.

9. Watts, *Melody Maker*.

10. Frank Mastropolo, "50 Years Ago: Simon & Garfunkel Record 'The Sounds of Silence'," ultimateclassicrock.com.

11. Watts, *Melody Maker*.

12. Paul Zollo, "Song Talk Interview," http://www.artgarfunkel.com/articles/songtalk .html.

13. Unterberger, *Turn! Turn! Turn!*, 178–79.

14. *Let's Sing Out!* (series), CTV, Feb. 17, 1966.

15. Faithfull, *Faithfull*, 50.

16. Leitch, *The Autobiography of Donovan*, 81.

17. Greenwald, *Go Where You Wanna Go*.

18. Ibid.

19. Ibid.

20. Ibid.

21. Unterberger, *Turn! Turn! Turn!*, 226.

22. David Leaf, "Paul McCartney Comments," album liner notes, http://albumlinernotes .com/Paul_McCartney_Comments.html.

23. Carol Kaye, "Carol Kaye on Bass, Brian and the Beach Boys," Abbeyrd's Beatles .com, http://abbeyrd.best.vwh.net/carolkay.htm.

24. King, *A Natural Woman*.

25. Ibid.

26. Weller, *Girls Like Us*, 176.

27. King, *A Natural Woman*.

28. Emerson, *Always Magic in the Air*.

29. Weller, *Girls Like Us*, 177.

30. Emerson, *Always Magic in the Air*.

31. King, *A Natural Woman*.

32. Emerson, *Always Magic in the Air*.

33. Rogovoy, *Bob Dylan*, 24.

34. Dylan, *Chronicles*, 115.

19. IT CAME FROM THE GARAGE

1. Dave Marsh, "Will Success Spoil the Fruit?" *Creem*, May 1971.

2. McNeil and McCain, *Please Kill Me*, 18.

3. Nardwuar, "Nirvana vs. Nardwuar," Nirvana Club, Jan. 4, 1994, http://www.nirva-naclub.com/info/articles/01.04.94.html.

4. Kubernik, *Canyon of Dreams*, 83.

5. Ken Sharp, "David Marks of the Beach Boys—In His Own Words," RockCellar Magazine.com, September 2013; Steven Gaines, *Heroes and Villains: The True Story of the Beach Boys*, 50.

6. John Lennon, "Blind," *Melody Maker*, Dec. 11, 1965.

20. ANARCHY AND ANDROGYNY, BRITISH STYLE

1. *Amazing Journey: The Story of The Who*, directed by Paul Crowder, Murray Lerner (Universal, 2007), DVD.

2. Ibid.

3. Cawthorne, *The Who and the Making of Tommy*, 45.

4. Cohn, *Awopbopaloobop Alopbamboom*, 179.

5. Library of Congress, *Respectfully Quoted*, 343.

6. Townshend, *Who I Am*.

7. Ibid.

8. Ibid.
9. Fiegel, *Dream a Little Dream of Me,* 91.
10. Richards and Fox, *Life*, 157.
11. Gottlieb, *Do You Believe in Magic?*, xii.
12. Wenner, "Jagger Remembers."
13. Brown with Tucker, *James Brown*, 153.
14. Bockris, *Keith Richards*, 51.
15. Andersen, *Mick*, 41.
16. Ibid., 340.
17. Ibid., 59.
18. Whiteley, *Sexing the Groove*, 67.
19. Wyman, *Stone Alone*, 359.
20. Norman, *Mick Jagger.*
21. Sanchez, *Up and Down with the Rolling Stones.*
22. Norman, *Mick Jagger.*

21. GOT TO KEEP ON MOVING

1. Martin Luther King, Jr., "The Voice of Martin Luther King, Jr.," *New York Times*, April 7, 1968.
2. Frank James, "Martin Luther King, Jr. in Chicago," *Chicago Tribune*, Aug. 5, 1966.
3. Cleary, *I Put a Spell on You.*
4. Jo Freeman, "Making the Revolution—in One County," seniorwomen.com, http://www.seniorwomen.com/articles/freeman/articlesFreemanLowndes.html, 2009.
5. Jeffries, *Bloody Lowndes.*
6. Miles, *Hippie.*
7. "Johnson Signs Voting Rights Act," History.com, history.com, http://www.history.com/this-day-in-history/johnson-signs-voting-rights-act.
8. "The Prize," We Shall Overcome: Historic Places of the Civil Rights Movement, http://www.nps.gov/nr/travel/civilrights/prize.htm.
9. Smith, *Cosby*, 57.
10. Cleary, *I Put a Spell on You*, 100.
11. Ibid., 117.
12. Edye Hughes, "Black Is Beautiful 50-Anniversary: A Movement That Went Viral Before Digital Technology," Black Copy, March 1, 2012, http://eldhughes.com/?s=Black+is+beautiful.
13. Benjaminson, *The Lost Supreme*, 78.
14. Sean Hillegass, "Percy Sledge Inspired by Former Relationship, Wrote Hit Song," *The Standard Report*, Nov. 12, 2004, http://archive.today/6sQYt.
15. Ritz, *Divided Soul*, 107.
16. Justin Driver, "Pillar of Ire" (book review), *The New Republic*, April 29, 2002, http://www.newrepublic.com/article/pillar-ire.

17. Amiri Baraka, *The Last Giant: The John Coltrane Anthology* liner notes, Rhino Records, 1993.

18. Prince Buster & Determinations, "They Got to Come," YouTube video, https://www.youtube.com/watch?v=vKfOAMDCnPM, retrieved June 25, 2014.

19. Heather Augustyn, *Ska: The Rhythm of Liberation*.

20. Clinton Hutton, "Forging Identity and Community through Aestheticism and Entertainment: The Sound System and the Rise of the DJ," *Caribbean Quarterly* (2007).

21. Augustyn, *Ska*.

22. Roy Black, "Hits from an Ice Cream Parlour—Leslie Kong's Beverly's Plays Foundation Music Role," *Jamaica Gleaner*, Feb. 9, 2014, http://collectorskornernow.com/leslie-kong/.

23. Robert Nicholls, "Black & White & Blue (Beat)," The Mod Generation, www.themodgeneration.co.uk/2010/10/black-white-blue-beat.html.

24. D. M. Collins, "Jimmy Cliff: Boom! Smash! It Went Smash!," *L.A. Record*, April 9, 2012, http://larecord.com/interviews/2012/04/09/jimmy-cliff-boom-smash-it-went-smash.

25. Ibid.

26. Nick Warburton, "Jimmy Cliff & the New Generation," Garage Hangover, April 20, 2012, http://www.garagehangover.com/jimmycliff/.

27. *Marley*, directed by Kevin Macdonald (Shangri-La Entertainment, 2012), DVD.

28. *Caribbean Nights: The Bob Marley Story*, directed by Charles Chabot and Jo Mendell (BBC, 1982), DVD.

22. WARHOL MEETS THE VELVET UNDERGROUND AND NICO

1. Stein and Plimpton, *Edie*, 229.

2. Unterberger, *White Light/White Heat*, 82.

3. Thompson, *Your Pretty Face Is Going to Hell*, 3.

4. Warhol and Hackett, *Popism*, 145–46.

5. Stein and Plimpton, *Edie*, 229.

6. Bockris, *Warhol*, 227–28.

7. Stein and Plimpton, *Edie*, 285.

8. Bockris, *Warhol: The Biography*, 236.

9. Warhol and Hackett, *Popism*, 108.

10. Lauren Gioia and Dan Abernethy, "Sotheby's Contemporary Art Evening Auction Totals $266,591,000," sothebys.com, 2012, http://www.sothebys.com/content/dam/sothebys/PDFs/Contemporary%20Post%20SalePR%20May12.pdf.

11. Doggett, *Lou Reed*.

12. Bockris, *Uptight*.

13. Cale and Bockris, *What's Welsh for Zen*.

14. James Mills, "John and Karen, Two Lives Lost to Heroin," *Life*, Feb. 26, 1965.

15. Cale and Bockris, *What's Welsh for Zen*.

16. McNeil and McCain, *Please Kill Me*, 17.

23. ACID OZ

1. Hofmann, *LSD, My Problem Child.*
2. Marc Lewis, "My Kool Acid Test," *Newsweek*, March 26, 2012.
3. Troy Hooper, "Operation Midnight Climax: How the CIA Dosed S.F. Citizens with LSD," *SF Weekly*, March 14, 2012, http://www.sfweekly.com/2012-03-14/news/cia-lsd-wayne-ritchie-george-h-white-mk-ultra/3/.
4. "LSD, Magic Mushrooms, and CIA Mind Control Experiments," *ABC News Closeup*, 1979, http://www.youtube.com/watch?v=XW5g597t0ZE.
5. Stevens, *Storming Heaven.*
6. Lee and Shlain, *Acid Dreams*, 79.
7. Greenfield, *Dark Star*, 70–71.
8. Ginsberg, *Planet News: 1961–1967.*
9. Sandison and Vickers, *Neal Cassady*, 297.
10. Ibid., 300.
11. Doggett, *Are You Ready for the Country.*
12. Draper, *Rolling Stone Magazine: The Uncensored History*, 50.
13. Perry and Miles, *I Want to Take You Higher*, 36.
14. Jann S. Wenner and Charles Reich, "The Rolling Stone Interview: Jerry Garcia, Part 1," http://www.jannswenner.com/Archives/Jerry_Garcia_Part1.aspx.
15. Graham and Greenfield, *Bill Graham Presents*, 199.
16. Perry and Miles, *I Want to Take You Higher*, 25.
17. Perry, *The Haight-Ashbury.*
18. Whitsett, *Erotic City*, 70.
19. Ken Kesey, "Allen . . . ," www.intrepidtrips.com/pranksters/ginsberg/.
20. Charters, *The Portable Sixties Reader*, 208–12.
21. Stevens, *Storming Heaven.*
22. Doggett, *There's a Riot Going On.*
23. Ibid.
24. Sloman, *Steal This Dream*, 59.
25. Wolfe, *The Electric Kool-Aid Acid Test*, 175.
26. Ibid., 172.
27. Lee and Shlain, *Acid Dreams*, 121.
28. Greenfield, *Dark Star*, 60–61.
29. Dennis McNally and Lou Tambakos, booklet for Grateful Dead box set *The Golden Road (1965–1973)*, Rhino Records, 2001.
30. Troy, *Captain Trips*, 27.
31. Wyman, *Stone Alone*, 359.
32. Greenfield, *Dark Star*, 60–61.
33. Ibid., 73–74.
34. Ibid., 71.
35. Perry and Miles, *I Want to Take You Higher*, 45.

36. Miles, *Hippie*, 54.

37. Perry and Miles, *I Want to Take You Higher*, 25.

38. Thompson, *Fear and Loathing in Las Vegas*, 68.

24. RUBBER SOUL

1. Beatles, *The Beatles Anthology*, 158.

2. Bellman, *The Exotic in Western Music*, 294.

3. MacDonald, *Revolution in the Head*, 165.

4. Badman, *The Beatles*, 190.

5. Gill, *Bob Dylan*.

6. Jonathan Cott, "John Lennon: The Rolling Stone Interview," Nov. 23, 1968, http://www.rollingstone.com/music/news/john-lennon-the-rolling-stone-interview-19681123.

7. Miles, *Paul McCartney*, 270–71.

8. Ibid.

9. Mitchell Glazer, "Growing Up at 33 1/3: The George Harrison Interview," *Crawdaddy*, 1977, http://www.beatlesinterviews.org/db1977.0200.beatles.html.

10. Rosen, *The* Billboard *Book of Number One Albums*, 77.

11. Spignesi and Lewis, *100 Best Beatles Songs*, 108.

12. Miles, *Paul McCartney*, 210.

13. Sheff, *All We Are Saying*, 178–79.

14. Spignesi and Lewis, *100 Best Beatles Songs*, 246.

15. Lennon, *In His Own Write*.

16. Gould, *Can't Buy Me Love*, 305.

17. Unterberger, *Turn! Turn! Turn!*, 180.

18. Maureen Cleave, "How Does a Beatle Live? John Lennon Lives Like This," *London Evening Standard*, March 4, 1966.

19. Sheff, *All We Are Saying*, 193.

20. Davies, *The Beatles*, 275.

21. Doggett, *There's a Riot Going On*.

22. Lewisohn, *The Complete Beatles Recording Sessions*, 13.

23. Miles, *Paul McCartney*, 272.

24. Steve Marinucci, "Mysterious Beatles 'Rubber Soul' Photo Gets Huge Buzz," *The Examiner*, Jan. 22, 2013, http://www.examiner.com/article/mysterious-beatles-rubber-soul-photo-gets-huge-buzz.

25. CHRISTMAS TIME IS HERE

1. Sally Kempton, "Super Anti-Hero in Forest Hills," *Village Voice*, April 1, 1965.

2. Ronald W. Dworkin, "Psychotherapy and the Pursuit of Happiness," *The New Atlantis*, 2012, http://www.thenewatlantis.com/publications/psychotherapy-and-the-pursuit-of-happiness; Herman, *The Romance of American Psychology*.

3. Fritz Redlich and Stephen R. Kellert, "Trends in American Mental Health," *The American Journal of Psychiatry* (January 1978).

4. *What's New Pussycat?*, directed by Clive Donner (Famous Artists Productions, 1965), DVD.
5. Michaelis, *Schulz and Peanuts*, 300–302.
6. Lee Mendelson, "Willie Mays and A Charlie Brown Christmas," Charles M. Schulz Museum, *Jean Schulz's Blog*, March 9, 2012, https://schulzmuseum.org/willie-mays-and-a-charlie-brown-christmas/.
7. Michaelis, *Schulz and Peanuts*, 347.
8. Ibid., 350.
9. *A Christmas Miracle: The Making of* A Charlie Brown Christmas (Trailer Park, 2008), DVD bonus feature.
10. Ibid.
11. Zollo, *Songwriters on Songwriting*, 8.
12. Rogan, *The Byrds*, 128.
13. Ibid., 619.
14. Badman, *The Beach Boys*, 104.
15. Don Traynor, "Brian Pop Genius!" *Melody Maker*, May 21, 1966.
16. Hartman, *The Wrecking Crew*, 151.
17. George Leonard, Jr., & Another vs. School Committee of Attleboro & Others, mass-cases.com, http://masscases.com/cases/sjc/349/349mass704.html.
18. Michael E. Young, "In '66, Their Hair Triggered a To-Do: Stylish Marcus Proved an Ally in Band's Battle to Keep Long Locks," *Dallas Morning News*, March 4, 2002.
19. Turner, *The Man Called Cash*.
20. Gilmore, *Stories Done*, 196.
21. Hilburn, *Johnny Cash*; Streissguth, *Johnny Cash*, 129.
22. Ribowsky, *Signed, Sealed, and Delivered*, 30.
23. Ibid., 63.
24. *Martin Freeman Goes to Motown*, directed by Sara Tiefenbrun (BBC, 2009), DVD.
25. Ribowsky, *Signed, Sealed, and Delivered*, 55.
26. Echols, *Hot Stuff*, 13.

EPILOGUE: STRIKE ANOTHER MATCH, GO START ANEW

1. Norman, *Mick Jagger*.
2. Rogan, *The Byrds*, 158–63.
3. Frank F. Furstenberg Jr., "History and Current Status of Divorce in the United States," *The Future of Children*, 1994, http://futureofchildren.org/futureofchildren/publications/journals/article/index.xml?journalid=63&articleid=409; Associated Press, "Premarital Sex Trends," *New York Times*, April 17, 1985, http://www.nytimes.com/1985/04/17/garden/premarital-sex-trends.html.
4. "Selected Notifiable Disease Rates and Number of New Cases: United States, 1950–2011," table, Centers for Disease Control, http://www.cdc.gov/nchs/data/hus/2012/039.pdf.
5. Gottlieb, *Do You Believe in Magic?*, 147.

6. *Ronald Reagan Speaks Out against Socialized Medicine*, 1961, LP.

7. Longley, *Deconstructing Reagan*, 76.

8. Hall, *American Patriotism, American Protest*, 134.

9. Krugman, *The Conscience of a Liberal*, 95.

10. Dallek, *The Right Moment*, 190.

11. Lewis, "My Kool Acid Test."

12. *Berkeley in the Sixties*, directed by Mark Kitchell (P.O.V. Theatricals, 1990).

13. "United States Military Casualties of War," Wikipedia.com, http://en.wikipedia.org /wiki/United_States_military_casualties_of_war.

14. Gottlieb, *Do You Believe in Magic?*, 153.

Bibliography

BOOKS

Adrahtas, Tom. *Diana Ross: The American Dream Girl: A Lifetime to Get Here*. Bloomington, IN: AuthorHouse, 2006.

Alteveer, Ian, Rebecca Lowery, Marla Prather, and Mark Rosenthal. *Regarding Warhol: Sixty Artists, Fifty Years*. New York: Metropolitan Museum of Art, 2012.

Andersen, Christopher. *Mick: The Wild Life and Mad Genius of Jagger*. New York: Simon and Schuster, 2012.

Augustyn, Heather. *Ska: The Rhythm of Liberation*. Lanham, MD: Scarecrow Press, 2013.

Badman, Keith. *The Beach Boys: The Definitive Diary of America's Greatest Band, on Stage and in the Studio*. Milwaukee, WI: Hal Leonard Corporation, 2004.

———. *The Beatles: Off the Record*. London: Omnibus, 2009.

Beatles, The. *The Beatles Anthology*. London: Chronicle, 2000.

Bellman, Jonathan. *The Exotic in Western Music*. Lebanon, NH: Northeastern University Press, 1998.

Benjaminson, Peter. *The Lost Supreme: The Life of Dreamgirl Florence Ballard*. Chicago, IL: Chicago Review Press, 2009.

Bennett, Lerone. *Before the Mayflower: A History of Black America*. New York: Penguin, 1984.

Bissell, Tom. *The Father of All Things: A Marine, His Son, and the Legacy of Vietnam*. New York: Random House, 2009.

Black, Johnny. *Classic Tracks Back to Back: Singles and Albums*. New York: Thunder Bay Press, 2008.

Bockris, Victor. *Keith Richards: The Biography*. New York: Da Capo Press, 2003.

———. *Uptight: The Velvet Underground Story*. London: Omnibus Press, 2009.

———. *Warhol: The Biography*. Cambridge, MA: Da Capo, 2003.

Booth, Stanley. *Keith: Standing in the Shadows*. London: Macmillan, 1996.

Bowman, Rob. *Soulsville, U.S.A.: The Story of Stax Records*. New York: Schirmer Trade Books, 1997.

Branch, Taylor. *At Canaan's Edge: America in the King Years, 1965–68*. New York: Simon and Schuster, 2006.

Braunstein, Peter, Phillip E. Carpenter, and Anthony O. Edmonds. *The Sixties Chronicle*. Lincolnwood, IL: Publications International, 2007.

Brokaw, Tom. *Boom!: Talking About the Sixties: What Happened, How It Shaped Today, Lessons for Tomorrow*. New York: Random House, 2008.

Bronson, Fred. *The Billboard Book of Number 1 Hits*. New York: Billboard Books, 1992.

Brown, Donald. *Bob Dylan: American Troubadour*. Lanham, MD: Rowman and Littlefield, 2014.

Brown, James, with Bruce Tucker. *James Brown: The Godfather of Soul*. London: Fontana/Collins, 1988.

Brown, Peter, and Stephen Gaines. *The Love You Make: An Insider's Story of the Beatles*. New York: McGraw Hill, 1983.

Browne, David. *Fire and Rain: The Beatles, Simon and Garfunkel, James Taylor, CSNY, and the Lost Story of 1970*. Philadelphia, PA: Da Capo Press, 2011.

Burke, Ken, and Dan Griffin. *The Blue Moon Boys: The Story of Elvis Presley's Band*. Chicago, IL: Chicago Review Press, 2006.

Cale, John, and Victor Bockris. *What's Welsh for Zen: The Autobiography of John Cale*. New York: Bloomsbury USA, 2000.

Cantwell, David. *Merle Haggard: The Running Kind*. Austin: University of Texas Press, 2013.

Cawthorne, Nigel. *The Who and the Making of Tommy*. New York: Unanimous, 2005.

Charters, Ann. *The Portable Sixties Reader*. London: Penguin, 2003.

Clapton, Eric. *Clapton: The Autobiography*. New York: Three Rivers Press, 2008.

Clayson, Alan. *The Yardbirds: The Band That Launched Eric Clapton, Jeff Beck, and Jimmy Page*. Milwaukee, WI: Backbeat Books, 2002.

Cleary, Stephen. *I Put a Spell on You: The Autobiography of Nina Simone*. Cambridge, MA: Da Capo Press, 2003.

Cohn, Nik. *Awopbopaloobop Alopbamboom: The Golden Age of Rock*. St. Albans, UK: Paladin Press, 1970.

Coplon, Jeff. *The First Time: Cher: As Told to Jeff Coplon*. Darby, PA: Diane Publishing Company, 2001.

Cott, Jonathan. *Dylan on Dylan: The Essential Interviews*. London: Hodder and Stoughton, 2006.

Dallek, Matthew. *The Right Moment: Ronald Reagan's First Victory and the Decisive Turning Point in American Politics*. New York: Oxford University Press, 2004.

Dallek, Robert. *Flawed Giant: Lyndon Johnson and His Times, 1961–1973*. New York: 1998.

Dang Phong, ed. *The History of the Vietnamese Economy, Vol. 2*. The Institute of Economy, Vietnamese Institute of Social Sciences, 2005.

Davidson, Sara. *Loose Change: Three Women of the Sixties*. Oakland: University of California Press, 1997.

Davies, Hunter. *The Beatles: The Authorised Biography*. London: Heinemann, 1968.

Davies, Ray. *Americana: The Kinks, the Road, and the Perfect Riff*. London: Ebury Publishing, 2013.

Des Barres, Pamela. *I'm with the Band: Confessions of a Groupie*. Chicago, IL: Chicago Review Press, 2005.

di Perna, Alan. *Guitar Masters: Intimate Portraits*. Milwaukee, WI: Hal Leonard Corporation, 2012.

Dillon, Mark. *Fifty Sides of the Beach Boys: The Songs That Tell Their Story*. Toronto: ECW Press, 2012.

Doggett, Peter. *Are You Ready for the Country: Elvis, Dylan, Parsons, and the Roots of Country Rock*. New York: Penguin Group, 2001.

———. *Lou Reed: The Defining Years*. London: Omnibus, 2012.

———. *There's a Riot Going On: Revolutionaries, Rock Stars, and the Rise and Fall of the '60s*. New York: Grove, 2009.

Draper, Robert. *Rolling Stone Magazine: The Uncensored History*. New York: Doubleday, 1990.

Dylan, Bob. *Chronicles: Volume One*. New York: Simon and Schuster, 2004.

Echols, Alice. *Hot Stuff: Disco and the Remaking of American Culture*. New York: W. W. Norton and Company, 2010.

Egan, Sean. *The Rough Guide to the Rolling Stones*. London: Rough Guides, 2006.

Einarson, John. *Mr. Tambourine Man: The Life and Legacy of the Byrds' Gene Clark*. San Francisco, CA: Backbeat Books, 2005.

Emerick, Geoff, and Howard Massey. *Here, There, and Everywhere: My Life Recording the Music of the Beatles*. New York: Gotham, 2007.

Emerson, Ken. *Always Magic in the Air: The Bomp and Brilliance of the Brill Building Era*. New York: Penguin, 2006.

Evanzz, Karl. *The Judas Factor: The Plot to Kill Malcolm X*. New York: Thunder's Mouth Press, 1992.

Faithfull, Marianne. *Faithfull: An Autobiography*. New York: Little Brown, 1994.

Farber, David. *The Columbia Guide to America in the 1960s*. New York: Columbia Press, 2001.

Ferrari, Michelle. *Reporting America at War: An Oral History*. Hyperion, 2003.

Fiegel, Eddi. *Dream a Little Dream of Me: The Life of Cass Elliot*. Chicago: Chicago Review Press, 2007.

Gaines, Steven. *Heroes and Villains: The True Story of the Beach Boys*. New York: New American Library, 1986.

George, Nelson, and Alan Leeds, eds. *The James Brown Reader: Fifty Years of Writing about the Godfather of Soul*. New York: Plume, 2008.

George, Nelson. *The Death of Rhythm and Blues*. New York: Penguin, 2003.

Gill, Andy. *Bob Dylan: The Stories Behind the Songs 1962-1969*. London: Carlton Books, 2011.

Gillett, Charlie. *The Sound of the City: The Rise of Rock and Roll*. Cambridge, MA: Da Capo Press, 1996.

Gilmore, Mikal. *Stories Done: Writings on the 1960s and Its Discontents*. New York: Simon and Schuster, 2008.

Ginsberg, Allen. *Planet News: 1961-1967*. San Francisco: City Lights, 1971.

Gleason, Ralph J. *The Rolling Stone Interviews*. New York: St. Martin's Press, 1981.

Goldman, Albert. *Elvis*. New York: Avon, 1981.

Gottlieb, Annie. *Do You Believe In Magic?: Bringing the Sixties Back Home*. New York: Simon and Schuster, 1988.

Gould, Jonathan. *Can't Buy Me Love: The Beatles, Britain, and America*. New York: Random House, 2008.

Graham, Bill, and Robert Greenfield. *Bill Graham Presents: My Life Inside Rock and Out*. Cambridge, MA: Da Capo, 2004.

Gray, Michael. *The Bob Dylan Encyclopedia*. New York: Bloomsbury Academic, 2006.

Greenfield, Robert. *Dark Star: An Oral Biography of Jerry Garcia*. New York: Harper-Collins, 2012.

Greenwald, Matthew. *Go Where You Wanna Go: The Oral History of the Mamas and the Papas*. New York: Rowman and Littlefield, 2002.

Gregory, Dick. *Callus on My Soul: A Memoir*. New York: Dafina Books, 2000.

Guralnick, Peter. *Careless Love: The Unmaking of Elvis Presley*. New York: Little, Brown, 1999.

———. *Dream Boogie: The Triumph of Sam Cooke*. New York: Back Bay Books, 2006.

Hajdu, David. *Positively 4th Street: The Lives and Times of Joan Baez, Bob Dylan, Mimi Baez Fariña, and Richard Fariña*. New York: Farrar, Straus and Giroux, 2001.

Hall, Simon. *American Patriotism, American Protest: Social Movements since the Sixties*. University of Pennsylvania Press: Philadelphia, 2011.

Hartman, Kent. *The Wrecking Crew: The Inside Story of Rock and Roll's Best-Kept Secret*. New York: Thomas Dunne Books, 2012.

Hayward, Keith. *Tin Pan Alley: The Rise of Elton John*. London: Soundcheck Books, 2013.

Herman, Ellen. *The Romance of American Psychology: Political Culture in the Age of Experts*. Berkeley: University of California Press, 1996.

Heylin, Clinton. *Bob Dylan: The Recording Sessions, 1960–1994*. New York: St. Martin's Press, 1996.

Hilburn, Robert. *Johnny Cash: The Life*. New York: Little, Brown and Company, 2013.

Hjort, Christopher. *So You Want to Be a Rock 'n' Roll Star: The Byrds Day-by-Day, 1965–1973*. London: Jawbone Press, 2008.

Hofmann, Albert. *LSD, My Problem Child: Reflections on Sacred Drugs, Mysticism, and Science*. Ann Arbor, MI: MAPS, 2011.

Holloway, Karla F. C. *Passed On: African American Mourning Stories, A Memorial.* Durham, NC: Duke University Press, 2003.

Hyatt, Wesley. *The Billboard Book of Number One Adult Contemporary Hits.* New York: Billboard Publications, 1999.

Jackson, Laura. *Paul Simon: The Definitive Biography.* New York: Kensington Publishing, 2002.

Jeffries, Hasan Kwame. *Bloody Lowndes: Civil Rights and Black Power in Alabama's Black Belt.* New York: New York University Press, 2009.

Jennings, Waylon, and Lenny Kaye. *Waylon: An Autobiography.* New York: Hachette, 1996.

Jones, Landon Y. *Great Expectations: America and the Baby Boom Generation.* New York: Ballantine Books, 1981.

Kahn, Ashley. *A Love Supreme: The Story of John Coltrane's Signature Album.* London: Penguin, 2002.

Kane, Larry. *Ticket to Ride.* Philadelphia, PA: Running Press, 2003.

Kelley, Kitty. *His Way: The Unauthorized Biography of Frank Sinatra.* New York: Bantam Books, 1987.

King, Carole. *A Natural Woman: A Memoir.* New York: Grand Central Publishing, 2012.

Kingsbury, Paul, Michael McCall and John W. Rumble, eds. *The Encyclopedia of Country Music: The Ultimate Guide to the Music.* New York: Oxford University Press, 2012.

Kooper, Al. *Backstage Passes and Backstabbing Bastards: Memoirs of a Rock 'n' Roll Survivor.* New York: Backbeat, 2008.

Kot, Greg. *I'll Take You There: Mavis Staples, the Staple Singers, and the March up Freedom's Highway.* New York: Scribner, 2014.

Krugman, Paul. *The Conscience of a Liberal.* New York: W. W. Norton and Company, 2009.

Kubernik, Harvey. *Canyon of Dreams: The Magic and the Music of Laurel Canyon.* New York: Sterling, 2009.

Lambert, Philip. *Inside the Music of Brian Wilson: The Songs, Sounds, and Influences of the Beach Boys' Founding Genius.* New York: Continuum Books, 2007.

Lee, Martin A., and Bruce Shlain. *Acid Dreams: The Complete Social History of LSD— the CIA, the Sixties, and Beyond.* New York: Grove Press, 1992.

Leitch, Donovan. *The Autobiography of Donovan: The Hurdy Gurdy Man.* New York: St. Martin's, 2005.

Lennon, John. *In His Own Write.* New York: Simon and Schuster, 2000.

Levy, Joe. *Rolling Stone's 500 Greatest Albums of All Times.* New York: Wenner, 2005.

Lewisohn, Mark. *The Complete Beatles Recording Sessions.* London: Hamlyn, 1988.

Library of Congress. *Respectfully Quoted: A Dictionary of Quotations.* Washington, DC: Courier Dover Publications, 2010.

Longley, Kyle. *Deconstructing Reagan: Conservative Mythology and America's Fortieth President.* Armonk, NY: M.E. Sharpe, 2007.

McClelland, Edward. *Nothin' but Blue Skies: The Heyday, Hard Times, and Hopes of America's Industrial Heartland.* New York: Bloomsbury, 2013.

MacDonald, Ian. *Revolution in the Head: The Beatles' Records and the Sixties.* Chicago, IL: Chicago Review Press, 2007.

McGonigal, Mike. *Well Down Freedom Highway: The Staple Singers' Masterpiece.* New York: Feedback Press, 2012.

McMillian, John Campbell. *Beatles vs. Stones.* New York: Simon and Schuster, 2013.

McNeil, Legs, and Gillian McCain. *Please Kill Me: The Uncensored Oral History of Punk.* New York: Grove Press, 2006.

Marcus, Greil. *Like a Rolling Stone: Bob Dylan at the Crossroads.* New York: Public-Affairs, 2005.

Marsh, Dave, with John Swenson. *The Rolling Stone Record Guide.* New York: Random House, 1979.

Marsh, Dave. *The Heart of Rock & Soul: The 1001 Greatest Singles Ever Made.* New York: Da Capo, 1989.

Medved, Michael, and David Wallechinsky. *What Really Happened to the Class of '65?* New York: Random House, 1976.

Michaelis, David. *Schulz and Peanuts: A Biography.* New York: HarperCollins, 2007.

Miles, Barry. *Hippie.* New York: Sterling, 2005.

———. *Paul McCartney: Many Years from Now.* London: Secker and Warburg, 1998.

Montague, Nathaniel. *Burn, Baby! Burn: The Autobiography of Magnificent Montague.* Chicago, IL: University of Illinois Press, 2003.

Moon, Elaine Latzman. *Untold Tales, Unsung Heroes: An Oral History of Detroit's African American Community, 1918–1967.* Detroit, MI: Wayne State University Press, 1994.

Morocco, John. *Thunder from Above.* Boston, MA: Boston Publishing Company, 1984.

Nash, Graham. *Wild Tales: A Rock & Roll Life.* New York: Crown Archetype, 2013.

Nelson, Willie, and Bud Shrake. *Willie: An Autobiography.* New York: Cooper Square Press, 1988.

Norman, Philip. *John Lennon: The Life.* New York: Random House, 2009.

———. *Mick Jagger.* New York: Ecco/Harper Collins, 2012.

———. *Shout! The Beatles in Their Generation.* London: ElmTree, 1981.

Painter, Melissa, and David Weisman. *Edie: Girl on Fire.* New York: Chronicle Books, 2007.

Patterson, James T. *The Eve of Destruction: How 1965 Transformed America.* New York: Basic Books, 2012.

Perry, Charles, and Barry Miles. *I Want to Take You Higher: The Psychedelic Era 1965–1969.* San Francisco, CA: Chronicle Books, 1997.

Perry, Charles. *The Haight-Ashbury: A History.* San Francisco, CA: Wenner Books, 2005.

Polan, Brenda, and Roger Tredre. *The Great Fashion Designers.* New York: Berg, 2009.

Polizzotti, Mark. *Bob Dylan's Highway 61 Revisited.* New York: Continuum, 2006.

Posner, Gerald. *Motown: Music, Money, Sex, and Power.* New York: Random House, 2002.

Priore, Domenic. *Riot on Sunset Strip: Rock 'n' Roll's Last Stand in Hollywood.* London: Jawbone Press, 2007.

Quirk, Lawrence J. *Totally Uninhibited: The Life and Wild Times of Cher.* New York: William Morrow and Co., 1991.

Ribowsky, Mark. *Signed, Sealed, and Delivered: The Soulful Journey of Stevie Wonder.* Hoboken, NJ: John Wiley and Sons, 2010.

Richards, Keith, and James Fox. *Life.* Boston: Little, Brown and Company, 2010.

Ritz, David. *Divided Soul: The Life of Marvin Gaye.* Cambridge, MA: Da Capo Press, 1991.

Robinson, Smokey. *Smokey: Inside My Life.* New York: McGraw-Hill, 1989.

Rodriguez, Robert. *Revolver: How the Beatles Reimagined Rock 'n' Roll.* Milwaukee, WI: Hal Leonard Corp., 2012.

Rodriguez, Robert, and Stuart Shea. *Fab Four FAQ: Everything Left to Know about the Beatles . . . and More!* Milwaukee, WI: Hal Leonard Corp., 2007.

Rogan, Johnny. *The Byrds: Timeless Flight Revisited.* New York: Rogan House, 1998.

Rogovoy, Seth. *Bob Dylan: Prophet, Mystic, Poet.* New York: Scribner, 2009.

Rolling Stone Magazine. The Rolling Stone Illustrated History of Rock & Roll. New York: Random House, 1992.

Rosen, Craig. *The Billboard Book of Number One Albums.* New York: Billboard Books, 1996.

Rubin, Jerry. *DO IT!: Scenarios of the Revolution.* New York: Simon and Schuster, 1970.

Sanchez, Tony. *Up and Down with the Rolling Stones.* New York: Da Capo Press, 1996.

Sandison, David, and Graham Vickers. *Neal Cassady: The Fast Life of a Beat Hero.* Chicago, IL: Chicago Review Press, 2006.

Schaffner, Nicholas. *The British Invasion: From the First Wave to the New Wave.* New York: McGraw-Hill, 1982.

Scoppa, Bud. *The Byrds.* Scholastic Book Services, 1971.

Sheff, David. *All We Are Saying.* New York: St. Martin's Press, 2000.

Shelton, Robert. *No Direction Home: The Life and Music of Bob Dylan.* Milwaukee, WI: Backbeat Books, 2011.

Shrimpton, Jean. *Jean Shrimpton: An Autobiography.* London: Ebury Press, 1990.

Sisk, Eileen. *Buck Owens: The Biography.* Chicago: Chicago Review Press, 2010.

Sloman, Larry. *Steal This Dream: Abbie Hoffman and the Countercultural Revolution in America.* New York: Doubleday, 1998.

Smith, Ronald L. *Cosby: The Life of a Comedy Legend.* Amherst, MA: Prometheus Books, 1997.

Smith, Suzanne E. *Dancing in the Street: Motown and the Cultural Politics of Detroit.* Cambridge, MA: Harvard University Press, 2000.

Smyth, Daniel Joseph. *Freedom of the Press and National Security in Four Wars: World War I, World War II, the Vietnam War, and the War on Terrorism.* Ann Arbor: ProQuest, 2007.

Spector, Ronnie. *Be My Baby: How I Survived Mascara, Miniskirts, and Madness—or, My Life as a Fabulous Ronette*. New York: Harmony Books, 1990.

Spignesi, Stephen J., and Michael Lewis. *100 Best Beatles Songs: A Passionate Fan's Guide*. New York: Black Dog and Leventhal, 2009.

Spitz, Bob. *Dylan: A Biography*. New York: W.W. Norton and Company, 1989.

Stanton, Mary. *From Selma to Sorrow: The Life and Death of Viola Liuzzo*. Athens: University of Georgia Press, 1998.

Stein, Jean, and George Plimpton. *Edie*. New York: Knopf, 1982.

Sterling, Christopher H. *The Concise Encyclopedia of American Radio*. New York: Routledge, 2011.

Stevens, Jay. *Storming Heaven: LSD and the American Dream*. New York: Grove Press, 1987.

Streissguth, Michael. *Johnny Cash: The Biography*. Cambridge, MA: Da Capo, 2006.

———. *Outlaw: Waylon, Willie, Kris, and the Renegades of Nashville*. New York: HarperCollins, 2013.

Sullivan, Steve. *Encyclopedia of Great Popular Song Recordings, Volume 2*. Lanham, MD: Scarecrow Press, 2013.

Thompson, Dave. *Your Pretty Face Is Going to Hell: The Dangerous Glitter of David Bowie, Iggy Pop, and Lou Reed*. New York: Hal Leonard Corp., 2009.

Thompson, Hunter S. *Fear and Loathing in Las Vegas: A Savage Journey to the Heart of the American Dream*. New York: Random House, 2010.

Thompson, Wayne. *To Hanoi and Back: The U.S. Air Force and North Vietnam, 1966–1973*. Washington, DC: Smithsonian Institution Press, 2002.

Tilford, Earl H. *Setup: What the Air Force Did in Vietnam and Why*. Maxwell AFB, AL: Air University Press, 1991.

Townshend, Pete. *Who I Am: A Memoir*. New York: HarperCollins, 2013.

Troy, Sandy. *Captain Trips: A Biography of Jerry Garcia*. Thunder's Mouth Press, 1994.

Turner, Steve. *The Man Called Cash: The Life, Love, and Faith of an American Legend*. Nashville, TN: Thomas Nelson, 2004.

Unterberger, Richie. *Eight Miles High: Folk-Rock's Flight from Haight-Ashbury to Woodstock*. Milwaukee, WI: Backbeat Books, 2003.

———. *Turn! Turn! Turn!: The '60s Folk-Rock Revolution*. San Francisco, CA: Backbeat Books, 2002.

———. *White Light/White Heat: The Velvet Underground Day by Day*. London: Jawbone, 2009.

Vincent, Rickey. *Funk: The Music, the People, and the Rhythm of the One*. New York: St. Martin's/Griffin, 1996.

Warhol, Andy, and Pat Hackett. *Popism: The Warhol Sixties*. New York: Penguin, 2007.

Weller, Sheila. *Girls Like Us: Carole King, Joni Mitchell, and Carly Simon and the Journey of a Generation*. New York: Atria Books, 2008.

Werner, Craig Hansen. *Higher Ground: Stevie Wonder, Aretha Franklin, Curtis May-field, and the Rise and Fall of American Soul.* New York: Crown Archetype, 2007.

White, Donald W. *The American Century: The Rise and Decline of the United States as a World Power.* New Haven, CT: Yale University Press, 1996.

White, Timothy. *Catch a Fire: The Life of Bob Marley.* New York: Henry Holt Paperbacks, 2006.

Whiteley, Sheila. *Sexing the Groove: Popular Music and Gender.* Abingdon, UK: Routledge, 2013.

Whitsett, Josh Sides. *Erotic City: Sexual Revolutions and the Making of Modern San Francisco.* New York: Oxford University Press, 2009.

Wilentz, Sean. *Bob Dylan in America.* New York: Doubleday, 2010.

Wilson, Mary. *Dreamgirl and Supreme Faith: My Life as a Supreme.* New York: Rowman and Littlefield, 2000.

Wolfe, Tom. *The Electric Kool-Aid Acid Test.* New York: Bantam Books, 1976.

———. *The Kandy-Kolored Tangerine-Flake Streamline Baby.* New York: Farrar, Straus and Giroux, 1965.

Wyman, Bill. *Rolling with the Stones.* New York: DK Pub., 2002.

———. *Stone Alone: The Story of a Rock 'n' Roll Band.* New York: Viking, 1990.

Zollo, Paul. *Songwriters on Songwriting.* Cambridge, MA: Da Capo Press, 2003.

REPORTS

King Jr., Martin Luther. "Southern Christian Leadership Conference Annual Report, 1965." http://www.thekingcenter.org/archive/document/sclc-annual-report-mlk-1965#, accessed August 27, 2014.

Knowles, Jon. "The Birth Control Pill—A History." http://www.plannedparenthood.org/files/1213/9611/6329/pillhistory.pdf, accessed August 27, 2014.

McCone, John Alex. "Violence in the City—an End or a Beginning? A Report by the Governor's Commission on the Los Angeles Riots, 1965." http://www.usc.edu/libraries/archives/instress/mccone/contents.html, accessed June 25, 2014.

PERIODICALS

Albuquerque Tribune

American Jewish History

The American Journal of Psychiatry

Brown Daily Herald

Chicago Tribune

Crawdaddy

Creem

Dallas Morning News

Eye Magazine

Guitar World Acoustic

Houston Press
Life
Los Angeles Times
Melody Maker
Metro Times
Mojo
Newsweek
New York Herald Tribune
New York Magazine
New York TimesPlayboy
Rock Cellar Magazine
Rolling Stone
San Francisco Chronicle
Village Voice
Washington Post

WEB PAGES AND WEBSITES

Abbeyrd's Beatles Page
http://abbeyrd.best.vwh.net/

Alan Cackett: Americana, Roots, Country, & Bluegrass Music
www.alancackett.com

Album Liner Notes
www.albumlinernotes.com

The Beatles Bible
www.beatlesbible.com

Beatles Music History
www.beatlesebooks.com

The Beatles Ultimate Experience: The Beatles Interviews Database
www.beatlesinterviews.org

Brown Daily Herald
www.browndailyherald.com

Centers for Disease Control and Prevention (CDC)
www.cdc.gov

CNN
www.cnn.com

The Economist: Intelligent Life
www.moreintelligentlife.com

Express: Home of the Daily and Sunday Express
www.express.co.uk

Garage Hangover
www.garagehangover.com

The Guardian
www.theguardian.com

History
www.history.com

History News Network
www.hnn.us

Houston Press
www.houstonpress.com

The Huffington Post
www.huffingtonpost.com

InfoPlease
www.infoplease.com

Intrepid Trips
www.intrepidtrips.com

Jann S. Wenner
www.jannswenner.com

Los Angeles Times
www.latimes.com

MailOnline.com
www.dailymail.co.uk

The Mini Skirt Revolution
theminiskirtrevolution.wordpress.com

The Mod Generation
themodgeneration.com

Music Radar: The No. 1 Website for Musicians
www.musicradar.com

The New Atlantis: A Journal of Technology and Society
www.thenewatlantis.com

New Republic
www.newrepublic.com

Newsday
www.newsday.com

New York Times
www.nytimes.com

NFC: The Internet Nirvana Fan Club
www.nirvanaclub.com

No Depression: The Roots Music Authority
www.nodepression.com

NPR: National Public Radio
www.npr.org

Pan-African News Wire
www.panafricannews.blogspot.com

Parade
http://parade.condenast.com/

PBS
www.pbs.org

Perfect Sound Forever
www.furious.com/perfect

Performing Songwriter
http://performingsongwriter.com/

P. F. Sloan
www.2.gol.com/users/davidr/sloan

Presidential Recordings Program
whitehousetapes.net

Rock & Roll Hall of Fame
www.rockhall.com

Rolling Stone
www.rollingstone.com

The Root
www.theroot.com

Saga
www.saga.co.uk

Senior Women Web: An UnCommon Site for UnCommon Women
www.seniorwomen.com

SF Weekly
www.sfweekly.com

The Singer: Art Garfunkel
www.artgarfunkel.com

Slate
www.slate.com

Sotheby's
www.sothebys.com

Time Is on Our Side: The Rolling Stones Forever
www.timeisonourside.com

Ultimate Classic Rock
ultimateclassicrock.com

Ventura County Star
www.vcstar.com

Wall Street Journal
online.wsj.com

WarholStars.Org
www.warholstars.org

Washington Post
www.washingtonpost.com

Whole Earth Catalog
www.wholeearth.com

Wikipedia
www.en.wikipedia.org

FILMS AND TELEVISION
Amazing Journey: The Story of the Who. Directed by Murray Lerner and Paul Crowder. Spitfire Pictures, 2007.

American Masters. Season 18, Episode 2: "James Brown: Soul Survivor." Directed by Jeremy Marre. American Masters, 2003.

Berkeley in the Sixties. Directed by Mark Kitchell. P.O.V. Theatricals, 1990.

Breakfast at Tiffany's. Directed by Blake Edwards. Jurow-Shepherd, 1961.

Caribbean Nights: The Bob Marley Story. Directed by Charles Chabot and Jo Mendell. BBC, 1982.

A Charlie Brown Christmas. Directed by Bill Melendez. United Feature Syndicate, 1965.

A Christmas Miracle: The Making of A Charlie Brown Christmas. Trailer Park, 2008.

Eyes on the Prize: Bridge to Freedom 1965. Directed by Callie Crossley and James A. DeVinney. Blackside, Inc., 1987.

Eyes on the Prize: The Time Has Come 1964–66. Directed by James A. DeVinney and Madison D. Lacy. Blackside, Inc., 1987.

Eyes on the Prize: Two Societies 1965–68. Directed by Sheila Curran Bernard and Samuel D. Pollard. Blackside, Inc., 1990.

Ho Chi Minh: Vietnam's Enigma. Produced by Gary Tarpinian. Actuality Productions, 2000.

Legends: Dennis Wilson: The Real Beach Boy. Directed by Matt O'Casey. BBC Four, 2010.

Let's Sing Out (Series). Produced by Syd Banks. CTV, Feb 17, 1966.

Live and Swingin': The Ultimate Rat Pack Collection. Produced by Paul Atkinson, Jimmy Edwards, and Robin Hurley. Bristol Productions, 2003.

"LSD, Magic Mushrooms, & CIA Mind Control Experiments." *ABC News Closeup*. Directed by Richard Roy. ABC, 1979.

Marley. Directed by Kevin Macdonald. Shangri-La Entertainment, 2012.

Martin Freeman Goes to Motown. Directed by Sara Tiefenbrun. BBC Television, 2009.

No Direction Home: Bob Dylan. Directed by Martin Scorsese. Spitfire Pictures, 2005.

Produced by George Martin. Directed by Francis Hanly. Grounded Productions/BBC, 2011.

Rat Pack: The True Stories of the Original Kings of Cool. Directed by Carole Langer. A&E Home Video, 2001.

Standing in the Shadows of Motown. Directed by Paul Justman. Lions Gate, 2003.

What's New Pussycat? Directed by Clive Donner. Famous Artists Productions, 1965.

Index